Australia's Major Cities

Tony Duboudin and Brian Courtis

Prentice Hall Travel

New York • London • Toronto • Sydney • Tokyo • Singapore

THE AMERICAN EXPRESS ® TRAVEL GUIDES

Published in the United States by
Prentice Hall General Reference
A division of Simon & Schuster, Inc.
15 Columbus Circle
New York, NY 10023

PRENTICE HALL and colophon are
registered trademarks of Simon &
Schuster, Inc.

First published in the United
Kingdom as *Cities of Australia* by
Mitchell Beazley International Ltd
Michelin House, 81 Fulham Road
London SW3 6RB

Edited, designed and produced by
Castle House Press, Llantrisant,
Mid Glamorgan CF7 8EU, Wales

First published 1987 as *The American
Express Pocket Guide to Australia*.
This new and expanded edition
published 1992.

© American Express Publishing
Corporation Inc. 1992
All rights reserved including the right
of reproduction in whole or in part in
any form

Library of Congress Catalog
Card Number 92-060353

ISBN 0-13-028739-3

The editor, authors and publisher
thank the State Government Tourist
Authorities of, respectively, the
Australian Capital Territory, New
South Wales, the Northern Territory,
Queensland, South Australia,
Tasmania, Victoria and Western
Australia; also Fran Madigan at the
Australian Tourist Commission in
London and Debbie Hindle at Scott
Gold Blyth, London for their
assistance during the preparation of
this edition. Warm thanks are due
also to Neil Hanson, David Haslam,
Hilary Bird and Tim Charity.

FOR THE SERIES:
General Editor:
  David Townsend Jones
Map Editor: David Haslam
Indexer: Hilary Bird
Cover design:
  Roger Walton Studio

FOR THIS EDITION:
Edited on desktop by:
  Sharon Charity
Art editor:
  Eileen Townsend Jones
Illustrators:
  Sylvia Hughes-Williams,
  Karen Cochrane
Gazetteer: Anne Evans
Cover photo: James Davis

FOR MITCHELL BEAZLEY:
Art Director: Tim Foster
Managing Editor: Alison Starling
Production: Sarah Schuman

PRODUCTION CREDITS:
Maps by Lovell Johns, Oxford,
  England
Typeset in Garamond and
  News Gothic
Desktop layout in Ventura
  Publisher
Linotronic output by
  Tradespools Limited, Frome,
  England

Contents

Culture, history and background

Basic information

Planning and tours

A to Z

Maps

How to use this book

Few guidelines are needed to understand how this book works:

- For the general organization of the book, see CONTENTS on the pages preceding this one.
- Wherever appropriate, chapters and sections are arranged alphabetically, with headings appearing in **CAPITALS.**
- Often these headings are followed by location and practical information printed in *italics.*
- As you turn the pages, you will find subject headers, similar to those used in telephone directories, printed in CAPITALS in the top corner of each page.
- If you still cannot find what you need, check in the comprehensive and exhaustively cross-referenced INDEX at the back of the book.
- Following the index, a LIST OF STREET NAMES provides map references for all roads and streets mentioned in the book that are located within the areas covered by the main city maps.

CROSS-REFERENCES

These are printed in SMALL CAPITALS, referring you to other sections or alphabetical entries in the book. Care has been taken to ensure that such cross-references are self-explanatory. Often, page references are also given, although their excessive use would be intrusive and ugly.

FLOORS

We use the European convention in this book: "ground floor" means the floor at ground level (called by Americans the "first floor").

KEY TO MAP SYMBOLS

CITY MAPS	ENVIRONS MAPS
▨ Major Place of Interest or Important Building	▪ Place of Interest
▢ Built-up Area	▢ Built-up Area
▨ Park	▨ Wood or Park
† Church	═○═ Highway (with access point)
(Mosque	
✡ Synagogue	══ Highway (under construction)
⊞ Hospital	
i Information Office	━━ Main Road
⊠ Post Office	━━ Secondary Road
⌾ Police Station	── Other Road
↞ Parking Lot	══ Railway
→ One-way Street	✚ Airport
⊞⊞⊞ Stepped Street	✗ Good Beach
── Monorail (Sydney only)	
- - - Ferry	

KEY TO SYMBOLS

☎	Telephone	⛔	Facilities for disabled people
Tx	Telex		
Fx	Facsimile (fax)	⪻	Outstanding views
★	Recommended sight	≋	Swimming pool
⚉	Good value (in its class)	⪻	Good beach nearby
⇌	Parking	⦿	Tennis
☑	Free entrance	⬨	Sauna
⬛	Entrance fee payable	⬥	Spa
📷	Photography forbidden	⚹	Golf
✗	Guided tour	⬮	Fishing
☕	Cafeteria	♉	Gym/fitness facilities
☀	Special interest for children	☵	Conference facilities
⌘	Hotel	▣	Refrigerator in room
☐	Cheap	⅄	Bar
⫍	Inexpensive	☰	Restaurant
⫎	Moderately priced	⬤	Good for wines
⫏	Expensive	⌑	A la carte available
⫐	Very expensive	⬛	Set (fixed-price) menu available
AE	American Express		
◈	Diners Club	●	Disco dancing
⬤	MasterCard	♪	Nightclub
VISA	Visa	⬚	Temporary membership

PRICE CATEGORIES

These are denoted by the symbols ☐ (cheap), ⫍ (inexpensive), ⫎ (moderately priced), ⫏ (expensive) and ⫐ (very expensive). For **hotels** and **restaurants** they correspond approximately to the following actual local prices, which give a guideline **at the time of printing**.

Prices for **hotels** vary considerably across each category: prices in Sydney, Melbourne and Canberra are the most expensive, those in Perth, Adelaide and Brisbane are near-average, and those in Hobart, Launceston, Darwin and Alice Springs are the least expensive. Prices **outside** the main cities are lower. Naturally, prices rise, but hotels and restaurants tend to remain in the same price category.

(Australian dollars: A$)	Corresponding to approximate prices for **hotels** *double room with bath; single rather cheaper*	for **restaurants** *meal for one with house wine or BYO bottle*
⫐ very expensive	over A$250	over A$75
⫏ expensive	A$170-250	A$50-75
⫎ moderately priced	A$125-170	A$35-50
⫍ inexpensive	A$75-125	A$20-35
☐ cheap	under A$75	under A$20

About the authors

British-born **Tony Duboudin** is a freelance writer and editor. Formerly chief subeditor of *The Age,* Melbourne, he has also worked on the foreign desk of *The Times,* London, and from 1983-85 was the *Times* correspondent for Australia. He has lived and worked in Australia since 1968.

Also hailing originally from Britain, **Brian Courtis** is a freelance arts and entertainments writer who has lived and worked in Australia since 1969. Formerly television critic of *The Age,* Melbourne, and journalist on the *Daily Express,* London, his assorted career has included TV scriptwriting, working as deckhand on an ocean-going yacht, and working on the media arrangements for the Pope's 1986 visit to Australia.

In this volume's predecessor (*The American Express Pocket Guide to Australia,* written in collaboration by the same authors and published in 1987), **Stephen Taylor** contributed the original chapters on the Australian Capital Territory, New South Wales and Queensland, and **Kim Lockwood** contributed the original chapter on the Northern Territory.

A message from the series editor

In designing *American Express Cities of Australia* we aimed to make this brand-new edition simple and instinctive to use, like all its sister volumes in our new, larger paperback format.

The hallmarks of the relaunched series are clear, classic typography, confidence in fine travel writing for its own sake, and faith in our readers' innate intelligence to find their way around the books without heavy-handed signposting by editors.

Readers with anything less than 20:20 vision will doubtless also enjoy the larger, clearer type, and can now dispense with the mythical magnifying glasses we never issued free with the old pocket guide series.

Our authors **Tony Duboudin** and **Brian Courtis**, together with editor **Sharon Charity**, have worked enormously hard to ensure that this edition is as accurate and up to date as possible at the moment it goes to press. But time and change are forever the enemies, and in between editions we appreciate it when you, our readers, keep us informed of changes that you discover.

As ever, I am indebted to all readers who wrote during the preparation of this book. Please remember that your feedback is extremely important to our efforts to tailor the series to the very distinctive tastes and requirements of our sophisticated international readership.

Send your comments to me at Mitchell Beazley International Ltd, Michelin House, 81 Fulham Road, London SW3 6RB; or, in the US, c/o American Express Travel Guides, Prentice Hall Travel, 15 Columbus Circle, New York, NY 10023.

David Townsend Jones

Australia's Major Cities

The lucky country

Sun, sea, a bountiful soil and vast mineral wealth combine with a stable political system to give Australia an unmatched sense of well-being and comfort. It is a nation that at times borders on smugness — a land blessed with vast wealth that has rightly earned the title of the "Lucky Country."

Because of its close historic and cultural ties with Europe, Australia in many ways often resembles the old continent. Europeans are always finding little corners of Australia that remind them of home, be it mountains, plains, or sea. Likewise, American visitors identify the style of life with California, and South Africans equate the vast open spaces of the Outback with the veldt. Australia can be all things to all people. But this constant, and faintly patronizing comparison with other, "older" countries is misleading, for Australia's origins go back more than 40,000 years, and recent discoveries suggest that the earliest traces of man may be in Australia.

The continent has virtually every type of scenery. Although rarely beautiful in the picture-postcard sense, it frequently has a grandeur and variety unmatched by anything in other countries. It ranges from the pleasant green pastures of the southern part of the state of Victoria and the island of Tasmania to the vast, forbidding desert and spinifex of the Simpson Desert, which covers parts of three states (Western Australia, South Australia and Queensland) and the Northern Territory. In between those extremes, Australia has tropical wetlands and crocodile-infested areas in the Northern Territory, and some of the wildest, most remote mountain landscape to be found anywhere on earth — areas where people have disappeared without trace — that offer first-class skiing comparable with some of the best Europe has to offer.

The kangaroo, the instantly recognizable national symbol, exemplifies the country's unique wildlife, which has evolved independently for millions of years. This isolation is similarly reflected in the flora of the continent, which has also developed its own unique ways of coping with the harsh climate and vast extremes of temperature of the world's driest land mass.

Visitors arriving in this land of plenty, particularly those who have passed through some Asian countries *en route,* may find the economic contrast stark. Couple this with the unconcern that is still often shown by Australians for their regional neighbors, veering sometimes toward outright hostility, and it is tempting to suppose that the nation is wholly indifferent to the Pacific region.

And in some respects that is true. For Australia is an oddity — an ethnically European nation with a Western democracy, surrounded by non-European nations in a region that has few Westminster-style governments. Other than self-interest, Australia has little in common with its neighbors, and still looks to Europe and the United States for inspiration in most fields. In recent years Australia has changed, under the impact of migration, in particular from Asia, but still it clings tenaciously to its European heritage.

The stereotype is of a land of hard-bitten, hard-riding, hard-drinking frontiersmen. In fact this is the most urbanized nation in the world — truly the home of the large city. A visit to Australia means exploring one or several cities, for they as much reflect the real Australia as does the laconic sheep or cattle farmer in the Outback, lording it over thousands of empty square kilometers. The great cities are generally pleasant, handsomely laid out, functional and clean — certainly much cleaner than London or New York. But outside the city centers they lack soul, seeming to stretch aimlessly for kilometer after kilometer. The average Australian city is the epitome of suburbia — and the ambition of the average Australian still goes not much further than owning his own home on a quarter-acre piece of land. That said, the cities do have much to offer, notably the inner areas of Sydney, such as the imaginatively preserved Rocks area, and Melbourne, which has some fine Victorian inner suburbs, such as Carlton and North Melbourne. And all Australian city centers contain numerous fine examples of modern architecture.

As a nation Australia takes pride in its achievements and sometimes ignores the costs and mistakes. The childlike pride in having the tallest building or the largest department store in the southern hemisphere, for example, suggests a lack of maturity in a society that still tends to venerate sportsmen ahead of artists.

But it should also be said that Australians are an extremely generous people. They possess a wry sense of humor and a laconic turn of phrase. They have a healthy disregard for authority and a great distaste for exaggeration, showing off and other displays of what they call "side." Putting on "side" is an Australian expression applied to those who have an inflated sense of their own importance... and there is nothing an Australian likes better than deflating such people. They are a phlegmatic and unemotional lot, and the fact that voting is compulsory is a fair indication of their generally apathetic attitude to politics and, more particularly, politicians, who are usually assumed to be less than honest.

Also characteristic is their overwhelming need to be liked and their strong desire for approval, particularly by foreigners. This is the so-called "cultural cringe," a belief that anything from outside of Australia must be good and, by definition, anything home-grown must be inferior. Although this attitude is now fading, it remains a strong national trait. Thus you are likely to be asked, sometimes within hours of arrival, what you think of this or that local manifestation. Provided you are not too critical, Australians will very quickly warm to you, particularly if you are willing to seek their help.

The Australian way of life is relaxed and the tempo easy. Blessed with vast natural wealth, originally through wool and meat and, more recently, mineral resources, Australia has never really had to extend itself to enjoy a good standard of living. Only in the past decade or so have the harsher realities of the outside world begun to impinge, and even now there remains a refreshingly unquenchable optimism in the future.

The richness of the language as it is spoken in Australia is among the cultural surprises awaiting those who think they speak the Queen's (or American) English. For Australians enjoy manipulating and, some might argue, doing great violence to the language. They also love abbreviating names and titles, evolving slang (and keeping existing slang alive) and creating expressions.

In many ways the Australian has taken up the London cockney's tradition of creating and preserving slang. This national disposition has a lot to do with Australia's penal beginnings, for many of the early convicts came from the poorest parts of London. Coupled with a desire to mark themselves apart from the authorities, the injection of some Aboriginal words and the additional spice of Irish phrases and expressions (many of Australia's early guests were political prisoners from the various "troubles" in that unfortunate island), this led to the evolution of the unique and rich Australian phraseology and style of speech.

For the visitor the challenge of understanding can be all part of the fun of a visit to Australia. So if a local, for example, asks if you would like to come down to the rubbidy (pub) tomorrow arvo (afternoon), or come around and rip the scab off a few blueys (open the ring pull on some cans of Fosters lager), you will understand the scale of the challenge.

Australia has come a long way since Charles Darwin made this unflattering comment about the country when he departed its shores in 1845 on the *Beagle:*

> Farewell, Australia! you are a rising child, and doubtless some day will reign a great princess in the South; but you are too great and ambitious for affection, yet not great enough for respect.
> I leave your shores without sorrow or regret.

Most visitors now depart Australia feeling that they have experienced a country that is truly different, one that has, so far, avoided or been spared many of the problems that beset the rest of the planet. It is a country where the government is stable, pollution is light, traffic still flows relatively freely, you can eat the food and drink the water without fear, the people are basically friendly and honest, the cities have not yet been taken over by the less desirable elements, and the sun is always shining somewhere. In short, Australia is how the rest of the world ought to be but is not.

Australia has in a way become a princess but not, one suspects, in the manner Darwin envisaged. It has certainly gained the affection of millions who have visited her shores.

Culture, history and background

Landmarks in Australia's history

c 40000BC: The first Aborigines are thought to have traveled across the land bridge from Asia.

c 1542: The Portuguese probably sighted Australia when exploring the East Indies. **1606**: The Dutchman Wilhelm Jansz, sailing from Java in the Dutch East India Company ship *Duyfken,* passed s of Papua New Guinea and sighted the w coast of Cape York Peninsula. He mapped part of the coast. **1616**: Dutch sea captain Dirk Hartog landed at Shark Bay on the coast of Western Australia.

1642-43: Abel Tasman sighted the sw coast of Tasmania, which he named Van Diemen's Land. **1688**: The pirate ship *Cygnet* sailed along the NW coast of Australia. On board was William Dampier, whose subsequent book published in England did much to excite interest in "New Holland."

1770: Captain James Cook in *Endeavour* sighted the E coast of the continent near what is now Cape Everard. He claimed the land for the Crown. **1788**: The First Fleet arrived at Botany Bay with 1,044 people, including 568 male and 191 female convicts plus 13 children, under the command of Captain Arthur Phillip. A few weeks later the settlement was moved 14.5km (9 miles) to the N to Port Jackson.

1790: The New South Wales Corps was formed in England to guard convicts. **1792**: The colony came under the control of the officers of the NSW Corps, especially their leader John Macarthur. Macarthur adopted measures designed to benefit himself and his fellow officers. The Corps retained control until 1795 when a new governor arrived. The clique controlled the colony's economy largely through monopoly of the trade in rum, which was *de facto* currency. **1806**: William Bligh became governor and tried to break the power of the NSW Corps, but his stern measures led to a rum rebellion and his arrest. The military ruled the colony for two years. London vindicated Bligh but removed him.

1824: The city of Brisbane was founded. **1825**: Tasmania was detached from NSW and created as a separate colony. **1829**: Britain formally claimed possession of the entire continent. Perth was founded. Newspaper compositors on *The Australian* newspaper staged Australia's first strike.

1834: A group of Tasmanians began colonization of what later (in 1851) became the colony of Victoria. **1835**: The Tasmanians, under the leadership of John Batman, bought 240,000ha (600,000 acres), the land on which Melbourne now stands, from the local Aborigines. **1850:** The British Parliament approved the Australian Colonies Government Act, extending a large measure of self-government to the colonies.

1851: Gold was discovered in NSW and Victoria, sparking a rush. **1854:** The Eureka Stockade, an armed insurrection at Ballarat, in which 30 died, led to some reforms of the colony's repressive legislation. **1856:** South Australia introduced universal suffrage for men. The stonemasons' societies agreed with their employers on a 48-hour week, working 8 hours a day — the first such agreement in the world and forerunner of much social experiment and enlightened legislation.

1859: Queensland separated from NSW and became a new colony. **1860-61:** Robert O'Hara Burke and William John Wills traveled from Melbourne to the Gulf of Carpentaria, completing the first crossing of the continent from s to n.

1894: South Australia became the first colony to introduce votes for women and thus the first to introduce truly universal suffrage. **1899:** A meeting of the colonial premiers in Melbourne resolved objections from NSW to the proposed federal constitution for a single nation. **1900:** The draft constitution was approved by London and received the Royal Assent. **1901:** The Commonwealth of Australia came into existence.

1908: Canberra was selected as the site for the national capital. **1910:** The first federal Labour government under Andrew Fisher was elected. **1914:** At the outbreak of World War I, Australia pledged its support for Britain "to the last shilling." **1915:** The Anzacs landed on the Gallipoli peninsula in the Dardanelles. A bitter campaign, conceived by Winston Churchill, ended in stalemate, with great loss of life. **1916:** The country was bitterly divided by a referendum on universal conscription, which was defeated. **1917:** A second referendum was defeated. Australia retained a volunteer army.

1927: The Duke and Duchess of York (later King George VI and Queen Elizabeth) opened the new Federal Parliament in Canberra. **1930:** Amy Johnson became the first woman to fly solo from England to Australia. **1932:** Sydney Harbour Bridge was opened.

1939: World War II began. Again Australia supported the Allies. **1942:** The Japanese bombed Darwin, killing 240 people. **1945:** The war ended.

1946: Australia accepted United Nations trusteeship over the Territory of New Guinea. **1949:** The Labour government was defeated by a coalition led by Robert Menzies (Liberal Party) and A.W. Fadden (Country Party). **1950:** Australia, New Zealand and the US signed the ANZUS pact for mutual defense in the Pacific. Menzies tried to outlaw the Communist Party, but a referendum was unsuccessful. Australia sent troops to the Korean War. **1954:** Vladimir Petrov, a Soviet diplomat in Canberra, defected. **1956:** The Olympic Games were held in Melbourne.

1965: Menzies committed Australian troops to fight in Vietnam. **1966:** Menzies announced his retirement and was succeeded by Harold Holt. Australia adopted decimal currency. **1967:** Harold Holt drowned in a swimming accident. **1968:** John Gorton took over as Prime Minister. **1971:** Gorton was succeeded by William McMahon as Prime Minister. **1972:** Gough Whitlam led Labour to power, breaking a 23-year monopoly by the Liberal-Country Party coalition. **1974:** Cyclone Tracy devastated Darwin.

1975: Governor-General Sir John Kerr dismissed the Labour government, sparking the most serious political crisis in the country's history. Malcolm Fraser succeeded as caretaker Prime Minister, a position he consolidated in elections held in December when he won a majority in both Houses of Parliament. **1978:** Sir Robert Menzies died.

1983: The Labour Party under Bob Hawke defeated the Liberal-Country Party coalition after Fraser called an election 9 months early. **1984:** An early election was called and Labour was re-elected with a reduced majority. **1987:** Labour again won an early election, against a divided opposition. **1991:** Bob Hawke, serving a record fourth term for Labour as Prime Minister, directed the Australian Naval Task Force to take action against Iraq in the Persian Gulf. **1992:** Former Treasurer Paul Keating became Prime Minister after toppling Hawke in a party coup.

Aborigines: the first Australians

I think of land as the history of my nation. It tells me how we came into being, and what system we must live. My great ancestors, who lived in the time of history, planned everything that we practise now.
(Aboriginal leader Galarrwuy Yunupingu)

Aboriginal Australians were the first people on the subcontinent, inhabiting the Australian mainland and Tasmania for at least 40,000 years before the arrival of the Europeans some 200 years ago. The generic name given to cover their diverse tribes and cultures comes from the Latin *ab origine,* meaning "from the beginning."

There are several theories concerning the origins of the country's earliest descendants. Some believe that the Aborigines derived from Java Man; others that they come from three distinct groups: the Tasmanoid, the Murrayian and the Carpentarian. A third, more recent and popular theory is that the Aborigines are racially homogeneous — that they are members of the unique Australoid race. Their forefathers are said to have migrated s from Asia, moving from island to island, having set off from the N as early as 50,000 years ago.

Evidence of the way in which those early inhabitants of the subcontinent lived and died is scanty, although recent discoveries have begun to drop pieces into the historical jigsaw puzzle. The cremated skeleton of a woman found at Lake Mungo in western NSW has been carbon-dated at about 26,000 years old, and subsequent excavations have revealed stone tools dating back a further 10,000 years or more.

Archeological evidence suggests that the earliest groups of Aborigines lived around the coastal areas and along the main river systems, where there was ample and easily acquired food, as seminomadic hunters and food gatherers, each tribe claiming certain specific rights over the territory

16

they roamed. Their relationship with the land was, and is, extraordinarily complex.

These first Australians, who initially shared the land with now extinct animals such as the giant marsupial diprotodon, the flightless genyormis and the giant kangaroo, rapidly adapted to their environment. They learned how to live with the land, the punishing climate and the flora and fauna around them; and the skills they learned were passed from generation to generation. In extended family groups they netted fish and collected seeds, berries, grubs, succulent honey ants, lizards and small marsupials. The men hunted emus and kangaroos, often using a harpoon-shaped spear attached by cord to a woomera (or spear-thrower). Also in their armory were nonreturning boomerangs, for use either as clubs or as lethal missiles. In the coastal areas of the N, dugong and turtle were important sources of food for the family, and a feast of charred barramundi or goanna, served up on a bark plate, was a welcomed treat.

The Aborigines used the natural materials around them for their shelters and their weapons. They discovered the times of the year when certain fruits and plants could safely be eaten, where water might be found in times of drought, and how to thrive in conditions that would be considered deadly by most inhabitants of the planet. They learned how to read the Outback and developed an intimate knowledge of the landscape. To incoming Europeans, the Aborigines' finely honed skills in gathering food and water, navigation and tracking, often seemed supernatural.

Few would deny today that European colonization had a ruinous effect on Aboriginal society. From the beginning, huge tracts of land were "settled," fenced or insensitively developed by the Europeans; sacred Aboriginal sites were abused and destroyed; families were enslaved and murdered; and the traditional life of a people civilized in ways beyond the understanding of the colonizers was fractured beyond repair. No attempt was made to understand the Aboriginals' feeling of "responsibility" for the land. The Europeans took the view that the Aborigines had done nothing to "develop" Australia and thus had no rights to the land.

The Aborigines resisted the invasion and, in the battles that followed, some Europeans and many Aborigines died. There were shootings, spearings and a great deal of misery. In Tasmania, the Aborigines were eventually wiped out. In the Northern Territory, groups of Aborigines were massacred or poisoned by Whites as recently as 1928. It is estimated that when Europeans first settled there were about 300,000 Aborigines throughout Australia; they comprised 500 tribes speaking about 200 different, distinct languages. Today, there are about 160,000 Aborigines, living mainly in rural areas.

In the early part of this century some steps were taken to provide assistance and protection for the Aborigines. Settlements and reserves were established and, with the best of intentions, government handouts to Aborigines were begun. Social welfare, religious do-gooding and government assimilation policies, however, quickly added to the troubles of a society linked closely with the land, tribal authority and self-sufficiency. Alcohol and a sense of rootlessness infected Aboriginal life. Not

17

until the mid-1960s did most Australians really begin to understand, and show concern, that the Aboriginal people and their rich and ancient culture were in extreme danger.

Today, clumsily but steadily, Blacks and Whites appear at last to be working together to counteract the effects of those bad times.

THE DREAMTIME

Aboriginal tribes, although not all holding the same religious beliefs, share several basic principles. Among them is the concept of The Dreamtime, or The Dreaming, a timeless continuum in which ancestral heroes first emerged from the night to create everything. The land existed without shape or life until these spirit-beings produced oceans, springs, billabongs (waterholes), mountains, sky, sun, moon, stars and the laws that govern existence. (There are parallels with the first chapter of Genesis in the Old Testament — and with the Christian idea of Heaven.) The Aboriginal ancestor heroes also gave the people their own tracts of land, along with languages and social institutions. And the Aborigines believe the influence of these Dreamtime spirits remain with them today as a spiritual power in the land, in certain sites, and in some animals and plants.

The relationship between man and land is given special emphasis in the belief that for a child to be born, a spirit from one of these sites must first enter the mother's womb to give the child life. That site is the source of the person's life force and, consequently, he or she is inseparably connected with it, the spirit returning to the site at death.

Through ceremony, the land, animals, plants and the sacred sites, the spiritual power of the past is believed to flow into the living Aborigine. During many ceremonies, the Aborigine not only re-enacts the actions of his ancestor hero, but he *becomes* that ancestor hero.

To the Aborigine, then, the Dreamtime is far from imaginary. It is the very basis of his life.

MAGIC AND MEMENTOES

Bound up with the Dreamtime and their faith in ancestral powers is a strong Aboriginal belief in what outsiders would simply call "magic." This magic might be used to improve the food supply, nurse a sick person back to health, or punish someone who has defied tribal authority. Even today, magistrates and judges in Australian courts take into consideration the tribal judgments that those Aboriginals appearing before them will also face. This might range from a spearing to banishment from tribal land.

The most feared form of magic known to Aborigines has been "pointing the bone." A medicine man would point a sharpened animal or human bone toward the victim and deliver a ritual chant. The victim, believing the bone was piercing his body, invariably collapsed and died. Similarly *kurdaitcha* (medicine) men, wearing moccasins of marsupial fur, emu feathers and cord, would approach their victims with certain ritual movements, and have the same devastating effect. Awareness that a *kurdaitcha* man had been appointed to carry out a sentence was often enough to cause an Aborigine hundreds of kilometers away to collapse and die. The power of suggestion was apparently supreme.

In the past 20 years a greater appreciation and awareness of the complexities of Aboriginal life has grown, both in Australia and abroad. Aborigines have found that by making much of their traditional art and crafts available for sale they can supplement the economies of many Aboriginal communities and keep alive ancient traditions.

In recent years, however, laws have been introduced to protect the treasured, sacred objects of Aboriginal and Torres Strait Islander heritage. Australia will not allow the export of bark and log coffins, human remains, rock art or carved trees. Aboriginal leaders, with Government support, have visited museums and private collectors around the world, trying to recover heads, bones and objects of religious significance stolen from them by Europeans in less enlightened times. They have had varying degrees of success. Among the relics that have been returned was the head of an Aborigine known as "Shiny." It was brought back to Hobart in March 1990 after being displayed for 150 years in a glass jar in Dublin's College of Surgeons.

Among the more fascinating objects readily available to collectors visiting Australia are:

The didjeridu   A difficult-to-play musical instrument made from eucalypt branches hollowed out by termites. Painted with distinctive designs, the didjeridu makes a low, fascinating, droning sound, familiar to those who know Aboriginal music. It ranges in size from 80-150cm (31-59 inches) and, traditionally, is played only by men.

The boomerang   Both a weapon and a clapping instrument used in the accompaniment of songs and dances. There are both returning and nonreturning boomerangs. The nonreturning kind has a shallow curve at one end and is a powerful hunting and fighting weapon. Returning boomerangs are occasionally used in hunting, but more often as an enjoyable form of competitive entertainment.

The coolamon   A general-purpose dish, made from native soft wood. It can be about 85cm (33 inches) long and generally has high sides. Aboriginal women use it for carrying water or food, as a bowl for food preparation, or as a bassinet or cradle for a baby.

LAND RIGHTS

Since the late 1960s, the question of Aboriginal land rights has emerged as a major political issue. The diverse requirements of farmers, miners and traditional "owners" of the land have created much friction. For in a European sense, the Aborigines do not own land: the land owns them. In Australia this has been a point of conflict and misunderstanding among city and rural Blacks and Whites right to the present time.

The Aboriginal Land Rights (Northern Territory) Act 1976 pioneered land rights legislation throughout the country. It provided a legal framework for Aboriginal groups to lay claim to unalienated Crown land on the grounds of traditional attachment. In South Australia, Victoria and NSW, titles to former reserves have been turned over to Aboriginal leaders. Perhaps the most dramatic "hand-over," however, took place on

November 11, 1983, when the Prime Minister announced the transfer of the title of the Uluru National Park (Ayers Rock-Mt. Olga) to the traditional owners. The agreement recognized that this area, one of Australia's most famous tourist spots, would continue to be protected as a national park.

Australia's formerly disenfranchised Aborigines are gaining a greater ability to determine and control their own destiny. Their red, yellow and black Aboriginal flag is seen more and more around the country today — the black in it symbolizing the people; the red, the color of the earth; and the yellow, the warmth and optimism of the sun. The flag is an important mark of identity for a people who are beginning to show once again a pride in the accomplishments of their past.

THE FUTURE

It is becoming clear to Australians that cash, by itself, is not going to solve the 200-year-old Aboriginal problem. Instead of blindly handing out social welfare checks, which have often bred a sense of hopelessness among recipients and resentment among others, Canberra has now embarked on a more promising strategy of reconciliation, involving a ten-year investigation of ways in which to redress the overwhelming disadvantages suffered by Aborigines.

Aboriginal groups have received support for broadcasting and telecommunications, providing modern links for communities in the remotest areas. Deep in the Outback, the Walkman provides broadcasts to Aborigines in their own languages. Government funding has also been allocated to support and maintain Aboriginal languages, many of which would otherwise have been in danger of disappearing altogether.

Intolerance still exists. There are still many racial difficulties. One of Australia's major concerns has been the number of Aborigines who have apparently committed suicide while in prison. This has been the subject of the Royal Commission into Aboriginal Deaths in Custody. Urban and rural police have been the target for many accusations of racism, especially in the poor inner-city Sydney suburb of Redfern. Poor education and poor training in the police force has been blamed for some of the incidents. But a lot of the trouble has been rooted in political neglect.

Times are changing. Many community leaders have committed themselves to improving racial relationships within Australia. There is a great resurgence of interest in Aboriginal life among many non-Aboriginal Australians. Artists, actors, sportsmen and women, and pop stars like Yothu Yindi and Archie Roach, have worked hard to break down any perceived barriers. In the 1990s, racial incidents tend to create a healthy furore. Australians are outraged when they hear of them, no longer accepting such behavior as a way of life. For the original people of Australia, the future is looking brighter than the immediate past.

> The law of history says that we must not take land, fight over land, or give land, and so on. My land is mine only because I came in spirit from that land, as did my ancestors. My land is my backbone.... My land is my foundation.
> (Galarrwuy Yunupingu)

Australia's architecture

The basic homes of the early convict parties were primitive hip-roofed box shelters, rectangular in plan, with the whole of the outer wooden face daubed with a heavy coat of mud to keep out wind and rain. The mud, applied with a trowel, was coated with pipe-clay, or white-washed with lime made by burning oyster shells. Roofs were thatched with reeds from nearby swamps. Inside there was a fireplace of heavy mud and sandstone; the smoke rose through a chimney built from timber coated heavily with clay. A packed earth or clay floor lay below.

Coarse clay bricks began to be made a few months after the arrival of the First Fleet. The earliest construction with any real pretension to architectural quality, the Governor's official residence, was a two-story design of brick set in lime and sheep "hair" mortar.

FROM PRIMITIVES TO COLONIALS

But whether they were built of brick, wattle-and-daub or slabs, the early buildings were unstable monuments to European man. The mud of the mortar covering the wattles simply washed out in Sydney's torrential rain, and for years walls sagged and chimneys collapsed. Poor construction was to plague the colony for a decade or more after the First Fleet's arrival.

Australia's first town planner was Lieutenant William Dawes, one of whose first duties was to design **Parramatta**, near Sydney, a "plan of grace, balance, charm and utility." In 1794 Captain John Macarthur, formerly an officer with the NSW Corps and a prosperous, hard-working landowner, moved into a farmhouse, **Elizabeth Farm**, on 250 acres (101ha) of land overlooking the Parramatta River. Elizabeth Farm, built of brick, with a hipped roof covered with swamp-oak shingles cut from local trees, was the primitive prototype of country farmhouses throughout NSW. Extended and altered, it still serves as a private home and is the oldest building in Australia.

When **Lachlan Macquarie** first took up his duties as the new Governor-in-Chief in 1810, he was appalled by the poor state of the buildings in the colony. His first act was to insist that Sydney's streets should be at least 66 feet (20m) wide and that no building should be erected closer than 20 feet (6m) to the street. Macquarie called for better construction throughout the colony, and stipulated the use of brick or stone, and that buildings should preferably be of two stories wherever possible. In his travels through the state, he particularly encouraged the building of inns, well aware that such hotels would play a major role in the opening up of the countryside. The oldest hotel in Australia, the appropriately named **Macquarie Arms** in Windsor, NSW, was built in 1811 under the Governor's direction.

In Macquarie's plans for country towns, priority was also given to sites for churches, courthouses and, eventually, schools. Unfortunately, these building regulations were introduced on a local basis — and this pattern of local building control has bedeviled Australian architects and builders to this day.

In 1816 **Francis Howard Greenway**, that arrogant, malicious and vain man but imaginative, thorough and professional architect, was appointed Civil Architect and Engineer in NSW. He had been despatched there for life for an act of forgery. Within six years, he had singlehandedly created what was to be Australia's finest early architectural heritage. Greenway designed and supervised the completion of an enormous number of buildings, ranging from a lighthouse to a hospital, to a large school. He initiated plans for town sewers, a water supply, fortifications and bridges.

Greenway designed his buildings in the Georgian style that had been favored in and around Bristol at the time he left the West Country of England. He added his own highly personal touches, and his architecture was both stylish and forceful. Among the surviving examples of his work are the

St Matthew's Church

St Matthew's Church of England (built 1817-20) and **rectory** (1823-25) at Windsor, NSW, and the **Hyde Park Barracks** in Sydney (1819). They are straightforward, uncomplicated edifices, with simple, clever touches to add variety to the generally plain body of the buildings.

Temperature changes in the new land could be severe, prompting in some country homesteads the beginnings of a new indigenous architecture. The veranda, borrowed from the East, was used as both a means of access to rooms and a cool and shady place for the inhabitants. Together with an overhanging roof and supporting columns, it helped create a low-lying building in harmony with the climate and the landscape.

The years 1822-40 produced the riches of the Colonial period of architecture in Australia. The prevailing style was still Georgian, but eventually it was supplanted by the more elaborate Regency fashion, featuring walls of stone or plastered brick.

In Van Diemen's Land (Tasmania), however, there were other developments. Many fine buildings, utilitarian but attractive, were designed and erected by, among others, **John Lee Archer**, the

Lacy wrought-iron **balconies** are a characteristic 19thC form

Colonial Architect, a former colleague of Charles Beazley and John Rennie, with whom he had designed London's Waterloo and Southwark bridges. Archer's most successful works were his elegant bridges and military buildings, but his excellence can also be seen in his design for several churches, the **Treasury offices** in Hobart, and hospitals, schools and lighthouses. Recent restoration work shows these buildings to great effect.

In 1837 **Colonel William Light**, the Surveyor General appointed by the South Australian Company, began laying out, around the Torrens River, what many feel is Australia's noblest town design. Light's plan for **Adelaide** involved a series of rectangular grids of broad streets wrapped in a swathe of natural parkland.

Meanwhile in Sydney an Australian high society was emerging that was determined to copy what was going on "at home." So Australian Regency, a simplified version of the imposing style popularized in Regency Britain by John Soane, was introduced. A good example is **Elizabeth Bay House** (1832-37), designed by **John Verge**, where the portico roof is an impressive balcony reached by French windows on the upper floor. On public buildings, however, just as in Britain, the Classical or Gothic style remained in favor. A strong proponent was **Edmund Blacket**, who designed the **St Mark's Church of England** at Darling Point in 1848.

In the 1840s a NSW settler introduced a building practice destined eventually to spread around the world. He built double-layered stone walls and left out the normal rubble core. Brick veneer — a protecting sheath of brickwork placed around a timber interior — was another Australian technique that emerged by the 1850s. The first brick veneer building in the world, erected near Swan Hill in 1850, developed eventually into **Tyntyndyer**, one of the finest farming homesteads in Victoria.

GOLD AND THE VICTORIANS

The gold rush era of the 1850s changed the face of Australian architecture dramatically. As the harsher realities of the goldfields hit home, some discovered that there was an easier-found crock of gold in the building of hotels, homes, churches, warehouses and offices, all of which were urgently required. In Melbourne, s of the Yarra at Emerald Hill, tens of thousands of people were living uncomfortably in a shanty town of tents. Italianate terraces and mansions, with cast-iron lacework balconies, stained glass, columns, towers, turrets and plaster ornamentation, became the fashion among the wealthy, particularly in Melbourne. Some very fine examples of these lacework buildings are still to be found in the suburbs of Carlton, South Melbourne and Albert Park.

Mid-19thC **Queensland timber home**

In the 1850s, a distinctive style of architecture began to develop in **Queensland**. Timber homes, with airy latticework exterior walls, were built on raised platforms (see illustration on previous page), with high stumps or stilts supporting them, providing coolness as well as protection against snakes and floods.

The most prominent architect in Sydney was **Edmund Blacket**, designer of the **Great Hall** at the **University of Sydney**, probably the finest Gothic Revival building in Australia. But Blacket traveled farther afield. His buildings can be found from Brisbane and Geelong to **St George's Cathedral** in Perth.

Melbourne, then the younger city, attracted **William Wardell**, who had built at least 30 churches before he migrated to Australia. His first commission in Melbourne was for the huge Roman Catholic **St Patrick's Cathedral** (illustrated on page 245), which became the largest and most impressive in the country. Wardell was appointed Government Architect for Victoria in 1859.

But it was another architect, **Joseph Reed**, who made the biggest impression on the appearance of Melbourne. Reed created the original Classical design for the **Melbourne Public Library** in 1854; the follow-

Ripponlea

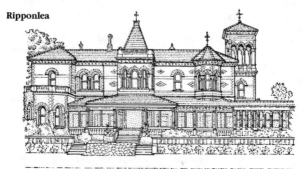

ing year he designed the **Town Hall** for Geelong. His work includes one of Melbourne's best-known mansions, **Ripponlea** in Hotham St., in Elsternwick (one of his smaller commissions), more than 20 church buildings of all denominations, many of the University of Melbourne buildings, ten banks, the Town Hall, the Weather Bureau, the Trades Hall, the Exhibition Building and many others.

RISING TO THE FUTURE
"Safe" passenger elevators arrived in Australia in the 1870s, enabling architects to design upward and answer the demand for more rooms on less land. By the 1890s there were several buildings of ten or even 12 stories. Although the new high-rise buildings had many critics, the main problems were overcome and, with developments in steel and reinforced concrete, the first authentic skyscrapers went up in the 1920s.

Following the depression years of the 1890s, a style known as "Queen Anne" predominated in domestic architecture. In this, the red brickwork of walls was openly displayed and Classical moldings were carved, not in timber, but wholly in brick. Terra-cotta-tiled roofs topped it off in inner-suburban Melbourne and Sydney; elsewhere they used iron roofs painted red.

In 1912, a young American architect, **Walter Burley Griffin**, submitted the winning design in the Australian government's international competition for a national capital. Griffin's imaginative design for **Canberra** used natural features of the land, a geometric sweep of wide roads and the lake that now bears his name. A leader in the style known as **Functionalism**, he designed Newman College (1918) in the University of Melbourne, then went on to plan the NSW town of **Griffith**.

Australia Square Tower, Sydney

The arrival in 1947 of **Harry Seidler** — an Austrian-born, American-trained architect who had studied under **Walter Gropius** — attracted much attention. He designed a highly sophisticated International-style home for his parents at Turramurra, an outer suburb of Sydney. And it was Seidler's work, seen in all its glory in the soaring glass-and-concrete **Australia Square Tower** in Sydney, that inspired so many of today's Australian architects.

Among them was the late **Sir Roy Grounds**, who designed the **Victorian Arts Centre** in Melbourne, illustrated on page 247, and the domed **Academy of Science building** in Canberra. Another disciple

Academy of Science Building, Canberra

was Danish architect **Joern Utzon**, whose skills will be recognized forever in the graceful splendor of the magnificent exterior sails of the **Sydney Opera House** (see illustration on page 108 and cover picture).

In the boom years of the 1980s, the rivalry between Melbourne and Sydney continued to inspire exhilarating changes to the skyline of both cities. There were attempts, however, to maintain within new buildings some of the glories of the past, occasionally with bizarre results.

One of the most remarkable developments, **Melbourne Central** (see SHOPPING in VICTORIA), opened late in 1991 when Australia, like much of the Western world, was in recession. The huge retail development, which covered a restored historic building, Shot Tower, with a 20-story glass cone, was largely the creation of Japanese architect **Kisho Kurokawa**.

25

At the heart of a great explosion of political edifices in **Canberra** is Richard Thorp's extraordinary **New Parliament House**, the city's central landmark (see illustration on page 88). This spectacular building, which apppears to erupt from the land, has as its peak an 81m (266-foot) flagmast, the largest stainless steel structure in the world. The New Parliament House was built from 300,000 cubic meters of concrete — enough to build 25 Sydney Opera Houses. Grass ramps cover much of the building, from which there are spectacular views all over the city.

In the mid-1980s, property developers clamored to fill Australia's skyline with office developments, almost as if to defy the signs of hard times ahead. By the early 1990s, glass, aluminum and concrete canyons cast their shadows over most of the state capitals, with ubiquitous "for lease" signs flagging the futility of it all.

But architects, and Australians in general, were taking a new pride in "Australian design" by the end of the 1980s. It meant different things, of course, to different people. To some it was Phillip Cox's Yulara Resort, almost a Bedouin-tent fantasy in the desert near Ayers Rock; to others it was more modest development, homes and offices that took the best design ideas from the past to create buildings that seemed to blend with the climate and landscape.

The arts in Australia

I come with strength of the living day,
And with half the world behind me;
I leave you alone in your cultured halls
To drivel and croak and cavil:
Till your voice goes farther than college walls
Keep out of the tracks we travel!
(Henry Lawson, *To My Cultured Critics*)

Ever since the arrival of the First Fleet, the cultural life of Australia has explored and drawn upon the everyday interests of "ordinary," working Australians, focusing firmly on those local matters that interest most of the people. That is hardly to say that the world's finest arts and entertainment have swept by unappreciated Down Under: far from it. The intellectual treasures of Europe, America and Asia have always been devoured eagerly by a largely immigrant population anxious to stay in touch with its cultural roots, and have also provided inspiration for generations of local artists, writers and performers. And a glance around the world's stages and galleries quickly lays to rest any suggestion that Australians have not marched enthusiastically, and with great success, to contribute to the great international artistic movements and traditions of the 20thC.

But even with the ebb and flow of styles and attitudes, popular icons have unfailingly remained the most truly Australian source of cultural inspiration. In literature, poetry, theater, painting, dance and cinema, it has been the bush, the race meeting, the beach, the Anzacs, the pub, the railways, the surfies, milk bars, the exotic fauna and, more recently, cityscapes that have produced, from the fresh palette this country offers, a picture that is distinctively Australian. Artists raised in the European tradition have had to learn both how to interpret a new landscape and to foster a new appreciation for it.

Australians, too, caught in the often patronizing, inevitably smothering embrace of the old mother country, were slow to recognize their own gifts and their own gifted. The "colonial cringe," that apologetic deference to the critics of London and New York, has been a long time departing. Artistic activity in Australia was until recently bedeviled by the local audience's tendency to believe that the home-grown product could only be inferior to the overseas version. For many years talented Australians felt obliged to go into artistic exile, daring to return home only when word of their triumphs abroad was received by the Australian press.

In the 1950s, a startling transformation began. Australia produced artists who were not only well-known internationally, but who drew unequivocally upon their Australian background. But from 1970 onward, this interest accelerated dramatically, and a vigorous new growth in arts activity became evident. Australians, wealthier and more traveled than in the past, came to realize that what they had on their own soil matched, if it did not surpass, the quality of the imported product.

Today, with government and private-industry sponsorship, and the support of an increasingly ardent audience, the arts in Australia flourish as never before.

THE WRITERS

Australian literature began to achieve a national identity around the turn of the century, when a romantic patriotic sentiment was helping to encourage the birth of a new nation. In 1901, when the separate colonies united to form the Commonwealth, there were only 3.5 million Whites in the country, 95 percent of them British and xenophobic. The bush provided the most vivid contrast with what was normal for most of those fresh Australians, and it was to the bush ballads of A. B. "Banjo" Patterson (1864-1941) and the poems and short stories of Henry Lawson (1867-1922) that they turned for their nationalistic fuel. These writers, and others of the kind, found their audience through the likes of the Sydney-based *Bulletin,* a magazine that encouraged examination of Australian rather than European subjects. The *Bulletin,* founded in 1880, continues today as a weekly news magazine.

The short story remained a popular form long after Lawson: there have been fine examples from such Australian writers as Alan Marshall, Frank Moorhouse and, more recently, Peter Carey and Tim Winton. The bush ballads of Banjo Paterson *(The Man From Snowy River, Clancy Of The Overflow, The Man From Ironbark* and, of course, *Waltzing Matilda)* and others helped establish poetry as a popular form; but through such poets as Kenneth Slessor and, much later, Judith Wright, both the techniques and subject matter changed considerably. Australian novelists who have attracted world attention with distinctively Australian themes include Henry Handel (Ethel Florence) Richardson, Xavier Herbert, Martin Boyd, Thomas Kenneally and Peter Carey. The country's best-known writer, however, was Patrick White, whose non-naturalistic approach to his subject matter initially disconcerted many local critics. White, the author of *The Tree Of Man, Voss, The Solid Mandala* and *The Twyborn Affair,* was awarded the Nobel Prize for Literature in 1973. An alert, witty, and somewhat cantankerous observer of Australian life in his final years, he died in 1990.

THE STAGE

The theater, which first drew its popular audiences during the gold rushes of the 1850s, has enjoyed mixed fortunes over the years. In the 1870s, impresario J. C. Williamson came to Australia, and his company's melodramas proved as popular then as its imported comedies and musicals would in the 1960s. But the cinema boom of the 1920s and then the Depression of the 1930s had an adverse effect on the box office.

It was in the 1950s that "Australian theater" received its first big boost, with the establishment of the government-assisted National Institute of Dramatic Art (NIDA). Ray Lawler's trilogy *The Summer Of The Seventeenth Doll* was produced in 1955, achieving critical success in Australia and then in New York and London. Alan Seymour's biting Anzac Day exploration, *One Day Of The Year,* followed.

By 1970 every state capital had a permanent professional drama company; and Australian actors, unlike their predecessors Peter Finch, Leo McKern, Judith Anderson and Diane Cilento, no longer found it necessary to go into exile to receive due acclaim. Today the plays of David Williamson *(The Removalists, Don's Party* and *The Perfectionist),* Dorothy Hewett, Jack Hibberd and Alexander Buzo, and the performances of Judy Davis, Robyn Nevin, Colin Friels, Peter Cummins and Freddie Parslow attract wide, sophisticated audiences at home.

Dance has a young and growing following in Australia although, with the exception of Edouard Borovansky's company in Melbourne, it was not until the early 1960s that local companies went beyond performance to creation in ballet. The Australian Ballet Company made its debut in 1962 and two years later helped establish the Australian Ballet School. In 1965, Sir Robert Helpmann and Dame Peggy Van Praagh, then the company's artistic directors, organized its first overseas tour. International acclaim and overseas awards have followed. In dance theater, the Sydney Dance Company, under director Graeme Murphy, has played to packed houses with exhilarating original productions.

MUSIC

Australia now has fully professional orchestras in all state capitals, as well as those that work with the Australian Opera and the Australian Ballet. There are also youth orchestras, the Australian Pops, chamber groups, and many popular ethnic groups. Standards vary considerably, and provide the critics with a fruitful source of argument. Musica Viva, which was founded in 1946 to encourage understanding of chamber music in the country, presents subscription concerts of overseas and distinguished Australian artists, which are particularly popular. And, with the proliferation of new and comfortable "arts centers" and concert halls, attendances have risen dramatically.

From the tradition of the country's best-known composers, Percy Grainger and Malcolm Williamson, have come Peter Sculthorpe and Barry Conyngham, and, from the pop music/movie world, Bruce Smeaton and Peter Best. Australian music of all kinds offers great variety. The country's rock stars, who include INXS, AC-DC and Kylie Minogue, have achieved fame in both Europe and North America, and jazz, from Don Burrows and exciting young players James Morrison and Allan Zavod, is currently going through one of its periodic revivals.

And opera? It may be all that sunshine and clear air, but Australia has always enjoyed a world-famous reputation for its opera sopranos. From Dame Nellie Melba to Dame Joan Sutherland, these singers have surprised and delighted audiences everywhere. At home they have helped create a large following for opera. Today the productions of such companies as the Australian Opera and the Victorian State Opera are often sold out months ahead.

THE VISUAL ARTS
With the early European explorers and settlers of Australia came documentary artists — the equivalent of today's photojournalists — whose often bizarre interpretations of the continent's landscape and fauna may have been of dubious scientific value, but certainly created curiosity in Europe.

The Heidelberg School, which was founded in the 1880s by Tom Roberts and Frederick McCubbin, and named after the area of Victoria that was favored by its members, was Australia's first distinct school of painting. Its artists painted in what they saw as an Impressionist style, striving to capture the unique lights and atmosphere of the Australian bush.

But the country's isolation from the European centers of art encouraged many artists to travel overseas for experience and, at the turn of the century, Roberts, Arthur Streeton and Rupert Bunny were among those who made the pilgrimage. Post-Impressionist, or Modernist, art provided one of the great controversies in the Australian art world between the two World Wars, but gradually gained acceptance through the work of Russell Drysdale and William Dobell. A younger colleague of these artists, Sidney Nolan, became better known overseas, but to reach that wider audience he found it necessary to travel to London in 1953.

From Nolan, and his Ned Kelly and Gallipoli paintings, there followed, again in the late 1960s and 1970s, a period of rapid expansion in both painting and sculpture. Private galleries bloomed; dealers and collectors pounced on Australian paintings. Artists such as Brett Whiteley, Fred Williams and Jeffrey Smart attracted interest around the world. Sculptors such as Tom Bass, Inge King and Stephen Walker, answering the demand for art around public and commercial buildings, provided outstanding work at home.

THE CINEMA

Cinema may seem the most recent of Australia's lively arts. In fact Australia was a pioneer of the world's movie industry. The oldest surviving relic is a clip of the 1896 Melbourne Cup by French photographer Maurice Sestier. In 1900 Melbourne enjoyed the world premiere of *Soldiers of the Cross,* a Salvation Army movie which, with the gusto of a C. B. De Mille epic, attracted an audience of 4,000 and had women in the first-night audience fainting in the aisles. *The Story Of The Kelly Gang* (1906) was Australia's first full-length feature. From the time of its premiere to 1960, Australian movie-makers produced more than 330 films. After World War II, however, the local movie industry slumped, hit by American imports and the arrival of television in 1956.

In 1970 the government formed what has since become known as the Australian Film Commission, introducing tax incentives to movie investors. Australian films began to attract worldwide interest, winning awards and critical acclaim, particularly for direction and cinematography. Movies such as *Picnic at Hanging Rock, My Brilliant Career, The Man from Snowy River, Mad Max: The Road Warrior, Careful He Might Hear You, Crocodile Dundee, Death in Brunswick* and *Proof;* directors such as Peter Weir, Fred Schepisi, George Miller, Gillian Armstrong and Bruce Beresford; and actors such as Judy Davis, Mel Gibson, Jack Thompson, Nicole Kidman, Genevieve Picot, Bryan Brown and Paul Hogan have emerged as compelling attractions both at home and abroad.

ABORIGINAL ARTS

The traditional arts of Australia — those of the Aboriginal people — have been the most underrated and least understood of all by the new arrivals. Only in the past few decades have the subtleties and skills, the passions and depths, and the beautiful mysteries of this non-European tradition received the attention they deserved. Aboriginal paintings, sculpture and carvings, which often tend to be related to the religious myths and beliefs of what the Aborigines know as "the Dreamtime," are now protected by law throughout the country. Aboriginal music consists mainly of singing and chanting and, perhaps accompanied by the sound of the *didjeridu* and clicking-sticks, may be heard at a *corroboree,* a song-and-dance performance that might include sacred as well as secular themes. Ceremonial and sacred sites in the Outback contain paintings and carvings, of which the earliest so far found is believed to be about 20,000 years old.

Today bark paintings and intricately designed totems, in natural ocher colors, are produced for sale. Different peoples specialize in different crafts. The Pitjantjatjara of the western desert, for example, are well known for their wood carvings. The government-funded Aboriginal Arts Board, among others, helps preserve and promote Aboriginal culture, arts and crafts.

FESTIVALS

Most of Australia's major cities today hold large-scale annual arts celebrations, as well as more general events such as, in March, Melbourne's Mardi Gras-style Moomba Festival. The Adelaide Festival of the Arts, which began in 1960, is still the country's major arts festival, although the competition from Melbourne and Perth is growing fierce. Adelaide's festival takes place in three weeks over February to March, every second year. The Festival of Perth, which has been running since 1953, is held around the same time annually. The plush Victorian Arts Centre, the newest and possibly the most progressive major arts center in Australia, has become the setting for both Melbourne Summer Music and, inspired by Gian Carlo Menotti's Spoleto Festival, the annual Melbourne International Festival of the Arts. And Sydney, with the spectacular A\$102 million Sydney Opera House at its heart, enjoys its Festival of Sydney every year in sunny January.

These festivals, and the opening of luxuriously appointed arts centers and theaters in the 1970s and 1980s, have attracted new audiences and enthusiasm from top international performers. Ultimately, new ideas and provocative alternatives will emerge from the current thriving arts activity. Today, Australians simply appear to be enjoying the show.

Australian wine

The Australian wine industry has come a long way from the days of Emu sherry. It is now recognized across the wine-drinking world as a serious producer of quality wines that stand comparison with the best that many older-established producers can offer. Moreover, Australian wine is still surprisingly inexpensive by world standards.

Australia and the grape go back to the very beginnings of European settlement, vine cuttings being among the specimens brought out with the First Fleet. However, despite its long history, the industry has only begun to be taken seriously outside Australia in the past 20 years, although at home good wine has been appreciated by a select few for decades.

The advent, more than 20 years ago, of the wine cask (or wine box, as it is known in Britain), claimed as an Australian invention, brought wine to the masses, and consumption started to take off. More than 60 percent of Australia's consumption is now "cask" wine, usually made from Sultana grapes grown in irrigated areas such as the Riverina of NSW and the Sunraysia area of northwestern Victoria.

Despite the wine snobs who despise cask wine, which could be truly called Australia's *vin ordinaire,* it has allowed wine drinking to become an everyday habit in very many Australian homes. Retailing for between A\$6 and A\$7 (\$4.5-\$5/£2.60-£3) the 4-liter cask represents outstanding value and, for the price, excellent quality — certainly far superior to much of the *vin ordinaire* drunk in France.

The cask-led wine boom has meant that Australians now consume 21.4 liters per head a year, well ahead of countries such as Britain and the US, but still way behind such nations as France and Italy. However, it is for quality that Australian wines are now making a name for themselves.

In the late 1940s and 1950s few people believed that Australia could produce anything other than indifferent fortified wines, as the climate was too hot for the production of quality table wine. Technology and research enabled Australia to overcome that problem. The next problem to confront the wine industry was that of names. The general belief was that Australian-produced wine had to correspond to a French wine type, hence "Australian claret" or "Australian Burgundy." For some time now, however, Australian wine has been labeled and sold on its merits by grape varieties, and the era of the "varietal" wine is well established.

Most good-quality wines have labels that carry a wealth of information, including grape type, alcohol by volume (a legal requirement in most states), and grape sugar level at harvest, as well as a brief description of the type of wine and what food it would partner best.

In the past two decades there has been an enormous increase in the number of small or so-called "boutique" wineries run by dedicated experts or self-taught *vignerons*. These wineries have been in the van of developing varietal wines and matching grape types to regional climates and in some cases even microclimates.

The boutique wineries have grown up in such areas as the **Yarra Valley**, about 50km (30 miles) N of Melbourne, and in the **Hunter Valley** of NSW, as well as the **Barossa** and **Clare** valleys of South Australia. The **Margaret River** area SW of Perth in Western Australia has emerged as one of the most exciting new wine regions, producing some magnificent reds as well as fine white wine. This pioneering work has not been confined to the boutique wineries, and some of the older established wineries, such as Brown Bros of NE Victoria, have made great strides in cool fermentation techniques.

South Australia is the leading wine-producing state. Most of the state's production is concentrated in an area around Adelaide. The **Barossa Valley**, starting about 50km (30 miles) NE of the city, is the most famous of the state's wine districts. Settled by German immigrants in the 1840s, it retains a distinctly Germanic air. There are more than 35 wineries in the valley, nearly all open for tasting. Farther N of the city is the **Clare Valley**, an area of rolling hills and farmlands spotted with fine wineries.

The odd man out in South Australia is the **Coonawarra** district, in the extreme SE of the state and isolated from the other major wine regions. A narrow strip of volcanic soil about 10km (6 miles) long, the so called terra rosa, produces arguably some of Australia's finest red wines. A good Coonawarra Cabernet Sauvignon can hold its own with some of the finest products of Bordeaux.

The **Hunter Valley**, which starts about 200km (125 miles) N of Sydney, has a justifiable reputation as one of the country's leading regions. Its full-blooded reds are much in demand. The Hunter Valley has achieved great results with its small plantings of Semillon grapes, but as these white wines are much sought-after they can be hard to find. They are well worth the effort.

Australia's wine industry is full of surprises and contradictions. For example, wine from heavily irrigated areas has tended to lack class, yet the "Sauternes" produced by De Bortolis of Griffith in the NSW Riverina irrigation area have been favorably compared with the products of Château Yquem.

The other delight is, of course, the civilized habit that Australian wineries have of offering prospective customers a taste of their latest product. The cellar-door sales and tasting are a tradition, and some wineries are more generous than others — a trap if one is driving.

Sparkling wine, it should be noted, is now so inexpensive as to be almost an everyday drink. All the better makes are produced by the traditional *méthode champenoise*.

The interest shown by such world-famous names as Rémy Martin, who have acquired interests in Australian producers, and a string of international awards in London and other centers, are sure signs that the local industry has come of age.

Australian wildlife

Nature has crammed Australia with an extraordinarily diverse range of animals, birds, plants and creatures of the sea — an inheritance so richly rewarding that the tourist or new arrival may initially be surprised by the blasé attitude of many native Australians to the beautiful, colorful and often bizarre creatures about them.

The visitor need not feel so restricted. The rainforests of the N, the wild flowers of Western Australia and the rugged lake district of Tasmania offer their own unique pleasures. And in the Great Barrier Reef, Australia has a haven for marine life of almost every shape, size and color.

FAUNA
Australia is famous for its **marsupials**. There are more than 170 species in the country, classified into 13 "families" of which the largest is the **kangaroo**. More than 45 species thrive here, including the smaller **wallabies**. They are all herbivorous, but can be found in a complete range of habitats throughout Australia. They range in size from the big Red Kangaroo, which may be more than 2m (6½ feet) tall, to the small Rat Kangaroo, about 30cm (12 inches). Visitors who want to see kangaroos in the wild, rather than in the wildlife sanctuaries near the major cities, should plan a trip that takes them away from cultivated farmland and toward the bush. The best time for sighting 'roos, and if you're lucky their young, the joeys, is at sunrise or nearing sunset. There are numerous locations, often signposted as a warning to drivers, around each state capital.

Other marsupials include the **koala** (often and wrongly called the koala bear), the **possum**, the **numbat**, the **marsupial mole**, the **bandicoot**, the **wombat**, the **Tasmanian devil**, and the **thylacine**, or **Tasmanian tiger** (now generally considered extinct).

That unique Australian marsupial, the koala, is one of the country's best-known and most popular animals. Its natural habitats are the forests and woodlands, where it spends its time almost exclusively up a particular species of eucalypt, living contentedly drowsy on a nutritious but mildly narcotic gum leaf. Wombats live in burrows and are known by graziers for their stubborn attitude to fence-poles; rather than detour around one, the wombat simply claws underneath until it collapses.

Australia contains the world's only two **monotremes**, those animals that lay eggs instead of giving birth to their young and are regarded as primitive links between reptiles and mammals. One of these is the **duck-billed platypus**, which is found in freshwater areas of eastern Australia but is shy and difficult to see outside a wildlife sanctuary. When the body of this animal was first taken from the colonies to London at the end of the 18thC, it seemed so bizarre that it was dismissed by many as a fake, a trick that had been sold to gullible travelers. The other monotreme is the **echidna**, or **spiny ant-eater**, a porcupine-like animal that grows to about 45cm (18 inches) in length. Australia's **crocodiles**, found in the estuaries and freshwater lakes of northern and northeastern Australia, have acquired some notoriety in recent years not only because of the Paul Hogan movie but also because of several fatal attacks on people in Queensland and the Northern Territory. There are two types: the generally nocturnal **estuarine crocodile**, which grows to 7m (23 feet) in length and has been responsible for the attacks on humans, and the **freshwater crocodile**, which grows to about 3m (10 feet) and is considered harmless. From 1972 the crocodiles have been protected, but a rise in the number of attacks has brought several calls for a broad culling.

Australia has about 450 of the world's known species of **lizard**, the largest of which, the **Perentie goanna**, grows to 2.5m (8 feet). There are more than a hundred species of **snake**, only a few of which are really dangerous to man. However, two of the snakes likely to be encountered in the most populated areas of the eastern seaboard, the **brown** and the **tiger** snakes, have respectively the second and fourth most poisonous venom of any snake in the world. The highly poisonous **taipan** is Australia's biggest venomous snake, growing to about 2m ($6\frac{1}{2}$ feet) in length. (Antivenom is available at most major hospitals.)

Among imported animals, **camels** are still to be found wild in the Northern Territory.

FLORA

Legislation protects Australia's wild flowers as well as the country's wildlife. Native species may be bought in plant nurseries, but it is generally forbidden to pick Australian flowers in the forest or bush. One seen everywhere is **acacia**, which includes about 700 species of Australian **wattle**. The **golden wattle**, *acacia pycnantha,* is featured on the Australian coat of arms and is the country's floral emblem. Among other well-known native plants is the **waratah**, with its vivid scarlet flowers.

Although the overseas visitor may notice many familiar European and American trees in Australian cities, native **eucalypts** make up about 90 percent of the country's forests and a large proportion of the woodlands. **Baobabs**, only found in the arid country of the NW of Western Australia and in the Northern Territory, have huge bottle-shaped trunks in which moisture is stored. Another spectacular tree is the **Moreton Bay fig**, a sprawling rainforest plant that grows to 40m (130 feet) in height and sends the "tentacles" that make up its trunk in all directions.

BIRDS
Particularly to Europeans accustomed to a more subdued palette, much of Australia's birdlife appears to have been painted by an artist with a manic desire to experiment with every color in the rainbow. And outside the cities, the shattering din of early-morning birdcalls will astound the first-time visitor.

There are some 700 species of birds in Australia, about 400 of which live within the island continent. Others are migratory, spending a part of the year in the country and the remainder overseas. To the bird-lover, the treasures of Australian flight are its **cockatoos** and **parrots**, of which there are 60 species. Among the more prolific cockatoos are the silvery, red-headed **gang-gangs** of southeastern Australia, the pink-and-gray **galahs**, and the white-and-yellow-plumed **sulfur-crested cockatoo**. Another colorful species of parrot to be found in the E of the country is the **rosella**, which lives in forests and woodlands, where it nests in the hollows of trees. At the other end of the scale from such friendly small parrots as the native **budgerigar** is the **emu**, the second-largest bird in the world. It can grow up to about 1.4m ($4\frac{1}{2}$ feet) tall; like the ostrich and its native relative the **cassowary** it does not fly, but can run at speeds of up to 40kph (25mph). The **southern cassowary**, which has a vivid blue neck and a flat, black, horny crown on its head, grows up to about 1.5m (5 feet) tall and can be found in northeastern Queensland.

Australia has ten species of **kingfisher**, the best known of which is the **kookaburra**, whose unique call resembles human laughter. Kookaburras are found throughout eastern Australia. Over the years, they have also been called "laughing jackass," "the bushman's clock" and "ha ha pigeon." Other familiar natives include the **frogmouth**, a nocturnal bird with flat, crumpled bills surrounded by bristles, and **bellbirds**, which are so called because of their pinging, chimelike calls.

One family of birds, the **diggers**, has devised a unique way of adapting to the harsh climate, incubating its eggs by burying them in mounds of soil and decaying vegetation. The **scrub fowl**, **brush turkey** and **mallee fowl** are all diggers.

Finally, Australia has its **black swans**, which have been known to Europeans since Dutch explorer Willem de Vlamingh first saw them in 1697, near what was later to become Perth. These large, elegant birds with distinctive red beaks breed in colonies, unlike the white swans, which live in pairs.

FISH
There are about 20 "families" of **shark**, most having representatives in Australian coastal waters. Their presence, particularly along the eastern seaboard, is a good reason for swimmers to frequent patrolled or protected beaches. Great whites, blue pointers, tiger sharks and whaler sharks have attacked people, and hammerhead sharks have come

under suspicion. On the other hand, Australians also regularly attack the local sharks, eating shark meat as "flake" in their fish 'n' chips.

There are some 3,000 different species of fish in Australian waters. In and around the coral reefs that bracket Australia from both oceans is a multitude of exotic, brilliantly colored fish. But it is in the colder waters that commercial fishermen catch such fish as **snapper**, **flounder**, **trevally** and **John Dory**. The best-known of Australia's freshwater fish is the **barramundi**, although this Aboriginal name is given to several species. The most common use is for the **giant perch**, a restaurant delicacy; it grows to 1.8m (6 feet) long and can weigh 50kg (110lbs). The **Murray cod**, **Murray perch** and Tasmania's **trout** are also among the country's finest food and sporting fish.

Marine life to stay well away from? **Rays** are plentiful in Australian waters, their tails often armed with serrated spines that can inflict painful wounds. Avoid the highly poisonous **porcupine fish**, **bluebottles** (the jellyfish also known as the **Portuguese man-of-war**) and the **blue-ringed octopus** (in or out of the water). These are to be found in waters ranging from warm-temperate to tropical. And it is wise not to handle the **crown-of-thorns starfish**, whose poisonous spines can become embedded. The crown-of-thorns, which feeds on coral polyps, infested large areas of the Great Barrier Reef in the 1970s, causing great concern and sparking off several scientific investigations.

AND THINGS THAT BITE AND CRAWL . . . .

Everything thrives in the Australian climate, including some insects and crawly creatures that endear themselves only to producers of television wildlife documentaries.

There are about 1,700 species of **spiders** — cobweb, sheet-web and orb-web weavers. They include the **redback**, which is poisonous and related to the black widow spider of North America, and the **Sydney funnel-web**, an aggressive and venomous spider that lives in a funnel-shaped web across a shallow burrow.

Australia also has about 1,500 species of **ant**. In the N of Australia, **termite** mounds are often seen; they are built up to 7m (23 feet) high.

An immediately noticeable pest is the **fly**. There are more than 6,250 species, the house variety and biting bush-flies among them. Their presence is responsible for the too-familiar wave across a person's face that has become known as "the Australian salute."

Far more attractive to the visitor are the 11,000 species of **butterflies** and **moths** that thrive in Australia. **Witchetty grubs**, which are a delicacy to tribal Aborigines and may be offered to the visitor in some parts, are the larva of the large **cossid moth**.

Sport in Australia

Sport to many Australians is life and the rest a shadow....
To play sport, or watch others play, and to read and
talk about it is to uphold the nation and build its character...
(Donald Horne, *The Lucky Country*)

Horne's analysis was written in the 1960s, but his findings are no less true today. Australians are close to being fanatical about playing sport, and, as spectators, take to all forms of it. Take the America's Cup (which Australia did in 1983 to end 112 years of American domination). Interest in the Cup became a national passion when *Australia II,* skippered by John Bertrand, beat the American entry *Liberty,* skippered by Dennis Connor, and the nation was transfixed again by Connor's gutsy recovery of the trophy in the stiff breezes off Fremantle four years later.

HORSERACING

Australia's love of horseracing is perhaps best illustrated by the way it reacts to its most famous race, the Melbourne Cup, which began in 1861 and is held on the first Tuesday in November at Melbourne's Flemington Racecourse. The Cup, the highlight of Victoria's Spring Racing Carnival and a public holiday in Melbourne, is considered one of the most colorful races in the world by turf enthusiasts. It draws a crowd of more than 100,000, attracts some of the most bizarre fashions seen outside a Fellini movie, offers more than a million dollars in prize money, and around the country everything comes to a standstill while it is run.

There are currently more than 450 flat- and harness-racing tracks throughout Australia; the better-known include Rosehill, Randwick and Warwick Farm in NSW, Caulfield and Flemington in Victoria, Eagle Farm and Albion Park in Queensland, Victoria Park in South Australia, Elwick in Tasmania, and Ascot and Belmont in Western Australia.

Visitors may note TAB (Totalizator Agency Board) shops, with windows for computerized betting on race meetings, in all cities. The state-controlled betting organization, TAB, is comparable to New York State's off-track betting system. Its original totalizator, or pari-mutuel machine, and the photo-finish camera used on the tracks, were both invented in Australia.

CRICKET

The great summer sport in Australia is cricket, both for spectators and for players. Australian fanaticism for the game is only matched by that among the followers of its greatest rivals, the West Indies and England. The fierce rivalry with the English probably goes back to 1882, when "the colonies" won their first cricketing match "back home" in England. From that arose The Ashes, an urn containing the ashes of a burned cricket stump. These now remain permanently in the Members' Pavilion at Lord's Cricket Ground in London, but the term "The Ashes" has come to stand for cricket's ultimate prize. Rivalry between the two countries reached its peak in 1933, in "The Bodyline Series." The English, facing what promised to be an unassailable performance from Australia's greatest batsman, Don Bradman, decided to bombard the Australian batsmen with short-pitched deliveries.

The series created a great wave of anti-English sentiment. Politicians in both countries became involved; Australian unionists called for a boycott of British goods. Ultimately, "bodyline" changed the game. The rules were modified and batsmen began padding their bodies against future bowling onslaughts. England won the Ashes that year, but Australia, under the brilliant leadership of Bradman, bounced back in the next series.

Cricket was raised to full professional status, and nudged rudely into the TV Age, with World Series Cricket, which was launched by Australian magazine and television magnate Kerry Packer in the 1970s. WSC, inspired perhaps by what had been happening in televised sport in the US, introduced such innovations as floodlit night cricket, colored kit and big incentives for star performers such as bowler Dennis Lillee and batsman Ian Chappell. The changes caused shudders among cricketing "purists" on both sides of the globe.

FOOTBALL
Australians enjoy four kinds of football, with a passion verging on the religious. Amateur Rugby Union is played enthusiastically throughout the country; professional Rugby League is the main spectator sport in Queensland and NSW; soccer, although increasingly popular in schools, is still mainly favored by immigrants; and Australian Rules, a spectacular game said to stem from Gaelic football, attracts the biggest crowds and is played in Western Australia, South Australia, Tasmania and Victoria.

SPORT FOR THE PARTICIPANT
Australians, it seems, are game for anything that moves, provides a challenge, calls for stamina, needs a stopwatch, and allows the ecstasy of victory. And there may be a *special* need to be satisfied Down Under. When you live so far away, it can be comforting to make the rest of the world stand up occasionally and take notice.

The spin-off of Australia's sporting excellence is that sporting facilities are generally superb and extensive and often cost a fraction of what visitors can expect to pay in their own country. This, coupled with a benign climate, makes Australia, to use that well-worn cliché, a sportsman's paradise. Virtually every town or small community has its tennis courts, and golf courses too are surprisingly plentiful. For example, a country town of 8,500 people about 200km (125 miles) NE of Melbourne typically has 20 lawn tennis courts, more than half a dozen squash courts, a golf course and numerous other facilities.

Sport in country areas is even more important than in the cities, as it is the hub of social activity. Although tennis courts in Australia are frequently leased or owned by clubs, facilities are usually available for visitors under the status of temporary membership or on a simple rental basis as a member's guest. There are also many public courts, generally owned by the local municipality. Hotels, if they do not have their own tennis courts, can usually arrange for guests to rent local courts.

Public indoor tennis courts have mushroomed in state capital city suburbs in recent years. They are easy to rent during the day, but it may be hard to get a court in the evening without reserving some days ahead. Squash is also extremely popular, and there are courts for rent in most suburbs, again more easily during the day than in the evening.

Golf is a game enjoyed by all classes of Australian society. By world standards it is inexpensive. Japanese visitors find the cost of golf in the country so cheap that a few games can go a long way to paying for their air fare when compared to green fees payable in their own country.

Australian courses are among the finest in the world. Around Melbourne, for example, is a sandy belt of land near Port Phillip Bay that boasts some of the finest courses anywhere. These so-called sandbelt courses are a delight. Many municipalities have their own public courses of a high standard and charge reasonable green fees, around A$5-A$10 (US$3.50-7.50/£2-4 sterling).

Increasingly visitors to Australia are heading N to the Great Barrier Reef for skin diving (some of the best in the world), sailing through the reef islands, and big-game fishing for marlin, which attracts the wealthy and famous. In Queensland, with its subtropical-to-tropical climate, you can waterski, sailboard, sail, skin dive, swim, surf and fish to your heart's content. Sailboards, surf boards, canoes or pedal craft and so on can be rented at most resorts, in Queensland and around the country.

For the adventuresome, cross-country horseback riding in the Australian Alps in Victoria and NSW is increasingly popular, particularly since the movie *The Man from Snowy River* made the area better known to visitors and locals alike. And skiing in the Snowy Mountains of NSW is becoming increasingly popular.

Virtually all the equipment needed for the more common sports can be rented in Australia, so it is pointless to burden yourself with bulky items such as surfboards and skis. The real prerequisite for a sporting holiday in Australia is plenty of enthusiasm, particularly if playing against the locals. For Australians like only one thing more than playing, and that's winning.

TENNIS AND OTHER SPORTS

Between 1956 and 1970 there were ten all-Australian Wimbledon finals. In the 1960s and 1970s Australian tennis champions included Ken Rosewall, Lew Hoad, Roy Emerson, Neale Fraser (now coaching the Australian Davis Cup squad), Rod Laver and John Newcombe; and in 1987 Pat Cash triumphed memorably at Wimbledon. Australia has also produced a number of world-ranking women players, including that supreme player Margaret Court, who won at Wimbledon in 1963, and the skillful part-Aboriginal player Evonne Goolagong, winner in 1971 and 1980.

In sports such as swimming and golf, Australia is hardly less pre-eminent, with fine facilities from its pools and tracks to some of the most delightfully landscaped courses imaginable. There have been notable successes too in auto-racing, cycling, sailing, and in the increasingly competitive international surfing events.

Basic information

Before you go

DOCUMENTS REQUIRED

Visas are required for all visitors to Australia except those from New Zealand. Visa applications should be accompanied by a recent passport photograph signed on the back by the applicant, and the applicant's **passport**, valid for the duration of his or her stay in the country. A **tourist visa** is valid for up to 6 months and precludes the visitor from taking a job in Australia. There are also **working-vacation visas**, normally valid for 6 months, intended for young people aged 18-25 who wish to take occasional jobs while traveling and learning more about the country. Visitors must pay a departure fee of A$10 as they leave.

Vaccination certificates are not normally required unless you arrive from a country affected by yellow fever, smallpox, cholera or typhoid.

Visitors can use their valid **driver's license** in Australia for an equivalent class of vehicle. The license must be carried when driving. **International driver's licenses** are recognized in all states. Those planning an extended stay must obtain a valid license from the state licensing authority: inquire at any police station.

TRAVEL AND MEDICAL INSURANCE

The cost of **medical treatment** in Australia is high. Except for certain countries with which Australia has reciprocal agreements, such as the UK and New Zealand, health care costs are not covered by the local health system called **Medicare**.

Visitors from the UK are covered under Medicare, which provides basic hospital care (in public wards) and a percentage (varying, but about 70-80 percent) of the "common fee" charged by doctors for a range of services. This fee is based on an agreement between the government and the Australian Medical Association, but is not binding on doctors, who may, but rarely do, charge whatever fee they think fit. The "common fee" is the basis on which refunds from the government under the Medicare system are calculated. The reciprocal arrangement only covers treatment needing to be carried out immediately. It will not necessarily cover the entire cost of treatment: some medication, for example, will be charged to you.

Visitors from countries with which no reciprocal agreement exists, and those wanting anything more than the most basic coverage, are strongly advised to take out private **insurance**. Make sure that the policy covers

repatriation: costs are high for special arrangements to fly a sick person from Australia to the UK or the US.

For US citizens the **IAMAT** (International Association for Medical Assistance to Travelers) is worth joining, and membership is free. It has member hospitals and clinics throughout the world, including six in Australia, and a list of doctors who will call, for a fee. It also provides information on health risks overseas. For further information, and a directory of doctors and hospitals, write to: **IAMAT** *(417, Center St., Lewiston, NY 14092, USA)*.

Health care in Australia is comparable, and in some respects superior, to that available anywhere else. Visitors intending to stay longer than 6 months may enroll in the Medicare system.

MONEY

The unit of currency is the **dollar** (A$), which is split into 100 cents. There are coins for 2 cents, 5 cents, 20 cents, 50 cents, A$1 and A$2, and notes for A$5, A$10, A$50 and A$100. There is no restriction on the amount of currency that can be brought into Australia, but A$5,000 is the maximum that can be taken out of the country in cash.

Carry cash in small amounts only. **Travelers checks** issued by American Express, Thomas Cook and major international banks are widely accepted. Banks, including those in the suburbs of the large cities, have a daily exchange rate for the major world currencies. Make sure you read the instructions included with your travelers checks. It is important to note separately the serial numbers of your checks and the telephone number to call in case of loss. Specialist travelers check companies such as **American Express** provide extensive local refund facilities through their own offices or agents.

Australians have embraced plastic money wholeheartedly and all the major **charge/credit cards** such as American Express, Diners Club International, Visa and MasterCard are accepted. Most shops and restaurants accept at least two cards and more often three or more. The most widespread card is the domestic **Bankcard**, issued and administered jointly by the major Australian banks. Anyone planning an extended stay can obtain a Bankcard if they open a local bank account. American Express offices will change cardmembers' personal checks in a foreign currency.

CUSTOMS

Visitors can bring in duty-free all personal effects, except tobacco goods, alcoholic drinks and perfume, for use during their stay or to take out of the country when they leave. Receipts may need to be produced for expensive electronic goods such as cameras, video machines, tape recorders and watches.

The duty-free allowances for Australians and visitors are generally similar to those in most other countries. Only people over the age of 18 are eligible for the duty-free allowance.

Tobacco   200 cigarettes *or* 250 grams of cigars *or* 250 grams of tobacco.

41

Alcoholic drinks   1 liter of wine *or* 1 liter of liquor.
Perfume   15fl.oz./425g/450cc.
Other goods   All goods brought into Australia are subject to customs duty, but concessions enable most goods to be landed free or at little charge. However, goods ineligible for concessions attract a high combined rate of duty and sales tax.

Such items as goods made to order and not collected before leaving the country — for example, footwear, clothing and jewelry — attract the full customs and sales tax, as do goods dispatched from shops on the visitor's behalf and goods sent as freight intended to arrive on the same aircraft or ship as the visitor. Usually goods brought for the visitor's personal use or goods that have been owned or used for 12 months do not attract any sort of duty or sales tax.

Items made from a number of endangered species, such as alligator and crocodile, big cats, snakes and lizards, zebra and rhinoceros, are forbidden as imports into Australia. Further information can be obtained from Australian diplomatic missions.

US/UK INFORMATION SERVICES

The **Australian Tourist Commission** has much useful information for prospective visitors. It has offices in the following locations:
New York   31st Floor, 489 Fifth Ave., New York, NY 10017 ☎(212) 687-6300
Chicago   Suite 130, 150 North Michigan Ave., Chicago, IL 60601 ☎(312) 781-5150
Los Angeles   Suite 1200, 2121 Avenue of the Stars, Los Angeles, CA 90067 ☎(213) 552-1988
London   Gemini House, 10-18 Putney Hill, Putney, London SW15 ☎(081) 780-2227

QUARANTINE REGULATIONS

Australian quarantine regulations are among the world's strictest. As exports of rural produce run to around A$6,000 million a year (Australia's second largest income earner after minerals), the concern with keeping animal diseases at bay is understandable. Australia has never experienced an outbreak of foot-and-mouth disease: on its open ranges, such an outbreak would be a disaster and difficult to control. There has been only one known case of rabies, in the 19thC, and many other animal diseases are unknown. To maintain this disease-free environment, imports are banned of: meat, cooked or raw; plants or seeds; animals, alive or dead; reptiles; fish; birds; any animal product such as semen; biological specimens; and soil. The penalties for breaking these rules can be severe. Many an Italian or Greek family returning to Australia with a favorite salami has ended up in court facing heavy fines. Even baby food containing meat must be surrendered at the airport.

Because of Australia's unique flora and fauna, illegal trade in the export of **birds**, particularly members of the parrot family, is lucrative and the penalties correspondingly severe. The unlicensed export of all flora and fauna is forbidden.

Visitors entering Australia must complete a customs and quarantine form, and all aircraft landing in Australia are sprayed with insecticide. The first-time visitor may be amused or alarmed by the sight of uniformed men, in summer usually wearing shorts, walking down the aisle of an aircraft with aerosol cans in each hand spraying the air, but the danger to Australia's valuable sheep and cattle industries is real, and at least quarantine officers now use a low-irritant spray and warn passengers to cover their noses with a handkerchief. Many Qantas aircraft now have inbuilt sprays that have done away with the need for the quarantine officers.

To protect the fruit and wine industries, it is forbidden to move most fruits and certain plants from one state to another. On some borders, particularly between Victoria and South Australia, Department of Agriculture officials are on hand to ensure compliance with the law, and to see that all fruit is dumped. At most state border crossing points, notices advise travelers of what they can take across.

GETTING THERE
By air   Most international carriers fly into the major Australian state capitals. The national airline **Qantas** (Queensland and Northern Territory Aerial Services), which flew its first passenger in 1922, operates the Kangaroo Route daily between Australia and Britain and Europe in conjunction with **British Airways**. The route is the longest in the world. Qantas and British Airways operate services into Sydney, Melbourne, Perth, Adelaide and Brisbane. Qantas also operates flights into Darwin and Cairns. There are direct flights from Australia to the major capitals of Europe, Asia and the US.

Airlines operating to Australia include: Qantas, British Airways, Singapore Airlines, Cathay Pacific, KLM, United, Continental, Lufthansa, JAT, Alitalia, Olympic, Japan Air Lines, Garuda, Air New Zealand, UTA, Air Caledonia, Thai International, Malaysian Airline System, Air Canada, Philippine Airlines, Air Lanka, All Nippon, South African Airways, Lauda Air, Virgin Atlantic, Air Vanuatu and Air Niugini.

Jet lag   One of the unavoidable problems of any journey to Australia is jet lag. For travelers from Europe the problem can be particularly acute, as the minimum time spent in the air is about 24 hours, and quite often the journey takes nearer 30 hours. For travelers from the West Coast of the US the journey of around 15 hours is not quite so draining, particularly as westbound travel is less disorientating than eastbound. However, either journey will leave you tired. Several precautions during the flight will minimize the effects of jet lag: drink lots of fluid, avoid alcohol, eat sparingly, at stopovers get out of the plane and walk around, and try to get some sleep, if only a catnap.

One of the best ways to recover rapidly is to stay awake for the first day in Australia and to try to adjust as quickly as possible to local time. This is particularly important for European travelers, who have lost nearly half a day *en route* and will probably have arrived short of sleep at the start of a new day in Australia. Manage to stay awake for that first day, get to bed at an early hour, and recovery can be quick. Try to resist the temptation to go out and launch at once into your vacation.

By sea There are no scheduled liner services, although several cruise ships call at Australian ports. The *Queen Elizabeth II* frequently calls on round-the-world cruises, as do several other cruise liners. Passage can be arranged on the few general-cargo, noncontainer vessels that visit Australia.

CLIMATE

Australia has a wide range of climate, from temperate in the southern island state of Tasmania to tropical (monsoonal) in the far N of Western Australia, Queensland and the Northern Territory. Two-fifths of the continent lies N of the Tropic of Capricorn, and in some parts the rainfall can exceed 2,500mm (200 inches) a year; yet Australia is the driest continent on earth. Paradoxically, every year people are lost in the mountains and there are frequent deaths from exposure on cross-country skiing trips. But this is also a land where people can die of exposure in the desert.

The southern part of the country has a temperate, Mediterranean-like climate with four seasons. It is characterized by cool winters, hot summers (especially in January and February), and mild springs and falls. Spring and fall can be the best times to visit the eastern seaboard and Western Australia. In the tropical N there are two seasons, a hot, wet season, with rain falling mainly in February and March during the prevailing monsoons, and a warm, dry season with a prevalent SE trade wind blowing.

CLOTHES

The choice of clothes to take will obviously be governed by the season. For the summer, shorts and short-sleeved shirts for men and light, cotton dresses for women should certainly be included, together with swimsuits. The rules of dress are relaxed, although some first-class hotels expect a collar and tie, if not a jacket, for men, and a dress for women, to be worn at dinner. In summer it is customary, particularly in the far north of Australia, for men at work to wear shorts and long, white walking socks, with a collar and tie.

Summer nights can be cool, particularly in Victoria and Tasmania, so the inclusion of a light sweater even in summer is advisable. For winter, warmer clothes are needed and a raincoat should be included. If planning a winter visit to the mountains of the Great Dividing Range, waterproofs and warm clothes are essential, just as they would be in any mountain region in winter. If planning a journey to the Outback, footwear is important: boots or similar should be worn, not just as a support but also as a sensible precaution against the possibility of stepping on snakes, which have a habit of basking in the sun on clear ground.

GENERAL DELIVERY/POSTE RESTANTE

Central post offices in the state capitals have general delivery counters where mail can be collected. All post offices, even in the remotest areas, will hold mail for collection. Normally some form of **identification**, such as a passport or international driver's license, is required when collecting mail.

Getting around

FROM AIRPORTS TO CITIES
Private bus services run from all state capital airports to the city centers. Fares vary according to distance and are payable on boarding the bus. **Taxis** are available at all state capital and most regional airports. As competition is keen at most large airports, there is rarely a shortage.

By and large, unlike their counterparts in some countries, Australian taxi drivers do not try to take advantage of newly arrived international travelers. Passengers are not, for example, asked to pay for return fares for the cab to get back to the taxi stand or airport.

FLYING
Australia's **domestic air services** are excellent and extensive. Until the abolition of the "two-airline policy" that allowed the two major internal airlines — **Ansett**, partly owned by Mr Rupert Murdoch's empire, and **Australian Airlines**, formerly Trans Australia Airlines and government-owned — to operate parallel services to most centers, air travel in Australia tended to be more expensive than in comparable countries. Now, with an "open skies" policy, the major airlines face competition from several new competitors. One, Compass Airlines, took to the skies only to close down after less than a year of operation. At the time of writing, hopes of a rescue operation are high, although it is not certain if or when Compass will take to the air again. Whatever happens, the effects of increased competition have been felt, and heavy discounting of fares has become a fact of life.

The situation now is similar to the early days of airline deregulation in the United States. In addition to the two major airlines, **Eastwest Airlines** has extensive services in NSW, Western Australia and Queensland. East-west also flies to Norfolk Island, the Australian dependency and home to descendants of the Bounty Mutiny. It has concentrated on the vacation and leisure market, leaving the two larger airlines to cater to the business traveler. It offers an extensive range of vacations, particularly in Queensland and Tasmania. Eastwest is a subsidiary of Ansett and its services can be reserved through that airline.

The other major carrier is the regional airline **Kendell**, which operates feeder services into both Melbourne and Adelaide from outlying centers. Kendell too offers an array of vacation packages, specializing in country packages. These range from a three-day package to Tasmania, taking in the wilderness areas of Cradle Mountain and the Gordon and Franklin Rivers out of Melbourne, to Kangaroo Island, off the coast of South Australia, where you can walk, cautiously, among the basking sea lions on the beach. Other packages take in the opal mining center of Coober Pedy *en route* to Ayers Rock, or offer the chance to camp on the Nullarbor Plain, and to view from a helicopter the Great Southern Right Whales backing in the Great Australian Bight. Kendell is also owned by Ansett, and its flights can be reserved through the parent airline.

All major airlines offer standby and advance purchase fares on major trunk routes. Standby fares offer savings of 20 percent on regular econ-

45

omy fares. Tickets are issued at the airport and you fly when a seat becomes available as allocated by the standby desk. Standby is best suited to people with a flexible itinerary who don't mind waiting and can use off-peak flights. In the new deregulated environment all airlines offer special off-peak discounts, which can be as much as 50 percent off the normal fare, in addition to standby.

RAILWAY SERVICES
Because of intense colonial rivalry, NSW, Victoria and Queensland once all had different gauges. After Federation things improved, but it was not until the early 1960s that it became possible to travel between Melbourne and Sydney without having to change trains at Albury, just across the border in NSW. Today it is possible, by using a number of rail links, to travel from northern Queensland to the se corner of Western Australia.

Despite the early confusion, Australia today boasts one of the few remaining great train journeys in the world, the **Indian Pacific** linking Sydney and Perth, a journey of nearly 4,000km (2,500 miles) that takes three nights (65 hours) and includes the world's longest stretch of straight railway line, which runs without a bend for 478km (299 miles) across the Nullarbor Plain. The Indian Pacific service started in 1970, shortly after the completion of the standard-gauge link between Western Australia and the eastern part of the country. It has proved highly successful, with reservations for journeys during some periods of the year needed up to 12 months ahead.

The other great train journey in Australia is the **Ghan**, which runs between Adelaide and Alice Springs. The line has been upgraded, as has the rolling stock, and is now safe from the occasional washouts caused by the infrequent but torrential rains that sometimes plague the Outback, which played havoc with the track laid on fragile soil.

The last link in the network of standard-gauge rail lines joining all mainland state capitals was completed in 1982, fulfilling a dream that started at the time of Federation.

Other major sectors are: **Melbourne to Sydney**, with an overnight service; **Melbourne to Adelaide**, overnight; **Sydney to Brisbane**, overnight; **Brisbane to Cairns**, overnight; **Adelaide to Alice Springs**, overnight; **Sydney to Canberra**, daylight service; **Sydney to Alice Springs**, two days (47 hours); and **Adelaide to Perth**, two days (42 hours). Sleeping accommodations are available, for a surcharge, on most of the overnight services. Reservations for seats and sleeping cars are recommended for all major services at all times, especially the Indian Pacific and Queensland services.

Within the states, railway services link most major centers in NSW and Victoria, and narrow-gauge services connect many outlying centers in Queensland. Services in South Australia and Western Australia are not as widespread. Both Melbourne and Sydney have extensive suburban railway services, and travel during the morning and afternoon rush hours presents the same problems of overcrowding faced by most commuters in large cities.

46

BUSES

Several nationwide bus companies operate services between the state capitals that are far more economical, if considerably more tiring, than air travel. Not counting the $4\frac{1}{2}$-hour Sydney-Canberra route, the shortest is around 10 hours (Melbourne-Adelaide). The Adelaide-Perth journey takes a bone-numbing $36\frac{1}{2}$ hours. All inter-capital buses are equipped with WCs and water fountains, and some companies operate luxurious double-decker vehicles and screen video movies during the journey. The major bus lines operating express inter-capital services are **Bus Australia**, **Pioneer** and **Greyhound**.

Although bus travel point-to-point can be wearing, **touring** by bus can be an excellent way of seeing Australia. The three major inter-capital bus companies operate tours, and several other specialist companies offer a wide variety of vacation packages, including some that provide for a bus journey one way and a return trip by air. The bus tours range from two-day outings to a 56-day circumnavigation of Australia.

Most tours feature an informed commentary from the drivers (now known as "coach captains"), with frequent stops and overnight accommodations in motels. Daylight touring is the rule — buses aim to arrive by nightfall, allowing time for a shower and a sightseeing walk.

For the more adventurous there are **camping tours** and **safaris**. These are more basic forms of bus travel in the Outback, with overnight stops at campgrounds equipped with showers and laundry facilities, which take the place of motels. All food, camping gear and sleeping equipment is carried on the bus or 4-wheel-drive vehicle. The duration of such tours can range from 2-38 days, or more. Popular with young people, offering a sense of adventure and a good chance to get to know people quickly and make friends, they can be recommended for the young-in-spirit, although hardly for those addicted to home comforts.

TAXIS

Australian taxis are basically standard sedans. The great majority are radio-controlled. They can be hailed in the street or rented at taxi stands, which are clearly indicated in city streets. At night and on weekends taxis can be hard to find.

Like their counterparts the world over, Australian taxi drivers are mines of local knowledge and information. The standard of driving is good and the taxi system is well policed and monitored. Taxi drivers must display their license with a photograph and number inside the cab. A single passenger is expected to sit in the front with the driver — all part of the egalitarian spirit of Australia. Drivers do *not* expect to be tipped unless they have rendered a special service. However, drivers do expect you to talk to them about anything and everything: you are considered to be a snob or worse if you fail to enter into a conversation.

Most major state capitals operate a **two-tier charge system**, with a day rate and a more expensive night rate. The rate is displayed inside the taxi; lights on the taxi sign on the roof indicate which rate is in operation. During the day a single light indicates the cheaper rate; at night both lights are illuminated to indicate the night rate. Taxi drivers can ask one

47

passenger if they would mind sharing the taxi and fare with another going in a similar direction. There is no obligation to accept the sharing arrangement, although it is customary to agree.

Fares vary slightly from city to city, but basically there is a flag-fall charge (the standard charge for renting, which comes into force when the driver turns on the meter) and then a combination of kilometers and time. A national taxi credit-charge system called **Cabcharge** issues credit-type cards or a book of credit vouchers to account holders. The system is mainly intended for business people, but, as it operates nationwide, may be worth considering for visitors on extended trips. There is an accounting fee on each monthly bill for the service. Many taxis now accept **American Express Cards** in payment for fares.

GETTING AROUND BY CAR

Behind the wheel of a car, many Australians change from fairly tolerant creatures into something far less attractive. In addition to fast and aggressive driving, they sometimes show a marked reluctance to obey traffic laws and lane discipline, which can be disconcerting for visitors accustomed to highway driving in Europe or the US. The result is that Australia has one of the highest accident rates of any country in the world. The national road death toll is some 2,800 killed a year out of a population of a little more than 17 million.

Australians drive on the left-hand side of the road. **Traffic signs** are easy to follow, being mainly self-explanatory and pictorial, and are similar to those used internationally. There are some local specialties, such as the sign warning that kangaroos cross some roads, and another alerting drivers to the possibility of slow-moving koalas or wombats crossing. Speed limits are 60kph ($37\frac{1}{2}$ mph) in built-up areas and 100kph ($62\frac{1}{2}$ mph) in nonurban areas, unless speed-limit signs indicate otherwise. Increasingly sophisticated methods are employed to detect drivers breaking the law. Some states use radar speed-checks coupled with cameras, which allow police to detect speeding drivers without having to stop them. A photograph showing the offending car's license plate provides sufficient evidence and a fine is imposed. Similarly, at some intersections cameras photograph cars that jump red lights; police then prosecute on the evidence of a photograph. The wearing of seat belts by the driver and all passengers is compulsory in all states.

Every state in Australia has its own **automobile club** similar to the AAA in the US, or the AA or RAC in Britain, and all operate breakdown services. Membership of one entitles visitors to reciprocal services from those in other states. (Addresses of the various automobile clubs are given under state capitals in the A TO Z.)

Parking meters are as much the bane of people's lives in Australia's major cities as they are in New York and London, and traffic wardens employed by the city councils are as universally unpopular.

Traffic laws are basically the same throughout Australia, but with some local state variations. In Melbourne, for example, trams cannot be passed on the right, and at most city intersections, where two tram tracks cross, right turns must be executed from the left-hand side of the road *after* the traffic lights have changed. This is intended to prevent obstruction of trams by cars turning right. Such intersections have large warnings to alert drivers to the right-turn rule, with a diagram showing how to execute the turn. Again, in some states vehicles turning left are obliged to yield to all other vehicles. Before taking to the road it is advisable to consult the state automobile club for advice: most provide leaflets explaining local traffic laws.

Australia's main **highways** are popularly known by name rather than route number, although on many maps route numbers are shown, and often both the route number and the highway's name. In the Outback, distances between gas stations can be great.

OUTBACK TOURING

For those who want to see the "real Australia" and get off the main roads in the **Outback**, there are certain precautions to take. Always inform someone of where you are going and when you expect to arrive. Always carry ample **water**, enough for at least three or four days, and note that the radiators of most modern cars now contain a poisonous anticorrosive agent that precludes using the water for drinking in an emergency. Always carry a few **spare parts**, such as a fan belt, spark plugs, tire repair kit and spare tire.

If you should become bogged down or have a breakdown, **do not leave your car**, which provides shade and is more easily spotted both from the air and the ground than a lone human. To help conserve body fluid, do not move about in the heat of the day. Always carry a spade in case you get bogged down.

To obtain water, dig a hole about 1m (3 feet) deep, place a tin or other container in the center of the hole and firmly pack around it any live vegetable matter you can gather (leaves, spinifex, saltbush etc.). Cover the hole with a sheet of plastic secured firmly at the corners, then place a pebble in the middle of the stretched plastic directly above the container. The heat of the sun will distill moisture from the live vegetable matter, and water will condense on the underside of the plastic sheet, gently run down and drip into the container. Using this method it is possible to distill $\frac{1}{2}$ liter (1pt) of drinkable water in 24 hours, which could mean the difference between life and death.

RENTING A CAR

Most large international **car rental companies** operate in Australia and have desks at state capital airports and agents at regional airports. The car rental market is extremely competitive, so it is advisable to shop around for the best deal. For example, some rental companies offer discounts to people paying with American Express Cards. Most offer either an unlimited-kilometers flat charge or a free initial distance followed by a charge per kilometer. Compulsory third-party insurance is included with the rental, and additional insurance covering collision damage and personal injury can be taken out for an extra fee.

Basic rentals require the car to be returned to the place of rental, but one-way rentals can be arranged, although there may be a fee to cover the cost of returning the car to its base. Both Ansett and Australian Airlines will make in-flight arrangements for a car to be available at your destination. The major car rental companies operating in Australia are **Avis**, **Hertz**, **National** and **Thrifty**. There are also several cheaper rental companies, however, which offer sound, older cars; they have such names as **Rent a Bomb** or **Rent a Wreck** and can be found in the *Yellow Pages*.

GETTING AROUND ON FOOT
The inner areas of most Australian cities lend themselves to walking, but once outside the central area the charm diminishes for pedestrians. The vast suburban sprawls that grew after the end of World War II were designed primarily for citizens with cars.

In cities and built-up areas **crosswalks (pedestrian crossings)** are plentiful. It is best, however, to use a crossing controlled by lights — on an uncontrolled crossing the battle of wills with the average Australian driver can be both trying and dangerous. It is an offense to jaywalk.

TOUR OPERATORS
Australia's four main internal airlines, **Ansett**, **Australian Airlines**, **Eastwest** and **Kendell**, offer a range of vacation packages and tours. So too do the major bus lines, **Pioneer**, **Greyhound**, **Australia Pacific**, **Bus Australia** and **AAT**. The state automobile clubs also operate travel departments and offer package tours (see under individual state capitals in the A TO Z). Look too for specialist tour operators who concentrate on particular destinations such as the Northern Territory; contact the relevant state tourist office for a list.

For those seeking the unusual, **Australian Himalayan Expeditions** *(377 Sussex St., Sydney, NSW, 2000 ☎ (02) 264 3366, map 3 E2; Suite 602, Wellesley House, 126 Wellington Parade, East Melbourne, Vic., 3002 ☎ (03) 419 2333, map 11 C5; c/o Thor Adventure Travel, 40 Waymouth St., Adelaide, SA, 5000 ☎ (08) 212 7857, map 8 D3)* has white-water rafting expeditions and hot-air ballooning, to name just two energetic options. Another operator, **Peregrine Adventures** *(343 Little Collins St., Melbourne, Vic., 3000 ☎ (03) 602 3066, map 10 C3)*, specializes in vacations-with-a-difference, such as cross-country skiing, bushwalking, rafting, canoeing or sailing.

Several smaller operators provide a personalized service and concentrate on one area. For example, **Bogong Jack** *(P.O. Box 209, Wangaratta, Vic., 3677 ☎ (057) 212 564)*, a husband-and-wife team, can arrange weekend (or longer) cycling trips around the wineries of northeastern Victoria, staying at country pubs, or, in winter, snowshoe expeditions and cross-country ski camping trips above the snow line, spending nights camped in special tents.

On-the-spot information

WITH BUSINESS IN MIND

Australian business is going through a period of extraordinary change. The era of the quick buck, with overnight entrepreneurs dazzling the world on far-too-easy credit, has gone. There is an air of caution as the country heads toward the mid-1990s. But that does not mean a lack of opportunities, or a cool reception for those who come here on business.

Among the biggest trends today is the steady dismantling of the protectionist barriers that have sheltered Australian manufacturing industry for most of the period since World War II. Products and cost structures in Australia must now be internationally competitive or they will go to the wall.

Australia's major sources of income are still coal, iron ore, wheat, wool, sugar and beef, but tourism is now Australia's biggest single export earner and is expected to attract more than A$25 billion by the year 2000.

The rising wealth of Asian nations is affecting both the focus and style of Australian business. Australian executives are becoming increasingly sophisticated in dealing not only with their major trading partner, Japan, but also with other competitive players on the Pacific Rim. More than 75 percent of Australian export growth over the next five years will come from sales to key Asian countries.

The international business executive is well catered to in the capital cities of Australia. Distances here have ensured that clear communications have always been a priority. **Convention facilities** are plentiful, from the Barrier Reef islands to Alice Springs. **Printing**, **secretarial** and **satellite teleconferencing** services are readily available and first class in all states. Most of the bigger **hotels** are experienced in handling business demands, from calls for interpreters to personal valets. There are many **private secretarial bureaux**, and many **"quick print" shops**, offering fast photocopying, facsimile services and basic printing, at reasonable rates.

Australian business practices can sometimes appear deceptively casual to the European or American eye. But behind the use of first names and the general bonhomie is a weighing-up of values and opportunities that is every bit as sharp as you will find anywhere. An Australian chief executive places a great deal on the shake of a hand, although these days his or her lawyers tend to be a little fussier about the paperwork that follows.

For those business visitors who intend to do a great deal of traveling within Australia, the services of the domestic airline executive "clubs" may prove invaluable. Both Ansett's **Golden Wing** (☎ (03) 668 1211) and the **Australian Airlines Flight Deck** (☎ (03) 666 3460) have reciprocal rights with many international airlines. Membership, however, allows, as well as priority aircraft seating, such business-related facilities as private conferencing rooms at airports, phones and work stations, free facsimile and photocopying, valet parking and a limousine service, as well as mobile phone rental. Drinks and light meals are provided, and business desks in the clubs can deal with last-minute secretarial needs.

For business visitors with specific queries on trading matters, the **Australian Trade Commission (Austrade)** (☎ *(02) 581 2555 in Sydney, (03) 284 3111 in Melbourne)* will offer broad and detailed assistance. Go to the **Australian Customs Service** office in each state capital for information on licensing and quotas on imports. There are also offices of the **Australian Chamber of Manufacture** and **Chambers of Commerce** in each capital city. The **Australian Stock Exchange** branches in Melbourne, Sydney and Perth are open to visitors.

Useful business magazines and newspapers in Australia include the daily *Australian Financial Review,* the weekly *Bulletin* and *Business Review Weekly (BRW)* magazines, and the monthly *Australian Business.* And, for those who really want to brush up their local knowledge before any negotiations, the **Commonwealth (Australian Government Publishing Service) Bookshop** in each capital city offers for sale a comprehensive list of official publications and statistics.

PUBLIC HOLIDAYS

Most public holidays are taken nationwide, but there are state-by-state and local differences. For example, in Victoria only the Melbourne Metropolitan region has a public holiday for the Melbourne Cup horse race, on the first Tuesday in November.

The public holidays are: **New Year's Day** (January 1); **Australia Day** (January 26); **Labour Day** (first Monday in March in Western Australia and Tasmania, second Monday in March in Victoria); **Canberra Day** (ACT only — third Monday in March); **Good Friday**; **Easter Saturday**; **Easter Monday**; **Easter Tuesday** (Victoria and Tasmania only); **Anzac Day** (April 25); **Labour Day** (Queensland and Northern Territory only — first Monday in May); **Adelaide Cup Day** (South Australia only — third Monday in May); **Foundation Day** (Western Australia only — first Monday in June); **Queen's Birthday** (all states except Western Australia — second Monday in June); **August Bank Holiday** (NSW, ACT and Northern Territory only — first Monday in August); **Melbourne Show Day** (Melbourne Metropolitan area only — last Thursday in September); **Labour Day** (first Monday in October in NSW, ACT and Western Australia, second Monday in October in South Australia); **Melbourne Cup Day** (Melbourne Metropolitan area only — first Tuesday in November); **Christmas Day**; **Boxing Day** (December 26).

TIME ZONES

Australia has three time zones: **Eastern Standard Time** (US EST plus 14 hours, GMT plus 10 hours) covering Queensland, NSW (except Broken Hill), Victoria and Tasmania; **Central Standard Time** (US EST plus $13\frac{1}{2}$ hours, GMT plus $9\frac{1}{2}$ hours) covering South Australia, Broken Hill and the Northern Territory; and **Western Time** (US EST plus 12 hours, GMT plus 8 hours) covering Western Australia. **Daylight Saving** (or Summer) Time operates in Victoria, NSW, South Australia and Tasmania but not in Queensland, the Northern Territory or Western Australia; in the eastern states the clocks go forward at the end of October and back in March or April. Each state decides independently, and they can be up to a month out of sequence with each other. It is best to check on arrival.

BANKING HOURS
Banks are open from Monday to Thursday from 9.30am to 4pm, and on Fridays from 9.30am to 5pm. Most **foreign exchanges** operate as part of large organizations such as American Express and Thomas Cook and have slightly longer opening hours than banks. There are exchange counters operated by the banks at the major **international airports**. Most larger **hotels** will gladly exchange travelers checks and major currencies.

American Express also has a **Moneygram** ® money transfer service that makes it possible to wire money worldwide in just minutes from any **American Express Travel Service** office. This service is available to all customers and is not limited to American Express Card members. Payment can be made in cash, or with an American Express Card with a Centurion Credit Line, an American Express Optima (SM) Card, Visa or MasterCard.

ACCOMMODATIONS
Hotel accommodations in Australia range from international 5-star standard to a room in a country pub with a washbasin along the corridor. The most common style of accommodation is the motel; they are widespread and generally of a good standard.

The average motel unit has its own bathroom facilities, color TV set, bedside clock, radio and refrigerator, as well as a table, a couple of chairs and an armchair. Most motels provide an electric kettle, tea, coffee and milk so that guests can make a hot drink. Breakfast can be served in the unit or, in larger, better-standard motels, in a dining room; the more basic motels lack dining rooms, and breakfast will be the only meal served.

Three large nationwide chains, **Flag Inns**, **TraveLodge** and **Best Western**, offer a standard that is acceptable in all cases, with some distinguished motels featuring in each chain. At the top end of the scale, for example, is Sydney's **Regent Hotel**, which ranks among the world's best; it overlooks Circular Quay and offers an unrivaled view across Sydney Harbour (with prices to match the view).

A new trend in family accommodations has emerged in the form of serviced efficiency (self-catering) apartments. Several have appeared in the capital cities, offering one- or two-bedroom apartments within a hotel-style complex. A good example is **Gordon Place** in Melbourne, a magnificent Victorian building, completely modernized. It offers a range of apartments, all with superb modern kitchens, from studio apartments through to two-bedroom apartments with separate living rooms.

HOTEL RESERVATIONS
Most of the state capitals operate **hotel reservation services**, and information is usually available at airports, railway stations and bus depots. Large motel chains with free reservation services, such as **Flag Inns**, **Best Western** and **TraveLodge** can reserve ahead.

53

FOOD AND DRINK

Australians, in the local argot, like their tucker. Restaurants abound in all the major cities, and Australians eat out frequently. Melbourne, for example, supports no fewer than 1,600 restaurants covering some 60 different cuisines.

But what of the homegrown product? Someone once remarked that the only truly Australian gift to the world was pavlova, a meringue topped with cream and banana, passion fruit or whatever one wishes. Once, the average Australian's idea of a "good feed" was roast lamb and two vegetables. Now, it is possible to eat as well in Melbourne or Sydney as in any major city in the world. Nor are other Australian cities in any sense lacking.

Melbourne and Sydney boast at least one restaurant for every major cuisine, and most minor ones, that the world has fostered. There are good examples of Greek, Italian, Lebanese, Turkish, Afghan, French, German, all styles of Chinese, and even Nepalese restaurants. The predominant styles are Italian, Chinese and French. The latest arrival is Vietnamese cuisine, which has spread rapidly and begun to displace the ubiquitous Chinese restaurant as the place for an inexpensive evening out. This internationalization of the Australian diet is a direct consequence of the huge influx of immigrants from all over Europe and Asia that have arrived since World War II.

Most restaurants offer an à la carte menu; the fixed-price menu is still a rarity but is gaining in popularity. Main courses usually include vegetables or salad in the price, although some, more expensive, restaurants list vegetables separately. (If they are not shown separately you can safely assume they are included.) It is customary to leave a tip: around 10-12 percent is considered acceptable.

In most states there are two types of liquor license available for restaurants: the full license and the Bring Your Own (BYO) license. Victoria, and more particularly Melbourne, abounds in BYO establishments (see DINING OUT in MELBOURNE, page 252), but the system is not as widespread in other states. In this guide, restaurants that have a **BYO** license or **no** license are indicated; if nothing is indicated the restaurant can be assumed to have a **full** license.

FAST FOOD Australians are fast-food addicts. McDonald's, Kentucky Fried Chicken and PizzaHut grace many suburbs.

The indigenous snack food, though, is a meat pie eaten with liberal amounts of tomato sauce. This is the staple diet of football fans at matches in winter, and there is truly an art to eating a hot and often somewhat soggy pie while balancing tomato sauce on top. A local variation in South Australia — a pie floater, consisting of the above-mentioned pie in a bowl of pea soup — poses an even greater challenge.

PUB FOOD The other great traditional eating habit is the **counter lunch** (or dinner), which the British know as a pub meal. The term "counter" is self-explanatory, although few pubs now expect their customers to eat sitting up at the counter; most provide tables.

Food in many pubs is increasingly upscale. It is no longer rare to find venison, quail or lobster on the menu. But most pubs offer first-class, economical meals, seeking to make a profit out of bar sales and to cover only their costs on the food. More traditional pubs, particularly in inner-city areas and suburbs, often erect a blackboard on the sidewalk to advertise the day's offerings and prices. Mostly the fare is unambitious: sausages, chicken, lamb chops — but servings are usually generous and the food is wholesome if unimaginative.

Pub lunches generally run from noon until 2.30pm. Dinner (or tea, as some Australians call any meal eaten after 4pm) is served from 5.30 or 6pm to 8 or 8.30pm. See also AUSTRALIAN WINE on page 31.

Public houses — called "hotels" in Australia — have slightly different opening hours from state to state, but as a rule open from around 10am to 10pm from Monday to Saturday; they also open for around six hours on Sunday, although hours vary. Licensed restaurants can serve liquor with meals seven days a week.

SHOPPING HOURS

In most Australian cities, the standard shopping hours are from 9am to 5.30pm from **Monday to Thursday**, from 9am to 9pm on **Thursday or Friday** (the late-shopping night varies from state to state), and on **Saturday** from 9am to 12.30 or 1pm. Some supermarkets remain open until 9pm or 10pm every weekday. Certain categories of shops, such as garden nurseries, bookstores, milk bars and convenience stores, open seven days a week; some convenience stores, which are often fran-chised American operations such as 7 Eleven and Food Plus, are even open 24 hours a day. In addition, in certain tourist areas shops stay open 7 days a week. The federal system in Australia places responsi-bility for shopping hours with state governments, which causes vari-ations between states.

WHAT TO SHOP FOR

Clothes The range of casual and leisure clothes available is remark-able. Traditional Australian **bush gear** — the clothes worn by shearers and station hands — has become highly fashionable. Similarly, the Akubra hat, the traditional Outback headgear thrust into prominence by Australian golfer Greg Norman, has become something of a fashion item in Australia and the US. The bush gear and hat are unique to Australia and in general can only be bought within the country.

Australian designer names to look out for include Trent Nathan, Perri Cutten, Anthea Crawford, Marianna Hardwick and Adele Palmer. De-signer Ken Done, whose internationally available work covers items as diverse as bed linen, towels, cosmetic bags and T-shirts, has a unique Australian style reflecting the relaxed nature of his country. His work is popular among teenagers and the early-20s, and is well regarded in the US and Europe.

Souvenirs The standard of Australian souvenirs has risen markedly in recent years. Well-made, high-quality local souvenirs are available through outlets with aggressively Australian identities and names to match, such as the **Australiana General Store** and **Antipodes** (see WHERE TO SHOP in MELBOURNE, page 257). Worth looking out for are:

55

Emergency information

EMERGENCY SERVICES
For **Police**, **Ambulance** or **Fire** ☎000 and ask for the service required.

OTHER MEDICAL EMERGENCIES
Doctors and dentists are listed in the *Yellow Pages* of the telephone directory. The doctors come under the heading *Physicians*, dentists under *Dentists*.

LATE-NIGHT PHARMACIES
Late-night pharmacies are plentiful in the major cities, and most suburbs have at least one open until 9pm every night seven days a week. There are also some 24-hour pharmacies in most cities. Pharmacies are listed in the *Yellow Pages*.

AUTOMOBILE ACCIDENTS
- Do not admit liability.
- Ask to see the other driver's license and the name of his insurance company; exchange names and addresses.
- If someone has been injured, call the police and stay until they arrive.
- Ask any witnesses to remain, or ask them for their names and addresses.

CAR BREAKDOWN
If your car breaks down, you should call the breakdown servive number of the **automobile club** listed for the state you are in (see under individual state capitals in the A TO Z). A **rental car** could be registered in any state and will have membership in the automobile club of its state of registry. However, state organizations offer full reciprocal services; when you contact the local service organization, simply state the name of the organization and your membership number. They will then either send a breakdown unit of their own or contact the nearest affiliated garage with a breakdown service. Be as specific as possible when giving your location to the emergency breakdown number.

LOST PASSPORTS
If you lose your passport, contact the state police and inform your consulate at once.

LOST TRAVELERS CHECKS
Inform the police immediately, then follow the instructions provided with your travelers checks, or contact the issuing company's nearest office. Contact your consulate or **American Express** if you are stranded with no money.

items made in Australian woods (Huon pine from Tasmania, Queensland blackwood, myrtle, and others) such as napkin rings and bowls; sheepskin goods such as coats, boots, gloves, hats and rugs; and leatherwork such as handbags.

Antiques   Australians have fallen in love with antiques almost on the same scale as Americans and Britons. Sadly, there is a shortage of genuine Australian antiques, and much of the stock available in the many antique shops is either directly imported by the containerload from Great Britain and Europe or consists of local pieces no older than the early 20thC or the Art Deco or Art Nouveau periods. It is still possible to find genuine Australian antiques — but at a price. One local 19thC specialty was the mounting of emu eggs, often in silver. Some of these display excellent workmanship and are sought after by collectors, and consequently command a high price.

HOW TO SHOP

Bargaining is not welcomed. Australians do not bargain and do not expect visitors to, either. They do, however, shop around extensively, and visitors will find wide variations in price.

There is no value-added or sales tax at the retail level, so the price marked on goods is what you can expect to pay. Most shops accept one or more of the major charge/credit cards. "Lay by," a system of putting down a deposit on goods and paying for them interest-free over a period up to three months while they are held at the shop, is widespread. Anyone staying more than a few weeks may find the system useful. For more details, see the WHERE TO SHOP section for each city.

CUSTOMS AND ETIQUETTE

Australians pride themselves on the egalitarian nature of their society, most of them believing they are the equal of anyone. Consequently they immediately use Christian names, almost as if that demonstrates their equality. Men generally call one another "mate," and the greeting "G'day" is almost universal. Do *not* expect to be called "sir" or "madam" and you won't be disappointed, as Australians have an abiding dislike of anything that smacks of servility.

Many of Australia's social customs revolve around drinking. Buying a "shout" (round) in the pub is considered essential good manners. Similarly, when invited out to dinner at someone's house, it is polite to arrive with a small gift, usually a bottle of wine, or perhaps a box of chocolates for the hostess.

RUSH HOURS

Although times differ from city to city, the early-morning rush hour starts earlier the farther N one goes. Because of the heat in the tropics, Brisbane, for example, comes to life at least half an hour earlier than Melbourne. Generally, however, the rush hour starts around 7am and lasts until 9am. In the evening the traffic starts to clog at around 5.15 to 5.30pm, until about 7pm. Friday nights in summer, when people go away for the weekend, tend to be worse than other peak periods.

POST AND TELEPHONE SERVICES

Post offices, denoted by a sign carrying the legend **Australia Post** in red, are widespread. Each post office also has the **post code (zip code)** for its area prominently displayed together with the town's or suburb's name. They open Monday to Friday 9am-5pm. The **central post office** in each capital city has a counter open 24 hours a day and is usually still referred to as "The GPO" (for "General Post Office"), although the postal system has been renamed Australia Post. **Mail boxes** are painted red and are identical to those used in Great Britain. Many milk bars sell a range of the most commonly used stamps.

Public telephones, which are located at post offices and in the street, are subject to vandalism, as they are in other parts of the world. A local call costs 30 cents. Phone booths take 10, 20 and 50 cent coins. In addition, certain phone booths accept **Phonecards** and major charge/credit cards. Phonecards can be purchased at post offices in a number of denominations. Inserted into a slot in the telephone, they allow callers time up to the limit of the card's value. The amount used is automatically deducted from the card, which can be used again until credit is exhausted. All calls outside a certain radius are classified as long distance. Long-distance numbers are prefixed by an **STD** (Standard Trunk Dialing) code. STD codes for all cities and towns in Australia are listed in telephone directories.

PUBLIC LAVATORIES (REST ROOMS)

These are few and far between in most Australian cities, although there are one or two gems of Victorian cast-iron *vespasiennes* in the Paris style in Melbourne and Sydney. Many people resort to the large department stores, which usually have generous facilities. Most rail stations have WCs for men and women, and public houses are often used in an emergency by passers-by.

ELECTRICITY

Current is 240/250v, AC 50Hz. Australia uses 3-pin power outlets. Most hotels have special plugs for 110v shavers. Universal adaptors for overseas appliances are obtainable in most large department stores.

LAWS AND REGULATIONS

A law peculiar to Australia is the system of **Total Fire Ban** days in summer. Under this system it is an offense on designated days to light a fire in the open or allow one to remain burning. These days are usually announced 24 hours in advance but can be imposed at shorter notice, and are designated according to forecast weather conditions such as high winds and dry conditions accompanied by high temperatures. Penalties for ignoring a Total Fire Ban are severe and differ from state to state, but typically they can be a fine of A$5,000 or imprisonment for 2 years, or even both. Southeastern Australia, particularly the states of Victoria and South Australia, is one of the most flammable regions in the world (think of the Ash Wednesday bushfires of 1983, which claimed more than 70 lives), so the concern with fire is understandable.

Penalties for importing **drugs** are severe. The laws governing trafficking and possession differ from state to state; those in Queensland are considered the toughest. **Cigarette** smoking is prohibited on public transportation in most states, as well as in most government (State and Federal) buildings. The transportation of **fruit and vines** across most state borders is strictly forbidden.

TIPPING
Tipping is not generally customary in Australia and no service charge is added by hotels or restaurants. It is customary to tip a waiter around 10 percent for good service, but taxi drivers, barbers and porters do not expect it. Porters at rail terminals have set charges, but hotel porters do not and can be tipped at the discretion of the guest.

DISABLED TRAVELERS
The law in most states requires all new buildings to provide for disabled people such facilities as ramps and special WCs. Many buildings erected in the past decade have included them, and in the wake of the Year for the Disabled many local authorities upgraded their provision for disabled people. Both the major internal airlines offer disabled travelers special assistance such as priority boarding and assistance with wheelchairs.

For booklets listing facilities in each state capital, write to the **Australian Council for Rehabilitation of the Disabled (ACROD)** *(P.O. Box 60, Curtin, ACT, 2605 ☎(06) 82 4333).*

There is no national reference point for information for disabled people, but most **state tourist authorities** have information about the facilities available at leading tourist destinations. Other sources of information are the **state departments of health**, whose telephone numbers can be found in the front of each capital city's telephone book under the "State Government" listing. The **Commonwealth Department of Youth, Sport and Recreation** publishes a book, available from the department, listing facilities for the disabled at a number of tourist destinations around the country.

Useful addresses

TOURIST INFORMATION
Australian Tourist Commission   Head Office: 81 William St., Woolloomooloo, NSW, 2011 *(☎(02) 360 1111, map 4D4);* branch office: 5 Elizabeth St., Sydney, NSW, 2000 *(☎(02) 233 7233, map 3C3).*
American Express   A valuable source of information for any traveler in need of help, advice or emergency service. There are American Express customer card service offices in all the capital cities. Main addresses and telephone numbers:
- **Sydney** — American Express Tower, Sydney, NSW, 2000 ☎(02) 239 0666, map **3**D3

- **Melbourne** — 105 Elizabeth St., Melbourne, Vic., 3000 ☎(03) 608 0333, map **10**C3
- **Adelaide** — 13 Grenfell St., Adelaide, SA, 5000 ☎(08) 212 7155, map **8**D3
- **Perth** — 1 Howard St., Perth, WA, 6000 ☎(09) 426 3777, map **15**C4
- **Brisbane** — 131 Elizabeth St., Brisbane, Qld, 4000 ☎(07) 221 7815, map **16**D2
- **Canberra City** — Centrepoint, Canberra, ACT, 2600 ☎(06) 47 7750, map **1**B4
- In addition there are a number of **American Express Travel Service** offices around the country at which it is possible to cash personal checks in an emergency (see under individual state capitals in the A TO Z).

State Government Tourist Bureaux   See under individual state capitals in the A TO Z. In addition to the main offices, most State Government Tourist Bureaux have branches in other major capital cities and are listed in telephone books.

CONSULATES
Most major countries have consular representation in the state capitals. Their addresses are listed in the telephone book under "Consuls" (in the alphabetical section).

GOVERNMENT DEPARTMENTS
Federal and state government departments are listed together with local councils at the front of all telephone books.

TELEPHONE INTERPRETER SERVICE
The Telephone Interpreter Service's number, in the front section of the telephone book, has useful numbers, such as the Ministries of Immigration, Foreign Affairs and Ethnic Affairs, for non-English-speakers. This section is written in 12 languages.

STATE AUTOMOBILE CLUBS
See under individual state capitals in the A TO Z.

Planning
and tours

When to go

Right now is the ideal time to visit Australia, for in such a large country clement weather can be found somewhere throughout the year. But there are times when some places are best avoided. For example, beach resorts can be extremely crowded during the school-vacation periods of January, Easter, the last week of June and first week of July, and the last week of September. Queensland's beaches are particularly busy at Easter and during the period from September to October, when families from the southern states take advantage of the warmer weather in the N (Australia has recently adopted a 4-term school year). Yet although by Australian standards resorts are packed during the school vacations, to Europeans they must seem relatively uncluttered. Nothing in Australia compares with a crowded Spanish beach in August, or Blackpool on a British bank holiday.

While many people are taking their vacations in January, the cities tend to be far less crowded, rather like Paris during August. Many factories and businesses close down entirely for some or all of the month. The closures often start a day or so before Christmas, and commercial life does not return to normal until the end of January or the beginning of February

THE DRIEST CONTINENT
Generally Australia is dry and hot, becoming progressively hotter and drier the farther inland you go. There are vast areas of desert in the center that see no rainfall for years — even decades — on end. Average rainfall is about 418mm (about 16 inches), as against the world average of 660mm (26 inches). Just how dry the continent is can be gauged from the total outflow of Australian rivers, which barely amounts to that of just one of the major South American rivers.

Rainfall is unevenly distributed. Areas such as the desert center receive less than 127mm (5 inches) a year, and achieve that level only because the average is increased by torrential downpours every few years. Conversely, areas of Tasmania and N Queensland receive more than 2,500mm (nearly 100 inches) a year.

THE SEASONS
In the northern tropical area, summer and fall are the wet seasons and little rain falls in winter and spring. The rain in the northeastern part of the country is produced by the NW monsoon, and in the NW by the

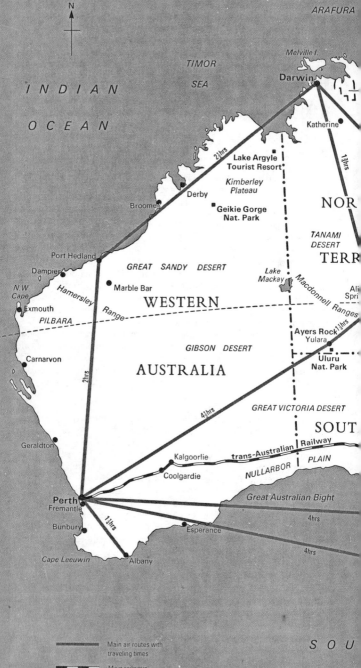

ARAFURA

Melville I.

TIMOR
SEA

Darwin

I N D I A N

Katherine

O C E A N

2¾hrs

Lake Argyle
Tourist Resort

1½hrs

*Kimberley
Plateau*

NOR

Broome

Derby

■ Geikie Gorge
Nat. Park

*TANAMI
DESERT*

TERR

Port Hedland

GREAT SANDY DESERT

*Lake
Mackay*

Macdonnell Ranges

Dampier

*N.W
Cape*

Hamersley

• Marble Bar

WESTERN

Ali
Spri

Exmouth

PILBARA

Range

GIBSON DESERT

Ayers Rock 1½hrs
Yulara

Carnarvon

AUSTRALIA

2hrs

*Uluru
Nat. Park*

GREAT VICTORIA DESERT

4½hrs

SOUT

Geraldton

GREAT VICTORIA DESERT

trans-Australian ‖ Railway

Kalgoorlie

NULLARBOR *PLAIN*

Coolgardie

Great Australian Bight

Perth
Fremantle

4hrs

Bunbury

1½hrs

Esperance

4hrs

Cape Leeuwin

Albany

▬▬ Main air routes with
traveling times
▬▬ Main railways

0   200   400   600   800km
0   250   500miles

S O U

O C

SEA

Torres   Strait

Cape York

CAPE YORK
PENINSULA

Gove
Peninsula

kadu
. Park

Weipa

PACIFIC

OCEAN

Groote
Eylandt

Gulf   of
Carpentaria

1¾hrs

Barkly
1⅓hrs   Tableland

ERN

Cairns

CORAL
SEA

1½hrs

vils Marbles
Nat. Park

Townsville

Great   Barrier
4hr

GREAT

Whitsunday
Group
Mackay

ORY

Mt. Isa

1hr

Tropic of Capricorn

QUEENSLAND

DIVIDING

2¾hrs

1¾hrs

Rockhampton

SIMPSON
DESERT

5hrs

RANGE

2¾hrs

Bundaberg

Sunshine
Coast

2hrs

Lake Eyre

Coober
Pedy

AUSTRALIA

Flinders
Ranges

4¾hrs

Darling

Brisbane

Gold
Coast

arcoola

Port
Augusta

Broken
Hill

NEW   SOUTH

1¼hrs   WALES

1¾hrs

RANGE

Coffs
Harbour

1¼hrs

Whyalla

1⅓hrs

Eyre
ninsula

Mildura

DIVIDING

Newcastle

Adelaide

1¾hrs
Murray

Wagga
Wagga

Sydney

Kangaroo I.

1hr

VICTORIA

A.C.T.   CANBERRA

2hr
GREAT

Mt. Gambier

Bendigo

1hr

Portland

Geelong

Melbourne

1¾hrs

TASMAN

Bass   Strait

SEA

HERN

1hr

AN

Devonport

Launceston

TASMANIA

Hobart

cyclone season, which can be erratic and unpredictable. In the southern part the climate resembles that of the Mediterranean: rainfall is more evenly distributed, occurring mainly in winter and spring, and summer and early fall tend to be dry.

Severe wintry cold spells are very unusual except in the mountains of the SE and in Tasmania. But even then temperatures drop only at nighttime to a few degrees below freezing. Daytime subfreezing temperatures are usually confined to the peaks and plateaux above 1,000 meters (3,280 feet).

The southeastern coastal strip is generally more temperate than inland. Once N of the Great Dividing Range, which runs from Queensland to South Australia at varying distances roughly parallel to the coast, temperatures tend to be both higher and lower than in the coastal cities. Hence it can freeze overnight in winter, but in daytime the temperature can possibly rise to 18°C (about 65°F). In summer the temperature can climb well above 40°C (about 105°F) on days when on the southern coast it might be a hot 32°C (90°F).

Except in the SE and the extreme SW, summers range from hot to very hot, with maximum temperatures of above 38°C (100°F) common inland from about November to mid- or late March. January and February are the hottest months in the southern states, when the state capitals usually experience a few days of above 38°C (100°F) temperatures. In the far N, November and December are hottest.

The northern third of the continent in most years experiences a number of severe cyclones accompanied by torrential rain, which frequently causes flooding. Cyclone Tracy, which devastated Darwin in 1974, was an example of the most severe type of cyclone that can hit the area. Luckily, the vast majority cross the coast in uninhabited regions.

SKIING
Predominantly a land of sunshine, Australia is less well known for its skiing. Few people outside the country realize that it has more skiable slopes than the Swiss Alps, although the Australian season is much shorter.

The major ski areas are concentrated in Victoria and NSW, and there are minor resorts also in Tasmania. The ski season is short but intense — it opens in June, although often snow has yet to fall at that time, and lasts until early September, or in some years late September. Facilities are generally first-class.

Calendar of events

Every year seems to bring new festivals and entertainments. The daily newspapers in Sydney, Melbourne and other capital cities have information-packed supplements on upcoming events, and there is a helpful booklet, *Australia: A Traveller's Guide,* published by the Australian Tourist Commission.

In this calendar, the seasons are merely a rough guide, generally meaning little in the subtropical N of Australia, where the year is more simply divided into the Big Wet and the Dry.

WINTER: JUNE, JULY, AUGUST

It's playtime in the N, with the festivities moving along from the **Alice Springs camel races** into the dubious delights of the **Darwin Beer Can Regatta** in June and, in August, **Henley-on-Todd**, a mock yacht race on the dusty dry bed of the Todd River at Alice Springs. The **Townsville Pacific Festival** offers a more traditional mix of art exhibitions, sports competitions, fireworks and carnival at the end of August and beginning of September. The fitter and more energetic may feel inspired to enter the 14km (9-mile) **Sydney City-to-Surf fun run**, a mini-marathon that takes thousands of amateur joggers and a considerable number of professional runners rushing from the city heat to the beach in August.

SPRING: SEPTEMBER, OCTOBER, NOVEMBER

This is the season for Australia's major sporting events. In Melbourne, the close of the football season is celebrated at the end of September with the **AFL Grand Final**, an Aussie Rules spectacular for which tickets are at a premium. The **Australian Grand Prix**, Adelaide's auto-racing carnival, follows (make hotel reservations well in advance), and then it's back to Melbourne for the horses and Victoria's **Spring Racing Carnival** in November. Do your best to get to the **Melbourne Cup** at Flemington, one of Australia's most colorful occasions. It takes place on the first Tuesday in November.

More cerebral pleasures can be enjoyed during the **Melbourne International Festival of the Arts**, a presentation of fine dance, theater, opera, music and the visual arts. Meanwhile, in South Australia's Southern Vales, there is feasting and wine tasting in the annual **McLaren Vale Bushing Festival**, which in October welcomes in the release of the new vintage wines.

SUMMER: DECEMBER, JANUARY, FEBRUARY

Sydney Harbour never looks more colorful than on Boxing Day, with the start of the **Sydney-to-Hobart Yacht Race**. The competing yachts are surrounded by flotillas of spectator craft, and maritime chaos inevitably ensues. At the other end of the course the **Tasmania Fiesta** begins; the annual cultural and sporting festival is held in conjunction with the world-famous yacht race and runs from December through January

This is arts festival time. At the end of December and well into January, the **Festival of Sydney** takes place. The **Melbourne Summer Music** festival at the Victorian Arts Centre sounds sweetly around the end of the month (January 26 being Australia Day). The **Festival of Perth**, with concerts, art exhibitions, theater, film and television, is held from mid-February, and (on even-numbered years) the **Adelaide Festival of the Arts**, Australia's most prominent cultural celebration, takes us into the first few weeks of March. This is also the heart of the **cricket season** and, whether it is a Test or a World Series Cricket one-day match, tickets should be easily available for most games. And in January there is the annual **Hahndorf Scheutzenfest** in South Australia, a German-style beer, food and folk-dancing festival, and, at the end of the month, the **Australasian Country Music Awards Festival** in Tamworth, NSW.

FALL: MARCH, APRIL, MAY

In Melbourne it's **Mardi Gras** time, with the annual **Moomba Festival** getting into full swing at the beginning of March. Normally staid Melbournians let their hair down for the Moomba parade and days and nights of free entertainment, fun fairs, fireworks and surfing events alongside and on the Yarra River. A little farther N, in the old Victorian goldfields, the **Ballarat Begonia Festival** is a floral celebration in March, with arts and sports events.

In April, Australians all around the country commemorate **Anzac Day**, the annual day of remembrance for those who died in World War I, World War II, Korea and Vietnam. Servicemen march at dawn to memorials in towns and cities.

Where to go

The main difficulty about planning a vacation in Australia is that there are so many choices. Broad decisions must be made before you travel, and personal priorities must be well defined. This book aims simply to present and help you select some of the options.

The sheer vastness and emptiness of the continent can be hard to grasp. At 7.68 million sq.km (nearly 3 million square miles), almost the size of the continental US, 25 times larger than the British Isles and three-quarters the size of Europe, Australia is one of the most sparsely populated countries in the world, with about 1.84 people per sq.km. Two-fifths of the continent lies N of the Tropic of Capricorn.

The distances between population centers are also enormous. Two examples: Brisbane and Perth are separated by more than 3,600km (2,250 miles) by air, a distance greater than that between London and Moscow; Perth is virtually closer to Singapore than it is to Sydney, and is generally accepted as being the most isolated city of significant size anywhere in the world.

Because of the vast distances, a coast-to-coast driving vacation is out of the question. However, Australia is very well geared to the fly-drive concept, which involves flying to a center, collecting a rented car for the duration of your stay, then returning it and flying on to another center. Both the main domestic airlines, Ansett and Australian Airlines, have arrangements with car rental companies — Avis and Hertz respectively — and the other major international rental companies are all represented at most major airports.

Australia is a long way from almost anywhere else, and it takes a long time to get there even by air. But, given careful advance planning, the rewards can be considerable. More than in most countries, it would be quite pointless to arrive without planning where and what you want to visit and establishing a priority list of sights you don't mean to miss.

For touring purposes Australia divides up roughly into four regions. There is the "Top End," comprising the Northern Territory and the northern parts of Queensland and Western Australia; NSW and the southern part of Queensland; Victoria, the southern part of South Australia and Tasmania; and the rest of Western Australia. Obviously some of these areas overlap, so that any combination can be put together to make up a vacation itinerary.

A number of sights and places should be on everyone's list of priorities: **Ayers Rock**; the **Great Barrier Reef** and the **Whitsunday Islands**; part of the **Outback**, preferably in the Northern Territory; **Sydney**, if only to see the **Opera House**; **Tasmania**, for a little bit of England in the southern hemisphere and some wonderful early colonial architecture; **Ballarat** and **Bendigo**, Victoria's golden cities; and **Western Australia**, for magnificent beaches and a sense of isolation possible to experience in few other places on earth.

Tours

The extended A TO Z in this book, which covers all the important centers and touring regions in Australia, provides a menu of options for the visitor. Arranged alphabetically by state, each begins with a general introduction to the state and its capital city. Then follows a full description of the capital, arranged alphabetically by subject — what to see, where to stay, eat, drink and shop, and where the best recreation and entertainment can be found — and a selection of excursions by rented car (many of them also feasible by public transportation) out of the city. Some of the excursions are short one-day or half-day trips. Others involve at least one overnight stop, and accommodations are then suggested. There are also concise pointers on how to arrange more ambitious expeditions, such as trips into the Outback.

Many readers, however, will find the routes suggested in the following PLANNING pages useful as a more focused planning foundation. They are based on some of the most popular touring areas — Victoria, southern NSW, and South Australia E of Adelaide; Tasmania; the coast between Sydney and Brisbane; Western Australia S and E of Perth; and the W coast between Perth and Port Hedland. Outside the state capitals, many of the places mentioned in these routes are described in the excursions for the relevant state (in the A TO Z).

Most visitors fly into either **Sydney** or **Melbourne**. Both cities are well worth a stay of several days. Subsequently, a drive N or S to the other city can form a good introduction to driving and touring in Australia.

ROUTE 1: SYDNEY — MELBOURNE
Maps 6 and 5 on pages 126-7 and maps 13 and 12 on pages 262-3. Allow 2 days. Recommended stop: Merimbula or Eden.

Two major roads link Australia's largest cities. The Hume Highway follows the direct inland route and offers a far less interesting although fast link between Sydney and Melbourne. Favored by heavy trucks, it is much the busier road. It is largely four-lane highway in Victoria and is generally excellent until the NSW border; thereafter the quality deteriorates. (Because each state is responsible for the upkeep of its roads, quality can vary quite considerably from state to state.) A detour off the Hume Highway can be made, S of Goulburn, to visit **Canberra**, the national capital.

The Princes Highway, on which this suggested itinerary of 1,042km (651 miles) is based, takes the more picturesque and longer coastal route. It is designated Route 1, which circles nearly the entire continent. Leaving Sydney heading S, the highway skirts the Wollongong region, which, with Port Kembla and neighboring communities, is one of the country's major steel- and coal-producing areas and also one of the largest urban areas in NSW outside of Sydney.

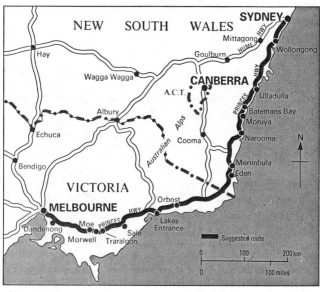

68

The highway then continues down the coast through the fishing and resort towns of **Ulladulla** and **Batemans Bay** before reaching **Moruya**, once a gateway to the Araluen goldfields and now a quiet resort. **Narooma** is a popular fishing resort, well known for its mud oysters. **Merimbula**, another popular vacation resort, is famous for its game fishing and oysters, which are cultivated under license in the river estuary. The coast from Ulladulla to Merimbula offers a wide variety of scenery with areas of bushland and forest that delight bushwalkers; white surfing beaches, hills, lakes and inlets are set against a backdrop of mountains. It is known as the **Alpine Coast** because of the proximity of the mountains of the Australian Alps, which form part of the Great Dividing Range.

Eden, the next town, is an important fishing center, with one of the largest fleets in the country. In the 19thC it was a whaling center, and the local museum has one of only two skeletons extant of a killer whale. Just 56km (35 miles) s of Eden is the Victorian border. From Eden the highway moves inland, the countryside changing quite dramatically as the road enters the heavily timbered and undulating region known as **East Gippsland**. From the NSW border to Orbost the road is forested on both sides. The area is home to the mountain ash, which is a variety of eucalyptus and the tallest hardwood tree in the world. Some examples have measured above 91m (300 feet); one, in 1880, reached a massive 114.3m (375 feet).

Take care along this stretch of road, particularly at night, for animals, chiefly kangaroos and wombats — slow-moving marsupials about the size of a medium-sized dog — have a habit of slowly crossing the highway at night and being mesmerized by headlights. Harmless, gentle creatures, they can do a lot of damage to a car that hits them.

From Orbost to Sale the route is timbered on the northern side into the mountains of the **Great Dividing Range**. The highway next touches the coast at **Lakes Entrance**, which marks the beginning of a vast saltwater lake system, offering unrivaled waters for cruising and fishing. Cutting inland again to Sale, the countryside now becomes more rural, with numerous farms, mostly dairy, before the road enters **LaTrobe Valley.**

Here industry blends into farmland, town into country. Power stations, located as near as possible to their source of brown coal, rear up startlingly out of rural vistas. The valley is also a rich dairying region: it is not uncommon to see Jersey and Friesian cows grazing within a few hundred yards of a smoke-belching chimney. Not surprisingly, the rural bliss is marred by higher-than-average pollution created by the burning of fossil fuels. The valley has several large towns that grew up mainly to house power station workers — Traralgon, Morwell, Moe and other smaller conurbations, all classic company towns, although, as it happens, the company is a state utility, the State Electricity Commission (SEC) of Victoria.

The Princes Highway enters Melbourne through the industrial area of Dandenong, center for much of the Australian car manufacturing industry.

A detour to spend two days in Canberra can easily be made on this journey by taking Route 52, the Kings Highway, just N of Batemans Bay, to Queanbeyan and then to Canberra. Alternatively the Federal Highway, which links Canberra and Sydney, can be reached by taking the Illawarra Highway from Shellharbour and driving through Goulburn to the national capital.

From Canberra it is possible to drive s on the Monaro Highway to Cooma and rejoin the Princes Highway at Bega. This route goes through the magnificent mountain country of the **Great Dividing Range**, close to where *The Man from Snowy River* was filmed.

ROUTE 2: MELBOURNE — THE KELLY COUNTRY — MURRAY RIVER — GREAT OCEAN ROAD — MELBOURNE

*Map **12** on page 262, and maps **8** and **9** on pages 184-5. Allow minimum of 10 days. Recommended stops: Wangaratta, Echuca or Swan Hill, Mildura, Renmark, Adelaide, Mt. Gambier or Port Fairy or Warrnambool.*

Victoria, Australia's smallest mainland state, is blessed with a network of generally well-maintained secondary roads that lead through rich rural country to places of scenic appeal or historical interest. And, for the Melbourne-based visitor, most are within a comfortable day's drive of "home." This circular tour takes in the countryside over which the bushranger Ned Kelly once roamed, as well as the mighty **Murray River** and the spectacular **Great Ocean Road**.

Drive the 235km (147 miles) N from Melbourne along the Hume Highway to the prosperous agricultural and dairy center of **Wangaratta**, a suitable first-night stopover. From here, the dual attractions of fine wines from nearby vineyards and the Kelly memorabilia are within easy

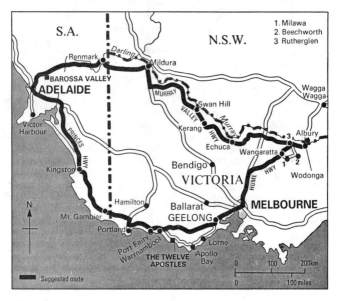

reach. Local wineries, such as those of Brown Brothers at nearby Milawa and All Saints at Rutherglen, welcome visitors with a "taster" and the cellar-door opportunity to buy wines that compete favorably with the best from Europe and northern California.

Around here, too, it is impossible to forget that this was "Kelly country." In the 1870s, Ned Kelly and his gang waged their own private war on the authorities. Kelly was finally captured at Glenrowan, near Wangaratta, after a gun battle and was tried and hanged in Melbourne in 1880. The picturesque town of **Beechworth**, where the much-romanticized Kelly was once imprisoned, is well worth a visit.

Travel on northward to the NSW border and the towns of Wodonga and Albury. Then veer NW along the Murray Valley Highway to **Echuca**, once a busy inland port packed with paddle steamers and barges laden with wool and wheat for the world. Echuca has restored its wharf area and from here visitors can enjoy a paddle-wheeler cruise up the Murray. Both Echuca and **Swan Hill**, another famous old paddle-steamer port farther up the Murray, offer a range of accommodations to suit most tastes. At Swan Hill, a paddle steamer has been converted into a riverside restaurant, offering such delights as kangaroo-tail soup, damper (unleavened bread) and, for the truly courageous, witchetty grubs.

The next stop is the city of **Mildura** at the heart of the Sunraysia district, a region of citrus groves, wines and dried fruit. The mild climate makes Mildura a favorite winter resort, where fishing and water sports provide major attractions. Local delicacies worth sampling include the Murray cod, Murray perch, and "yabbies," or freshwater crayfish.

From Mildura it's a rather flat, fast trip across the South Australian border into **Renmark**. (Make sure the tank is full and that you have checked the water.) Like other Murray River towns, Renmark offers all the major facilities needed by visitors. Rental houseboats (with 4-6 berths) are available for those who want to explore the river more intimately. Nearby is the famous wine-growing district of the **Barossa Valley**, for those with time for a detour.

From the elegant city of **Adelaide**, turn SE and take the Princes Highway for the 455km (285 miles) to **Mt. Gambier**, a city well known for its crater lakes. One, the **Blue Lake**, changes color to a vivid blue in springtime. Cross the Victorian border, heading for **Warrnambool** (Port Fairy, just before it, was one of actor Lee Marvin's shark-fishing haunts); then drive along the Great Ocean Rd. to enjoy magnificent seascapes, superb beaches and pleasant fishing villages. On the drive to Apollo Bay and Lorne, a major attraction is **The Twelve Apostles**, a formation of rocky islands along the coast. Melbourne is a few hours away, with a freeway speeding up the journey on the other side of Geelong.

ROUTE 3: SYDNEY — MELBOURNE — ADELAIDE — BROKEN HILL — SYDNEY

*Map **6** on page 127, maps **13** and **12** on pages 262-3 and maps **8** and **9** on pages 184-5. Allow at least 10 days if driving Sydney-Melbourne-Adelaide, otherwise 8 days. Recommended stops: Merimbula or Eden, Melbourne, Warrnambool or Port Fairy or Mt. Gambier, Adelaide, Broken Hill.*

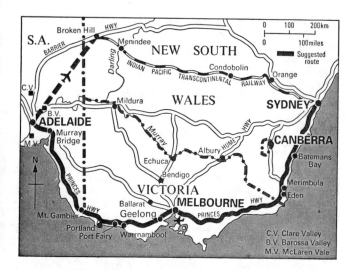

This four-center tour offers a chance to see the two largest cities, together with Adelaide and its surrounding wine-growing districts, the most extensive in Australia. It also offers a taste of the real Outback around Broken Hill, before a leisurely train journey back to Sydney.

Having driven from Sydney to Melbourne (see ROUTE 1), there is a choice of either flying to Adelaide or continuing by road (following in reverse the final stages of ROUTE 2) via the Princes Highway, which goes inland until it reaches the port of Warrnambool and then follows the coast to just N of Portland before again cutting inland to Mt. Gambier in South Australia. The road follows the coast again but slightly inland before coming into Adelaide via Tailem Bend and Murray Bridge.

From Adelaide, that most graceful city on Gulf St Vincent, tours can be made to the **Barossa Valley**, **Clare Valley** and **McLaren Vale** wine-growing districts. All these areas are within an easy day's or half-day's drive from Adelaide. South Australia — and the area around Adelaide particularly — produces some of Australia's finest wines, which now attract world attention. Virtually all wineries have cellar-door sales and offer tastings to visitors, wine purchased at the winery usually entailing a saving on normal retail prices. A visit to the wineries for a tasting has become a great Australian tradition, and most of them are open 7 days a week.

Adelaide and the surrounding wine districts having deserved perhaps three or four days, leave the rented car and fly to **Broken Hill**, only an hour distant but worlds away from the sedate setting of Adelaide. It is in NSW, but operates on Central Time, 1 hour behind the rest of NSW.

Broken Hill sits on one of the world's largest lodes of silver, lead, zinc and other metals, and has been mined over a continuous length of 7km (about $4\frac{1}{2}$ miles). It is still operating nearly 100 years after it was first discovered. An oasis in the middle of a semidesert region, Broken Hill has known no other existence but mining. Increasingly, however, it is attracting tourists. Here are just a few of the attractions: a fully working mine; a ghost town within a half-day's drive of the "Hill," used for many movies and TV series, including *Mad Max II* and *A Town Like Alice;* camels to ride; and the headquarters of the Royal Flying Doctor Service to visit.

From Broken Hill a connection can be made with the Indian Pacific transcontinental rail service to **Sydney** to round off the tour.

ROUTE 4: AROUND TASMANIA
See map on page 205. Allow 2 nights for ferry crossing and minimum of 5 days in Tasmania. Recommended stops: Launceston, St Helens, Hobart, Strahan, Burnie.

Tasmania, a compact island packed with apple orchards, rugged hills and fast-flowing rivers, is often overlooked. Yet it is easy to get to and comfortable to get around. This tour needs careful planning, however, and for those really pressed for time, it may be easier to forget the ferry and fly in from Melbourne (or Sydney) to Launceston, pick up a rented car on arrival and adapt the tour as relevant.

A completely different type of journey begins in Melbourne with a 14-hour overnight crossing on the Bass Strait passenger/vehicle ferry *Abel Tasman*. The ferry takes you into **Devonport** on the N coast of the island. To the E, 90 minutes' drive away, is Launceston, Tasmania's second-largest city, noted for its restored colonial buildings, its gardens and parks, and many nearby scenic attractions. Hotels and motels are commendable and, with the Launceston Country Club-Casino as an evening attraction, this may be the place for a first overnight stop. From Launceston the visitor can enjoy a trip on the chair lift over **Cataract Gorge**, the historic **Franklin House** and **Entally House**, or, with a little more effort, the trout-crammed lakes and peaks of the **Central Plateau**. This last is a joy for bushwalkers, fishermen and photographers alike.

From Launceston, travel 169km (105 miles) E along the Tasman Highway to **St Helens**, a beach resort popular for its nearby bush walks, swimming and surf. Turning S, the road goes through **Scamander**, known for its good fishing, and **Bicheno**, an old whaling town that prides itself on the quality of its crayfish. To the S the clean white beach of **Coles Bay** is close by, with the imposing red granite peaks known as **The Hazards** towering from the sea. Just beyond, **Freycinet National Park**, a picturesque peninsula of bays, beaches and walking tracks, offers campgrounds, guesthouses and cottages.

Back on the highway, continue S to **Hobart**, Tasmania's charming capital, with its scattering of sandstone homes and freshly restored government buildings. There is more than enough to keep the most impatient traveler here a day or two: among the many attractions are Constitution Dock, Battery Point, Mt. Wellington, Salamanca Place, Wrest Point Casino and the old Port Arthur penal settlement about 100km (63 miles) to the SE.

From Hobart, take the NW route up the Lyell Highway to the mining town of **Queenstown** and, 39km (24 miles) farther on, the fishing port of **Strahan**, which once bustled with international shipping. The rugged W coast here is untamed, raw and beautiful. Not far from Strahan is the white water of the Gordon and Franklin Rivers, the delight of skilled rafters.

The last leg is northward along the Murchison Highway and on to **Burnie**, a deep-water port that is Tasmania's fourth-largest center. Note the **Pioneer Village Museum**, a re-creation of a commercial center of a typical northern Tasmanian town about the turn of the century. From Burnie, the Devonport ferry terminal is within easy reach.

ROUTE 5: SYDNEY — COFFS HARBOUR — TWEED HEADS — COOLANGATTA — BRISBANE
Maps 6 and 7 on pages 127 and 154. Allow 2 days. Recommended stop: Port Macquarie or Coffs Harbour.

One of the most pleasing scenic drives for the traveler based in Sydney is the route N following the sun along the Pacific Highway toward the Queensland border.

Escaping the Sydney suburbs may seem a little tiresome, but before too long picturesque **Gosford** is reached. **Newcastle**, busy and industrial although far from grim, is 175km (110 miles) N of Sydney, and from then on the road is dotted with pleasant coastal resort towns. To the right are the long sandy beaches and spectacular headlands of the Myall Lakes National Park, which lies on the coastal side of the Pacific Highway about 16km (10 miles) E and extends about 45km (28 miles) along the coast, occupying the region between the sea and Myall Lake. For those not in a hurry, the park offers camping sites, excellent fishing and swimming.

The sparkling Pacific Ocean surf gives rise to year-round vacation playgrounds: **Port Macquarie** leads to **Nambucca Heads**, then **Coffs Harbour**, a favorite overnight stopping place surrounded by rich banana plantations.The warm, subtropical climate encourages the cultivation of tropical fruits and sugar cane. Together with the dramatic mountain peaks and unexpected valleys of the nearby **Great Dividing Range**, it makes for some delightful driving.

North of Coffs Harbour, there are the varying attractions of towns such as **Grafton**, **Byron Bay** and **Tweed Heads** to sample before crossing the NSW border and reaching the Queensland **Gold Coast**, one of Australia's busiest, most exuberant playgrounds. The 32km (20-mile) strip of white sandy beach is lined with resort hotels, luxury apartments, restaurants, clubs and shopping malls. **Surfers Paradise** is the major resort.

Just 65km (40 miles) N is Queensland's capital, **Brisbane**. Bustling and prosperous, it has lately begun to show increasing respect for its fine old colonial buildings. It is well served with modern hotels and fine restaurants (where you may be able to taste that most delicious fish, the barramundi).

Distance dictates everything in Australia. Brisbane is 1,031km (644 miles) N of Sydney as the cockatoo flies; **Cairns**, a popular gateway to

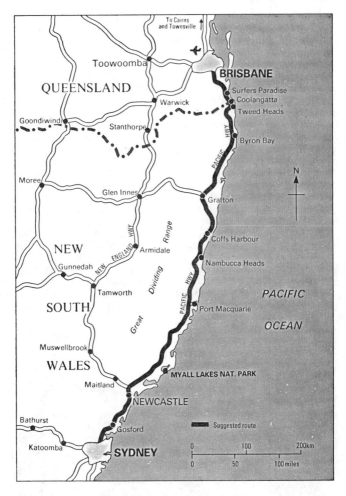

the **Great Barrier Reef** and an ideal touring base for the islands, the rainforest, and picturesque **Port Douglas**, is 1,710km (1,069 miles) farther N of Brisbane. Leave the car in Brisbane and fly the rest of the way

ROUTE 6: PERTH — MARGARET RIVER — ALBANY — ESPERANCE — KALGOORLIE — PERTH
Maps 14 and 15 on pages 282-3. Allow 2 weeks. Recommended stops: Mandurah, Busselton, Margaret River, Manjimup, Albany, Jerramungup, Esperance, Norseman, Kalgoorlie, Southern Cross or Northam.

Western Australia contains only 1.4 million people and yet is three times the size of Texas and bigger than any country in Europe. There may be few people between the barren plains of the Nullarbor desert and the Indian Ocean, but there is certainly a good deal to see. This tour takes in the most populous and fertile region of the state, the sw, offering comfortable drives through the wild-flower areas (August-October), leading on to the chance to strike gold around Kalgoorlie.

Drive to Fremantle and then s to **Mandurah**, a resort town where the pelicans nest and dolphins frolic. From the rural-industrial town of Bunbury, 175km (109 miles) s of Perth, it is a short distance to the beach resort town of **Busselton** on Geographe Bay.

Nearby, and well worth exploring, is the **Margaret River** wine-growing area, where some of the country's most surprisingly subtle prize-winning red and white table wines have been produced in recent years. Plan it well and you may be able to get to Leeuwin for the annual visit to a winery by an orchestra. The organizers of this Glyndebourne of the grape, held in January or February, can cater to an audience of 12,000, but the chance to hear visitors such as the Royal Philharmonic Orchestra, the Berlin Statskapelle or the Royal Danish Orchestra playing among the gumtrees and vines is highly sought after; so reserve in advance.

Return to the Bussell Highway and, traveling s from Margaret River, detour inland along the Brockman Highway to the small town of **Nannup**, nestled in tall pine forests beside the **Blackwood Valley**. Follow the scenic route eastward to **Bridgetown**, which lays claim to having Australia's only public jigsaw puzzle gallery. Here also you can see

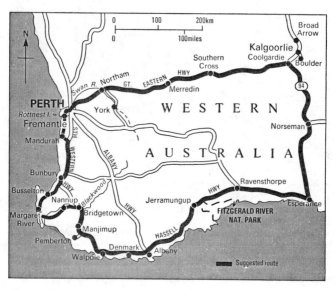

Blechyden House, the old home of a pioneer farmer, or arrange a tour of local orchards where apples, nectarines, plums and peaches are grown.

From Bridgetown travel s along the South Western Highway to **Manjimup**, sampling the unique scenery of the karri forests. Here, see the Four Aces: four huge karri trees, more than 300 years old, growing in a line. Nearby, delicate, pastel-colored wild flowers grow between giant trees that soar up to 80m (260 feet) high. Karri trees, one of the world's finest hardwoods, provide a deep reddish-brown, strong timber. They blossom every 3 years, and their nectar makes a delicately flavored honey, much sought after.

If time is with you, take the 32km (20-mile) detour from the road s of Manjimup westward to **Pemberton**. Here (if you're game!) you can climb the highest tree lookout in the world: the Gloucester Tree, 61m (195 feet) above the ground.

Then return to the South Western Highway, traveling SE to the small settlement of **Walpole**, where there are outstanding panoramic views, and then eastward to **Denmark**, where the calm waters of the inlets and the protected beaches provide delights for both the fisherman and swimmer. Denmark offers another surprise, for at Winniston Park is held one of the country's most outstanding collections of antiques.

Fifty-three kilometers (33 miles) farther E is the town of **Albany**, site of the first White settlement in Western Australia (in 1826). This former whaling port is located around an eye-catching, although now relatively underused, harbor, surrounded by lush green hills that reminded the early settlers of the English countryside. The traveler is well cared for in the historic town, where accommodations are clean, modern and economical. Allow ample time to explore Albany Whaleworld museum; see how the pioneers lived at Strawberry Hill Farm, the old Gaol, the Old Post Office and the Residency.

After this, the alternatives are to return to Perth by the direct route NW along the Albany Highway — 408km (255 miles) of well-made road that most Australians would consider a comfortable day's drive — or, for hardier, more adventurous travelers, a journey that takes you farther E.

For the latter, the Hassell Highway travels NE through rugged scenery into the **Hassell National Park** and on to **Jerramungup**. It is a solid, relatively unspectacular drive 110km (69 miles) onward to **Ravensthorpe**, although invitingly to the s is the **Fitzgerald River National Park**, an oasis for fishermen, swimmers and golfers.

Eventually, you arrive in the small coastal resort of **Esperance**, a rural town, with spectacular coastal scenery, that has proved popular with miners, artists and bushwalkers alike. The land surrounding Esperance is a rich farming area, producing beef, lamb, wool, wheat, oats and barley. The town itself was named by French explorer D'Entrecastaux in 1792 after his ship *L'Esperance*.

Travel N up the Esperance Highway and then Route 94 and you move into the red dust and rich mining sites around **Norseman** and, eventually, **Kalgoorlie** — hard driving and hard country, with the occasional 'roo or emu. The attractions of this rugged land reveal themselves to the miners, geologists and bushwalkers who know it best, and may not be immediately clear to the drive-through tourist.

Fascinating Kalgoorlie, which today has the feel of the old American frontier about it, in the 1900s dazzled the world with its gold. Most of the original buildings are retained and the main street is still known as the Golden Mile. And ghost towns abound nearby.

On the way out N to **Broad Arrow**, for example, once a bustling community, the gambling hall where the miners still play "two up" (a game in which participants bet on "heads" and "tails" for two thrown pennies) is one of the few signs of life.

More astonishing still is the ghost town of **Coolgardie**, to the sw, surrounded by the old mullock heaps (residues of gold mining, some still containing recoverable gold) of long-gone miners. Photographs in a museum there show the dramatic consequences when the gold runs out; even a town of 20,000 can disappear "overnight."

From Coolgardie, it's another long 188km (118-mile) and solid drive to the w, along the Great Eastern Highway to the gold town of **Southern Cross**. Gold was first discovered here in 1888, and buildings left in the town help it retain a turn-of-the-century atmosphere. A curiosity: all the streets in Southern Cross bear the names of either stars, planets or constellations.

West lies the heart of the wheat belt, the center of which is the town of **Merredin**, 259km (162 miles) E of Perth. This old railway town is especially beautiful in November when hundreds of jacaranda trees burst into bloom. Travel onward to reach the lush green paddocks of the **Avon Valley**. From **Northam**, the only inland town in the state with a continuously flowing river through its center, there is a final, pleasant 100km (63 miles) before the circuit ends back in Perth.

ROUTE 7: PERTH — GERALDTON — CARNARVON — EXMOUTH — PORT HEDLAND

Maps **14** and **15** on pages 282-3. Allow 2 weeks. Recommended stops: Geraldton, Kalbarri, Denham, Carnarvon, Exmouth, Onslow, Port Hedland.

Another possibility for the more adventurous visitor based in Perth is the journey N across the Tropic of Capricorn to the rugged and immensely rich mining territory of Western Australia's **Pilbara** region. It is essential to seek local advice before embarking on this tour, since the journey takes you through remote regions prone to flash-flooding or other exceptional conditions. The Royal Automobile Club of Western Australia (RACWA) will recommend that you carry certain **spare parts** for your car and **extra drinking water**, and will provide you with information on the roads and climate.

Taking the route N through the lush wine-growing **Swan Valley**, the first major point of interest is the city of **Geraldton**, 424km (265 miles) up the Brand Highway from Perth. The rich, green countryside here reminds many British immigrants of a sun-drenched Mediterranean version of Wales.

Geraldton, an attractive town that offers first-class motel and hotel accommodations, is a crayfish port as well as a popular resort among

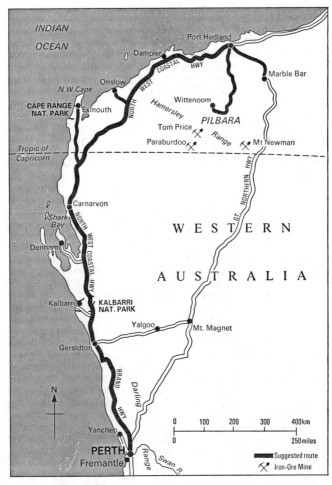

coastal sports fishermen. More than 400 boats fish for rock lobsters off the coast here, providing local fishermen with a major export to the US. To the N, detouring from the North West Coastal Highway, is the **Kalbarri National Park**, famous for its spring wild flowers. At Kalbarri, 167km (104 miles) from Geraldton, there is a campsite beside the ocean and, in the right spot, the fisherman can easily draw in a feast of delicious tailor fish and whiting.

The landscape N of Geraldton is harsh, often covered to the horizon in low purplish spinifex scrub. Snakes, foxes, hawks and eagles provide occasional distraction for the traveler. But from this seeming wilderness, you must detour for the spectacular. One such detour from the highway N leads to **Monkey Mia**, near Denham on Shark Bay; here "tame" dolphins come in to the beach to be fed by hand.

Back on the highway, continue N. *En route,* be a little careful if you see Old Man Emu up ahead investigating the road; he is not particularly bright. A blast on the horn may simply send him sprinting along the highway... in the same direction that you are traveling!

Surrounded by banana plantations, the sultry subtropical town of **Carnarvon**, 483km (302 miles) from Geraldton, offers motel accommodations and the opportunity to sample the sweet delights of the barramundi fish and ice-cold beer.

Move on N to experience unique wilderness landscapes; when alone on the highway here it's worth pulling over for a moment simply to experience "absolute silence," a memorable vacuum interrupted only by your heart beating or a cranky goanna sounding in the spinifex scrub.

Another detour, due N off the main highway, leads through the rust-red dust to Exmouth and the US naval communications base at North West Cape. Here, in the **Cape Range National Park**, are peaks and gorges, a small-scale Grand Canyon that literally takes the breath away.

Crossing the Tropic of Capricorn, the road leads more and more into sparsely populated territory. This is land run by farmers and miners where huge iron-ore deposits are mined at Tom Price, Paraburdoo and Mt. Newman. The **Pilbara**, as this part of the country is known, is rich with iron ore and mineral deposits. It is pioneer country and remains a land only for the more adventurous. Journeys to the major centers often require long drives that might be unthinkable in Europe.

From the North West Coastal Highway another 82km (51-mile) detour w will take you to **Onslow**. It is a journey worth making. Onslow is a pleasant, tree-shaded coastal town that offers excellent fishing and safe swimming. The town was the farthest point s in Western Australia to be bombed by the Japanese in World War II. It was also the mainland base for Britain's nuclear tests in the Monte Bello islands.

From Onslow, rejoin the main highway to reach the sunny destination of **Port Hedland**, where bulk carriers line up to take Australia's mineral riches to Japan, South Korea and the world. E from Hedland, the visitor is within reach of the small town of **Marble Bar**, which has the reputation for being the hottest place in Australia and one of the hottest in the world. Another day excursion due s from Hedland might be **Wittenoom**, noted for its colorful gorges.

It is a rugged journey, but visitors who make it to Port Hedland go away knowing truly that they have been to Australia's wild west, a land still untapped of all its riches.

GETTING INTO THE OUTBACK
And what, you may ask, about **Alice Springs**, **Darwin**, the **Kimberleys** and some of the more remote parts of the great subcontinent? How about a trip out to **Ayers Rock** or a drive through the territory made familiar by *Crocodile Dundee?*

Given time, visitors can indeed travel to many exotic and untouched locations in Australia. Given that time, however, they are more likely to follow the Australian pattern of using aircraft to get to the main centers (such as Alice, Darwin or Cairns) and then travel on by 4-wheel-drive, preferably escorted, into the bush.

For the adventurous there are **safari tours** in which a visitor can "rough it" in style. These involve 4-wheel-drive vehicles, camping out, with catering provided, and may venture off from civilization for a couple of weeks into the spectacular landscapes of the Kakadu National Park, Katherine Gorge and Ayers Rock.

Another way of coming to terms with the vastness of Australia is to take an **air safari** with a group of friends. A light aircraft, with a pilot-guide, can move you from city to Outback cattle station or tropical island all within a matter of hours. With a group reservation, it need not be beyond the average tourist's pocket.

For those who prefer their vacation to be only slightly more civilized than that portrayed in the movie *Deliverance,* there are now dozens of reputable companies that offer trips into the unknown. Ranging from 5-star service to help-yourself, these Outback safaris offer the whole gamut from riding white-water rafts to flirting with crocodiles, from bounding after wild pigs and buffalo in the Northern Territory to delighting in exotic orchids and rare birdlife, or from abseiling down gorges to inspecting rarely-seen Aboriginal art painted on rocks thousands of years ago. Those who do not mind roughing it might even go "walkabout" in the desert country to help find the relics of expeditions by the brave or merely foolhardy in the last century.

But be warned — such traveling is only for the most hardy.

The Australian Capital Territory

The ACT is an Australian oddity: a fragment chipped off the block of New South Wales; a lovely, pastoral plain on which was imposed a purpose-built capital charged with the task of establishing national unity. From here, in splendid isolation, the federal administration runs a country the size of the US, but with one-twentieth the population.

To all intents and purposes, the ACT, with a total population of only 278,000, is Canberra. And Canberra itself is a potent symbol of regionalism in Australia, being the compromise solution to the intense rivalry between Sydney and Melbourne over which city would be the federal capital. In the end, the design owed nothing to either, being the work of Walter Burley Griffin, an American landscape architect who in 1912 won a city planning competition.

His concept has been meticulously executed. Canberra is a gracious and clean city. The tempo of life is unhurried, there are no slums, and the crime rate is low. It is spacious too, with a happy harmony between ambitious architecture and Burley Griffin's leafy, garden layout.

Despite its at times sterile atmosphere, Canberra has much to commend it, particularly for the student of modern architecture. The new Parliament House (illustrated on page 88) is a *tour de force* comparable with Sydney's Opera House. The High Court of Australia'and the Australian National Gallery, both situated beside Lake Burley Griffin, are fine examples of 20th century civic buildings.

Still, oddities persist. This is Australia's capital, but it does not have an international airport. Few of the politicians and civil servants who live here for most of the year regard it as home. And despite its immaculate civic countenance and the pleasures of the climate (clean, crisp air at 2,000 feet), it is rare that Canberra enchants the visitor. A young city, after 60 years it has yet to find an identity.

For all that, it is not without interest and stimulus. Visit, for example, the Australian War Memorial. Looking around these somber exhibits, the question raises itself naggingly: how was it that Australian (and New Zealand) soldiers paid the heaviest price of all combatant nations in a terrible war fought on the other side of the world, while remaining to the end a volunteer army?

Only time will tell if Walter Burley Griffin's grand design is to be judged worthy of being a capital city or just another administrative enclave. Increasingly, however, Australians are seeing Canberra as a truly *Australian* city, born since Federation and, as an enormous growth in tourism testifies, a real statement of national identity and pride.

82

Canberra

ORIENTATION

The Sydney/Melbourne feud over federal pre-eminence was resolved slightly in favor of the former. The ACT is enclosed entirely within New South Wales, and is 304km (190 miles) by road from Sydney, compared with 655km (409 miles) to Melbourne. Its total area is 6,200sq.km (2,400sq. miles).

Burley Griffin planned a city divided by a lake, with the commercial and residential areas to the N of it, and the political/diplomatic centers to the s. The concept remains intact, although the population has boomed from the 25,000 he envisaged to more than ten times that number, and satellites have sprung up on all sides.

Wherever one turns in Canberra, the eye is presented with a vista. But Canberra is above all a city of political edifices, which can in some ways be seen as Australia's answer to Brasilia. Embassies, reflecting the nature of their homelands, have made a diplomatic Disneyland out of one corner of the city, while massive concrete hives thrust through the city's greenery elsewhere, housing the public-service worker bees of one department or another.

PRACTICAL INFORMATION

Maps 1 & 2 (see pages 84-85)

☎**STD (area) code**   06

Airport   ☎243 5911 (domestic services only); Ansett ☎245 6511; Australian ☎268 3333

Rail station   Wentworth Ave., Kingston ☎295 1555 (country services only)

Car rental   Avis ☎249 6088; Budget ☎248 9788; Hertz ☎249 6211

Australian Capital Territory Tourism Commission   Northbourne Ave., Dickson, ACT, 2602 ☎249 7577

American Express Travel Service   Centre Point, P.O. Box 153, City Walk, Petrie Plaza, Canberra City, ACT, 2601 ☎247 2333

National Roads and Motorists Association (NRMA)   92 Northbourne Ave., Canberra City, ACT, 2601 ☎243 8800

SEEING THE CITY

For a comparatively small city in terms of population, Canberra covers a great deal of territory, and getting around it is not easy. Public transportation is not good, and, although taxis can be hailed in the city center, it is very advisable to reserve by telephone *(☎46 0444)* from the political/diplomatic sector, across Lake Burley Griffin. Moreover, to see the sights, taxi fares could cost you as much as renting a car. Signposting is poor, and a street directory is essential. The main **tourist information center** is on Northbourne Ave., Dickson, between Wakefield Ave. and Antill St. *(☎249 7577)*.

Two commercial operators run guided tours that include BLACK MOUNTAIN, the WAR MEMORIAL and the old and new PARLIAMENT HOUSES: **Murrays** *(☎295 3611)* and **Monarch Tours** *(☎259 1686)*.

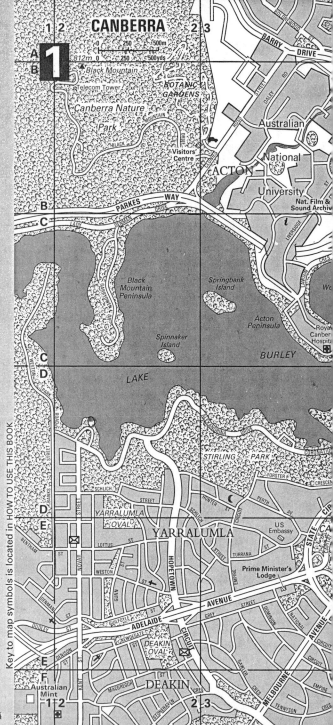

CANBERRA

0   250   500m
812m 0   250   500yds

Black Mountain
Telecom Tower

BOTANIC GARDENS

Canberra Nature Park

Australian

Visitors' Centre

National

ACTON

University

PARKES — WAY

Nat. Film & Sound Archive

Black Mountain Peninsula

Springbank Island

We

Acton Peninsula

Royal Canber Hospita

Spinnaker Island

BURLEY

LAKE

STIRLING PARK

CORONATIO

CRESCEN

SCHLICH

STREET

HUNTER

PERTH

AV

YARRALUMLA OVAL

YARRALUMLA

US Embassy

STATE

CA

LOFTUS

TURRANA

WESTON

HOPETOWN

Prime Minister's Lodge

AVENUE

STREET

GREY

EDMONDON

GUILFOYLE

ADELAIDE

CIRCUIT

NATIONAL

AVENUE

CIRCUIT

NEWDEGATE

DEAKIN OVAL

CIRCUIT

DUDLEY

DENISON

KENT

MACGREGOR

STONEHAVEN

DEAKIN

Australian Mint

MELBOURNE

EMPIRE

TENNYSON

Key to map symbols is located in HOW TO USE THIS BOOK

84

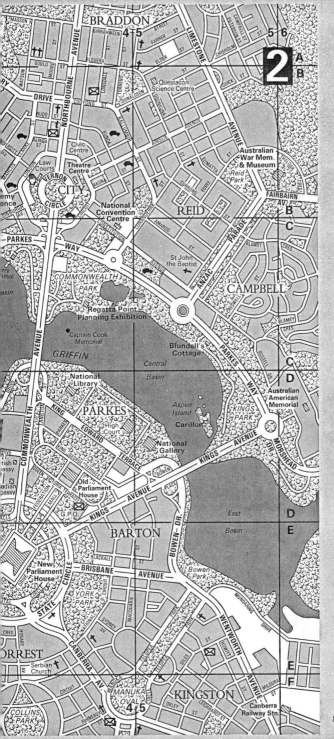

Sights and places of interest

AUSTRALIAN WAR MEMORIAL AND MUSEUM ★
Anzac Parade, Reid ☎*243 4238. Map 2B5-6* 🆔 ⅛ ✗ 💺 ➡ *Open
9am-4.45pm.*
This ugly but impressive and acutely poignant complex of buildings
includes an extensive war museum. It should be remembered that in
World War I, casualties from Australia and New Zealand were pro-
portionately higher per capita than from any of the combatant nations
over whose territory the war was actually fought. The memorial and
museum are a terrible reminder of that fact. Interestingly, more visitors
come here annually than to any other site in Australia except for
Sydney Opera House.

BLACK MOUNTAIN AND TELECOM TOWER ★
Off Clunies Ross St., West Canberra ☎*248 1911. Map 1B2* 🍴 💺 ➡ ◁€ *Open
9am-10pm.*
Visible from all over Canberra, the Telecom Tower offers the best view
of the city's layout on either side of Lake Burley Griffin. **Mt. Ainslie** in
the NE also offers a grand panorama.
   Black Mountain lies about 4km ($2\frac{1}{2}$ miles) W of the city center at an
altitude of 812m (2,664 feet). The tower rises another 195m (640 feet)
above the summit. Its primary function is as a transmitting station, but
there is ample provision for the public, with three viewing platforms and
a revolving restaurant.

BLUNDELL'S COTTAGE
Wendouree Drive. Map 2C5 ➡ *Open 10-4pm.*
The visitor could be forgiven for wondering why this undistinguished
little dwelling figures in Canberra tours. The reason is that the capital is
so patently of this century that any historical antecedents are, *ipso
facto,* remarkable. The cottage was built in 1858 by Robert Campbell, a
wealthy Scottish merchant, and the first settler in what is now the ACT,
for his plowman. Campbell's own fine residence, DUNTROON, is 2km ($1\frac{1}{4}$
miles) away. The cottage is furnished with period pieces.
   Combine this with a visit to the CARILLON. Access can be confusing and
is via Constitution Ave., not Parkes Way.

BOTANIC GARDENS
Clunies Ross St., West Canberra ☎*267 1811. Map 1B2* 🆔 ⅛ 💺 ➡ *Open
9am-5pm* ✗ *Sun 10am, 2pm.*
Situated on the eastern slopes of BLACK MOUNTAIN, this is the national
collection of native flora. The 40ha (99-acre) site contains a rainforest
and around 600 species of the ubiquitous eucalypt tree. There are set
walks of up to 1.5km (1 mile), including an Aboriginal trail with plants
labeled to explain how they were used by Aborigines.

CARILLON ★
Wendouree Drive. Map 2D5 ➡ *45min recitals Sun 2.45pm; Wed 12.45pm.*

Built on Aspen Island in LAKE BURLEY GRIFFIN, the Carillon was a gift from Britain to mark Canberra's 1963 golden jubilee, although it was only opened by Queen Elizabeth II in 1970. In effect it is a gigantic musical instrument, with 53 bells (the smallest of which is about 7kg/15$\frac{1}{2}$lbs and the largest 6 tonnes/13,230lbs), which are sounded by a single player from a baton keyboard. Chimes like those of Westminster in London sound on the quarter-hour. The island is a picturesque spot, and it is worth a visit for the view even if you miss the Wednesday and Sunday recitals.

DUNTROON MILITARY COLLEGE
Jubilee Ave., Duntroon ☎*275 9111* 🔲 ⬛ *Guided tours of college 2pm. Access to Duntroon House only on infrequent open days.*
Canberra's oldest property, built by a Scots merchant named Robert Campbell, is now incorporated in the Royal Military College The residence was built in 1833 and added to in 1862. It was acquired by the government when Canberra was selected as the site for the federal capital, and has been a military college since 1911.

LAKE BURLEY GRIFFIN
Maps 1 & 2.
The central waterway that separates Canberra City from the political and diplomatic enclave is named after the American landscape architect who designed the new capital. The lake, with 35km (22 miles) of shoreline, has become a focus for picnicking and boating. Other features are the CARILLON and the **Captain Cook Memorial**, which sends a jet of water to a height of 130m (426 feet).

NATIONAL GALLERY ★
King Edward Terrace, Canberra South ☎*271 2502. Map 2D5* 🔲 ⬛ ⬛ 🔪 💻 ⬛
Open 10am-5pm.
The youngest of Australia's major art collections, this was only started in the 1960s. Nevertheless, generous government grants have enabled the acquisition of significant and valuable works. A particular feature is the collection of paintings by postwar Australian artists, including a rightly renowned series by Sidney Nolan known as the *Ned Kelly* paintings.

NEW PARLIAMENT HOUSE ★
Capital Hill, Canberra South ☎*277 7111 or 277 5402. Map 2E4* 🔲 ⬛ ⬉ ⬛
🔪 *depart every 20mins between 9am and 4pm daily.*
Ambitious in concept, dramatic in scale and unprecedented in cost for an Australian public building, the New Parliament House is an affirmation of national pride and was opened during the bicentennial in 1988. One of only three surviving copies of the final and definitive version of the **Magna Carta** is on display.

The only other architectural endeavor with which it bears comparison is the Sydney Opera House. The Parliament House too has had its critics, as much for the huge budget blow-out (the final cost exceeded

A$1,000m) as for its architectural style. Built into the hillside, it has been compared to a bunker. Wags point out that because the building has been built into the surrounding hillside, and grass grows over what would otherwise be the roof, this is one of the few places in the world where you can walk over politicians.

The New Parliament House, with its marble-clad columns, marble staircases and magnificent halls and corridors, is built to last 200 years and beyond. The dimensions are remarkable, with an area of 40ha (99 acres), granite walls 460m (1,509 feet) long, and a flagpole 81m (266 feet) high.

It houses its own broadcasting studios, a covered car park for 2,000 vehicles, and some of the country's finest works of art. In the cruel economic climate of the early 1990s, the New Parliament House has been seen as both a financial folly and an optimistic architectural salute to Australia's future.

PARLIAMENT HOUSE ★
King George Terrace, Canberra South ☎ *272 1211. Map 2D4* ◀€ *Not open to the public.*
Unfortunately, after long service, no new role has been found for Canberra's first Parliament House, which, even when it was opened in 1927, was intended only as a provisional home for the federal legislature. Its planned life of 50 years exceeded 60, and required numerous extensions. Perhaps surprisingly under the circumstances, it is a quite handsome, low-slung building, with a striking view across LAKE BURLEY GRIFFIN up **Anzac Parade** to the AUSTRALIAN WAR MEMORIAL. It has been proposed to turn the building into a parliamentary museum, but at the time of writing its future was unclear.

ST JOHN THE BAPTIST CHURCH
Anzac Park, Reid. Map 2C5 ◛ *Open 9am-5pm.*
A charming Anglican church, which is all the more pleasant for its antiquity in surroundings of relentless modernity. Building on the church started in 1841, and the grounds, once part of the estate of DUNTROON, contain some interesting old graves. Although the interior is tiny, Queen Elizabeth II and Prince Philip attended divine service here in 1954.

Where to stay

Until quite recently, despite its status as the federal capital of Australia, Canberra offered a limited choice and distinctly moderate quality of accommodations. Things have improved, however, with the opening of the **Hyatt** in 1987 to supplement the only other 5-star hotel, **The Lakeside**.

The establishments listed below are in the northern/city-center sector, rather than the inconvenient southern/diplomatic quarter. Many get fully booked during the week, but on weekends the city empties and some hotels offer special rates.

CANBERRA CITY MOTOR INN

Corner of Northbourne Ave. and Cooyong St., Canberra City, ACT, 2601 ☎ *249 6911* ⊤⋈*62050* ⊠*247 8133. Map 2B4* ⊞ *72 rms* ⇌ ⊟ AE ⊕ ⊚ VISA ⇌ ⊡ ⍉
Location: Central, the city center being a short walk down Northbourne Ave. Part of an established chain that usually maintains a good standard of food and accommodations, this hotel can also be recommended for the convenience of its location.

CANBERRA INTERNATIONAL HOTEL

242 Northbourne Ave., Dickson, ACT, 2602 ☎ *247 6966* ⊠ *248 7823* ⊤⋈*62154* ⊞ *151 rms* ⇌ ⊟ AE ⊕ ⊚ VISA ⍓ ⇌ ⍉ ⚓ ⛾
Location: On Northbourne Ave., the main road from the N, but 2km ($1\frac{1}{2}$ miles) from the city. An inn with a spacious, airy feel to it because of the garden atrium, a pleasant spot to eat and drink. Rooms are comfortable but quite pricey.

THE HYATT HOTEL CANBERRA

Commonwealth Ave., Yarralumla, ACT, 2600 ☎ *270 1234* ⊠ *281 5998. Map 2D4* ⊞ *249 rooms* ⇌ AE ⊕ ⊚ VISA ⍓ ⛾ ⇌ ⊡
Location: On prestigious Commonwealth Ave. and a mere stroll from Parliament House, the Hyatt has good views of Lake Burley Griffin. Originally a hostel for politicians in the 1920s, when Canberra was but a country town, and later converted to a hotel, the building in which the Hyatt stands has recently been remodeled at great cost to give it 5-star status, while retaining its

old world atmosphere. A protected outdoor area overlooks the 12 hectares of gardens and parklands, where tea can be taken in a 1920s atmosphere. The much-acclaimed **Oak Room** restaurant (see DINING OUT) won the Australian Tourism Award for Fine Dining in 1990. Comfortable, in the Hyatt manner, but correspondingly expensive.

LAKESIDE HOTEL

London Circuit, Canberra City, ACT, 2601 ☎ *247 6244* ⊤⋈*6237 4* ⊠*257 3071. Map 2B4* ⊞ *216 rms* ⇌ ⊟ AE ⊕ ⊚ VISA ⍓ ⇌ ⊡ ⛾
Location: A few mins' walk from the commercial center, with views, once its exclusive preserve until the opening of the Hyatt, over Lake Burley Griffin. The Lakeside does brisk business, and getting a room on short notice during the week is usually difficult. It has benefited from the competition from Canberra's other 5-star hotel, the Hyatt, and can still lay claim to providing the capital's best-known top-class accommodations. Service is attentive.

OLIMS CANBERRA HOTEL ❂

Limestone Ave. and Ainslie Ave., Braddon, ACT, 2601 ☎ *248 5511* ⊤⋈*62988* ⊠*247 0864. Map 2B5* ⊞ *126 rms* ⇌ ⊟ AE ⊕ ⊚ VISA ⍓ ⊡ ⍉ ⛾
Location: To the NE of the center, but within walking distance for those who enjoy some exercise. One of Canberra's oldest hotels, formerly the Ainslie Rex, this hotel has since been refurbished when it was purchased by a small Australian chain. The central feature is a courtyard garden surrounded by ac-

commodation units, which include two-level suites and some self-contained rooms with their own cooking facilities.

COUNTRY COMFORT HOTEL
102 Northbourne Ave., Braddon, ACT,
2601 ☎*249 1411* ⓕ*249 6878*
☎*61516. Map 2A4* ▥ *78 rms* 🛏 ⥤ ⒶⒺ

▢ ▣ ▦ ▨ ▤ Ⓨ ◈ 🏊 ♨

Location: On Canberra's hotel strip, the
Northbourne Ave. main road, a brisk
10min walk from the center. The atmosphere is fairly formal, by Australian standards, in a hotel geared to the business visitor. A hostess will meet guests at the airport. Some may find the blue decor heavy.

Dining out

Fortunately, Canberra is better served for restaurants than it is for hotels. Indeed, there are some excellent eating spots, as might be expected in a major political and diplomatic center. The choice below has been made with convenience of location in mind.

EJ'S ♣
21 Kennedy St., Kingston ☎*247 4041.*
Map 2F5 ▥ ▭ 🛏 ⒶⒺ ▣ ▨ *Last orders*
10pm. Closed Sun.
Rather out of the way, but EJ's is a lunchtime institution with journalists and public servants. Dine in the courtyard or inside, from an inventive menu that changes daily.

FRINGE BENEFITS
54 Marcus Clarke St. ☎*247 4042. Map*
2B4 ▥ ▭ 🛏 ⒶⒺ ▣ ▣ ▨ *Last orders*
10pm. Closed Sun.
Canberra generally closes down quite early in the evening, and this latish-night brasserie is worth bearing in mind. If the food is not exceptional, the coffee is, and the environment is pleasant.

IMPERIAL COURT
40 Northbourne Ave. ☎*248 5547. Map*
2B4 ▥ ▭ 🍽 🛏 ⒶⒺ ▣ ▣ ▨ *Last*
orders 11.30pm.
A smart and comparatively pricey Chinese restaurant (although still reasonable by Canberra standards) but with some sumptuous food. Popular with the Orientals of the diplomatic

community, and with the local press corps.

THE LOBBY
King George Terrace ☎*273 1563. Map*
2D4 ▥ ▭ ⥤ 🛏 ⒶⒺ ▣ ▣ ▨ *Last*
orders 10pm. Closed Sun.
Situated within walking distance of the old PARLIAMENT HOUSE (see SIGHTS), and a favorite with its former denizens when it comes to fairly formal dining. The food is ambitious, and usually enjoyable. Prices are described by the establishment as "contemporary," i.e., on the higher side.

THE OAK ROOM
Commonwealth Ave., Yarralumla ☎*270*
1234. Map 2D4 ▥ ▭ ⥤ 🛏 ⒶⒺ ▣ ▣
▨
Situated in the HYATT HOTEL CANBERRA, the Oak Room won the Australian Tourism Award for Fine Dining in 1990. The expensive menu features several unusual offerings such as beef tournedos served with steamed oysters in small zucchini baskets on an oyster and cream sauce. It is becoming increasingly popular with politicians, because of its proximity to Parliament House.

Entertainment

Canberra regulars have been making disparaging remarks about the nightlife of the capital for decades. In truth, this is not a city that welcomes outsiders. There are a number of clubs, most of which admit only members of affiliated bodies. The diplomatic, political and media communities tend to be clubs in their own right. The visitor who steps out into the city center at night may wonder whether this is a ghost town. But not quite all is darkness, and what nocturnal sparkle there is can mainly be found at the following outposts.

CANBERRA THEATRE CENTRE
Civic Sq., London Circuit
☎*257 1077. Map 2B4* ⚥ ☰ AE ⓄⒹ VISA *Box office open Mon-Fri 10am-5.30pm and from 7pm.*

Eclecticism is the keynote at this, the capital's only arts center. Whether it is the Australian Opera or Elton John, Barry Humphries or Shakespeare, that Canberra is playing host to, the site is certain to be the Theatre Centre. Check the *Canberra Times* or call the box office.

JULIANA'S
Lakeside Hotel, London Circuit ☎*247 6244. Map 2B4* ⚥ Ⓞ ☰ 🕪 AE ⓄⒹ VISA *Open Tues-Thurs 5pm-midnight; Fri, Sat 5pm-3am.*

This discotheque at THE LAKESIDE HOTEL (see WHERE TO STAY) is favored by Canberra's young professionals. There are nice views too.

PRIVATE BIN
46-50 Northbourne Ave. ☎*247 3030. Map 2B4* ⚥ Ⓞ AE ⓄⒹ VISA *Open Mon-Fri noon until last customer leaves; Sat 6pm until last customer leaves; Sun 7pm until last customer leaves.*

A modern disco with light show, giant video screen and music at a level that is likely to damage the hearing. The Private Bin has a cocktail and champagne bar with a happy hour from 9-10 pm. Noisy and, like most other discos around the world, it is well liked by the younger set.

Where to shop

Canberra is not one of the world's great shopping centers, and any intended purchases of Australiana or souvenirs would be better made in a bigger city, such as Sydney or Melbourne. In any case, a visit to one of these is inevitable, because Canberra lacks an international airport.

However, one thing Canberra is noted for is secondhand bookstores. (On the road down from Sydney, incidentally, is one of Australia's largest and best, **Berkelouws**, about 4km/2½ miles before the town of **Berrima**.) The following establishments have rare and antiquarian books as well as collectable first editions and a general selection of good second hand volumes: **Gilbert's Books** *(Cinema Centre Arcade, Bunda St.* ☎*247 2032, map 2 B4, open Mon-Thurs 9.30am-5.30pm; Fri 9.30am-7pm; Sat 9.30am-1pm),* **Winchbooks** *(68 Wollongong St., Fyshwick* ☎*280 5304, open Mon-Sat 9am-5pm),* and **Miriam Brown Books** *(Unit 9, 57 Wollongong St., Fyshwick Plaza, Fyshwick* ☎*280 7666, open Mon-Sat 9am-5pm).*

Excursions

You can drive from the northern to the southern extremities of the ACT in an hour, so there is no question of lengthy excursions. But Canberra is well placed to visit parts of NSW, such as **Bateman's Bay** on the coast, about 150km (95 miles) by road (see page 136), or the **Snowy Mountains**, just over 260km (125 miles) away (see page 138).

The following easy drive is an introduction to the pleasant pastoral countryside around the capital, with wildlife and a little pioneer history thrown in.

SOUTH OF CANBERRA
125km (80-mile) round trip. Allow a day, although can be done in half.

Leave the city traveling westbound on the main highway, Parkes Way. At Clunies Ross St. there are signposts to BLACK MOUNTAIN and the BOTANIC GARDENS (see SIGHTS). The westbound highway becomes Lady Denman Drive. Turn off to the right at Tuggeranong Rd., then again at Cotter Rd., following signs for Cotter.

About 20km ($12\frac{1}{2}$ miles) from the city is **Cotter Reserve** recreation park, pleasant for river swimming and picnicking. From here the road turns s, passing through forestry range, and attractive sheep- and cattle-farming country. At **Tidbinbilla** the way is signposted to a large 5,000 ha (12,300-acre) nature reserve for domestic wildlife, offering picnicking and walks *(open 9am-6pm)*.

A few kilometers farther along the road, now signposted to **Tharwa**, is a turn-off for the **Gibraltar Falls**, 7km ($4\frac{1}{2}$ miles) away. The falls themselves are unspectacular, but this is a lovely and quiet spot to stop for a picnic lunch if you have not already done so.

The historical focus of this excursion is the 19thC homestead of **Lanyon**, which lies just N of Tharwa on the road back to Canberra. Construction of this splendid old farm home began in 1859, some years after Europeans started settling on the well-watered plains. Nestling among trees, stables and other outbuildings, Lanyon looks now as it must have then, a handsome colonial homestead in rich pastoral countryside. The job of refurbishing the interior with period furniture only began in 1980 and still continues. Also at Lanyon is the **Nolan Gallery**, which houses a permanent collection of paintings by Sir Sidney Nolan *(homestead and gallery both open Tues-Sun 10am-4pm)*.

Returning to Canberra, from the s on the Monaro Highway, it is possible to make a side trip to the **Canberra Wildlife Gardens**, a park with all the main Australian species of animals and a few others too. Turn off the highway at Mugga Lane, some 12km ($7\frac{1}{2}$ miles) s of Capital Hill; the wildlife gardens are about 5km (3 miles) up Mugga Lane on the right.

New South Wales

It can be hard today, when Sydney is accepted as one of the world's great cities, when her dazzling harbor and buoyant people seem to represent best the vigor and growth of the Pacific Rim region, to recall just how inauspicious were her origins. But for an understanding of this stylish, beautiful and brittle center of the Australian dream, it is important to remember those beginnings.

The name New South Wales was the idea of Captain James Cook, who jotted it down in his journal after landing on the eastern edge of the great Southern Land, whose coal-black soil, greenery and distant hills were somewhat reminiscent of South Wales, in 1770. Eight years later a pathetic band of exiles landed a few hundred yards away from where the Opera House now stands, to establish a concentration camp for the detritus of Georgian Britain. The first New South Welshmen were 756 convicts, 450 civilian and military personnel, and 58 women and children.

There was always another Australia, of course: a unique indigenous culture, and a land mass whose sheer vastness had about it something both elemental and mystical. But until well into the last century, to the hardy early settlers eking out an existence around Sydney Cove, this was, effectively, the new Australia.

So far as Sydneysiders are concerned, that remains the case today. From the squalid, frequently brutal, sometimes famine-stricken settlement, a city arose that, in many eyes, outshines for sheer beauty those other great harbor cities, Rio, San Francisco and Hong Kong. On a sunny afternoon, when a light breeze sends hundreds of sailing craft whipping across blue, glittering waters, and you can repair from the beach to an old sandstone pub by the harbor for refreshment, you have the essence of those qualities of life that make Australia, truly, the Lucky Country.

There are other reasons for the locals' not entirely unreasonable prejudice that this is the only part of Australia that matters. The population of NSW is a third of the national total, while more than a fifth of all Australians live in Sydney. The transformation in its ethnic makeup has been rapid and dramatic. Postwar immigration from Europe, and more recently from Asia, has made Sydney a more vivid and, perhaps surprisingly, a more tolerant place.

SYDNEY AND SYDNEYSIDERS

Sydney people are witty and shrewd, with a devastating eye for pretension, and a flair for vivid imagery in language. They are confident, exuberant, and quick to extend the hand of friendship. Theirs is not, however, a particularly compassionate society. In a city where success is revered and celebrities adored, there is little pity for the casualties of life in the fast lane, and woe betide the public figure who falls on his face.

Sydney is emphatically not the cultural desert that it was once supposed to be. It sustains the admirable national opera company, three orchestras, 22 major theaters, an extraordinary variety and spectrum of artists, an occasionally inspired movie industry, and enough rock and jazz musicians to keep feet tapping into 2001.

Primarily, however, Sydney's popularity has always come down to a simple outdoors formula. Here, after all, are the beaches of one's dreams, with all the trimmings — golden sands, bronzed bodies, endless sunsets and perfect waves: the Utopia of a hedonist or sun-worshiper.

THE INTERIOR
It is common enough for visitors to be so seduced by Sydney harbor and the beaches of NSW that the interior is forgotten. That is a mistake. For huge though the distances in travel are, a great deal is easily accessible in a day or two's outing from Sydney. Indeed, the main attractions of the New South Wales countryside lie within a 200-kilometer (125-mile) radius of the city.

Once the outer limits are cleared, you are in the bush, the infinite Australian hinterland of sandstone and eucalyptus trees. The lovely Hunter Valley, the main wine-producing region, is between 2 and 3 hours' drive away. Even closer are the Blue Mountains, which used to be a sort of summer retreat, and still attract more visitors annually than anywhere else outside the city. Within an easy hour's drive, to the north and the south, are two magnificent national parks, Ku-ring-gai Chase and the Royal National Park. Even an afternoon's rowing on the Hacking River at the Royal National Park is enough to get a taste of the grandeur of the bush.

The state divides into four natural regions. There is, self-evidently, the coast, with beaches running virtually its full 1,500-kilometer (950-mile) extent. Behind that lies a mountainous tableland known as the Great Dividing Range, which follows the line of the coast; until it was crossed in 1813 it formed an impenetrable barrier to exploration of the interior. Then come the pastoral western slopes of the range, where sheep farming is concentrated. Finally, there are the barren western plains, which cover more than two-thirds of the state, and are known simply as the Outback.

Within this diversity there are enormous contrasts, from the country's only wintersport resort, the Snowy Mountains in the south, to subtropical Byron Bay in the north, which make it possible to go skiing and surfing in the same week. Probably, though, you will want to time a visit according to the weather in Sydney.

WHEN TO GO
There is no categorically bad time to go to Sydney, where on average the sun shines 342 days a year. There is plenty of rain too, but it spreads itself around fairly obligingly. The winter months, from May to

August, are of course too cold for the beach, but the days are clear and this is a good time to be on an excursion to the Blue Mountains or the Southern Highlands, and spending the evening around a log fire in an old colonial hotel. The fall months of April and May can be the nicest time of all if you don't insist on swimming. Logically, however, most visitors will be coming to Australia in the summer, from late November to February, when the temperature in Sydney averages 21.7°C (71°F); the midsummer average is 25°C (77°F).

THE HARBOR

But what, besides its sunshine and beaches, and its people, is it that makes Sydney remarkable? In the end, Sydney is, quite simply, her harbor — all 240 kilometers (150 miles) of a shoreline of innumerable coves and bays, where tall-masted clippers and barques and great white P & O liners have been berthing for two centuries. The harbor is Sydney at her most elegant, and her most flagrantly materialistic. Yachting marinas such as Rushcutters Bay and Rose Bay are so full of sleek, gleaming craft that it seems everyone here must own a boat. Indeed, the ratio of Sydney boat owners to residents is reputed to be the highest in the world.

Property prices for houses along these eastern suburban shores fall into a similar category, the convenient million-dollar tag being a starting point. The older, leafy eastern suburbs of Paddington and Woollahra are less inclined to flaunt their wealth, and are generally more distinguished architecturally.

But Sydney's real structural wonders are found on the harbor, and are distinctively of this age. The 1950s design by a Danish architect for an opera house at the water's edge, dismissed variously as preposterous or just impractical, has become one of the landmark structures of the century, although the production process was so difficult that Joern Utzon has never returned to see the completed building.

An earlier landmark, the 1932 Harbour Bridge was, at 503 meters (1,650 feet), the world's largest single-span bridge for almost 50 years. The task of repainting it is such that workmen have no sooner finished at one end than they have to go back and start again at the other. As the bridge was unable to cope with the increasing flow of traffic, construction of the A$750 million Sydney Harbour Tunnel began in 1988. The tunnel, with its two 4-lane road links, extends for 2.3 km ($1\frac{1}{2}$ miles) between the Warringah Freeway, north of the Harbour, and the Cahill Expressway, south of the Harbour. Due to open in August 1992, it is expected to carry up to 60,000 vehicles a day.

THE FUTURE

NSW has a lot to be proud of. What its third century holds in store is anyone's guess, although certainly it will be different. The easy wealth that lay in the state's pastures and pits, and made this one of the richest of 20thC nations — "living off the sheep's back," they called it — is gone. Minerals are still being uncovered, the sheep still produce the finest wool in the world, and the seas of wheat still spread across the

95

land, but the realignment of world markets has changed the nation's economic priorities. European and American cartels with the benefit of high government subsidies, competing against Australian producers, have made life difficult for those on the land. NSW, like the rest of Australia, will have to discover a new formula for prosperity.

Sydneysiders have little doubt that they will. Optimism and tenacity are part of their credo, and if the mines and the farms are played out... well, something will come up. It always has before.

This, after all, is where the Lucky Country was born.

Sydney

ORIENTATION

Shorn of the descriptive prose that it inspires, Sydney is a riverside city of $3\frac{1}{2}$ million people, sheltered from the Pacific Ocean by two massive bluffs. It is the most remote of the world's great cities, being more than 24 hours' flying time from London, 19 hours from New York, 13 hours from Los Angeles and 10 hours from Tokyo.

Distances to other Australian state capitals are scarcely less tyrannical. Melbourne is 893km (558 miles) away by road, Brisbane 1,027km (642 miles) and Adelaide 1,431km (894 miles). The distances to Perth and Darwin are slightly absurd at 3,988km (2,492 miles) and 4,060km (2,537 miles) respectively.

Sydney is laid out along the northern and southern banks of the Parramatta River, the magnificent natural harbor of Port Jackson that gives the city its unique character. The harbor is Sydney's pulse, as well as its greatest vanity, and although expansion continues to the N, S and W, it remains the immutable center.

The southern sector has traditionally been the main residential area, stretching from the Pacific's edge at Bondi, through the leafy, affluent suburbs of Woollahra and Paddington to the western suburbs of Balmain, Leichardt, Strathfield and Parramatta.

To the N of the harbor, however, lie some of Sydney's prettiest residential areas, which have become even more sought-after since the development of the North Sydney business district.

PRACTICAL INFORMATION

Maps 3-6. See Sydney city maps (maps **3** and **4**) on pages 100-101 and Sydney environs (maps **5** and **6**) on pages 126-127

☎STD (area) code   02

Airport   Kingsford Smith (Mascot); Ansett ☎268 1111; Australian ☎693 3333; Eastwest ☎268 1166

Main rail station   Central, between Broadway and Elizabeth St., map **3**F2-3; contact NSW Rail Authority for inquiries about country and suburban services ☎219 8888/217 8819

Car rental   Avis ☎516 2877; Budget ☎339 8811; Hertz ☎(008) 33 3377

New South Wales Travel Centre 16 Spring St., Sydney, NSW, 2000 ☎231 4444, map **3**C3

American Express Travel Service American Express Tower, 388 George St., Sydney, NSW, 2000 ☎239 0666, map **3**D3

National Roads and Motorists Association (NRMA) 151 Clarence St., Sydney, NSW, 2000 ☎260 9222, map **3**C2

SEEING THE CITY

Sydney's public transportation nucleus is Circular Quay. From this point, where the First Fleet landed in 1788, ferries depart across the harbor for North Sydney, and buses and trains fan out across the city.

Taxi charges are reasonable, and given that many of Sydney's sights are within a 2km (1½-mile) radius, most visitors are inclined to take a cab rather than the bus.

An essential telephone number of general use, for information on anything to do with staying in Sydney, from accommodations to guided tours, and from shopping to how to register a complaint, is the **Tourist Information Service** *(☎669 5111, 8am-6pm).*

BUSES

Perhaps the best way to get acquainted with the city is through the **Sydney Explorer Bus** *(inquiries ☎231 4444).* This bus service, operated by the state transport authority, offers a one-day circuit of the 20 top tourist spots. The Explorer runs every 15 minutes or so from 9.30am-5pm daily, and for a modest fare you can travel the circuit at leisure, staying at any of the destinations for as long or as short a time as you like before reboarding. The 20km (12-mile) route starts from Circular Quay. Among its stops are the Opera House, the Royal Botanic Gardens, Hyde Park Barracks, Kings Cross, the Australian Museum, Elizabeth Bay House, Chinatown and The Rocks. *(For details and information about other city bus services ☎954 4422.)*

HARBOR CRUISES

The harbor is Sydney's greatest sight of all, and a trip out on the water is as good as obligatory. Transport authority ferries leave Circular Quay regularly, crossing the harbor to Manly and Taronga Park Zoo. The authority also offers full harbor cruises, with commentary, lasting more than 2 hours. *(Departure 1.30pm from Jetty #5 ☎247 4738.)*

Captain Cook Cruises, a private operator, offers a more expensive but also more pampered service, with refreshments *(departures 10am, 2pm).* This operator has also taken a leaf from the transport authority's book, and offers a **Harbor Explorer**, a cheaper five-stop ticket that you can use at your own pace: stops are the Opera House, The Rocks, Watsons Bay, Taronga Park Zoo and Pier One. *(For all Captain Cook departures from Jetty #6 ☎251 5007.)*

FROM THE AIR

A more hair-raising way of seeing Sydney is from the air. The **Red Baron** *(☎709 5943)* is a Sydney pilot who has painted his Tiger Moth scarlet in the manner of the World War I flying ace. You can choose between a 40-minute birds-eye view of the Harbour Bridge and a 1-hour flight.

ON FOOT
Ultimately, walking is the best way of all to see some parts of Sydney, and again the harborside is a convenient launching pad. For three suggested routes in the central city area, look at the CIRCULAR QUAY and THE ROCKS entries in SIGHTS.

CAR RENTAL
For excursions outside the city, you really need a car. In addition to the usual rental companies — such as **Avis**, **Budget** or **Hertz** *(see details on page 96)* — there are a number of organizations renting no-longer-immaculate but adequate vehicles at reduced rates. One such is **Rent-A-Bomb** *(☎ 281 3003)*.

Sights and places of interest

ART GALLERY OF NEW SOUTH WALES ◁€
Art Gallery Rd., The Domain ☎ 225 1700. Map 4D4 ▣ ⊀ ⬤ Open Mon-Sat 10am-5pm; Sun noon-5pm. Explorer Bus.
Sydney takes art seriously but not earnestly, as this excellent gallery shows. The original building, opened in 1885, is an architectural oddity, but has been imaginatively extended and offers a superb harbor view.

The fine collection of Australian art on show here includes early colonial paintings, significant works by the so-called Heidelberg School, including Tom Roberts and Arthur Streeton, and a few genuine master-pieces by Sir William Dobell — Australia's greatest portraitist — and Sir Russell Drysdale. There is also a section of Aboriginal and New Guinea art. Exhibitions of new Australian works change regularly.

AUSTRALIAN MUSEUM
William St./College St. ☎ 339 8111. Map 3D3 ▣ ⪜ ⬤ ✦ Open 10am-5pm. Explorer Bus.
This museum examines the unique anthropology and natural history of the Australian continent, with lucid exhibits on the tragic history of the Aborigines, and on marsupial fauna; the birdlife display is another strong feature. Its focus extends to the Pacific, and the Melanesian cultures in particular, with a re-created New Guinea village (Australia had responsibility for Papua New Guinea until independence in 1975). Although the museum is of a high standard, and has had a recent facelift, given such a heritage, it should be even better.

BEACHES
Sydney's beaches are as good as you will find in any city, and are the very embodiment of the Australian concept of hedonism. Harbor

beaches are sheltered from currents and surf, and consequently are favored by families and inexpert swimmers, although lifeguards always patrol the main beaches. City beaches are always crowded on weekends, and parking can be a problem. Don't concern yourself unduly about sharks on the popular beaches, as Sydney's last fatal attack was more than 20 years ago. It is wise, however, to arm yourself with insect repellant for the ubiquitous and relentless Antipodean fly!

It is even wiser to guard against the fierce Australian sun. Many Australians today, conscious of their country's proximity to the hole in the ozone layer and their unenviable record for having the world's highest incidence of skin cancer, protect themselves with sunblock lotions that help screen out the harmful ultra-violet rays. The bronzed-Aussie look hasn't completely disappeared, but only the foolish fail to cover up when the sun is at its highest. Topless sunbathing goes unremarked at most beaches.

HARBOR BEACHES

Camp Cove   This short, pretty stretch of beach near Watsons Bay can reasonably claim to be among Sydney's most picturesque and popular swimming spots. It is also a historically important location, as Captain Arthur Phillip and the First Fleet landed here to establish the penal colony of New South Wales in 1788.

Nielsen Park   This safe, pleasant beach at Vaucluse is set in a nature reserve. Walks among rock pools and a large, shady park make it popular for picnics. Particularly recommended for families.

Balmoral Beach   A long, sandy beach set in an attractive part of Sydney, near Mosman. It has grassy verges, and, at the western end, known as **Edwards Beach**, there is a shallow, rock swimming pool. (Ferry from Circular Quay to Taronga Park Zoo, then bus.)

Reef Beach   This officially designated nudist beach on the N side of Sydney Harbor National Park, near Manly, has been made inaccessible enough to discourage the voyeur, or even the merely curious. (Ferry from Circular Quay to Manly, then bus, then a hike.)

Manly   This popular northern suburb is a pleasant ferry ride away from CIRCULAR QUAY, and is well worth the effort involved in visiting it. Next to the harbor beach (whose calm waters are ideal for toddlers) is the **Manly Oceanarium** (see MANLY), which has performing seals and a shark-viewing aquarium (☎ 949 2644). Manly also has an ocean beach, just a stroll across the peninsula.

OCEAN BEACHES

Surfing is as Australian as iced beer and kangaroos, and does not necessarily require enormous expertise in all its forms. Riding a wave on your body can be as exhilarating as doing it on a surfboard, but be warned that the currents off the ocean beaches can be treacherous. You should only swim within the flagged areas, which are kept under observation by lifeguard crews, but in difficulty, wave an arm to attract attention.

Bondi   Australia's most famous beach (pronounced Bon-dye) is by no means the best. This rather ugly suburb in Sydney's E boomed after

Key to map symbols is located in HOW TO USE THIS BOOK

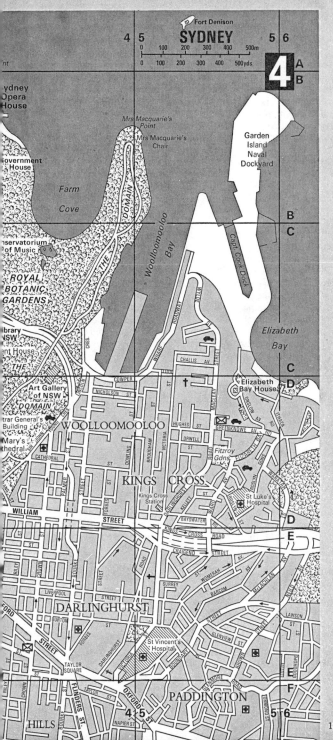

SYDNEY

Fort Denison

0 100 200 300 400 500m
0 100 200 300 400 500yds

4

Sydney
Opera
House

Government
House

Mrs Macquarie's Point
Mrs Macquarie's Chair

Garden
Island
Naval
Dockyard

Farm
Cove

Conservatorium
of Music

ROYAL
BOTANIC
GARDENS

Woolloomooloo Bay

Capt. Cook Dock

Elizabeth
Bay

Library
NSW
Parliament House
THE

Art Gallery
of NSW

THE
DOMAIN

Registrar General's
Building

St Mary's
Cathedral

WOOLLOOMOOLOO

COWPER ST
NICHOLSON ST

CHALLIS AV

Elizabeth
Bay House

ONSLOW AV

ITHACA RD

GREENKNOWE AV

HUGHES ST
ORWELL ST

Fitzroy
Gdns

ELIZABETH BAY RD

ROSLYN GDNS

KINGS CROSS

Kings Cross
Station

St Luke's
Hospital

WILLIAM STREET

BAYSWATER RD

KINGS CROSS ROAD

E

CRAIGEND STREET

WOMERAH AV

BARCOM AV

McLACHLAN AV

LIVERPOOL STREET

SURREY ST

DARLINGHURST

BURTON ST

GLENVIEW ST

LAWSON ST

St Vincent's
Hospital

TAYLOR SQUARE

OXFORD ST

PADDINGTON

HILLS

NAPIER ST

101

World War II, and on summer weekends is tightly packed with local residents. The best time to enjoy the surf and discover what made it popular is on a quiet weekday.

Coogee   Another popular beach in the SE, which has been memorably captured on canvas by Australian Impressionist painters. It is much busier these days, but the current is generally milder than at other Sydney ocean beaches. Recommended.

Tamarama   This beach, in an attractive setting, is for the young and body-proud. Sun-worship is more important here than the mundane business of swimming, partly because the currents can be dangerous.

Long Reef   Favored by adventurous swimmers — windsurfing, surfing and skin-diving are popular here, but beware of the current. The lagoon provides safer swimming.

CENTENNIAL PARK
Oxford St., Paddington. Map 6C5-D5 ▣ ✱ ▰ *Open sunrise-sunset.*
Founded in 1888 to celebrate the centenary of the arrival of the first settlers, this is Sydney's equivalent of London's Regents Park or New York's Central Park. There are acres of space in which to stroll, feed the ducks or have a snooze. You can also hire horses *(☎332 2770),* bicycles or tandems.

A visit to Centennial Park would not be complete without a stroll around the leafy eastern suburb of **Paddington**. Built during the Victorian period, this tree-lined residential area had, by the end of World War II, become a virtual slum. But the trend for restoring row houses, with their characteristic wrought-iron balconies, has made this one of Sydney's most fashionable suburbs. PADDINGTON VILLAGE CHURCH BAZAAR (see WHERE TO SHOP), off Oxford St., is a picturesque Saturday menagerie.

For lovers of Victorian architecture, the neighboring suburb of **Woollahra** has some even grander residences than Paddington.

CENTREPOINT (Sydney Tower) ★
Pitt St. ☎229 7444. *Map 3D3* ▨ ◁≈ ═ ✱ ʃ*hourly. Open Sun-Fri 9.30am-9.30pm; Sat 9.30am-11.30pm. Explorer Bus.*
Although no more attractive than any city tower, this one has the redeeming feature of a view that helps to fix in the mind's eye the complexities of the city layout. From the observation deck you can look westward up the Parramatta River, with its innumerable bays and coves, across the harbor to the suburbs of NORTH SYDNEY, and eastward up the harbor to the Heads, at the entrance of this magnificent natural harbor; so be sure to go on a clear day. There is a restaurant *(☎233 3722 Ⅲ),* for which reservations are essential.

CHINATOWN
SW Sydney. Map 3E2. Explorer Bus.
Less intriguing, perhaps, than its equivalents in San Francisco and London, Sydney's Chinatown is nonetheless an interesting district to wander in — and the best spot for an Oriental blow-out. There are dozens of restaurants, including the MARIGOLD (see DINING OUT) and the **Sun**

City *(Sussex St.* ☎ *261 1833)*. There are also a few specialty supermarkets, and a food-stall center in Dixon St., which offers a passable imitation of similar establishments found in Singapore.

CIRCULAR QUAY ★
Map 3B3 🚐 *Explorer Bus.*
If Sydney has a transportation nerve-center, this is it. Once, tall-masted barques and schooners arrived here from the mother country; now, ferry services depart across the harbor for the northern suburbs of MANLY and **Mosman**, and numerous bus services terminate here *(* ☎ *954 4422 for bus and ferry inquiries)*. The Sydney Explorer Bus and the Harbor Explorer both start here, and the city center is only a 15-minute walk away.

For all these reasons Circular Quay is an excellent place to begin your investigation of the city. It is also a good starting point for a number of central walks. Here are two suggested routes.

Walk A
Total distance about 5km (3 miles), broken up by lunch along the way.
Follow **Circular Quay East** to **Bennelong Point**, site of the OPERA HOUSE. Continue walking eastward along the harborside cove, through the BOTANIC GARDENS to **Mrs Macquarie's Chair**. A road, which also bears the name of this early governor's wife, then runs for approximately 1km ($\frac{1}{2}$ mile) s past the Charlton swimming pool to the ART GALLERY OF NEW SOUTH WALES, which has a good cafeteria for lunch. Even if you don't go in, pause to enjoy the Henry Moore sculpture of a reclining female figure, on the lawn. Return to the quay by striking back across the Botanic Gardens, or continue along Art Gallery Rd. until you emerge at HYDE PARK.

Walk B
Total distance about 2km (1 mile). Can also be combined with a visit to the Opera House, or undertaken separately.
On emerging from Circular Quay turn left and continue until you reach the bottom end of Macquarie St. It is a stiffish uphill walk to the top, but contains much Sydney history. (The less fit and energetic may prefer to take a taxi or a train — the nearest station is St James — to the top of Macquarie St. and walk downhill to Circular Quay.)

Starting from the bottom of the hill the first important building you come to, on the left, is the CONSERVATORIUM OF MUSIC. Farther along, on the right, are two elegant early town terraces, preserved as **History House** and the **Royal College of Physicians**. On the left is the LIBRARY OF NEW SOUTH WALES. In the next section of Macquarie St. are the PARLIAMENT HOUSE, the MINT MUSEUM and, finally, HYDE PARK BARRACKS. On the opposite side of the road to the barracks is ST JAMES CHURCH, dating from 1819.

Circular Quay is also a good starting point for visiting THE ROCKS, one of the best walking areas of Sydney.

CONSERVATORIUM OF MUSIC
Macquarie St. ☎ *230 1222. Map 3C3* 📷 *Open 8am-5pm. Closed Sat, Sun. Explorer Bus.*

The original design for this distinctive building was created in 1821 by
Francis Greenway (a former convict, and Australia's first recognized
architect) as stables for Governor Macquarie. "The Con," as it is known,
was established in 1916. During the school year it is open to the public,
and is a place for weekly lunchtime recitals and concerts (*☎ or check
the press for details).*

DARLING HARBOUR
SW Sydney. Map 3C1-D2.
This major redevelopment of the rundown docks area is the latest of
Sydney's major tourist attractions, although it continues to attract brick-
bats as well as bouquets. It covers 54ha (133 acres) and includes nightclubs, shops, restaurants, and, with more than 5,000 aquatic creatures,
the world's largest **aquarium**. Other attractions are THE POWERHOUSE
MUSEUM (*☎217 0111),* **The National Maritime Museum** (*☎552
2011* ▨ *open daily 10am-5pm)* and **The Chinese Garden**, the largest
of its kind outside mainland China. The Monorail, which glides through
Sydney's Central Business District on a 15-minute circular route, offers
a swift and scenic view of all the action *(for further information ☎552
2288).*

ELIZABETH BAY HOUSE ★
*7 Onslow Ave., Elizabeth Bay ☎358 2344. Map 4D5 ▨ ➡ Open
10am-4.30pm. Closed Mon. Explorer Bus.*
This splendid example of a colonial mansion has been maintained with
an eye for authenticity, setting the standard by which other historic
homes in Australia are judged.

"The finest house in the colony" (according to a contemporary record)
is handsomely sited in what is still an elegant part of central Sydney. It
was built in 1835 for Colonial Secretary Alexander Macleay, and was
originally set in 22ha (54 acres) of gardens, which ran down to the water's
edge of what is now a yachting harbor.

Principal features are the elliptical reception salon, with its grand
sweeping cantilevered stone staircase, the paneled dome ceiling, which
is naturally lit, and magnificent cedar doors. There are interesting exhibitions on aspects of colonial life, which are changed regularly.

FORT DENISON ★
*Map 4A5 ▨ ✗ compulsory ⋘ Maritime Services Board (☎364 2111, ext.
2157) organizes ferry tours from Circular Quay, departing 10am, 12.15pm, 2pm.*
This fortified island in the middle of Sydney Harbour is a poignant
reminder that in the 19thC it was feared that Australia faced invasion —
first by the US, then by Russia.

Allow $1\frac{1}{2}$ hours for a round trip of this island, 0.2ha ($\frac{1}{2}$ acre) in area and
less than 100m (328 feet) long, which was the first detention place in the
new penal colony, being used to hold convicts temporarily while a prison
was being built on the mainland. In this time it acquired its other name,
"Pinchgut", a vivid description of the agonies experienced by unrulier
convicts, who were placed there as punishment on near-starvation ra-

tions. The unheralded arrival in the harbor of American sloops around 1840 stimulated the concept of fortifying the rock, which gained momentum during the Crimean War. Fort Denison, named after the governor of the day, was completed in 1857.

The martello tower, barracks, battery and underground magazines are all accessible for viewing. Needless to say, the cannons were never fired in anger.

GEORGE STREET ★
Map 3C3-F2. Explorer Bus.
This is one of Sydney's earliest thoroughfares, which in a short section around Town Sq. contains three handsome historic buildings: ST AN-DREW'S CATHEDRAL, the **Town Hall** (built in Renaissance style and completed in 1874) and the **Queen Victoria Building**.

The history of the Queen Victoria Building is a cautionary tale in town planning, and it has taken Sydney nearly 90 years to appreciate the grandeur of this huge, Romanesque-style market complex. Completed in 1898, the sandstone building fell into neglect, and suffered major civic vandalism between World Wars I and II; by the 1950s there was a concerted move to have it demolished. In 1983 the huge task of restoration began, and was completed three years later at a cost of A$82 million. This splendid arcade of shops, boutiques and restaurants (see WHERE TO SHOP) is now a major Sydney sight.

This is also a convenient starting point for a city shopping expedition. The major stores DAVID JONES and GRACE BROTHERS, and the STRAND ARCADE, another complex of fashionable shops, are within easy walking distance of Town Sq. (see all these in WHERE TO SHOP).

HARBOUR BRIDGE ★
Map 3A3 ▣ ◀€ SE pylon and museum display open daily 9am-5pm. Explorer Bus.
Until the construction of the OPERA HOUSE, the "Old Coathanger" was Sydney's most instantly recognizable symbol. The spectacular N-S harbor link was completed in 1932 at a cost of a mere A$20 million. Now

that it is no longer capable of handling the traffic flow, a tunnel is being built under the harbor, for around A$750 million.

Pedestrians can reach the bridge by stairs from THE ROCKS, and although it is possible to walk across, the best view is from the top of the SE pylon.

Pier One, at the southern end of the bridge, has some attractions for children, such as a merry-go-round, and live entertainments, but **Luna**

Park, for decades Sydney's main amusement center, whose giant clown-like face grins still at the N bridge end, has now been closed down.

HYDE PARK

Elizabeth St. Map 3D3-E3 🔟 *Open sunrise-sunset. Explorer Bus.*

Its central location makes this park popular with city workers at lunchtime, and with the ubiquitous drunks. During the school vacation in January it becomes an amusement center. The Art Deco-style **Archibald Fountain**, designed by French sculptor François Sicard, caused a furore when it was unveiled in 1927 in memory of Australia's association with France in World War I. The **Anzac Memorial** is a moving reminder that Australia and New Zealand suffered a higher proportion of casualties in that conflict than any other combatant nation. The annual Anzac Day parade, commemorating the Gallipoli landing on April 25, 1915, culminates here.

Opposite the park, in Elizabeth St., is the **Great Synagogue**, a 19thC sandstone structure with fine detail.

HYDE PARK BARRACKS MUSEUM ★

Queens Sq., Macquarie St. ☎*217 0333. Map 3D3* 🔟 💽 *Open Wed-Mon 10am-5pm; Tues noon-5pm. Explorer Bus.*

This is the first product of what became a fertile partnership between Governor Lachlan Macquarie and Francis Greenway, the great convict architect of colonial Australia. This handsome 3-story structure, designed as accommodations for convicts, was completed in 1819, and so pleased the governor that he pardoned Greenway. The building has been converted into Sydney's main museum of colonial history, and displays there illustrate the Macquarie era and convict life.

Excellent-value lunches and teas are served at the **Barracks Square Café**.

KING'S CROSS

About 2km (1 mile) from city center. Map 4D5. Explorer Bus.

Sydney's sin center has benefited from a series of clean-up campaigns to get narcotic abuse off the streets. The main thoroughfare, **Darlinghurst Rd.**, can still be an ill-tempered, somewhat desperate spot late at night, but "the Cross" has some reasonable eating places, such as the BOURBON & BEEFSTEAK (see ENTERTAINMENT), and in addition to the strip joints and porn establishments, there is plenty of activity here. It contains many small hotels and guesthouses, which have made the area a center for young budget travelers. At the top end of Darlinghurst Rd. is the **El-Alamein Fountain**, an intriguing dandelionlike design.

MANLY ★

N of the city. Map 6B5. Ferry across the harbor from Circular Quay: departures on the $\frac{1}{2}$ hr.

This residential suburb of N Sydney, which is also a popular resort, is worth visiting just for the ferry trip. Manly's harbor beach, known as **South Steyne**, is particularly calm, but the ocean beach across the peninsula, **North Steyne**, can be dangerous at times, although the surf is good.

At the **Manly Oceanarium** *(West Esplanade* ☎ *949 2644* 📷 *open 10am-5pm)* there are seal performances *(noon and 2pm)* and a large tank with sharks, turtles and rays. You can have lunch at the MANLY PACIFIC PARKROYAL (see WHERE TO STAY).

MINT MUSEUM ★

Macquarie St. ☎ *217 0111. Map 3D3* 📷 *Open Thurs-Tues 10am-5pm; Wed noon-5pm. Explorer Bus.*

This is actually a museum of colonial history, from the perspective of the decorative arts. Fine furniture, made of indigenous red cedar, and silverware are among the most collectable Australian objects, and there are excellent examples here, as well as stamps, coins, earthenware and glass. The Mint building is part of what was once known as the Rum Hospital, which, like so many old New South Wales structures, was built during the governorship of Lachlan Macquarie, in a deal that involved granting the two citizens who funded the hospital a trade monopoly in the colony's favorite tipple.

NORTH SYDNEY

Map 6C4.

The commuter strain imposed on the HARBOUR BRIDGE and other city transportation resources were the mainsprings for the decentralization of Sydney in the 1970s and the rapid growth of the area immediately N of the bridge. North Sydney is today a busy center for insurance, computer firms, advertizing agencies, and film and television companies. A hive of offices, small restaurants, and winding streets, it has become a self-contained commercial center, attached to the main business district by road, rail and ferry. The nearby suburbs — **Neutral Bay**, **Cremorne**, **Mosman** and **Kirribilli** (where the Prime Minister lives when in Sydney) — are among the most pleasant of the city's residential areas.

OPERA HOUSE ★

Bennelong Point ☎ *250 7111 (general inquiries Mon-Sat 9am-9pm, Sun 9am-4pm), 250 7777 (reservations). Map 3B3* 📷 ♿ ✗ *at regular intervals from 9am-4pm* ◁€ *Explorer Bus.*

It is just as well to remember today, when this marvelous building is accepted as embodying modern Sydney style, that during a difficult gestation period it was often dismissed as the most pallid of all pachyderms.

When Joern Utzon's sketches won a design competition in 1957, it was generally estimated that the sails-on-the-harbor design (alternatively nuns-in-a-scrum) would cost around A$8 million and take no more than five years to build. In the event, it cost well over A$100 million, and took more than a decade.

All but the dourest Sydneysiders would agree today that it was worth waiting for. The city has gained a symbol even more distinctive than the

HARBOUR BRIDGE, as well as a splendid arts center. In addition to the opera theater there is a concert hall, drama theater and cinema.

The AUSTRALIAN OPERA company (see ENTERTAINMENT) generally offers vigorous and well-sung productions, and has staged some exhilarating triumphs in recent years *(for program details consult the press, or contact the box office)*. The **Bennelong** restaurant offers the same splendid setting, and reasonable value *(☎ 250 7578/250 7548 ▥)*.

PARLIAMENT HOUSE
Macquarie St. ☎ 230 2111. Map 3C3 ▣ ✗ of Upper and Lower Houses by arrangement, Mon-Fri 10am-3.30pm. Open 9.30am-4pm. Closed Sat, Sun. To inspect the interior or attend debates ☎ the Sergeant-at-Arms' office at the above number. Explorer Bus.

The state legislature is contained in this, Australia's oldest parliamentary building. With its large verandas, it resembles a classically colonial administrative block, but in fact used to be part of what was called the Rum Hospital. The other wing is now the MINT MUSEUM. The hospital was an inspired innovation by that indefatigable builder, Governor Macquarie, who, finding the public coffers empty, granted two wealthy citizens control of the rum trade in return for constructing a hospital.

POWERHOUSE MUSEUM
500 Harris St., Ultimo ☎ 217 0111. Map 3E2 ▣ ♿ ✿ Open 10am-5pm.

Australia's largest and possibly most popular museum is now part of the DARLING HARBOUR complex. It has 25 major permanent displays covering the decorative arts, science and social history. The collection reflects technological change since the Industrial Revolution, and contains participatory displays for children.

THE ROCKS ★
Map 3B3 ✗ Explorer Bus.

This is where it all began: Old Sydney, where the settlement founded by Captain Arthur Phillip after landing at Sydney Cove grew and developed. It was a rude society. Dimly lit streets were the haunts of grog traders, whores and sailors, and press gangs lurked among the alleys of the harbor. An outbreak of bubonic plague here in 1900 killed more than 100 people. All this is hard to imagine today, among these charming sandstone cottages and old pubs, and nowadays The Rocks offers one of the best walks in Sydney. Organized walking tours lasting 1 hour leave from **Argyle Centre** *(Argyle St.* ☎ *247 6678, at hourly intervals every morning).* If walking on your own, the **Rocks Visitors' Centre** *(104 George St.* ☎ *247 4972)* will provide maps.

Your first stop should be **Cadman's Cottage** *(110 George St.* ☎ *247 8861),* overlooking the harbor, which would be unremarkable but for the fact that it is Sydney's earliest surviving dwelling. Follow George St. N to the 19thC row houses known as **Sergeant Majors Row**, then turn left into Playfair St. for the shops of Argyle Terrace. At Argyle St. turn right and walk through the **Cut**, a tunnel carved out of cliff, to the **Holy Trinity Anglican Church** (the garrison church), which was built from the quarried rock, and consecrated in 1843. Along Argyle Pl. and Lower Fort St. are a range of handsome row houses from the Georgian and Victorian eras; also the **Colonial House Museum** *(53 Lower Fort St.* ☎ *247 6008).*

Back at Argyle Pl. is **Observatory Park**, on the far side of which is the handsome building of the **National Trust Centre**.

Refreshment, after thirsty work, is obtainable at two of Australia's oldest licensed establishments, the **Lord Nelson** *(19 Kent St.),* which has a pleasant upstairs restaurant, and the **Hero of Waterloo** *(81 Lower Fort St.).* There are a great number of shops in The Rocks — too many, in fact, particularly of those aimed at tourists.

ROYAL BOTANIC GARDENS ★
The Domain ☎ *231 8111. Map 4C4* 🔲 ✗ *Wed and Fri 10am; Sun 1pm* 🍴 🚃
◄€ *Open sunrise-sunset. Explorer Bus.*

This pleasant harborside attraction can be combined with a visit to the OPERA HOUSE. Other sights within walking distance are the ART GALLERY OF NEW SOUTH WALES, the CONSERVATORIUM OF MUSIC and the LIBRARY OF NEW SOUTH WALES.

The first colonists cultivated vegetables here, but from 1816 the 69ha (170-acre) site became established as a garden. Today it supports a fine collection of trees and tropical plants. It is an excellent spot for a nap on the lawn after a long walk, and has a prime view of the OPERA HOUSE. **Mrs Macquarie's Chair**, named after the wife of Governor Lachlan Macquarie, greatest of the early colonial administrators, is a rocky vantage point projecting into the harbor.

The **Domain** is another park, adjacent to the gardens. The main interest for visitors is the Sunday afternoon soapbox oratory — a local blood sport.

ST ANDREW'S CATHEDRAL
Town Hall Sq., George St. ☎ *265 1555. Map 3D3* 🔲 ✗ *after last two services and after 1.15pm Wed service. Open Mon-Fri 7.30am-6pm; Sat 10am-4pm; Sun 8am-8pm. Organ recitals Thurs 1.15pm, 1.45pm. Explorer Bus.*

The design of this Gothic Anglican cathedral, built in sandstone and consecrated in 1868, was based on two structures in Oxford, England. The nave and aisle were modeled on those at St Mary's Church, and the steeple on the tower at Magdalen College. Music is an important feature of worship here: the organ is a unique two-in-one combination, with sets of pipes from both the 19thC and 20thC; and the cathedral has one of the finest male-voice choirs in the country.

ST JAMES CHURCH ★

King St., Queens Sq. ☎ *232 3952. Map 3D3* 🚻 *Open 9am-5pm. Sun services 8am, 9am, 11am. Explorer Bus.*

A finely proportioned Anglican church by Francis Greenway, the convict-architect who designed many of Sydney's most notable buildings. Greenway and his patron, Governor Lachlan Macquarie, had already started building a courthouse on this site when a commissioner, sent out from London to restrain their civic ambitions, forced readjustments to projects already in hand. St James Church took the place of the courthouse. It opened in 1822.

ST MARY'S CATHEDRAL

College St. ☎ *232 3788. Map 3D3* 🚻 *✗ on request. Open Mon-Fri 6.30am-6.30pm; Sat 8am-7.30pm; Sun 6.30am-7.30pm. Sun services 9am, 10.30am, 6.30pm. Explorer Bus.*

Catholicism is the faith of the NSW political establishment, and this imposing structure, built on a fine site overlooking the **Domain** (see ROYAL BOTANIC GARDENS), is the headquarters of the faith in Australia. The cathedral has had a checkered history. The foundation stone of the first Catholic chapel was laid by Governor Macquarie in 1831, but was destroyed by fire in 1865. Three years later a new foundation stone was blessed, and building commenced on the ruin of the old structure; but St Mary's was not opened until 1928, and is still incomplete, the twin towers having no spires.

THE STATE LIBRARY OF NEW SOUTH WALES

Macquarie St. ☎ *230 1414. Map 3C3* 🚻 💻 ♿ *Open Mon-Fri 9am-9pm; Sat 9am-5pm; Sun and hols 11am-5pm. Explorer Bus.*

Sydney's main library overlooks the ROYAL BOTANIC GARDENS and contains what is arguably the finest collection of Australian history and reference books. The building, a blend of early sandstone and "hi-tech," has been reorganized to attract a far broader public than in the past. It encourages young readers with the latest electronic "user friendly" services, including hands-on computers. With exhibits, film screenings, voluminous research material and comprehensive databases, it has become more accessible to students of Australia's diverse heritage.

TARONGA PARK ZOO ★

Bradleys Head Rd., Mosman ☎ *969 2777. Map 6C5* 🚅 ♿ 💻 ✻ ⇇ *Open 9am-5pm.*

Situated in NORTH SYDNEY, overlooking the harbor, and a short ferry ride from CIRCULAR QUAY, Taronga Park is as attractive a setting as you could find for a zoo, and during the week a good spot for picnics. It also contains the finest collection of Australia's unique fauna. In recent years, animal enclosures have been gradually upgraded, with an emphasis on moving towards more "natural" landscapes. The **nocturnal** and **reptile houses** are both worth visiting. An aerial cable ride from the harborside is an option that makes the steep climb to the entrance easier and provides spectacular views. If you're in the city, a **Zoopass** ticket is available at Circular Quay; this covers ferry, bus, entry to the zoo, and a cable ride. Special features of Taronga include an entertaining **seal show** *(🔲1.15pm and 3.15pm, additional show Sun 11.15am)*, an **aquarium**, and the **chimpanzee park**.

VAUCLUSE HOUSE

Olola Ave., Vaucluse ☎337 1957. Map 6C5 🔳 💻 Open 10am-4.30pm. Closed Mon.

This historic home was once the residence of W. C. Wentworth, architect of the Australian constitution, and an explorer who was involved in the first successful crossing of the Blue Mountains.

The house, begun in 1803, is built in Gothic style, with turrets and castellations, and has been furnished with period pieces. The grounds, covering more than 8ha (20 acres), are among the main attractions, with period outbuildings and fine gardens. There is a small beach at the bottom of the grounds, and **Nielsen Park** beach (see BEACHES) is an easy stroll away.

VICTORIA BARRACKS

Oxford St., Paddington ☎339 3455. Map 6C5🔲 ✗by reservation only at 10.30am Wed.

Unlike HYDE PARK BARRACKS, which was built to accommodate convicts, this was a true military barracks, and was the headquarters of British colonial troops until 1871, when an Australian defense force was raised. The barracks is a handsome Georgian structure 225m (738 feet) in length, consisting of twin 2-story wings, and it remains a military headquarters and administrative center. Access to the public is confined to a free guided tour of the barracks and museum on Wednesday, shortly before the changing of the guard, and visits to the museum from 1.30-4pm on the first Sunday of the month. Reservations for both are essential.

Where to stay

The most common complaint about Sydney's best hotels was that there were too few of them. In the late 1980s, the city finally began to respond to the huge demand for international 4- and 5-star-standard accommodations. Today Sydney can boast many first-class international hotels. If there is anything to be disappointed about, it is that there are few time-proven establishments, and few that can offer an ambience to compare with the grand old hotels of Europe or the United States.

Most of the hotels described below are within easy reach of the sea — the distance from the city to the harbor beaches, for example, or to the eastern ocean beaches, such as Bondi, is less than 10km (6 miles) — although only one on the following list is situated right on the beach. All the others are conveniently located for central sightseeing. For good accommodations, which by Australian standards are expensive, it is advisable to reserve ahead.

Sydney has no shortage of the standard, clean — if basic — motel unit, which can be found all over Australia. Motels and motor inns, however, tend to be located out of the center, making car rental a near-necessity. Such accommodations can be found around the eastern beaches such as **Bondi**, **Coogee** and **Maroubra**, and in the N at **Manly** and **Dee Why**.

In addition to hotels and guesthouses, Sydney offers a range of efficiency (self-catering) serviced accommodations: establishments that provide simple, clean rooms with all basic amenities, such as TV and laundry (and often swimming pools and sauna), with the independence of private kitchens, crockery and cutlery. Examples below, chosen mainly for their convenience, are the FLORIDA MOTOR INN and HYDE PARK PLAZA.

CENTRA HOTEL

17 Blue St., North Sydney, NSW, 2060
☎*955 0499* ⊞*26644* ⊠*922 3689. Map*
6C4 ▥ *215 rms* ━ ⊟ 🆎 ⊡ ⓪ ▨ ⇌
⊟ ☕ ♨

Location: In the center of North Sydney's business district. The **Blues** restaurant offers good views of the harbor from an unusual perspective; if you prefer *al fresco* dining, there are umbrellas and tables by the pool. The hotel is within walking distance of the best view of the OPERA HOUSE, from Pelican Point, and not far from Balmoral Beach, probably the best on the lower N shore. There are two nonsmoking floors.

CENTRAL PLAZA

Corner of George St. and Quay St., Sydney, NSW, 2000 ☎*212 2544* ⊞*74862*
⊠*281 3794. Map 3F2* ▥ *114 rms* ━
⊟ 🆎 ⊡ ⓪ ▨ ⇌ ⊟ ☕ ✿ ⚓ ♨

Location: Opposite Central Station. The convenient location of this modern hotel in the SW of the city, a short walk from Chinatown and the Entertainment Centre, compensates for its uninspiring surroundings. Most of the rooms contain spa baths, and some suites have their own patio garden. There is a rooftop pool with a sauna and barbecue area. An elegant brasserie-style restaurant promises value for money.

FLORIDA MOTOR INN ✿

1 McDonald St., Potts Point, NSW, 2011
☎*358 6811* ⊞*21128* ⊠*358 5951. Map*
4C5 ▥ *89 rms* ━ 🆎 ⊡ ⓪ ▨ ⇌ ⊟
⌁

Location: Between Kings Cross and Potts Point, 5mins' taxi ride from the city. This motor inn, with its well-equipped apartments, is conveniently located in a pleasant residential area.

GAZEBO

2 Elizabeth Bay Rd., Elizabeth Bay, NSW, 2011 ☎*358 1999* ☒*121569* ☒*356 2951. Map 4D5* ▥ *400 rms* ⬛ ☰ AE ◉ ◎ ▦ ⬢ ☙ ◲ ☿ ☏ ♈ ☷

Location: In the heart of Kings Cross, overlooking Fitzroy Gardens and Elizabeth Bay. Taking a dip in the pool here can leave you breathless, not from exertion but at the panorama across the bay; for the glass-enclosed pool is on the 17th floor, at the top of a circular tower, an unmistakable landmark in downtown Kings Cross. Upper-level rooms also have fine views of the harbor and city.

HILTON INTERNATIONAL

259 Pitt St., Sydney, NSW, 2000 ☎*266 0610* ☒*25208* ☒*265 6065. Map 3D3* ▥ *605 rms* ⬛ ☰ AE ◉ ◎ ▦ ⬢ ☙ ◲ ☿ ☏ ♈ ♈ ☷

Location: In the heart of the city center, opposite the impressive Queen Victoria Building. This Hilton is surprisingly anonymous, buried within a shopping complex, but this does not detract from its elegant and comfortable interior. The chefs of the **San Francisco Grill Room** have won a number of awards; the hotel also has an Art Deco-style nightclub, and the magnificent **Marble Bar**, which, dating from the turn of the century, was a feature of the George Adam hotel originally on this site. There are two executive floors with extensive business services. Among the Hilton's newest features is a direct link to DARLING HARBOUR by Monorail.

HILTON INTERNATIONAL SYDNEY AIRPORT

20 Levey St., Arncliffe, NSW, 2205 ☎*597 0122* ☒*70795* ☒*597 6381. Map 6D4* ▥ *270 rms* ⬛ ☰ AE ◉ ◎ ▦ ⬢ ☙ ◲ ☿ ♈ ♈ ☷ ☿ ☏

Location: Opposite the international air terminal, about 20mins from the city. Obviously not the surroundings for a vacation, this is the executive traveler's domain, useful for quick stopovers or conferences, and providing the usual Hilton standards of efficiency and courtesy. For more relaxed moments,

there are squash and tennis courts — or take the opportunity of using the nearby 18-hole Kogarah Golf Course (in a suburb that calls contemporary wit and writer Clive James one of her sons). A shuttle service operates every half-hour to and from the airport and every 2 hours to and from the city center.

HYATT KINGSGATE ♨

William St., Sydney, NSW, 2011 ☎*356 1234* ☒*23114* ☒*356 4150. Map 4D4* ▥ *389 rms* ⬛ ☰ AE ◉ ◎ ▦ ⬢ ☙ ☿ ♈ ☷

Location: Towering over the Kings Cross district, offering spectacular views of the harbor and city, which are less than 10mins away. This might not be Sydney's most salubrious district, but the luxurious interiors of this fine, recently refurbished hotel, and its attentive staff, are a world away from the *risqué* street life. Its **Craigend** restaurant suggests the style of a splendid old Italian villa. Offering competition to another successful eating place, the SUNTORY (see DINING OUT), is the pricey **Chitose**, a Japanese restaurant with a *sushi* bar. The hotel is proud of patronage by sporting personalities, mainly golfers and cricketers.

HYDE PARK INN ♨

271 Elizabeth St., Sydney, NSW, 2000 ☎*264 6001* ☒*25304* ☒*261 8691. Map 3E3* ▥ *86 rms* ⬛ ☰ AE ◉ ◎ ▦ ☷

Location: Opposite Hyde Park, close to Sydney's shopping and business center. Owned by the Returned Services League, an association of former members of the armed forces, this hotel offers reductions to ex-servicemen. Nearly all the rooms, which are prettily furnished in soft pastel shades, have balconies overlooking the park.

HYDE PARK PLAZA ♨

38 College St., Sydney, NSW, 2010 ☎*331 6933* ☒*22450* ☒*331 6022. Map 3E3* ▥ *182 rms* ⬛ ☰ AE ◉ ◎ ▦ ⬢ ☷ ☿ ☏ ♈ ☷

Location: Overlooking Hyde Park on the corner of Oxford St., gateway to the eastern suburbs. Comfortable one-, two- and three-bedroom apartments that are ideal for families or business travelers. Served by a restaurant and cocktail bar.

INTER-CONTINENTAL

117 Macquarie St., Sydney, NSW, 2000 ☎230 0200 ⊠176890 ⊠251 2342. Map *3C3* ⅧⅢ 502 rms ⚊ ☲ 🆎 ⬙ 🔟 🎊 ☕ 🔊 ▣ 🍸 ⚲ ⚑ ⚓ ⚏

Location: Near the central business district, close to the Botanic Gardens and the Opera House. Sydney's stylish Inter-Continental, voted the city's leading deluxe hotel in the NSW Tourism Awards for Excellence in 1990 and 1991, was designed around the 19thC sandstone Treasury Building. The concept used here makes sensitive use of the features of the historic building to create an atmosphere combining the best of tradition and modernity. The palazzo-like central courtyard, surrounded by vaulted arcades of sandstone, is the focal point. Bedrooms on the upper floors have outstanding harbor views. Banquets and conferences can be accommodated in a selection of rooms, from the **Grand Ballroom** to the faithfully restored 19thC boardrooms.

JACKSON ✿

94 Victoria St., Potts Point, NSW, 2011 ☎385 5144 ⊠357 4935. Map *4D5* ⅢⅢ *20 rms* ⚊ 🆎 ⬙ 🚐

Location: On a pretty treelined street in Potts Point, close to Kings Cross, and two kilometers from the city. A carefully restored Victorian row house, classified by the National Trust, this small establishment offers comfortable but economical accommodations of a sort common in European guesthouses, but all too rare in Australia. Its attractive wrought-iron balconies, high, ornate ceilings and gleaming brass and cedar all add to the charm. The continental breakfast, which is included in the room price, is served in a sunny conservatory.

MACQUARIE PRIVATE HOTEL

Corner of Hughes St. and Tusculum St., Kings Cross, NSW, 2011 ☎358 4122

⊠357 1421. Map *4D5* ⅢⅢ *25 rms*

Location: In Kings Cross, less than 2km (1 mile) from the city. Kings Cross is the cheap-rate hotel district of Sydney, popular with young travelers. If you enjoy the raffish, and are not too fussy about frills, there is excellent value to be had here.

MANLY PACIFIC PARKROYAL ✿

55 North Steyne, Manly, NSW, 2095 ☎977 7666 ⊠73097 ⊠977 7822. Map *6B5* ⅢⅢ *170 rms* ⚊ ☲ 🆎 ⬙ 🔟 🎊 ⚲ ⚑ ▣ 🍸 ⚲ ⚑ ⚓ ⚏

Location: Overlooking one of Australia's most famous surfing beaches. This is one of the few luxury hotels in NORTH SYDNEY, situated in one of the city's most attractive suburbs. It offers the best of both worlds — sand and surf on the doorstep, and easy access to the center of Sydney, just 15 minutes away by hydrofoil.

MENZIES

14 Carrington St., Sydney, NSW, 2000 ☎20232 ⊠20443 ⊠290 3819. Map *3C2* ⅧⅢ *441 rms* ⚊ ☲ 🆎 ⬙ 🔟 🎊 ⚲ ⚲ ▣ 🍸 ⚲ ⚑ ⚓ ⚏

Location: In the city center, 5mins' walk from Circular Quay. The Holiday Inn chain has spent A\$15 million on refurbishing the Menzies, which had become something of a Sydney institution. The lobby now consists of gleaming black granite, oak paneling and mirrors; the lobby bar and stylish **Park Lounge**, where high tea is served from a silver service, look out over Wynyard Park. There are five restaurants, including the Japanese **Keisan**, a non-smoking floor, and 24-hour medical service.

METRO MOTOR INN ✿

Corner of Abercrombie St. and Meagher St., Chippendale, Sydney, NSW, 2008 ☎319 4133 ⊠26474 ⊠698 7665. Map *6C4* ⅢⅢ *34 rms* ⚊ ☲ 🆎 ⬙ 🔟 🎊 ▣

Location: Just outside the city in a light-industrial and residential district. There is nothing very distinguished about this or other Metro Motor Inns, which are characteristic of the ubiquitous Australian motel, but they generally offer value for money in clean and comfortable surroundings. The group maintains several establishments reasonably close to the city, but this one is particularly convenient, and close to Sydney University, DARLING HARBOUR and Sydney Entertainment Centre.

OLD SYDNEY PARKROYAL

55 George St., Sydney, NSW, 2000 ☎*252 0524* ⊠*72279* ⛵*251 2093. Map 3B3* ▥ *174 rms* ⬛ ⇌ ⒶⒺ ⊡ ⊚ ⟱ ⬥ ⚲
▤ ⅋ ⟡ ⚓ ⛴

Location: In the heart of the historic Rocks area, site of the first European settlement, and within easy walking distance of the city. This modern hotel's main attraction is its location in THE ROCKS area. It was converted a few years ago from a 1920s building, and its amphitheater-like interior gives a feeling of spaciousness. The ground-floor **Cove Café** looks out onto the pedestrian parade of The Rocks. Good breakfasts are another attraction.

THE PARK ON OXFORD ✿

16-32 Oxford St., Sydney, NSW, 2010 ☎*331 7728* ⊠*74824* ⛵*360 2583. Map 4E4* ▥ *133 rms* ⬛ ⇌ ⒶⒺ ⊡ ⊚ ⟱ ⚲
▤ ⅋ ⟡ ⚓ ⛴

Location: On the edge of the city, opposite the Ansett terminal in Oxford Sq. All-suite hotel with light and airy single- and two-bedroom apartments, in pleasant surroundings. Each suite has a fully-equipped kitchen, which includes a dishwasher, and the additional feature of 24-hour room service.

PARKROYAL AT DARLING HARBOUR

150 Day St., Sydney, NSW, 2000 ☎*261 4444* ⛵*261 8766. Map 3D2* ▥ *295 rms* ⬛ ⇌ ⒶⒺ ⊡ ⊚ ⟱ ⬥ ▤ ⇌ ⅋ ⛴

Location: In the city's southern commercial district, close to Chinatown and connected by walkway to Darling Harbour. This luxurious hotel provides an ideal base for those who want to combine business in the city with entertainment and the attractions of the DARLING HARBOUR complex. The Parkroyal, which offers guests a distinctively Aus-

tralian feel "with a touch of the tropics," boasts that its rooms have the best and largest marble bathrooms in Sydney. Restaurants include the contemporary **Arizona Bar and Restaurant** and **Day Street Café**. The hotel's business appeal includes in-room fax facilities.

RAMADA RENAISSANCE

30 Pitt St., Sydney, NSW, 2000 ☎*259 7000* ⊠*127792* ⛵*252 1999. Map 3B3* ▥ *562 rms* ⬛ ⇌ ⒶⒺ ⊡ ⊚ ⟱ ⚲
▤ ⅋ ⟡ ⟡ ⚓ ⛴

Location: At Circular Quay, in the heart of the city, close to the Opera House and other harborside attractions. A first-class hotel that has everything the international traveler could desire. The elegantly designed Renaissance incorporates Sydney's famous **Custom House**. There is fine dining at **Raphaels**, but a popular gathering place is the **Oyster Bar**, which serves only oysters, seafood and excellent Australian wines.

REGENT

199 George St., Sydney, NSW, 2000 ☎*238 0000* ⊠*73023* ⛵*251 2851. Map 3B3* ▥ *620 rms* ⬛ ⇌ ⒶⒺ ⊡ ⊚ ⟱ ⬥ ⚲ ▤ ⅋ ⛴

Location: Ideally situated — a stroll away from the Opera House, the historic Rocks area and the central business district. Thought by many to be Sydney's finest, the Regent has been ranked among the world's top dozen hotels. Service for business executives, including a business reference library, is unmatched in Sydney. Other features are **Kable's** restaurant, which is probably Sydney's best hotel restaurant, and executive suites with a personal butler.

RITZ-CARLTON

93 Macquarie St., Sydney, NSW, 2060 ☎*252 4600* ⊠*171221* ⛵*252 4286. Map 3C3* ▥ *106 rms* ⬛ ⇌ ⒶⒺ ⊡ ⊚ ⟱ ⚲ ▤ ⅋ ⟡ ⟡ ⚓

Location: In the CBD, opposite the Botanic Gardens. Extraordinarily attentive service is the hallmark of this smaller luxury hotel, which is the first to be operated by the Ritz-Carlton chain outside the US. Although the old-world charm of the restored stately government building that the Ritz-Carlton occupies can sometimes appear a little forced, the attention that guests receive more than makes up for it.

RUSHCUTTER TRAVELODGE

110 Bayswater Rd., Rushcutters Bay, NSW, 2011 ☎*331 2171* ⓕ*71524* ⓕ*360 4439. Map 4D6* ▥ *113 rms* ▰ ⇶ ⒶⒺ ⊕ ⓞ ⓦ ⩜ ⬛ ⊟ ⫿ ⫯ ⩳ ⛄

Location: In a quiet cul-de-sac overlooking picturesque Rushcutters Bay, within 3km (2 miles) of the city center. The main attraction here is the hotel's proximity to fashionable Double Bay, with its expensive boutiques and café life, and the beaches of the eastern suburbs. The TraveLodge stable has established a generally high reputation in the Pacific region for good value, and this is no exception. The hotel's **Waterview** restaurant has delightful views over Rushcutters Bay.

RUSSELL ✿

143A George St., Circular Quay, Sydney, NSW, 2000 ☎*241 3543* ⓕ*252 1652. Map 3B3* ▱ *30 rms* ⒶⒺ ⊕ ⓞ ⓦ

Location: The Rocks. Despite having few of the facilities required by business travelers, the Russell can confidently be recommended to anyone who appreciates the special pleasures that only a small establishment can offer. It was built in 1887 and is furnished in keeping with the period, but with a modern touch of great care and charm. Each room is different, offering a refreshing change from the conformity of large hotel chains. Besides the inclusive continental breakfast, light lunches and snacks are available during the day. Guests can watch the passing parade from the roof-top garden. One drawback: some rooms lack private bathrooms.

SEBEL TOWN HOUSE

23 Elizabeth Bay Rd., Sydney, NSW, 2011 ☎*358 3244* ⓕ*20067* ⓕ*357 1926. Map 4D6* ▥ *165 rms* ▰ ⇶ ⒶⒺ ⊕ ⓞ ⓦ ⩜ ⩳ ⊟ ⫿ ⫯ ⩲ ⛄

Location: On a quiet street in Elizabeth Bay, a few kilometers from the city and a stone's throw from Kings Cross. This hotel has fine views of the yachting basin, and is appreciated by celebrity visitors for its discretion and polished efficiency. The rooms are decorated with taste, and the suites, one of which was designed by Hardy Amies, are the height of simple elegance. The **Encore** restaurant claims to be able to prepare whatever a guest desires.

SHERATON WENTWORTH

61-101 Phillip St., Sydney, NSW, 2000 ☎*230 0700* ⓕ*121227* ⓕ*227 9133. Map 3C3* ▥ *443 rms* ⇶ ⒶⒺ ⊕ ⓞ ⓦ ⩜ ⩳ ⊟ ⫿ ⛄

Location: In the heart of the central business district. One of Sydney's old-established hotels, now managed by an international chain. It obviously has the business clientele in mind, with its facilities for large conferences. The rooms have been given the full Sheraton treatment, while retaining the Wentworth's unusual Art Deco curved bathrooms with marble floors. The main **Garden Court** restaurant overlooks an attractive willow tree garden.

SOUTHERN CROSS

Corner of Elizabeth St. and Goulburn St., Sydney, NSW, 2000 ☎*2820987* ⓕ*26324* ⓕ*211 1806. Map 3E3* ▥ *183 rms* ▰ ⇶ ⒶⒺ ⊕ ⓞ ⓦ ⩜ ⩳ ⊟ ⫿ ⫯ ⛄

Location: In the city center, close to Chinatown and the Entertainment Centre. Opened in 1983, having been tastefully converted from an old city office building, the Southern Cross has gained a reputation for fine service. An unusual feature is the **Cartoon Bar**, where the pick of Australian satirical humor is displayed.

SYDNEY BOULEVARD

90 William St., Sydney, NSW, 2011 ☎*357 2277* ⓕ*24350* ⓕ*356 3786. Map 4D4* ▥ *300 rms* ▰ ⇶ ⒶⒺ ⊕ ⓞ ⓦ ⩳ ⊟ ⫿ ⫯ ⩲ ⛄

Location: Between the city and Kings Cross. The Australian flagship of the

Southern Pacific Hotel group, this is one of Sydney's best hotels, with a young and courteous staff. It is hard to imagine that anyone would want to leave the *à la carte* restaurant on the 25th floor, as the outlook is genuinely breathtaking, giving an uninterrupted bird's-eye view of Hyde Park and the harbor; the food is highly regarded too, having won local awards. The **Williams** supper club offers *à la carte* dining as well as a disco.

WYNYARD TRAVELODGE
7-9 York St., Sydney, NSW, 2000 ☎*299 3000* ☒*26690* ☒*262 2416. Map 3C2*

▥ *205 rms* ⇔ ⇰ ▣ ▣ ▣ ▥ ▤ ♈
♨
Location: In the heart of the city, close to the main shops, and a few mins' walk from the historic Rocks area and Circular Quay. An informal, cheerful atmosphere, if sometimes a bit flurried because of its popularity with group tours. Features include a club lounge, exclusive to guests and friends; the **Kache** international restaurant on the 22nd floor, overlooking the city and harbor; and the more informal **Café on York**, a good place for observing Sydney folk.

Dining out

Sydney, once scorned by visitors as one of the world's great culinary deserts, has in the past decade welcomed an astonishing array of good restaurants. Indeed, food has been one of the city's major growth industries, stimulated by immigrant arrivals since World War II, bringing with them the cuisines of not only France, Italy and Greece, but those too of Lebanon, Vietnam, Malaysia and Thailand. The Australian palate has in the process been greatly educated.

Prices are mostly extremely reasonable, particularly by comparison with other service industries, and the overall standard is highly respectable — as it should be, given the quality of the available ingredients. The bounty of the sea, for example, is one of NSW's blessings.

The "ethnic" restaurants — Vietnamese and Thai, for example — often offer the best value. Many of these places are BYO unlicensed establishments to which you are invited to take your own liquor.

BALKAN II ♧
215 Oxford St., Darlinghurst ☎*331 7670. Map 4E4* ▥ ▭ ▣ ▣ ▣ ▥ *Last orders 11pm. Closed Mon. BYO license.*
A lively, crowded, fun place which, although a bit noisy, is nevertheless one of the best-value eateries in town. A large variety of charcoal grills is served, with fish being a particular favorite (try the grilled calamari with thick garlic sauce). A couple of doors down is the original **Balkan**, which only differs in not serving fish dishes.

BANGKOK
234 Crown St., Darlinghurst ☎*361 4804. Map 4E4* ▥ ▭ ▣ ▣ ▣ ▥ *Last orders*

9.30pm. Lunch Thurs and Fri 12.30-3.30pm; dinner Tues-Sat 6.30-10pm.
Thai food, sometimes subtle and aromatic, sometimes fiery and robust, is at last being given the recognition it is due. Many Thai restaurants in Australia follow a routine yet successful formula, and this is one of the best — certainly in Sydney.

BAYSWATER BRASSERIE ♧
32 Bayswater Rd., Kings Cross ☎*357 2177. Map 4D5* ▥ ▭ ▥ ⇰ ▣ ▥ *Open Mon-Fri noon-midnight; Sat-Sun 10am-midnight. Last orders 11.15pm.*
This is one of Sydney's smartest eating places, and although fashions change

so rapidly among the local socialites that it might be out of date next year, the food here is good enough to ensure that it will continue to satisfy its patrons. Careful attention to detail and a real concern for food are its strongest virtues. The decor, aimed at reproducing a French atmosphere, might strike some as too studied, but you can be assured of a good night out.

BEROWRA WATERS INN
Berowra Waters, 35km (21 miles) N ☎456 1027 ▦ ▬ ▬ ◈ AE ⬤ 🔲 VISA *Lunch Fri-Sat from 12.30pm, Sun from noon. Dinner Fri-Sat from 7.30pm. Closed Mon-Thurs.*

A ferry-ride across the Berowra Creek, an inlet of the Hawkesbury River N of Sydney, will bring you to what a number of Sydney folk swear is the finest restaurant in Australia. This may or may not be too grand a claim, but it is by common consent the best around Sydney. The Berowra serves French cuisine and changes its set menu every day. The prices are intimidating by Sydney standards, as is the distance of the drive home afterwards, but there is never a shortage of eager patrons, and reservation in advance is always necessary.

CHEZ OZ
23 Craigend St., Darlinghurst ☎332 4866. Map 4E5 ▦ ▭ AE ⬤ 🔲 VISA *Lunch Tues-Fri 12.30-3pm; dinner Tues-Sat 7pm-midnight. Last orders 10pm.*

One of the most imaginative and successful of Sydney's restaurants. This unashamedly Antipodean establishment was actually started by a family from Melbourne, who in the process may have made a point about restaurant standards in the two cities. The decor and exuberantly modern style of the place are distinctive, and, of course, the food — innovative and local — is good too.

CLAUDE'S
10 Oxford St., Woollahra ☎331 2325. Map 6C5 ▦ ▬ ▬ *No cards. Last orders 9pm. Closed Sun, Mon.*

For a gastronomic treat you can't do better in Sydney. The monthly Festival de la Fine Bouche draws gourmets who have otherwise given up on eating out, and its milk-fed goat sent the competition back to the cutting-board — not for the first time. Don't bother unless you have reserved.

CLEVELAND
63 Bay St., Double Bay ☎327 6877. Map 6C5 ▦ ▭ ▬ Y AE ⬤ 🔲 VISA *Lunch daily noon-3pm; dinner Sun-Thurs 6-11pm and Fri-Sat 6pm-midnight.*

Among the city's finest Chinese restaurants. This long-established favorite in trendy Double Bay receives praise for both its service and its innovative dishes. Enjoy the crisp-fried shredded beef, abalone with snowpea leaf, and heavenly mudcrab braised with chilli.

DOYLE'S ON THE BEACH
11 Marine Parade, Watsons Bay ☎337 2007. Map 6C5 ▦ ▭ Y ▬ ◈ ⬤ 🔲 VISA *Last orders 9.15pm.*

A Sydney institution, Doyle's enormous popularity might leave some visitors a bit perplexed. But oysters and very fresh fish and chips (French fries) are a firm favorite with Australians, and the Doyle family were frying fish long before anyone else here. Although there may now be more restaurants of this kind, few can match the location.

EJ'S
143 Macquarie St. ☎247 8558. Map 3C3 ▭ ▬ AE ⬤ 🔲 VISA *Lunch Mon-Fri noon-3pm. Breakfast and dinner functions by reservation.*

Something of a city institution, this fast and efficient restaurant has become a favorite of Sydney's politicians, money-dealers, and lawyers. Chef-owner Ron Hughes and his staff pride themselves on a French-styled menu that has a distinctly Aussie accent. It seats 60, and there is a private function room for 30 others.

FINE BOUCHE
191 Palmer St., East Sydney ☎331 4821. Map 4D4 ▦ ▭ Y ▬ AE ⬤ 🔲 VISA

Lunch Wed and Fri noon-2.30pm; dinner Tues-Sat 7-10pm.

Tony Bilson, who helped build the reputation of the Berowra Waters Inn, produces excellent, traditional French fare in this small, unpretentious restaurant. It is essential to reserve.

IMPERIAL PEKING HARBOURSIDE
15 Circular Quay, West, The Rocks ☎247 7073. Map 3B3 ▦ ▭ ▬ ▬ ⋘ AE ⬥ ◉ ▥ Last orders 10.15pm.

Set in an old restored warehouse in the historic Rocks area, the Imperial Peking not only boasts fine views of the harbor but some very superior, and expensive, food, and is, by general consent, Sydney's best Chinese restaurant. It specializes in seafood dishes of perfect freshness, in the admirable Chinese tradition, and has dinner "on the fin" in tanks waiting for a customer. This is one of four Imperial Peking restaurants in Sydney, and there's another in Manly.

KABLE'S
The Regent, 199 George St. ☎238 0000. Map 3C3 ▦ ▭ ▬ ▬ Y ▬ ⬤ AE ⬥ ◉ ▥ Last orders 10.30pm.

French-Canadian chef Serge Dansereau clearly delights in exploring the luxurious possibilities of local seafood, meats, cheese and fruit. Kable's offers grand hotel dining with light, innovative dishes. This is the perfect place for that special night out.

MARIGOLD ♥
299-305 Sussex St. ☎264 6744. Map 3E2 ▭ ▭ ▬ Y AE ⬥ ◉ ▥ Last orders 10.30pm.

Chinese diners are much in evidence here, particularly at lunchtime when the specialty of the house is yum cha, a meal consisting of a dazzling variety of savory oddments — dough and pastry with delicious fillings, which come in a seemingly endless procession of little bamboo baskets. The rest of the menu is also of a high standard.

MIXING POT ♥
178 St Johns Rd., Glebe ☎660 7449. Map 6C4 ▭ ▭ AE ⬥ ◉ ▥ Last orders

8.30pm. Closed Sat lunch; Sun; hols. BYO license.

Outdoor dining adds to the informal atmosphere of this old-established Italian favorite. The Mixing Pot is situated in the Glebe area (which has a remarkable number of restaurants). There are daily specials.

OASIS SEROS
495 Oxford St., Paddington ☎361 3377. Map 4F5 ▦ ▬ Y ▬ AE ⬥ ◉ ▥ Lunch Fri noon-2.30pm; dinner Tues-Sat 7-10pm.

The essential restaurant for the adventurous gourmet. Chef-owner Phillip Searle sometimes travels to surrealistic extremes in his presentation of what may be the most creative cuisine in Australia. This is not a place for the faint-hearted. Among the delights have been the seafood and noodle soups, salmis of pigeon braised with chestnuts, and heart-shaped tuna steak embraced by a fine dill-flecked pastry. Reservation is a must.

RAPHAEL'S
Ramada Renaissance, Level 2, 30 Pitt St ☎259 7000 ▦ △ ▭ ▬ Y AE ⬥ ◉ ▥ Lunch Mon-Fri noon-2.30pm; dinner Tues-Sat 7-11pm.

The emphasis is on luxury in all areas in this upmarket hotel dining room. Tables, elegantly spaced across a richly carpeted room, focus on displays of caviar and crystal. The food, modern Australian with a subtle Asian tang, is as exhilarating to the eye as to the tastebuds. The service is predictably first class.

LA RUSTICA ♥
435 Parramatta Rd., Leichardt ☎569 5824. Map 6C4 ▭ ▭ AE ⬥ ◉ ▥ Lunch Mon-Sat noon-3pm; dinner Mon-Sat 6-10pm. Closed Sun.

This Italian restaurant is situated a little out of town, in the heart of the Italian community. The food is simple, hearty fare, and as the restaurant is well patronized, seating can be tight when things get busy, as they often do — so reserve ahead.

119

SUNTORY

529 Kent St. ☎267 2900. Map 3E2 ▥
▢ ▥ ▱ ♈ ⌁ ≪ ⒜⒠ ⊡ ⓪ ⥂ *Last orders 10pm. Closed Sun; hols.*

This is the best Japanese restaurant in Sydney, and also among the most expensive of any type. It is full of businessmen clinching big deals — and Japanese, to whom it may actually seem cheap.

TAYLOR'S ♣

203-205 Albion St., Surry Hills ☎361 5100. Map 3F3 ▥ ▱ ▱ ⒜⒠ ⊡ ⓪ ⥂ *Lunch Fri 12.30-3.30pm; dinner Tues-Sat 7.30pm-midnight. Last orders 9.45pm.*

What sounds like a Devonshire tea-room is actually a superb North Italian restaurant. It gets top marks for the setting, as well as the food.

THE WHARF ♣

Pier 4, Hickson Rd., Millers Point ☎250 1761. Map 3B2 ▥ ▢ ♈ ≪ ⒜⒠ ⊡ ⓪ ⥂ *Last orders 11pm. Closed Sun.*

It is difficult to imagine any better value in Sydney than lunch at The Wharf, which is attached to the Sydney Theatre Company's residential stage. It is a bit out-of-the-way, but quite accessible for those who have been walking in THE ROCKS in the morning.

Entertainment

There is no need ever to be bored in Sydney. If by day it is the sheer beauty of the place that holds the attention, at night the energy and determination with which her inhabitants set about letting off steam are both remarkable and infectious.

Over the past 20 years, Sydney has established itself as a much-favored city on the international entertainment circuit, attracting the headliners of popular and classical music. But if Pavarotti, Harry Connick Jnr or INXS are not your bag, then take a look around. Sydney has 22 major theaters, a changing feast of cabaret shows and, around Kings Cross and Oxford Street, a swag of nightclubs and pubs with rock bands. On balmy summer nights, folk, jazz and rock music wafts from bars in Paddington, Balmain and The Rocks.

The best spot-guide to what is happening in the entertainment world is the *Sydney Morning Herald* newspaper. There is a comprehensive guide every day, and the Friday edition has a pull-out section called *Metro,* which outlines weekend attractions. The *Herald* also has a sharp nose for which nightclub is the current hot spot.

Performing arts

Opera, theater, and classical music all have strong followings. The AUSTRALIAN OPERA is a touring company, but spends most of the time at its incomparable local headquarters. While theater is variable as well as varied, SYDNEY THEATRE COMPANY productions can be relied upon. The youthful AUSTRALIAN CHAMBER ORCHESTRA receives rave reviews in Europe when it tours and is now gaining the recognition it deserves at home. The **A.C.O.**, **Musica Viva** (a chamber music company with an extensive educational wing), and the **Sydney Symphony Orchestra** all attract enthusiastic audiences to the Opera House.

AUSTRALIAN CHAMBER ORCHESTRA

50 Darlinghurst Rd., Kings Cross ☎357 4111. Map 4D5.

Young violinist Richard Tognetti has led this talented ensemble on extensive tours of Europe, Asia, and North and South America. Their appearances with John Williams, Barry Tuckwell and Australian soprano Yvonne Kenny have attracted glowing reviews in England, Austria and Yugoslavia. At the *Musikverein* in Vienna, that city's exacting critics were unanimous in praise. On home territory, under the sails of the SYDNEY OPERA HOUSE, you can expect a mix of traditional and innovative.

AUSTRALIAN OPERA

Opera House, Bennelong Point
☎information 250 7111, reservations 20525. Map 3B3 ☎ ᴀᴇ ◉ ◍ ᵛⁱˢᵃ

The national company is in residence at the Opera House twice a year, the summer season generally running from January to February and the winter season from June to October. Opera and Australia go together like oysters and lemon, and the country has a tradition of producing great sopranos, from Melba to Sutherland. Among spectacular recent successes have been performances of *Der Rosenkavalier* and the Elijah Moshinsky *Rigoletto*.

SYDNEY DANCE COMPANY

Pier 4, Hickson Rd., Millers Point ☎221 4811. Map 3B2.

Choreographer Graeme Murphy's innovative and dynamic young ensemble, who perform in both modern and classical styles, have changed the face of dance in Australia, and have also made an impact abroad. When the company is not touring, its main theater is the Opera House.

SYDNEY THEATRE COMPANY

Wharf Theatre, Pier 4, Hickson Rd., Millers Point ☎250 1777. Map 3B2 ☎ ᴀᴇ ◉ ᵛⁱˢᵃ

The city's premier drama company divides its time between two theaters. The Opera House theater is used for the big productions with popular appeal, and the Wharf, which is the STC's residential base, is used for staging new or experimental work. The STC is an eclectic outfit, and in recent seasons it has received acclaim with productions that range from the première run of David Williamson's play *Money and Friends* to a traditional *Much Ado About Nothing*. One of its big hits was Karin Mainwaring's *The Rain Dancers,* which starred film actor Bryan Brown. For pre-show meals, the **Wharf** restaurant (see DINING OUT) is highly recommended.

121

Nightlife

Wit and humor go down best, and there are enough club and pub cabarets featuring stand-up comics for a city twice the size. The standard tends to be high too, because the bad or mediocre are certain to be massacred.

Biggest crowd-puller of all is the pub rock scene, with almost 100 bands (mainly part-timers) working the local circuit. The band names are frequently more inventive than the music, but everyone still seems to have fun.

THE BASEMENT
29 Reiby Pl., Circular Quay ☎ 27 9727. Map 3C3 ☿ ♩ ⊐ AE ⊙ CD VISA Open Mon-Sat 7pm-3am.
A long-established jazz club, where the music is good and the atmosphere informal.

BOURBON & BEEFSTEAK
24 Darlinghurst Rd., Kings Cross ☎ 358 1144. Map 4D5 ☿ ⊐ AE ⊙ CD VISA Open 24hrs.
A bar-cum-eatery renowned among Sydney's insomniacs and bitter-enders, who crowd here into the wee small hours. This is the place to come when the party has gone on until dawn and you are looking for somewhere to have a last bottle of wine with a huge cooked breakfast.

BURDEKIN BAR
2 Oxford St., Darlinghurst ☎ 331 1046. Map 4E4 ☿ AE ⊙ CD VISA Last orders Mon-Sat 2am; Sun midnight.
This fashionable nightspot is the place where the seriously stylish of Sydney come for a late-night drink with friends after dinner. The decor is big, white and minimalist, but the place has an established reputation for friendly, careful service.

JULIANA'S
Hilton Hotel, 259 Pitt St. ☎ 266 0610. Map 3D3 ☿ ⊙ ♩ 🏢 AE ⊙ CD VISA Open Tues-Sat 9pm-3am.
This club-within-a-hotel offers a stylish night out. Top entertainers, including international names, perform at the dinner show, followed by a late disco. Inevitably, reservations are essential.

KINSELAS
383 Bourke St., Darlinghurst ☎ 331 3100. Map 4E4 ⊙ ♩ ⊐ 🏢 AE ⊙ CD VISA Open 5pm-3am.
A number of subtle changes made recently have kept this lively Sydney nightspot among the most fashionable for the 18-to-30 age range for more than a decade now. Late-nighters take a macabre delight in raving away in what used to be one of the city's biggest funeral parlors.

There are three bars, a disco, and a cabaret-theater where acerbic home-grown comics like Wendy Harmer can be enjoyed.

KIRRIBILLI PUB THEATRE
Broughton St., Milson's Point ☎ 560 5093. Map 6C4 ☿ Open Thurs-Sat from 8pm.
Anarchic and wildly offbeat humor is top of the menu at this comedy spot, where acts stand up and take on the house.

ROGUES
16-18 Oxford Sq., Darlinghurst ☎ 332 1718. Map 4E4 ☿ AE ⊙ CD VISA Open Tues-Sat 9.30am-3am.
Another popular venue for the late-night diners. Attached to the **Rogues Streetons** restaurant, this traditional nightclub attracts a diverse group of customers.

SELINA'S
Coogee Bay Hotel, 253 Coogee Bay Rd. ☎ 665 0000. Map 4D5 ☿ Open Fri, Sat 8pm-2am.
Selina's is one of the liveliest and steamiest among Sydney's many pub-rock spots.

Where to shop

If money is no object, there isn't much that can't be bought in Sydney, where only food is particularly cheap. But there are bargains to be had at the duty-free shops that operate in the city, which are a great bonus for tourists.

For quality goods there are the big stores and shopping arcades in an area roughly bordered by Hunter St., Park St., George St. and Phillip St. Just out of the center are the specialty shops and boutiques of Paddington and Double Bay, as well as those farther N along Military Rd. on the Lower North Shore. However, the shops mentioned below are mainly located in the city center.

Normal shopping hours are Monday to Friday 9am-5pm (with late opening on Thursday until 9pm) and Saturday 9am-noon (department stores until 4pm).

ABORIGINAL ART
Aboriginal artifacts must be the most original items available to the shopper in Australia, but if your purchase is old and has a sacred relevance it would be best to get the vendor to inquire about an export permit.

ABORIGINAL ART CENTRE DREAMTIME GALLERY
Argyle Arts Centre, 18 Argyle St., The Rocks ☎ *27 1380. Map 3B3* 🆎 💠 💳 💳
Bark paintings, modern acrylic dot paintings, baskets and numerous other items are on sale here, varying dramatically in price. There is another branch *(7 Walker Lane, Paddington)*, which concentrates on older artifacts.

ABORIGINAL ARTISTS GALLERY
Civic House, 477 Kent St. ☎ *261 2929. Map 3D2* 🆎 💠 💳 💳
This knowledgeable gallery has interesting exhibitions, from fabric designs to modern paintings, as well as various artifacts and bark paintings.

ANTIQUES
The largest concentration of antique stores in Sydney is along Queen St., Woollahra, just off Oxford St. But there are also a number of large antique centers around the city. These are the two largest.

SYDNEY ANTIQUE CENTRE
531 South Dowling St., Surry Hills ☎ *360 7020* 💳 🆎 💠 💳 💳
There are about 50 stalls in this large converted warehouse and basement, covering a wide range of mainly Victorian furniture, and objects ranging from large cedar tables to silver sauceboats. A coffee shop serves light refreshments.

WOOLLAHRA GALLERIES
160 Oxford St., Woollahra ☎ *327 8840. Map 6C5* 💳 🆎 💠 💳 💳
These galleries extend over three floors, with a small restaurant in the basement. As with other Australian antique markets, most stalls are unattended: prospective buyers inquire at a central desk near the entrance.

AUSTRALIANA

Most department stores and shopping centers have the usual koalas and T-shirts and cheap, tacky bits and pieces, but the AUSTRALIAN MUSEUM GIFT SHOP has a more novel selection. There are also many craft centers, such as the **Argyle Arts Centre** and others in The Rocks, that offer something different.

AUSTRALIAN MUSEUM GIFT SHOP

Corner of William St. and College St. Map 3D3 & ☑ ⒶⒺ ⒸⒹ 🆅🆂🅰

Finger- and glove-puppets of Australian birds and animals; unusual, locally-made jewelry; pieces of Australian rock; and lots of books on Australian fauna and flora, are on sale here.

COO-EE

98 Oxford St., Paddington ☎ *332 1544. Map 4F5* ⒶⒺ ⒸⒹ 🆅🆂🅰

An emporium of interesting Australian crafts, including fabrics made by the Tiwi Aboriginal group from islands off the coast, near Darwin.

DEPARTMENT STORES

The department store is a great Australian tradition, which produced some striking 1920s-30s architecture, such as the GRACE BROTHERS store in The Broadway. The city branch of DAVID JONES claims to be the finest department store in the world.

DAVID JONES

Corner of Market St. and Elizabeth St., and corner of Market St. and Castlereagh St. ☎ *266 5544. Map 3D3* & ☑ ⒶⒺ ⒸⒹ 🆅🆂🅰

Australia's answer to Harrods (or any other of the world's great stores), the lavishly decorated, recently renovated Elizabeth St. store specializes in female fashions. Its less glamorous Castlereagh store, next door, sells men's attire.

GRACE BROTHERS

436 George St. ☎ *238 9111. Map 3D3* ☑ ⒸⒹ 🆅🆂🅰

One of the secrets of the Grace Bros. stores' success is the staff — they are always cheerful, friendly and most obliging. As you would expect, this is the chain's showpiece.

DUTY-FREE SHOPS

These shops give you the chance to look around for the best deal before buying duty-free. Anyone with an air ticket out of the country can purchase in the dozens of such shops, specializing in electronic and photographic equipment. **Downtown Duty Free** *(84 Pitt St.* ☎ *232 2566, map 3C3* ⒶⒺ Ⓒ ⒸⒹ 🆅🆂🅰*)* is recommended for camera equipment.

MARKETS

Sydney's markets are hardly in the same league as its department stores, but they are pleasant enough places to while away a sunny afternoon.

BALMAIN MARKET
Corner of Darling St. and Curtis Rd., Balmain. Map 6C4 📺

In the grounds of St Andrew's Church. An untidy mixture of secondhand junk and the odd real antique, but it can be good fun. Open 7.30am-4pm Sat only.

PADDINGTON VILLAGE CHURCH BAZAAR
Village Church, Oxford St., Paddington. Map 6C4.

In fashionable Paddington (and near to Woollahra): a colorful, lively collection of innovative creations by young designers, together with secondhand clothes. Open 9am-4pm on Saturday only.

PADDY'S MARKET
Hay Street, Haymarket. Map 3E3.

There is a fruit and vegetable section as well as a large number of stalls selling cheap clothes, shoes, toys and other items. Open on Saturday and Sunday.

SHOPPING ARCADES

There are numerous centers crammed with expensive boutiques. A selection of the better ones is listed below.

BIRKENHEAD POINT
Cary St., Drummoyne ☎*81 3922. Map 6C4* ♿ 📺 ✴

This complex is situated on a peninsula overlooking the harbor, just a short drive out of the city.

CENTREPOINT
Corner of Market St. and Pitt St. ☎*231 6222. Map 3D3* ♿ 📺

Close to both the GRACE BROTHERS and DAVID JONES department stores, this center has four levels of nearly 200 shops, with the accent on modernity.

QUEEN VICTORIA BUILDING
455 George St. ☎*264 9209. Map 3D3* ♿ 📺 🄰🄴 🄾 🄲🄱

Erected to celebrate the jubilee of Queen Victoria in 1893, this truly glorious Victorian edifice was actually threatened with demolition in the 1950s. Now that it has been restored, it houses more than 200 shops, from the stylish **Bunda Fine Antiques** to the colorful clothes of Australian designer Jenny Kee. Fast food is available 24 hours a day.

STRAND ARCADE
George St., between King St. and Market St. ☎*232 4307. Map 3D3* 📺

Until the restoration of the QUEEN VICTORIA BUILDING, this arcade was considered to be the city's most elegant. Carefully reconstructed after a fire some years ago, it now accommodates some of Sydney's top clothes designers, and a delightful little shop that specializes in buttons.

SYDNEY ENVIRONS

Key to map symbols is located in HOW TO USE THIS BOOK

Excursions (1): Environs of Sydney

A number of Sydney's most striking attractions are outside the city proper. The following is a selection of places that, generally speaking, are close enough to Sydney to be quite easily encompassed inside a day. Combinations are possible. In one day's journey w of the city you could see both PARRAMATTA and WINDSOR. A tour of the HAWKESBURY RIVER could be turned into a full-blown excursion. In all cases, frankly, a car is necessary.

CAPTAIN COOK'S LANDING PLACE PARK

Captain Cook Drive, Kurnell, about 45km (28 miles) s of Sydney ☎ *668 9923. Map 6E5* 🔳 🚣 *Open 7am-7pm; museum 10.30am-4.30pm. Best by car; or slowly, by train to Cronulla, then bus to Kurnell.*

This historical site at Kurnell in Botany Bay tends to be overlooked, by locals as well as foreigners, possibly because it is a bit out of the way. This should not deter you, for despite industrial development, which blemishes the bay, the Landing Place Park is a pleasant and well-kept spot. It is within a half-hour's drive of the city, but allow longer if traveling by public transportation. Wood is provided for barbecuing; you can picnic and swim within sight of the spot where Cook first set foot on the Great South Land in 1770.

The small **museum** is a bonus attraction, illuminating the voyage of the *Endeavour,* and the lives of Cook and others who accompanied him in his discoveries.

GOSFORD

85km (52 miles) N of Sydney. By car, via Route 1.

Scenic and historic interest are the basis for this full-day excursion to the **Brisbane Water** region. Gosford itself has little to draw the visitor, but is a convenient center for the tour.

After crossing the HARBOUR BRIDGE (see SIGHTS) northbound, follow signs to the Pacific Highway and Hornsby. Join the Sydney-Newcastle tollway, which offers panoramic views of the Australian bush *en route* to Gosford.

Old Sydney Town *(Pacific Hwy, Somersby* ☎ *(043) 40 1104* 🔳 *open Wed-Sun 10am-5pm),* which is signposted from the first Gosford turn-off, is a living-theater reconstruction of the early days of the penal colony, featuring Redcoats and convicts, floggings and duels, and tall-masted ships in the harbor. There are picnic facilities and a restaurant.

Just N of Gosford on Route 83, you can visit **Eric Worrell's Reptile Park** *(* ☎ *(043) 28 4311* 🔳 *open 10am-6pm),* which has platypuses as well as deadly taipans, pythons and crocodiles. Check times of daily "milking" of venomous snakes.

Back in Gosford, before heading for the beach you might call in at **Henry Kendall Cottage** *(off Brisbane Water Drive* ☎ *(043) 25 2270* 🔳 *open Wed and weekends 10am-4pm),* a museum dedicated to a 19thC

Australian poet. Beaches that are within easy reach of Gosford include **Forresters** *(about 20km/12 miles N)*, **Terrigal** and **Avoca** *(about 16km/10 miles W)*.

Within 5km (3 miles) of Gosford, off Route 83 back to Sydney, **Brisbane Waters National Park** *(☎ (043) 24 4911 ▨ open sunrise-sunset)* offers views, walking and picnicking.

➡ On the way back to the city, you can visit one of Australia's best restaurants, the **Berowra Waters Inn** (see DINING OUT on page 118).

HAWKESBURY RIVER
50km (31 miles) N of Sydney. By car, via Route 1.

The first tentative steps of exploration in New South Wales were up the Hawkesbury River, and some of the earliest settlements were established along its banks. The river remains a scenic and historic highway to the interior, which can be seen by car, or at greater leisure by renting a cabin cruiser.

The following is a suggested one-day excursion around the mouth of the river. An itinerary for a tour of the historic towns on the upper reaches will be found under WINDSOR.

KU-RING-GAI CHASE NATIONAL PARK, on the banks of the Hawkesbury, is a convenient starting point. Cross the HARBOUR BRIDGE (see SIGHTS) northbound, following Route 1 (the Pacific Highway) to Hornsby and Mt. Colah, the entrance to the park. Ku-ring-gai has numerous walking trails, along with good picnic and barbecue sites. A recommended spot is **Cottage Point**, which is situated on the river; more information is available from the National Parks office *(☎ 457 9853)* at the entrance.

PALM BEACH is easily reachable from Ku-ring-gai Chase. To get there, follow the main road in the park, McCarr's Creek Rd., eastward until it joins the Barrenjoey Rd. Turn left (N) for Palm Beach. This splendid stretch of sand, 50km (31 miles) N of Sydney, is a favorite of the young and wealthy. Ideal for a comfortable day's excursion, it offers a moderate surf and, between the patrol flags, safe swimming. Nude swimming is permitted at the northern end.

Palm Beach lies at the edge of the Hawkesbury. From here ferries ply around the coves and inlets at the river mouth. An hourly service, starting at 9am, runs around one of the largest of these coves, the **Pittwater**, from the Public Wharf at **Pittwater Park** *(☎ 918 2747)*. It calls at a number of pleasant beaches that are actually in the Ku-ring-gai park, including the **Basin** (camping available) and **Great Mackerel Beach**, especially suitable for families. Ferries depart from the same wharf for **Patonga**, on the northern bank of the Hawkesbury, at 9am, 11am and 3.45pm.

More extensive river trips can be made by renting cabin cruisers and houseboats. This is an option well worth considering, as the Hawkesbury is not only a great river passing through some majestic scenery, but the most historic of Australia's waterways. The first governor, Arthur Phillip, explored it in 1789. Twenty years later, Governor Lachlan Macquarie compared the Hawkesbury with the Thames, and saw it as a civilizing highway into the interior.

129

No sailing license is required for renting a boat. Three days is quite enough for a leisurely trip as far as WINDSOR, about 140kms (88 miles) upstream. Standard equipment on cabin cruisers includes cooker, refrigerator, cutlery, crockery, 2-way radio and depth sounder. Details are available from **Halvorsen Boats** (☎ *457 9011*). Houseboats are slightly cheaper, from **Able Hawkesbury River Houseboats** (☎ *(045) 66 4299*).

Captain Cook Cruises (☎ *27 4548* Ⓣ🅇 *72316*) has 4-night trips up the river on the cruise vessel *Lady Hawkesbury*. One-day cruises run downstream from Windsor daily: for details, contact **Windsor River Cruises** (☎ *621 4154*).

KOALA PARK
84 Castle Hill Rd., West Penant Hills, 26km (16 miles) w of Sydney ☎484 3141. Map 5A2 🆇 ▣ ☀ ➤ Open 9am-5pm. By bus, Ansett Pioneer run full-day tours including the Blue Mountains ☎268 1881.

The continent's most cuddly inhabitants are a favorite with visitors. There are about 30 of them in 4ha (10 acres) or so of wildlife park, and feedings, with commentary by a member of staff, are held four times daily. The park also has other indigenous animals — kangaroos, wallabies, wombats and dingoes — and children can wander among the animals and feed them. WARATAH PARK ANIMAL RESERVE is a similar and in some respects better establishment, but the koala section here offers closer contact. But neither of these parks is close to the city or easily accessible by public transportation.

KU-RING-GAI CHASE NATIONAL PARK ★
Ku-ring-gai Chase Rd., Mt. Colah, 40km (24 miles) N of Sydney ☎457 9853 🆇 ⅄ ➤ ◁€ ✔▧ Open sunrise-sunset. By car, follow Route 1 across the Harbour Bridge to Hornsby and Mt. Colah.

This tract of splendid NSW bush, strung out along the banks and inlets of the HAWKESBURY RIVER, is the ideal place to take a picnic or barbecue food, and combine with a visit to WARATAH PARK ANIMAL RESERVE.

There are numerous animals in Ku-ring-gai too, including goanna lizards (an Aboriginal delicacy), koalas and possums. **Cottage Point** is an attractive spot for a picnic, and for launching off on a bush walk, either up the granite hills or following one of the creeks that flow into the river. More information on walks can be obtained from the National Parks office at the entrance, and they can give directions to Aboriginal rock engravings.

PALM BEACH ★
50km (31 miles) N of Sydney ➤ ◁€ By car, take the Harbour Bridge N, then follow Route 14 for Mosman, Manly, Dee Why, Narrabeen and Palm Beach.

This splendid stretch of sand, situated outside the city, makes an enjoyable and comfortable one-day excursion, and there are other good beaches to stop at along the way.

The main attractions of Palm Beach are its comparative quiet and the quality of its surf. There is nude swimming at the northern end, but newcomers are urged to swim only between the patrol flags, as the rip tides here are treacherous. A ferry-ride away you will find the safe, pleasant beaches of the **Basin** and **Great Mackerel Beach** in KU-RING-GAI CHASE NATIONAL PARK *(departures hourly 9am-4pm from the Public Wharf, Pittwater Park ☎ 918 2747)*.

PARRAMATTA

22km (13 miles) w of Sydney. Map 5B2. By car, via Route 32. By train, from Central station.
This busy extension of Sydney, which today has a population of 130,900, was founded in 1790 and is the second oldest European settlement in Australia. It has more than enough of interest to compensate for the drive required to get there, along what is arguably the ugliest stretch of road in Australia.

It can be a confusing place to find your way around, and it is worth stopping first at the **Tourist Bureau** *(corner of Prince Alfred Park and Market St. ☎ 630 3703)* for a map.

Parramatta was founded because the soil at Sydney Cove was unsuitable for growing vegetables, and the Experiment Farm was set up in 1798, literally to test the ground. Successful cultivation here by an ex-convict named James Ruse established that agriculture in the colony was viable. The **Experiment Farm Cottage**, built in the early 19thC *(9 Ruse St. ☎ 635 5655 ✉ open Tues-Thurs, Sun 10am-4pm)*, is also worth a visit.

If you visit only one historic building in NSW it should be **Old Government House** *(Parramatta Park ☎ 635 8149 ✉ opening hours as Experimental Farm Cottage— see above)*. It took some years to build, spanning the rule of three governors, and was completed in 1816 by Macquarie and his able aide, Francis Greenway. It was used as a boarding-house and a school, before being restored, first in 1909 and then in 1968. That work has now been tastefully accomplished, and the interiors are superb, with the colonial cedar furniture being a particular feature.

The **Elizabeth Farm House** *(Alice St. ☎ 635 9488 ✉ open Tues-Sun 10.30am-4pm)* is another early colonial building, lovingly restored.

The twin towers of **St John's Church** have been a distinctive feature of Parramatta since the 19thC, but the original 1804 structure has been added to.

➥ **Barnaby's** *(66 Phillip St. ☎ 633 3777 ▥)* is recommended for lunch.

ROYAL NATIONAL PARK ★

*Princes Hwy, Sutherland, 36km (22 miles) s of Sydney ☎ 542 0648 ▨ ▬ ✴ ◄
◄€ Open sunrise-sunset. By car, via Route 1, the Princes Hwy.*
This is an excellent spot in which to sample the pleasures of the Australian outdoors, with the comforts of Sydney not far away. The park has one or two magnificent beaches set amid tracts of bush. A car is

necessary, and you would do well to consult the parks official on entry, as there are numerous corners to explore.

Two suggestions follow. You could take a picnic hamper out on a weekday and follow the signs to **Wattamolla**, a lovely beach sheltered by cliff surrounds. Alternatively, stop at **Audley** on the Hacking River and rent a rowboat. Galahs, cockatoos and kingfishers inhabit the trees along the banks there, and a kilometer or so upstream it should begin to seem that you are in unexplored territory. (You can picnic anywhere along the bank.) This is one of the most pleasant ways to spend a sunny afternoon around Sydney.

WARATAH PARK ANIMAL RESERVE
Namba Rd., Terrey Hills, N of Sydney ☎ *450 2377* ▨ ▣ ✻ ◂▬ *Open 10am-5pm. By car, via Route 1, N to Terrey Hills.*
Australian animals are visible at close quarters here. You can wander in enclosures and feed kangaroos and emus, and there is also a koala enclosure, which makes it a good place for the obligatory Australian vacation snap. The park is a particular favorite with local youngsters, as it is the home of a wallaby named Skippy, a sort of Down Under television version of Lassie.

WINDSOR
56km (35 miles) NW of Sydney. By car, via Route 32 to Eastern Creek, then Route 61.
Windsor and its historic sister town of **Richmond** on the HAWKESBURY RIVER were among the first White settlements established after the founding of Sydney. Governor Macquarie clearly had the towns of England's River Thames in mind when he named them. As well as this easy one-day excursion by car, they can also be reached by river in a rented cabin cruiser (see HAWKESBURY RIVER). You can stop at the **Tourist Information Centre** *(Thompson Sq., Windsor* ☎ *(045) 77 2310, open 10am-4pm)* for a map. Thompson Sq. itself has some interesting Georgian buildings, such as the **Doctor's House**.

Other important buildings in Windsor include two designed by Francis Greenway, the **Courthouse** *(open Mon-Wed 10am-12.20pm; weekends 11am-noon, 1-4pm)* and **St Matthews Church**, dating from 1817, the oldest Anglican church in Australia. The nearby graveyard is worth a visit to let the old headstones tell their tales of pioneer life. At Richmond, the cemetery at **St Peters Church** is interesting.

▭ The **Richmond** *(315 Windsor St.* ☎ *(045) 78 3914* ▥ *open lunch Wed-Fri and Sun noon-2pm; dinner Wed-Sat from 6pm, last orders 9pm)* is recommended.

Excursions (2): Farther afield

Handsome a city as Sydney is, it gives no idea of the grandeur of the Australian countryside. Because the dimensions of internal travel are so vast, a great many Australians have never traveled outside their own home state, and the visitor can find himself intimidated into confining his stay to one locale. The following excursions are designed to show that much of beauty is accessible by car within a day or two of the city. With more time, various permutations indicated in the text become possible; for greater detail these should be discussed with the appropriate Visitor Centre.

It is as well to remember that although food and accommodations are in some cases as good as in Sydney, the general standard of service industries in the countryside is less exacting.

THE HUNTER VALLEY
430km (270-mile) round trip. Allow 2 days. Recommended stop: Pokolbin.
This excursion, to Australia's main wine-producing region, is popular on weekends, so aim for midweek and reserve accommodations in advance.

Cross the Harbour Bridge northbound and follow the Pacific Highway, Route 1. Then take the Sydney-Newcastle tollway, which is carved out of mountainside and offers magnificent views over KU-RING-GAI CHASE NATIONAL PARK and the HAWKESBURY RIVER; turn off the tollway for GOSFORD (see ENVIRONS for possible side-trips to all three), perhaps stopping at **Old Sydney Town** and following the signs to Peats Ridge. You are now at the start of the scenic route N to Cessnock, the main town of the Lower Hunter Valley.

The road, formerly the convict-built Great North Rd., dating from 1830, passes through settlements with characteristic Aboriginal names: Kulnura, Bucketty and Yalambie. To the W lies the **McPherson State Forest**, and a panorama of hills and bushland.

Wollombi, 30km (19 miles) SW of Cessnock, is a historic village much cherished by the National Trust. **St Michael's Church**, a sandstone structure, was built in 1843, and **St John's** dates from 1846. Almost every building in the village is from the last century, including the **courthouse** (1866), now a museum, and a **post office** (1850). It is a convenient as well as a picturesque spot for lunch.

The lovely, pastoral country here is set against a backdrop of the Watagan Mountains. It was once bushranger territory and also a ceremonial meeting place for local Aboriginal tribes. Wollombi is an Aboriginal word meaning "meeting of the waters."

Cessnock is an industrial town of little historic or architectural interest, but it is worthwhile to stop at the **Visitor Information Centre** *(Wollombi Rd. ☎ (049) 90-4477)* for information (including a map) on nearby **Pokolbin** (NW of Cessnock) and the vineyards of the Hunter Valley. Besides the scenery, the local wine is undoubtedly what makes the region worth visiting.

133

The Hunter Valley is Australia's oldest commercial wine-producing region: the **Wyndham** estate was established as long ago as 1828. What was once the hobby of a few gentleman growers, however, has expanded to become an important industry, ever since Australians and foreigners started becoming alert, around 15 years ago, to the quality of the local produce.

The custom here is to arm yourself with a map of the Pokolbin region showing the location of the 30 or so wineries, and to stop at a number of chosen establishments, where you are invited to taste and discuss wine with informed staff. You then make your way, carefully, back to your accommodations for a nap before dinner. Food and drink are among the pleasures of Pokolbin, and several recommendations are given at the end of this excursion.

The Lower Hunter has some of the country's biggest producers, and a few small establishments that turn out wines — good whites in particular — that are not available from retail outlets. The larger vineyards include **Tyrrells Vineyard** *(Broke Rd. ☎ (049) 98 7509, open Mon-Sat 8am-5pm)* and **McWilliams** *(Mt. Pleasant, Marrowbone Rd. ☎ (049) 98 7505, open 10am-4pm daily).* Among small producers offering a limited range of excellent wines and friendly, personal advice are **Petersons Vineyard** *(Mt. View Rd. ☎ (049) 90 1704, open daily)* and **Allanmere** *(Lovedale Rd. ☎ (049) 30 7387, also open daily).*

For a tour of the valley, the remainder of the day after arriving in the area from Sydney and the following morning are usually sufficient. It is pleasant countryside to see by bicycle. These can be rented at the **Trading Post** *(Broke Rd.)*, although the distances would make a serious bicycle tour of the wineries a hard slog. For horseback riding, inquire at the **Visitor Information Centre** at Cessnock.

What you do on leaving Pokolbin is a matter of choice. The following are a few options.

The Upper Hunter, centered on **Singleton** and **Muswellbrook**, is the gateway to New England, in the N of the state, which, with its green pastures, trout streams and the university town of **Armidale**, is indeed akin to the mother country. To the E of Armidale is some lovely, rugged country, riven by gorges, where good rainbow trout are to be caught in rivers with names such as the **Styx** and the **Guy Fawkes**. Bear in mind the distances, however. Armidale is 560km (350 miles) N of Sydney, and **Tenterfield**, at the top end of the New England region, is 750km (469 miles) away. If you are coming this far, telephone the **Tourist Information Centre** at Armidale *(☎ (067) 738 527)* for information on accommodations, fishing and any other details.

☜ **Peppers Guest House** *(Ekerts Rd. ☎ (049) 98 7596 Ⅲ⎕)* is a pleasant colonial-style guesthouse, tastefully kept, with good views and thoughtfully prepared food: it is recommended, although on weekends heavily reserved. The **Brokenback Motor Lodge** *(Hermitage Rd. ☎ (049) 98 7777 Ⅲ⎕)* has modern facilities and is both comfortable and popular. The **Pokolbin Wine Village Inn** *(Broke Rd. ☎ (049) 98 7600 Ⅲ⎕)* is a resort suitable for families.

☰ **Casuarina** *(Hermitage Rd. ☎ (049) 98 7562 Ⅲ⎕); **Blaxlands** *(Broke Rd. ☎ (049) 98 7550 Ⅲ⎕).*

THE SOUTHERN HIGHLANDS

370km (230-mile) round trip. Allow 2 days. Recommended stop: at entrance to Southern Highlands. Take a swimsuit.

Leave the city driving w on the hideous Parramatta Rd. as far as Ashfield, then turn left onto the Hume Highway. At Liverpool the industrial concentration starts to thin out, and you join the South Western Freeway, Route 31. In normal circumstances you should be in Mittagong, gateway to the Southern Highlands, in 2 hours or so.

Mittagong has numerous craft stores, but your main purpose here should be to visit the regional **Tourist Information Centre** *(Winifred West Park* ☎ *(048) 71 2888),* which can provide current advice, detailed information, and licenses to fish for trout in the highlands.

Bowral, just s and adjacent to Mittagong, is a garden township of great charm. Founded in 1860, it has some attractive colonial homes but no building of major architectural distinction. For lovers of cricket, the town's most distinguished building is at **28 Glebe St.**, the home of the young Donald Bradman. This remains a private residence, and plans to build a museum to perhaps Australia's most famous son, at the **Bradman Oval** cricket ground opposite the house, have not yet borne fruit. Bowral's busiest time is the annual October Tulip Festival.

Just 11km (7 miles) w of Bowral is the historic village of **Berrima**. This important National Trust site is the best-preserved example of an early New South Wales settlement, though some visitors might find its quaintness somewhat contrived. The pretty location on the banks of the Wingecarribee River was surveyed in 1830, when Berrima was envisaged as an inland city.

The major buildings are within easy walking distance of Market Place, where you can park. They include the **Courthouse** (1838), containing a surprisingly tawdry trial tableau, and two truly lovely country churches, **St Francis Xavier** (Catholic, 1851), built in sandstone in Gothic-revival style, and **Holy Trinity** (Anglican, 1849), which has stained-glass windows of great antiquity, brought here from a church in Cornwall, England.

Other structures worth inspecting are the entrance to old **Berrima Gaol**, in which were incarcerated German prisoners of World War I, and which is still used as a training center for young offenders, and **Bellevue House**, a home in Georgian style. Sadly, the old **Anglican rectory** is not open to the public. There is no shortage of eating places and watering holes back in the center of town.

From Berrima drive w the 10km (6 miles) to **Moss Vale**. Here Route 48, the Illawarra Highway, starts for the Southern Highlands proper, and it is around here that you will be looking for a place to spend the night.

The tour now enters terrain where the interest is scenic rather than historic, for the Southern Highlands is an agglomeration of mountains, swirling mists, lakes, rivers and waterfalls. From Moss Vale take the road sw to **Exeter**, a charming village, and **Bundanoon**, an area so evocative of Scotland that the clans come here for their annual April gathering to toss cabers, hurl haggis and dance to the pipes.

Bundanoon is also the entrance to the **Morton National Park**, 130,000ha (320,000 acres) of startling mountain landscapes. There is a

135

campground near the entrance, leading to a number of lookout points: **Echo Point** is to be recommended.

From Bundanoon, head back toward Moss Vale but turn off just before the town and follow Route 79 SE to the **Fitzroy Falls**, a plunge of more than 100m (330 feet) in three stages over sandstone cliffs. A license obtained at the Mittagong Visitor Centre entitles the holder to fish for trout at the Fitzroy Falls reservoir.

Two options now present themselves. You can get back to Sydney by turning N for Robertson and the Illawarra Highway (although you should try to stop at the lovely **Belmore Falls**) and thence E on Route 48 to **Wollongong** and the coast. This takes you back to Sydney in between 2 and 3 hours by a different and scenic drive.

The second option is preferable if you can spare an extra half-day and fancy a side trip to the sea. Continue from the Fitzroy Falls on Route 79 to **Kangaroo Valley**, across the picturesque 19thC **Hampden Bridge**. The **Pioneer Farm**, a reconstructed dairy farm opposite the bridge, offers interesting insights into Australian rural life in the 19thC.

About 10km (6 miles) farther SE along Route 79, it is worth making the short detour to the lookout point of **Cambewarra** (an Aboriginal word meaning "Smoke coming out of mountain"), which on a clear day offers a spectacular view from the edge of the highlands, an altitude of 678m (2,224 feet), out to sea.

A few kilometers on join the Princes Highway, Route 1, and turn S for **Nowra**, an undistinguished port town, and **Jervis Bay**. The bay, a Royal Australian Navy base, has a number of excellent beaches, including **Huskisson**, where you can also get a good pub lunch. After a leisurely swim here, Sydney is 190km (119 miles) N and easily reachable by dinner.

Farther S along the coast are some of what are arguably the best beaches in Australia, and in season you might do well to think of extending your excursion. **Ulladulla** is only 225km (140 miles) S from Sydney, and the ever-popular **Bateman's Bay** is about 280km (175 miles) to the S. Nor are swimming and skin-diving the only attractions. In the 1930s, the American novelist Zane Grey visited the fishing center of **Bermagui**, 380km (238 miles) S of Sydney, and his subsequent accounts of heroic tussles with giant marlin remain undisputed classics of fishing literature.

🐟 The **Milton Park Country House** *(Hordens Rd., Bowral* ☎ *(048) 61 1522* ⅢⅢ*)* offers gracious country-estate accommodations in pastoral surroundings, although children aren't welcomed. The **Solar Springs Country Club** *(96 Osborne Ave., Bundanoon* ☎ *(048) 83 6027* ⅢⅢ*)*, a health retreat, provides natural foods and optional fitness activities. **Ranelagh House** *(Illawarra Highway, Robertson* ☎ *(048) 85 1111* Ⅲ*)* is a rambling, eccentric guesthouse whose shabbiness is offset by its grand highland setting; unlicensed. Or try the **Braemar Lodge** *(Hume Highway, North Mittagong* ☎ *(048) 71 2483* Ⅲ*)*.

🍽 All handy for lunch in the center of Berrima: the **Surveyor General Inn** (which, for students of trivia, is Australia's oldest continuously licensed hotel), the **Victoria Inn** and the **White Horse Inn**.

For dinner: **The Colonial Inn** *(Hume Hwy, Berrima* ☎ *(048) 77 1389* ⅢⅢ*)*; **Hume House** *(Hume Hwy, Mittagong* ☎ *(048) 71 1871* ⅢⅢ*)*.

THE BLUE MOUNTAINS

270km (170-mile) round trip. A long one-day excursion, or, if extended to Jenolan Caves or Windsor, recommended stop at Blackheath or nearby.

These mountains, part of the Great Dividing Range, once posed so formidable a barrier to the interior that early explorations from Sydney were by sea rather than land. In 1791 a group of convicts took to the interior believing that thither lay China, and freedom. It was not until 1813 that the range was crossed. Since then, the Blue Mountains have been a favorite Sydney escape.

Head W on Route 32 to PARRAMATTA (see ENVIRONS) and Penrith. At **Springwood**, 74km (46 miles) W of Sydney, is the handsome **country home** of Norman Lindsay, an artist whose bacchanalian fantasies once outraged his compatriots *(open Fri-Sun 11am-5pm* ☎*(047) 51 1067)*. Today it is the house and gardens rather than the pictures that make the detour worthwhile — and there is a very pleasant tearoom here.

Your main destination is the town of **Katoomba**, 105km (66 miles) W of Sydney. Katoomba and, to the E, the neighboring centers of **Leura** and **Wentworth Falls** are strung out over about 10km (6 miles) at the edge of the **Jamison Valley**, with spectacular views over the **Blue Mountains National Park**, the second-largest such park in the state.

In Katoomba there is a **Tourist Information Centre** *(Echo Point* ☎ *(047) 82 1833, open 9am-5pm)*, which is useful for a map of the area and advice on bushwalks. This is also a good vantage point for the region's most enduring symbol, a rock formation called the **Three Sisters**.

A kilometer or so to the W is the **Scenic Skyway**, a cable car across a gorge with panoramic views, among them another formation, **Orphan Rock**. Also along the valley's edge and clearly signposted are **Sublime Point** and **Inspiration Point**, both with commanding views. (Incidentally, it is the dispersal of oil from eucalyptus forests into the atmosphere, intensifying the effect of light refraction, that makes these mountains appear so blue.)

Worth seeing are two waterfalls, the **Wentworth Falls** and **Leura Cascades**. Also at Wentworth Falls, **Yester Grange** *(Yester Rd.* ☎ *(047) 57 1110, open Wed-Fri 10am-4pm; Sat, Sun 10am-5pm)* is a restored Victorian house of characteristic Australian design.

If you are returning to Sydney the same day, the excursion will probably end in Katoomba. But don't leave before tea and cake at the **Paragon** *(Katoomba St.* ☎ *(047) 82 2928)*, a genuine 1930s Art Deco refreshment parlor and a Blue Mountains institution. If you are staying on, however, two establishments in **Blackheath**, 10km (6 miles) NW of Katoomba, are recommended (see the end of this excursion) for truly excellent food and accommodations, if you can get a reservation.

From the Blue Mountains, you could drive on the next day to the **Jenolan Caves**, by road about 75km (47 miles) SW of Katoomba. Tours of these spectacular underground limestone caves are conducted from 9.30am-5pm *(* ☎ *(063) 59 3311)*.

After returning to Route 32, you have a choice of routes back to Sydney. You can go directly E; however, going N for 10km (6 miles) or so gives you the option of returning to the city on Route 40 via WINDSOR (see ENVIRONS OF SYDNEY) and, just before it, **Richmond**. Even allowing for a stop in these historic Hawkesbury towns, you should still be back comfortably by the end of the second day.

✒ ☎ Both highly recommended, for comfort and excellent French cuisine: the **Cleopatra Guest House** *(4 Cleopatra St., Blackheath* ☎ *(047) 87 8456* ▥), which has only five rooms, and the **Glenella Guest House** *(Govetts Leap Rd., Blackheath* ☎ *(047) 87 8352* ▥).

Alternatively, try the following: the **Carrington** *(Katoomba St., Katoomba* ☎ *(047) 82 1111* ▥), the region's most popular hotel since the turn of the century (reopening in December 1992 after restoration work); the **Hydro Majestic** *(Great Western Hwy, Medlow Bath* ☎ *(047) 88 1002* ▥), another grand old establishment; the **Victoria & Albert Guest House** *(Station St., Mt. Victoria* ☎ *(047) 87 1241* ▥).

Specialized accommodations for disabled people are provided by the **Santa Maria Holiday Centre for Handicapped People** *(253 Great Western Hwy, Lawson* ☎ *(047) 59 1116)*.

THE SNOWY MOUNTAINS

It can come as a surprise to discover that New South Wales has a winter sports region within 200km (125 miles) of surf-swept beaches. The "Snowies," as the region is known to Australians, is unlikely ever to spark an exodus from the European Alps, but it is unique in Australia, and by common consent has certainly one resort of international standard.

The Snowy Mountains are no hop, skip and jump from Sydney. By road it is a round trip of more than 1,000km (600 miles) to Thredbo, the best resort, and when time is pressing it has, really, to be reached by air. Thus, although the **Kosciusko National Park** contains some glorious scenery (**Mt. Kosciusko**, at 2,173m/7,129 feet), is Australia's highest peak), we will concentrate here on brief advice on how to go about taking a winter vacation in NSW.

Cooma *(Visitor Information Centre* ☎ *(064) 521108)* is the main center of the Snowy region, and has the only airport. Neither of the two major domestic airlines flies to Cooma, the only service being one daily flight (two in mid-season) by **Air New South Wales** *(reservations* ☎ *268 1242)*.

During the season, which lasts from June to October, **Ansett Pioneer** runs bus services the 80-90km (50-55 miles) from the airport to the main resorts, **Thredbo**, **Perisher Valley**, **Smiggin Holes** and **Charlotte Pass**. The trip takes around 90 minutes.

Thredbo has the only genuine giant slalom course in Australia and generally has the most advanced runs, although conditions are less predictable here early in the season. Perisher Valley offers settled conditions and is recommended for cross-country skiing. All resorts have skis for rent, instructors, ski-tows and chair lifts, and a range of hotels and motels.

Skiing is becoming increasingly popular in Australia. To get a reservation at the height of the season can be awkward unless you go midweek or are able to take up a vacancy on short notice. For this reason a specialist winter vacation agency, which will endeavor to arrange a package to your needs, can be useful.

BROKEN HILL

This western Outback town was the site of the first of the great mineral finds that transformed Australia from a pastoral nation. Since the 1880s, and the mining rush to Broken Hill, innumerable other deposits have been found — indeed Australia sometimes seems just one vast quarry — but this remains the richest streak of silver, lead and zinc in the world. At the same time it is Outback, the true rugged heartland of Australia.

Broken Hill is actually closer to Adelaide, 508km (318 miles) away, than Sydney, 1,157km (723 miles). It is reachable by air daily from Adelaide with **Kendell Airlines**, and from Sydney with **Air New South Wales** on Sunday, Monday, Wednesday and Friday.

Leisurely travelers might be more inclined to go by rail. One of the world's great trains, the **Indian Pacific** *(reservations ☎217 8812)*, leaves Sydney for Perth at 3.15pm on Sunday, Thursday and Saturday, arriving at Broken Hill at 9am the next day. This is a very comfortable train with sleeping cars, lounge and dining cars, and the flavor of an epic rail journey. Broken Hill also connects by rail with Adelaide.

- See also ROUTES 1 and 3 and maps in TOURS on pages 68-73.

The Northern Territory

The Northern Territory is still, in parts, frontier country — the real Outback of Australia, still remote, still rough 'n' ready. But this vast, unspoiled expanse is home to a teeming diversity of flora, fauna and landforms unmatched anywhere else in the continent. The human inhabitants are no less varied in their origins. The Northern Territory has been aptly named "the land of God's eighth day" (after six days of making the world and one of rest He decided He could do better — so He made the Northern Territory).

The whole character of the Northern Territory, all 134 million hectares (331 million acres) of it, is one of startling contrast. It ranges from true desert in the southeast (the notorious Simpson Desert), through semi-desert in the southwest (the Gibson) and west (the Tanami), to the humid, tropical north with its majestic rivers, waterfalls, billabongs, lagoons and pounding surf.

Flora and fauna also differ according to the terrain. In the Red Centre, around Alice Springs, grow the stark-white eucalypts called ghost gums, and the unique salmon gum, its trunk and limbs a delicate pink salmon hue. These strange semidesert flora are entirely different from the lush vegetation of the well-watered north of the Territory.

Likewise, the fauna of the dry Centre — timid desert rats, lizards, dingoes and small marsupials — yield to large kangaroos, crocodiles, buffalo, jabiru, brolga and big sea eagles in the so-called Top End (the Territorians' way of distinguishing the water country of the northern third of the NT from the Centre).

Parts of the Northern Territory are still remote enough not to have felt the tread of the white man nor, indeed, in some of the more remote parts of the Arnhem Land Aboriginal Reserve, the Aboriginal.

The Territory (so-named by the locals, who call everywhere else in Australia "down south") is home to some of the world's most primitive people. These are the Aborigines of the desert to the far west of Alice Springs, the *Pintupi* and *Warlpiri,* who still live in the way their ancestors did, hunting lizards and other small game, as they move from one waterhole to another in the spinifex and sandhills of the Gibson and Great Sandy deserts.

HISTORY
The first seafarers discovered Port Darwin in 1839 (in Charles Darwin's ship, the *Beagle;* hence the city's name), and there are now 130,000 of these "European invaders" in the Northern Territory, as against about

20,000 Aborigines. Settlers made four unsuccessful attempts to establish a base on the north coast before John McDouall Stuart, the third-ever white man successfully to lead an expedition south to north across the continent, reached the coast in July 1862. A settlement was finally established at Port Darwin in 1869.

The Top End was gradually settled by people such as gold miners, cattlemen and traders, who moved here from the coast. Alice Springs was established as a relay station and telegraph office on the Overland Telegraph line that was pushed through from Adelaide to Darwin in 1872, with the first electric telegraph message being transmitted from London to Adelaide and other Australian colonial cities in August that year.

The NT was originally "the Northern Territory of South Australia." From 1911 it was taken over by the federal government. In 1922 an MP was instated, but without the right to vote. He was eventually given that right, although only on matters affecting the NT, and not on any financial bills. Full enfranchisement was only granted in 1968. There has been limited self-government since 1978, although the federal government retains control of uranium mining, Aboriginal matters, national parks and other areas considered to be of more than local significance. Full statehood, however, cannot now be far off.

THE TERRITORIANS
Since long before these constitutional wrangles were thought of, however, this land has been inhabited by the Aborigines; an introduction to their complex society and culture is given on page 16. Their music is compelling and haunting, their art is painstaking and diverse in form and meaning, and their myths and legends of the Dreamtime are as inventive and allegorical as any philosopher's attempts to explain humanity's existence. The visitor who takes the time to become acquainted with all this, and with the people themselves, will be richly rewarded.

The "new" Territorians — those who have lived here since 1869 — are a multiracial mixture. Origins represented include Indonesian, Malaysian, Filipino, Chinese, Timorese, Greek, Italian, Yugoslav, German, Cypriot, Sri Lankan, Indian, Fijian and, of course, British and American. They mix remarkably well, both at work and socially, and their children grow up and go to school together. The possibility of racial disharmony does not seem to exist here, and the Territorian's attitude toward life is still best described by the Australianism, "She'll be right, mate."

The fierce sense of equality, or pride, which is a characteristic of Australians everywhere, is especially noticeable in the Territory. A municipal ditch-digger will consider himself the equal of the mayor, although this attitude of "you're no better than me" and "mañana" can sometimes alienate visitors. "Sir" and "madam" are seldom-used courtesies, and the slightest impatience from a visitor can sometimes result in even slower service. But the Territory's flourishing tourist industry is forcing a gradual reappraisal of such ingrown attitudes.

This is Australia's real Outback, which richly repays the effort entailed in visiting it. The NT's many attractions are scattered over vast distances

141

of difficult terrain, to which this guide aims to provide only a series of pointers. Specific advice useful when planning your trip completes this introduction and is followed by two condensed city guides, to the Territory capital, DARWIN, and the southern center, ALICE SPRINGS. Using the cities as a base, many places in the Top End and the Red Centre can be visited. Some representative examples are suggested here.

GETTING THERE

Darwin and **Alice Springs** are the two bases that most visitors use for excursions to the Northern Territory. Both are served daily by major internal airlines from other state capitals, and by some international airlines.

The **"Ghan"** passenger train (named after the Afghan camel drivers who in the 19thC transported passengers through the Outback) provides a comfortable and interesting journey from Adelaide to Alice Springs, with facilities for passengers to take their vehicles with them.

Those who wish to drive at least have the advantage of using the **Stuart Highway**, stretching all the way from Adelaide to Darwin. The disadvantage is that the amount of time involved in this drive of some 3,000km (1,850 miles) inevitably shortens the time available for exploring places "off the beaten track." There are also regular long-distance bus lines serving the N, but the same problems of time and distance arise as with private vehicle travel.

GETTING AROUND

The airport bus will take you to your hotel or motel, but after this the easiest way of getting around Darwin and Alice Springs is by **taxi**. There are government-run buses too, but these are basically suburban commuter services.

The major car rental companies, **Avis**, **Budget** and **Hertz**, as well as several smaller companies, provide a good service in both cities. The rates are slightly higher than elsewhere, and it is advisable to reserve a car before arrival, especially in the high season (April to October).

Tour operators run bus and minibus trips for city sightseeing, day tours to places of interest out of town, and longer camping or bush-lodge "safari" trips to such attractions as **Ayers Rock** and **Kakadu National Park**. Car rental and bus tours can be arranged at hotel reception desks, travel agents and at NT Tourist Bureaux.

CLIMATE

The Northern Territory has two distinct climatic zones: the arid (or continental) in the Centre, and the monsoonal at the Top End.

The best time of year to visit both the Centre and the Top End is during the dry season (known as **the Dry**). This is the Australian winter (April to September), when, in the Centre, the nights are cold, falling as low as 0˚C (32˚F), and the days are cool-to-warm, with maximum temperatures from 25-30˚C (77-86˚F). From October to March, in the wet season (or **the Wet**) — something of a misnomer in the semiarid heart of Australia — the nights are still cool, but the days are fiercely hot.

In the N, dry-season days are perfect, with temperatures falling to about 20˚C (68˚F) at night and rising to about 30˚C (86˚F) during the day. The months that build up to the Wet (October to December) are hot and very steamy, as are the "let-down" months of March and April, and torrential rain (150cm — about 60 inches — a year) falls in December, January and February. The early months of the year are also the cyclone season, although there have been only three completely destructive cyclones in the past 100 years.

There are certain disadvantages in visiting the Top End in the Wet. Swimming in the sea, for example, is highly dangerous, as the monsoon brings with it lethal sea wasps and other stingers. And the remarkable wetlands, with such attractions as **Kakadu National Park**, are so extended by the heavy rain that the wildlife disperses over a wide area. In the Dry the waterholes contract and wildlife is concentrated in this area.

CLOTHING

Territorians dress sensibly. Men wear cotton slacks and short-sleeve, open-neck shirts during the Dry, and in the Wet, shorts and knee-length socks. Ties are generally worn only at official functions, and suits are worn only by visiting politicians or businessmen who don't know the procedure. In the Wet, women wear sundresses or cotton blouses with slacks or a skirt. You might need a sweater on mornings in the dry season (even some Top Enders resort to woolens when their temperatures "plunge" to 20˚C/68˚F in the early morning).

WARNINGS

In parts of the Territory, especially in the bush, flies are a menace, so it is essential to carry insect repellant at all times. Also, take seriously signs that warn against **swimming** in the **wet season** and against swimming where there might be **crocodiles**.

If traveling extensively out of the towns, find out where the **Aboriginal Reserves** are and make sure you don't enter them without the permission of the relevant Aboriginal council. There is, in fact, only one main "adventure" route that goes through a reserve, from Alice Springs to Halls Creek in Western Australia, through the **Tanami Desert** — a 4-wheel-drive-and-camping trip. In this case permission is not necessary, as long as the traveler does no more than buy gasoline, and perhaps an artifact or two from the shop at Yuendumu, an Aboriginal town on the route, and keeps moving. There is little to tempt the tourist to stay in Yuendumu, even *with* permission.

Darwin

ORIENTATION

The Territory's capital, Darwin is set on a harbor that is both beautiful and bigger than Sydney's. The city's population, which currently stands at 73,000, is the fastest-growing in Australia apart from that of the national capital, Canberra. Like the magnificent region in which it is set, Darwin is a city of contrasts. Going against the Australian norm, Darwinians play soccer in summer (their wet season) and cricket in winter (their dry season). The racial mix is as varied and harmonious here as it is in the rest of the Territory. You will find Darwinians of Chinese, Filipino, and particularly of Greek and Italian descent, with Aborigines also forming an integral part of the community.

Darwin's charm is all the more remarkable given its frequent brushes with devastation. Destroyed three times by tropical cyclones — in 1897, 1937, and on Christmas Day, 1974 by Cyclone Tracy — Darwin has risen like a phoenix from the rubble. Today it ranks among the world's most pleasant, small, tropical cities, with a variety of good shops, restaurants and beaches, and some interesting sights. And because Darwin is the NT's "front door" for visitors from Europe and Asia, and the base for those wishing to tour such Top End delights as KAKADU NATIONAL PARK (see page 147), hundreds of millions of dollars have recently gone into the development of new hotels and motels.

Points of interest include the **Museum of Arts and Sciences** *(Bullocky Point, Fannie Bay* ☎ *82 4211* 🖂*)*. This fine, air-conditioned building, at the city end of Fannie Bay, houses the most extensive collection of Aboriginal and non-Aboriginal art, natural history and social history in northern Australia; it also has a good licensed restaurant, **The Beagle** (see WHERE TO EAT), favored by locals for sunny lunches and relaxed dinners. Also of interest are the **East Point War Museum** *(East Point, Fannie Bay);* **Howard Springs** *(30km/18 miles) s on the Stuart Highway),* a big, natural spring and swimming complex; and for a day trip, take the ferry across the harbor to **Mandurah**, on the Cox peninsula, where you can have lunch and see displays of Aboriginal dancing and singing.

PRACTICAL INFORMATION

☎**STD (area) code**   089

Air   Daily flights by Australian Airlines and Ansett

Bus   Regular services by national companies; Ansett Pioneer and Greyhound offer unlimited-mileage 14-, 15- 30- and 60-day passes, allowing flexible travel to and around the NT

Car rental   Avis ☎81 9922; Budget ☎84 4388; Hertz ☎41 0944

NT Government Tourist Bureau   31 Smith St., Darwin, NT, 0800 ☎81 6611

American Express Travel Service   c/o Travelers World Pty Ltd, 18 Knuckey St., Darwin, NT, 0800 ☎81 4699

Automobile Association of the Northern Territory (AANT)   79-81 Smith St., Darwin, NT, 0800 ☎81 3837

Where to stay

Despite the burgeoning of its hotel industry in recent years, Darwin still offers a limited choice of accommodations in comparison with other major cities. Perhaps this is because many of the older establishments failed to survive the cyclone of 1974. For motels and cheaper accommodations, it is best to look well away from the city center.

ALL SEASONS ATRIUM
On the corner of Peel St. and The Esplanade, Darwin, NT, 0800 ☎41 0755 Tx85296 Fx81 9025 ▥ 140 rms ⬛ ▭ AE ▣ ▥ ▥ ⬛ ♺ ⬛

Location: Central; close to the harbor and city shops. Popular, airy hotel; rooms have private balconies. Some suites have kitchen facilities; in-house videos and room service are available.

BEAUFORT
The Esplanade, Darwin, NT, 0800 ☎82 9911 Tx84061 Fx81 5332 ▥ 196 rms ⬛ ▭ AE ▣ ▥ ▥ ⬛ ♺ ⬛ 𝖸 ♺ 𝗪 ⬛ ⬛

Location: Central, with fine views over Darwin Harbour. It looks like a series of pink and blue boxes, but this hotel complex comes up to the best international standards. Its many facilities include health studio, business center and 24-hour room service.

DARWIN FRONTIER HOTEL
Buffalo Court, Darwin, NT, 0800 ☎81 5333 Fx41 0909 ▥ 86 rms ⬛ ▭ AE ▣ ▥ ▥ ⬛ ⬛ 𝖸 ⬛

Location: 2km (1 mile) from city center. Originally known as the Territorian, this hotel enjoys harbor views, overlooks a golf course, nestles in green parkland. Across the road from the **Botanic Gardens**, a 5-minute walk from the beautiful white sands of **Mindil Beach**.

DARWIN TRAVELODGE
122 The Esplanade, Darwin, NT, 0800 ☎81 5388 Tx85273 Fx81 5701 ▥ 183 rms ⬛ ▭ AE ▣ ▥ ▥ ⬛ 𝖸 ⬛

Location: 10mins' walk from city center. Built in 1972, this conveniently located hotel is now one of Darwin's oldest new hotels. Similar in character to other TraveLodges, it has a good restaurant, bistro, swimming pool, and superb views from its top floor.

DIAMOND BEACH HOTEL CASINO
Gilruth Ave., Mindil Beach, Darwin, NT, 0800 ☎46 2666 Tx85214 Fx81 9186 ▥ 96 rms ⬛ ▭ AE ▣ ▥ ▥ ⬛ ♺ ⬛ 𝖸 ♺ ♺ ⬛ ⬛ O

Location: 1.6km (1 mile) from Darwin's center. A pleasant casino hotel, set on the beachfront.

HOTEL DARWIN
10 Herbert St., Darwin, NT, 0800 ☎81 9211 Tx85194 Fx819575 ▥ 70 rms ⬛ ▭ AE ▣ ▥ ⬛ 𝖸 ⬛

Location: In the heart of the city. Grand old hotel in the tropical/colonial style, with magnificent views across Darwin Harbour, and 24-hour room service.

MARRAKAI LUXURY APARTMENTS
93 Smith St., Darwin, NT, 0800 ☎82 3711 Tx85502 Fx81 9283 ▥ 23 apts ⬛ ▭ AE ▣ ▥ ⬛ ♺ ⬛

Location: Close to the city center. These are attractively designed, superior serviced private suites with kitchen facilities and much of what you will find in the big hotels. The ideal choice for those who prefer a little more privacy. A drycleaning service is offered.

SHERATON DARWIN
32 Mitchell St., Darwin, NT, 0800 ☎82 0000 Tx85991 Fx81 1765 ▥ 233 rms ⬛ ▭ AE ▣ ▥ ▥ ⬛ ♺ ⬛ 𝖸 𝗪 ⬛ ⬛

Location: City center. Opened in 1986, this modern hotel is a convenient 1-minute walk from the main shopping thoroughfare, Smith Mall. Its elegant **Flinders** restaurant features the Territory's finest haute cuisine.

Dining out

The fast-changing restaurant scene in this fastest growing part of Australia makes it hard to pick examples with real staying power. Good prospects, all licensed, include **Blue Blazer Restaurant** *(Seabreeze Hotel, 60 East Point Rd., Fannie Bay* ☎ *81 8433* ▥ ▣ ▣ ▣ ▥*)*, a true gourmet restaurant with magnificent views over Fannie Bay; **The Beagle** *(Museum of Arts and Sciences, Conacher St., Fannie Bay* ☎ *81 7791* ▥ ▣ ▣ ▣ ▥*)*, situated virtually on the beach overlooking Fannie Bay, with a colonial theme and waitresses in 19thC costume; and **Lee Dynasty** *(21 Cavenagh St., Darwin* ☎ *81 7808/81 2700* ▥ ▣ ▣ ▣ ▥*)*, an elegant Cantonese restaurant serving lunches and leisurely dinners.

Entertainment

In the vanguard of nightspots is the **Diamond Beach Hotel Casino** *(Gilruth Ave.* ☎ *46 2666)*. On Sundays, there's **Sunset Jazz** *(*☎ *462666, 4-8pm)*, on the lawns overlooking the beach. Within the casino complex is **Crystals**, a spacious disco with regular cabaret entertainment.

After-dark entertainment can also be found in the popular local night clubs, **1990s** and **Chloe's**, both in the Victoria Hotel complex *(*☎ *81 4011)*. Good bars include the **Top End Frontier Brewery Bar** and the **Sheraton Pub Bar**.

As well as its restaurants, clubs and bars, Darwin has several live theaters. Among them is **Brown's Mart** *(*☎ *81 5522)*, the **Cavenagh Theatre** *(*☎ *48 0049)*, and the **Darwin Theatre Company** *(*☎ *818424)*. They may not attract the grand productions of southern theaters, but they favor innovative productions and are well attended.

Where to shop

The city-center **Smith Street Mall** is a picturesque paved thoroughfare, lined with bougainvillea and palms. Numerous smaller arcades lead off it. On Saturday it is filled with the fragrance of *satays* and other Asian delicacies from open-air food stalls, and in the Dry there is live entertainment. **Casuarina Square**, in the northern suburbs, is vast: more than 200 specialty shops plus four major stores. Adjacent is Darwin's one-stop shopping center, **Casuarina Village**.

Excursion

KAKADU NATIONAL PARK ★
150km (93 miles) E of Darwin ✈ ✗ ♿ *Open all year; some roads in the park closed in wet season. By car, via Stuart Highway S for 35km (21 miles), then left on Arnhem Highway. By bus, contact tour operators in Darwin.*

Kakadu is a fascinating and mysterious place. Aboriginal rock art, towering escarpments, grasslands and wetlands, crocodiles, buffalo, birdlife in great variety, and unique flora are all to be found here. Previously unreachable by conventional vehicles in the Wet season, and an arduous journey even in the Dry, Kakadu is now a mere three hours' drive from Darwin.

Darwin tour operators run day trips to the park, which unfortunately tend to be tiring and inadequate because of the distances needing to be covered; but they can also arrange longer visits. Independent travelers either camp out in the areas designated by the National Parks and Wildlife Service or stay at the Four Seasons Cooinda Motel (see below), near the town of **Jabiru** (an incongruous support town for the big uranium mine in an area excised from the park), or at the Four Seasons Kakadu (see below), in the heart of the national park.

🛏 The **Four Seasons Cooinda Motel** *(near Jabiru* ☎ *(089) 79 0145* ▥ ▣ ▣ ▣ ▥ *)*, a wilderness lodge, small and basic, stands on the fabled Yellow Waters lagoon, where boat cruises can be arranged. The **Four Seasons Kakadu** *(Flinders St., Jabiru* ☎ *(089) 79 2800* ▥ ▣ ▣ ▣ ▥ *)* is a unique resort built in the shape of a crocodile and located in the heart of the national park. Both hotels are managed by Four Seasons on behalf of the Aboriginal owners, the local Gagudju people.

Alice Springs

ORIENTATION
Alice Springs is a thriving, fast-growing city with a population of 20,000 people. It is the starting point for most visitors on their way to the fabled AYERS ROCK and THE OLGAS (see EXCURSIONS) and the base for those interested in the lesser-known (but equally interesting) chasms, gorges and gaps in the **MacDonnell Ranges**, which surround the city. STANDLEY CHASM (see EXCURSIONS) is an easy day trip from "the Alice" (as the city is called locally).

Although John McDouall Stuart crossed the MacDonnell Ranges six times in his journeys to the N coast in 1860, 1861 and 1862, he saw neither the Todd River nor the plain on which Alice Springs stands. Those discoveries were made by surveyors plotting the Overland Telegraph route in 1870. The isolated town, consisting of a few shacks, a shop and hotel, was originally known as Stuart, but the telegraph station and post office were situated at a waterhole 3km (2 miles) away called Alice Springs. When the post office was transferred to the township, the name moved too.

Alice Springs has come a long way since those shantytown days. Today it can provide reasonable accommodations, good leisure facilities and a broad range of shops. Points of interest to visitors include the old **telegraph station** *(3km/2 miles N, off the Stuart Highway)* and **Pitchi Richi** *(Aranda Terrace* ☎*52 1931* 🚗 ⬅ *open 9am-sunset)*. This is central Australia's largest outdoor museum, a bird-and-flower sanctuary that also features remarkable **sculptures of Aborigines** by William Ricketts. Events in the Alice include **camel races** in May and, in late August, the **Henley-on-Todd regatta** on the bed of the Todd River, which runs through the town and is nearly always dry (see CALENDAR OF EVENTS).

PRACTICAL INFORMATION

☎**STD (area) code**   089
By car   1,529km (950 miles) s of Darwin on Stuart Highway
Air and bus   Daily services from southern capitals
Rail   The "Ghan" service takes 24 hours from Adelaide, the "Alice" service 48 hours from Sydney
Car rental   Avis ☎52 4366; Budget ☎52 4133; Hertz ☎52 2644
Northern Territory Government Tourist Bureau   51 Todd St., Alice Springs, NT, 0870 ☎52 1299

Where to stay

Alice Springs is quite well provided for in its range of places to stay, from expensive (by Northern Territory standards) to budget accommodations. Surprisingly, motels are generally not cheap.

OASIS FRONTIER RESORT ✿
10 Gap Rd., Alice Springs, NT, 0870 ☎*52 1444* 📠 *102 rms* ⬅ ⚒ 🆎 ⓪ ⓪ 🆅 🔥 ♿ ▱ 𝖸 ⚘ 🎾
Location: Just 6mins s of town center. This motel, which is set in several acres of lawns and aviaries, offers the best-value accommodations in Alice Springs.

SHERATON ALICE SPRINGS
Barrett Drive, Alice Springs, NT, 0870 ☎*52 8000* 📠*81091* 📠*52 3822* 📱 *235 rms* ⬅ ⚒ 🆎 ⓪ ⓪ 🆅 ♿ 🔥 ▱ 𝖸 ✈ ◈ ⚓ 🎾
Location: On SE edge of town. This ele-

gantly designed hotel complex blends in well with its surroundings. It is spread out over several acres of lawns, with an 18-hole golf course.

VISTA HOTEL ALICE SPRINGS
Stephens Rd., Alice Springs, NT, 0870 ☎*52 6100* 📠*81051* 📠*52 6234* 📱 *140 rms* ⬅ ⚒ 🆎 ⓪ ⓪ 🆅 ♿ 🔥 ▱ 𝖸 ✈ ◈ ⚓ 🎾
Location: Opposite Lasseter's Casino, s of town center. A popular hotel, nestled below the **MacDonnell Ranges**, which boasts a refreshing waterfall spa among its other attributes. These include barbecue facilities.

Dining out

The **Outback Winery** *(Petrick Rd.* ☎*55 5133* 📱 🆎 ⓪ ⓪ 🆅*)* is a thoroughly Australian-style restaurant, operated by Dennis Hornsby at his winery, Chateau Hornsby. The setting is open-air with a cover to protect patrons from rain or hot sun, and a small amphitheater features nightly Australian entertainment. It's all relaxed and friendly in the true Outback tradition.

Entertainment

There are few true late-night spots in the Alice. But **Bojangles** *(80 Todd St.* ☎ *52 2873)* is hugely popular (get in early!), yet surprisingly intimate. And at **Lasseter's Casino** *(Barrett Drive* ☎ *52 5066),* gamblers can also try their luck at a disco featuring stunning lighting; strict dress regulations demand neat, clean casual clothes.

Where to shop

The **Todd Street Mall** is a pleasantly landscaped pedestrians-only thoroughfare spanning two blocks and containing some 80 shops plus offices and banks; other arcades lead off, with one, **Ford Plaza**, providing late-night shopping until 9pm.

Excursions

ULURU/AYERS ROCK ★
450km (280 miles) by road sw of Alice Springs ▨ *ʏ* 🚌 *⟨⟨ Open all year. By air, from Alice Springs and Perth. By bus, from Alice Springs and Adelaide.*
Ayers Rock was named by the South Australian explorer W. C. Gosse in 1873. He wrote, "What was my astonishment when, two miles distant, to find it was an immense pebble rising abruptly from the plain... it is certainly the most wonderful natural feature I have ever seen." Ayers Rock is not, however, the biggest monolith known; that honor goes to the far less eye-catching Mt. Augustus in Western Australia.

Measuring 9km ($5\frac{1}{2}$ miles) in circumference and 348m (1,142 feet) in height, the Rock famously changes color through darkening shades of glowing red at sunset, reversing this spectacle at dawn; its color is affected too by the quality of the light and the mood of the weather. The stiff climb is rewarded by astonishing views of the endless red plain, sometimes covered, after a thunderstorm, by flowers. Walking trails around the base take in caves containing Aboriginal rock paintings, and **Maggie Springs**, where dingoes, lizards and other wildlife thrive.

The Rock, which is on the World Heritage list, is unquestionably the most impressive living symbol of Aboriginal ritual and myth. The tribespeople believe that within Ayers Rock their mythological heroes, who came into the country at the dawn of time, are resting, awaiting the moment to re-emerge. They believe each part of the mountain is a

149

creative symbol kept alive by a sacred rock python *(Wanambi)* living at a waterhole in *Uluru*, the Aboriginal name for the Rock.

☞   The **Four Seasons Ayers Rock** *(Yulara Drive, Yulara, NT, 0872* ☎ *(089) 56 2100* ▨ AE ⊕ ⊜ ▨ *)* is a handy 20km (12 miles) from the Rock, and runs a courtesy bus service from Yulara Airport.

☞   The **Sheraton Ayers Rock Hotel** *(Yulara Drive, Yulara, NT, 0872* ☎ *(089) 56 2200* ▨ AE ⊕ ▨ *)* is an eye-catching complex whose unique "desert sails" architecture provides a cooling oasis in the desert.

DEVIL'S MARBLES ★
400km (249 miles) N of Alice Springs ➤ ◈ *Open all year. By car, via Stuart Highway.*

These two groups of immense granite boulders cover several square kilometers and weigh thousands of tons. They range in shape from almost perfectly rounded boulders, stacked in precarious tiers, to rocks sliced clean in half by nature's knives.

THE OLGAS ★
25km (15 miles) w of Ayers Rock ▨ ✗ ➤ ◈ *Open all year. Getting there: see Ayers Rock.*

Ernest Giles was the first explorer to see the Olgas, and it was he who named them for the Queen of Spain. He wrote, "Mt. Olga displayed to our astonished eyes rounded minarets, giant cupolas, and monstrous domes. There they have stood as huge memorials of the ancient times of earth, for ages, countless aeons of ages, since its creation first had birth. The rocks are smoothed with the attrition of the alchemy of years, [but] Time, the old and dim magician, has laboured ineffectually here... Mt. Olga has remained as it was born."

Unlike the single dome of AYERS ROCK, the Olgas have more than a dozen separate heads, divided by deep clefts and water-filled gorges teeming with wildlife; the tallest peak, **Lotherio**, rises to a height of 546m (1,791 feet). The Aborigines know the Olgas, home of many myths, as *Katajuta* (many heads).

STANDLEY CHASM ★
50km (31 miles) w of Alice Springs ▨ ➤ ◈ *Open 8.30am-4.30pm. By car, via Larapinta Drive.*

This sheer cleft is a delightful subject for photographers, when the sun stands directly overhead and illuminates its red walls. The phenomenon lasts for only a few minutes in the middle of the day; but this vertical slice is only one of many spectacular gorges in the **MacDonnell Ranges**, a number of which have rocky waterholes and support much wildlife — and even wild flowers in spring.

Queensland

The "Sunshine State," they call it, and with good reason. Queensland is the center of Australia's vacation industry, having experienced the sort of growth in international tourism since the mid-1970s that is as pleasing to governments as it is alarming to environmentalists. Images of beaches so perfect they could only exist in a rum commercial, of a dazzling, silent world of coral reefs, of epic struggles with giant fish — all these have established Queensland firmly in the international register of desirable destinations. And fairly so, for the Sunshine State in nearly every way measures up to its reputation.

The omens for European settlement in Queensland were even less auspicious than elsewhere in Australia. Although the Queensland coast had been charted by Captain Cook in 1770, the first step toward establishing a colonial administration was taken only in 1824, more than three decades after the founding of Sydney, the purpose being to set up a last-resort colony for incorrigible offenders from New South Wales. By all accounts Brisbane's early years were ugly and brutal, and the commandant of the penal settlement, Captain Patrick Logan, has come down in Australian folklore as one of the most notorious of the many villains to be inflicted on Australia by the mother country.

Queensland's progress toward prosperity was founded on the land. A great pastoral industry evolved out of free settlement, as did agriculture. Sugar cane plantations larger than European principalities drew an immigrant labor force of Pacific Islanders, still a prominent section of the state's population. Minerals sustained the growth.

Today the source of much of the state's wealth is the sea, the lure for a tourist industry contributing 12 percent to the gross state product. And vast though the land area is — more than 1.7 million square kilometers, second in size only to Western Australia — the sea and the coast are what we are concerned with here.

WHEN AND WHERE TO GO

It is advisable to avoid the period from December to March if possible. Most visitors will find the climate, in the tropical north in particular, uncomfortably hot when it is not pouring with rain. There is danger too, on the beaches north of Gladstone, from the box jellyfish, which appears near the coast at this time and has a sting that has proved fatal as recently as January 1987.

Queensland is not an easy place to see. Its attractions do not present themselves conveniently close to the urban centers. The Great Barrier

Reef, which is the one reason above all others to visit Queensland, sprawls over a length of more than 2,000 kilometers (1,250 miles), and in places is well over 100 kilometers (60 miles) offshore. The islands so successfully promoted by the state authority, in an era when the tourist ideal seems to be to get away from absolutely everything, are in most cases by no means easily, or cheaply, accessible.

Queensland, it should be emphasized, is expensive for travelers who insist on the highest standard of accommodations and want to fly everywhere in order to save time. There is more than a whiff of the old Australian disease, protectionism, about the Queensland tourism industry. Even vacation packages to offshore destinations such as Heron Island, an exquisite coral cay with magnificent skindiving on the reef, are expensive enough for Queenslanders to save money by taking their vacations in Bali and Thailand.

But it is possible to travel independently, and with a flexible itinerary, and not spend a fortune, provided the visitor plans carefully, uses motels (many of which are moderate to inexpensive, but no less comfortable for that) and shops around for stand-by rates on island accommodations.

Be assured that the rewards that Queensland offers are well worth any effort entailed. To provide practical advice to this end, this section of the guide has been devised in a slightly different form. The state capital, Brisbane, is presented under the usual convenient A to Z headings, but a second part concentrates on information about getting to see the Great Barrier Reef, and visiting the islands.

QUEENSLANDERS

A word about your hosts: Queenslanders have a reputation among other Australians for a certain eccentricity, an image fostered by the former archly conservative government headed by Sir Joh Bjelke-Petersen, which in 1986 passed legislation forbidding the serving of alcohol to "drug-dealers, perverts and child-molesters." The state now has a Labour Government, the first for more than three decades.

At the same time, perhaps because they are only like simple and kind country people anywhere else, Queenslanders present a genuinely warm welcome to visitors. A great deal of spurious nonsense is written about "traditional Aussie hospitality." But in Queensland it really is true.

Brisbane

ORIENTATION

Brisbane, along with the rest of Queensland, is sometimes imagined by outsiders as being located beside a great white beach on the Pacific where the sun shines perpetually and the surf is always up.

This is a misleading impression. Over the past five years, Brisbane has been dragged out of its rural slumber with a building boom in the central area. Much of this reawakening resulted from the enormous national and international interest that the Expo in 1988 focused on the city. Such developments as the **Queen Street Mall**, with its open air cafés, Victorian-style **Myer** department store and street entertainers, have brought new life to the central area. The former Expo '88 site, a prime piece of real estate beside the Brisbane River and now known as the **Southbank** development, is being redeveloped with shops, hotels, residential apartments and parklands; it will certainly be the city's showpiece when completed in the next couple of years.

Like most early settlements in Australia, Brisbane was established and developed on the banks of a river, and the modern city is in fact more than 20km (12½ miles) inland from where the muddy waters of the Brisbane River empty into Moreton Bay. From the mountains of the **D'Aguilar Range**, some 35km (22 miles) to the w, you can look out to the bay, and the islands of Moreton and Stradbroke, which shelter it from the Pacific. The dazzling beaches of **Surfers Paradise** and the **Gold Coast** are about 70km (44 miles) to the s, and the **Sunshine Coast**, another vacation resort area, is about 110km (69 miles) N.

Brisbanites pride themselves on the rural identity of their state, and regard Southerners with a certain wariness. Geographically, however, they are closer to New South Wales and Canberra than to the northern areas of Queensland. The state border is a bare 100km (63 miles) away, the merest hop in Australian terms, and Cairns, the main city of the N, is almost twice as far away as Sydney, so that Brisbane folk themselves tend to be tagged Southerners in their own state.

Most of Brisbane's attractions are in a central, convenient location, and can be comfortably seen in 2-3 days. The city center is easily encompassed on foot, and, as the streets named after kings run parallel roughly N-to-s, and those named after the queens run w-to-e, it is hard to get lost.

PRACTICAL INFORMATION

Map 7 on page 154

☎**STD (area) code**   07

Airport   ☎860 8600; Ansett ☎854 2222; Australian ☎131 313

Railway station   Roma Street ☎235 1122, map **7**D2

Car rental   Avis ☎252 7111; Budget ☎252 0151; Hertz ☎221 6166

Queensland Government Travel Centre   Corner of Adelaide St. and Edward St., Brisbane, Qld, 4000 ☎221 6111, map **7**D2

American Express Travel Service   131 Elizabeth St., Brisbane, Qld, 4000 ☎221 7815, map **7**D2

Royal Brisbane Hospital

1 · 2 HERSTON ROAD 2 3 Exhibition 3
Exhibition Grounds
Station
GREGORY TERRACE
A A
B B

Newstead House

Municipal Golf Course

VICTORIA PARK

WATER ST
KENNIGO ST
WARRY STREET
LOVE ST

FORTITUDE VALLEY

Brunswick St. Station

WICKHAM

GIPPS

GOTHA ST.

TERRACE

UNION ST.

BOWEN BRIDGE ROAD

C GREGORY C

SPRING HILL

GLOUCESTER ST
BARRY PARADE

CENTENARY PLACE

ST
STREET

BRADFORD HWY

FORTESCUE ST
BOUNDARY ST
LEICHHARDT ST
WHARF

ALBERT PARK

BIRLEY ST
WICKHAM

ASTOR TERR.

Central Station

ANN

St Johns Cathedral

All Saints

Kangaroo Point

Customs Ho. Ferry

HOLMAN

TER.
UPPER

STREET
STREET
QUEEN ST

Customs House

C C
D

Roma St. Station
Transit Centre

Observatory

Anzac Square

EDWARD

EAGLE ST

ROMA STREET

Albert St. Uniting

ANN

QUEEN

G.P.O.

ALBERT

John Oxley Monument

NORTH QUAY

City Hall

CITY

Town

Edward St Ferry

ADELAIDE ST

QUEEN ST
ELIZABETH ST
CHARLOTTE ST
ALBERT ST

STREET

GEORGE

State Library

Treasury Building

Festival Hall

MARGARET ST

Edward St Reach

D D
E E

Museum & Art Gallery

BRISBANE

BOTANIC
Queensland Club

Coach Stn.

MELBOURNE ST

Queensland Cultural Centre

South Brisbane Station

South Brisbane Reach

RIVER

Parliament House

Old Government House

GARDENS

RIVERSIDE EXPRESSWAY

Conservatorium of Music

MONTAGUE ST
MERIVALE ST

MUSGRAVE PARK

E E
F

COLCHESTER STREET

SOUTH BRISBANE

RIVER TERRACE

LEOPARD ST

1 · 2 VULTURE 2 · 3 STREET 3

Royal Automobile Club of Queensland (RACQ)   300 St Paul's
Terrace, Brisbane, Qld, 4000 ☎253 2444, map **7B3**

SEEING THE CITY

The place for information of every kind, on Brisbane and the rest of
Queensland, is the **Queensland Government Travel Centre** *(196
Adelaide St., map* **7D2** *☎221 6111).*

The local transportation authority runs a sightseeing tour called **City
Sights** *(departs every half-hour between 9am-4pm Mon-Fri; inquiries
☎225 4444),* a city tour on buses decorated to resemble old Brisbane
trams. Specially marked stops dot the city, and passengers can break their
tour and resume their journey on a later bus. **Sunstate Day Tours** *(☎236
3355)* runs visits to Lone Pine Koala Sanctuary and other destinations.

A cruise on the Brisbane River offers another view of the city. Operators include **Miramar** *(☎221 0300)* and **Koala Cruises** *(☎229
7055),* which takes in Lone Pine Koala Sanctuary.

Ballooning offers a spectacular perspective of Brisbane and its environs *(inquiries ☎844 6671).*

Sights and places of interest

ALBERT STREET UNITING CHURCH ★
Corner of Albert St. and Ann St. ☎221 6788. Map **7D2** ▣ *✗(ask at office).
Open 7.30am-5.30pm.*

This 19thC gem of church architecture was formerly the Wesley Central
Mission, now attached to the Uniting Church in Australia. Situated in
the heart of the city, it once dominated the position overlooking CITY
HALL, but due to civic carelessness toward historic buildings (only too
common in Brisbane) it is now reduced in the landscape by surrounding high-rise structures.

The red-brick and white-sandstone exterior was completed in 1889
and is harmoniously proportioned. The interior, lined from ceiling to
pews with polished timber, is intimate and welcoming. The communion
and gallery rails are in cedar. There are some fine stained-glass windows.

ART GALLERY OF QUEENSLAND
Queensland Cultural Centre, South Bank, South Brisbane ☎840 7303. Map **7E2**
▣ *✗* ▣ ➡ *Open Thurs-Tues 10am-5pm; Wed 10am-8pm.*

It may come as a surprise to find this excellent collection of pictures in
what is, after all, a small city. Located in the modern surroundings of
the QUEENSLAND CULTURAL CENTRE on the s bank of the Brisbane River, the
state collection has been compiled over almost a century with discrimi-
nation and taste. It contains works by Renoir, Degas, Toulouse-Lautrec
and Picasso (all acquired in a 1959 windfall through a local benefac-
tor). But the real meat here is the important and comprehensive record
of Australian art, including major works by Frederick McCubbin and
William Dobell.

BOTANIC GARDENS
George St. Map 7E3 ▣ *Open sunrise-sunset.*
Situated at a pleasant and secluded end of George St. in the city, the gardens face two fine 19thC buildings, PARLIAMENT HOUSE and THE MANSIONS. Here the havoc wrought upon Brisbane's heritage in recent years can almost be forgotten. Palms in a subtropical setting, which extends down to the banks of the Brisbane River, make this an exotic spot in which to relax after a stroll through the city. Handsome though the gardens are, however, they have been overshadowed as a botanic exhibition by the more specialized displays lately established at MT. COOT-THA, although that is less conveniently located about 5km (3 miles) from the city.

CITY HALL
Adelaide St. ☎ *225 4048. Map 7D2* ▣ *⚌ (*☎ *225 4360). Open 8am-5pm. Closed Sat, Sun.*
This characteristic Late Empire hybrid of architectural styles, situated in the heart of the city, has been long regarded as its showpiece. Building started in 1920 and took 10 years. The **clock tower**, at 92m (302 feet) once Brisbane's highest point, has an observation platform that features in the conducted tour. Also contained within the Neoclassical framework are the rather grand foyer at the King George Sq. entrance and a civic art gallery and museum *(open daily 10am-5pm)*.

EARLY STREET VILLAGE
75 McIlwraith Ave., Norman Park ☎ *398 6866* ▦ ▣ ➡ *Open 10am-5pm.*
A private enterprise that appeals to Australians' fascination with heritage, this fails to live up to its promise. The so-called village is a collection of early Queensland structures, including a cottage, a general store and a pioneer hut. It also features the remains of **Auchenflower House**, a fine old mansion in which three state premiers lived, but which nevertheless was being demolished in the 1960s when two rooms were salvaged and brought here. The one structure of real significance on the site is **Eulalia**, but as this colonial home is a private residence it is not open to visitors. For what is on show, the entry fee is steep, and a visit to NEWSTEAD HOUSE might give a more rewarding insight into colonial life.

LONE PINE KOALA SANCTUARY
Jesmond Rd., Fig Tree Pocket ☎ *378 1366* ▣ ✱ ➡ *Open 8.30am-5pm.*
The biggest sanctuary in Australia for this delightful but vulnerable marsupial (the koala is not a bear at all) can be reached by ferry departing from North Quay at lunchtime daily *(inquiries* ☎ *378 1366)*. Lone Pine also has kangaroos and emus, which visitors may hand-feed.

THE MANSIONS ★
40 George St. Map 7E3 ▣ *Shopping arcade open in trading hours.*
This stately old terrace building near the BOTANIC GARDENS and PARLIAMENT HOUSE was completed around 1890 and has been refurbished, like

so many historic structures in Australia, as an arcade of shops. Yet this and the old **Salvation Army headquarters** in Ann St. (adapted for office accommodation) are the grandest remaining buildings of their type in Brisbane.

MOUNT COOT-THA AND BOTANIC GARDENS

Mt. Coot-tha Rd., Toowong ☎ *377 8898* 🔲 ▬ 🍴 ➡ ◀€ *Open 9am-5pm.*
About 8km (5 miles) w of the city is this large site, worth the drive as much for its fine views and picnic spots as for the gardens. From the summit of **Mt. Coot-tha**, overlooking Brisbane, you get a good idea of the layout of the city along the river banks, and a panorama of the hinterland stretching away to the distant **D'Aguilar Range**. The summit restaurant serves lunches, teas and dinner.

The new botanic gardens are at the foot of the mountain and include an enclosed tropical display. Also on the site is the **Sir Thomas Brisbane planetarium** *(two showings daily* ☎ *377 8896 for times).* The surrounding natural parkland is a popular local picnic spot, although quiet on weekdays. From the parking lot just beyond the turn-off for the summit, there are signposted walks to the **J. C. Slaughter Falls**.

NEWSTEAD HOUSE ★

Breakfast Creek Rd., Newstead ☎ *252 7373. Map 7B3* 🔲 🍴 ➡ ◀€ *Open Mon-Fri 11am-3pm; Sun 2-5pm. Closed Sat.*
This lovely old residence is the oldest house in Brisbane. The meticulous care given by a local heritage group, combined with its stately position overlooking the river, place it among the country's finest historic houses. Built in 1846 for a pioneer Queensland farmer, a Scot named Patrick Leslie, the original shell was extended and embellished over the decades. More recent residents were US servicemen during World War II, and, following the US President's visit here in 1967, an area behind the house is named **Lyndon B. Johnson Place** as a memorial to them. Restoration has been rounded off with the addition of period furniture and objects, many of them treasures in their own right.

THE OLD WINDMILL (The Observatory)

Wickham Terrace. Map 7C2. Not open to the public.
There is actually not a great deal to be seen of the oldest surviving building in Brisbane, but its history is interesting enough to warrant a visit. Built in 1829 by convicts under the supervision of Captain Patrick Logan, much-hated commander of the penal settlement established here for incorrigible offenders, it was designed as a windmill, and is sometimes called the Observatory. In fact it was not used as either, although it has functioned as a grain mill, a fire lookout, a signal station and, in 1840, as a gallows when two Aborigines were hanged from the windmill arm for murdering a government land surveyor.

PARLIAMENT HOUSE

George St. ☎ *226 7111. Map 7E3* 🔲 ✗ *compulsory: four tours daily, from 10.30am.*

157

This is an enduring symbol of the independence won by Queensland from New South Wales in 1854, when a design competition was launched for a state legislative chamber. The winning design, for a building in the grand French style and said to have been modeled on the Louvre, has been in use as a parliament since 1868 and is an altogether more splendid affair than its equivalent in New South Wales. The imposing stone facade and blackened copper domes are in picturesque contrast to the subtropical setting of palm trees and the adjacent BOTANIC GARDENS.

QUEENSLAND CULTURAL CENTRE
South Bank, South Brisbane ☎*inquiries 840 7229, reservations 840 7478. Map 7E2* ☒ *✗ hourly* ⬛ ⬟ *Open Thurs-Tues 10am-5pm; Wed 10am-8pm.*

The Cultural Centre's design is an ambitious concept modeled along the lines of London's South Bank, although arguably with greater architectural appeal. Like the South Bank, the Cultural Centre consists of a series of arts venues built on the banks of a major river. It includes a performing arts complex containing three auditoriums, now Brisbane's main venue for concerts, ballet, opera and drama (see ENTERTAINMENT), and homes for the ART GALLERY OF QUEENSLAND, the QUEENSLAND MUSEUM and the state library since 1982. Among the acres of space are a number of restaurants, bistros and plazas.

QUEENSLAND MUSEUM
Queensland Cultural Centre, South Bank, South Brisbane ☎*840 7635. Map 7E2* ☒ ⬛ ⬥ ⬟ *Open Thurs-Tues 9am-5pm; Wed 9am-8pm.*

Recently moved to the QUEENSLAND CULTURAL CENTRE, the museum is next to the ART GALLERY OF QUEENSLAND, with which it can be combined in a half-day visit. Main themes are anthropological and natural history, but many of the other exhibits are no less intriguing, such as the section on early Australian aviators such as Charles Kingsford Smith. (The *Southern Cross,* the aircraft in which "Smithy" made his crossing of the Pacific, is on show at Brisbane airport.) The museum also houses a display, including a film, on the continuing underwater excavation of the 18thC wreck of HMS *Pandora.* This British frigate was on its way home from Tahiti carrying captured mutineers from the *Bounty,* when it sank off the Queensland coast.

ST JOHN'S CATHEDRAL
417 Ann St., Fortitude Valley ☎*839 4766. Map 7C3* ☒ *✗ at 10am on Wed, Fri* ⬟ *Open Fri-Tues 10am-noon; Wed-Thurs 10am-3pm.*

Building of the headquarters of the Anglican Church in Queensland started in 1901 and is not expected to finish until the second decade of the 21stC. What appears at present to be a modern façade imposed on the old stonework is in fact the first stage of a western extension, to include a bell tower. The interior is spacious and grand.

TREASURY BUILDING ★
Corner of Queen St. and George St. ☎*224 2111. Map 7D2.*

This most imposing of Brisbane's old buildings was designed by John Clarke, the Colonial Architect, who also created the Treasury in Melbourne and whose liking for the Italian style is evident in the high arcades. Work started in 1885 but because of technical problems took more than 40 years to complete.

Where to stay

Brisbane's hotel standards have improved considerably in the past decade, and the city's reputation as an accommodation wasteland is no longer warranted. The addition of the HILTON, the SHERATON and two other international standard hotels, the BRISBANE CITY TRAVELODGE and GAZEBO RAMADA plus a number of good quality all-suite hotels such as the ABBEY have helped to place Brisbane on the hospitality map. This growth has been stimulated by the city playing host to Expo '88 and its emergence as a Pacific business center. In common with other Australian capital cities, Brisbane hotels rely for much of their Monday to Friday patronage on business travelers. Consequently, the visitor can find some outstanding bargains in weekend packages, even in the five-star chains, saving between 20 and 30 percent of the normal weekday cost. Your excursion to, say, the Sunshine Coast can then be taken during the week, when it will be less crowded anyway.

The city has a good selection of self-catering (efficiency) accommodations with the addition of a number of all-suite hotels. The ubiquitous motel is also well represented in the Queensland capital. Examples of all types of accommodations are featured below.

ABBEY HOTEL

160 Roma St., Brisbane, Qld, 4000 ☎*236 1444* 🖬*236 1134. Map 7D2* 🎟 *87* rooms 🛏 ⇌ 🆎 🔲 🚾 ⇱ ♈ 🎿 ⚲ ⌖
Location: Opposite Brisbane's Transit Centre allowing easy to buses and trains for day trips to the surf of the Gold Coast, just 45 minutes away. Another of Brisbane's recently completed all-suite hotels offering a more homey atmosphere than a normal hotel room with extra space as well as cooking facilities in your room. The 16-story Abbey offers excellent city views from the 10th floor upwards.

BRISBANE CITY TRAVELODGE ♣

Roma St., Brisbane, Qld, 4000 ☎*238 2222* 🖬*41778* 🖬*238 2288. Map 7D2* 🎟*191 rms* 🛏 ⇌ 🆎 🔲 🔘 🚾 ▣ ♈ ♈ ⚲ 🎿
Location: Above the new interstate rail

and bus terminal; although not in the very center, still close enough to be an easy walk. A member of the TraveLodge stable, which is tackling the big international chains in the Pacific by offering broadly comparable facilities and services at reduced rates. The **Drawing Room** restaurant is recommended.

CAMELOT INN ♣

40 Astor Terrace, Brisbane, Qld, 4000 ☎*832 5115* 🖬*45347. Map 7C2* 🎟*70* rms 🛏 🆎 🔲 🔘 🚾 ⇌ ♈ ⇱ ▣ ⚲
Location: On a quiet street, but close enough to the center to be walkable. Recommended for budget travelers. An unpretentious establishment offering all the benefits of a town apartment. Decor is the usual unimaginative standard motel style, but with well-equipped kitchenettes, a pool and laundry, it is hard value to beat.

159

GAZEBO RAMADA ✿

345 Wickham Terrace, Brisbane, Qld, 4000
☎*831 6177* ✉*41050* ℻ *832 5919.*
Map 7C2 ▥ *179 rms* ⊷ ⇒ AE ⊙ ⊚
▨ ⇎ 🖂 ∵ �

*Location: A commanding position
overlooking the city, a brisk 10mins
away.* The decor of this 4-star establishment was totally refurbished in
1990. Given the ungainly pyramid-like
structure, the interiors are surprisingly
spacious.

HILTON INTERNATIONAL BRISBANE

190 Elizabeth St., Brisbane, Qld, 4000
☎*231 3131* ✉*43476* ℻*231 3199. Map
7D2* ▥ *321 rms* ⊷ ⇒ AE ⊙ ⊚ ▨ &
⇎ 🖂 ∵ ☞ ℘ ♈ ♨ �

*Location: Central, between Queen St.
shopping mall and Elizabeth St.* This is
an impressive addition to Brisbane's
quality hotels. The most distinctive feature is the open-plan 25-floor interior, a
futuristic-looking atrium with balconies
on each floor looking down on the
lobby. The so-called **Wintergarden**, a
shopping arcade, covers three floors.
The business traveler will also find a
business center and three executive
floors.

LENNONS

66 Queen St., Brisbane, Qld, 4000 ☎*222
3222* ✉*40252* ℻*221 9389. Map 7D2*
▥ *150 rms* ⊷ ⇒ AE ⊙ ⊚ ▨ ⇎ ☞
♨ 🖂 ∵ �

*Location: Central, next to the Queen St.
shopping mall.* Old Queensland hotels
that have stood the test of time are an
endangered species. This is a hotel
name that goes back more than a century, although sadly the original building in George St. has, like many another
historic address in Brisbane, been demolished. Visitors to Australia longing
for a hotel that combines comfortably
aged leather and a certain style seek in
vain. Lennons, however, competes successfully with the big chains by offering
old-fashioned service.

MAYFAIR CREST ✿

King George Sq., Brisbane, Qld, 4000
☎*229 9111* ✉*41320* ℻*229 9618.*

Map 7D2 ▥ *406 rms* ⊷ ⇒ AE ⊙ ⊚
▨ & ⇎ 🖂 ∵ ☞ ♈ �

Location: Central, opposite City Hall.
The terrace café is a popular spot with
a Continental feel, overlooking the
throng of King George Sq. A youthful,
lively clientele is drawn to the facilities,
which include a nightclub, six bars and
four restaurants. A 24-hour TV news
service is on tap in all rooms.

PARKROYAL

*Corner of Alice St. and Albert St., Brisbane,
Qld, 4000* ☎*221 3411* ✉*40186* ℻*229
9817. Map 7D3* ▥ *149 rms* ⊷ ⇒ AE
⊙ ⊚ ▨ & ⇎ 🖂 ∵ ☞ ℘ ♈ �

*Location: A prime situation, within
easy walking distance of the city center
and Parliament, and with attractive
views over the Botanic Gardens.* The
Parkroyal's location is its biggest draw.
The terraced dining area overlooks the
BOTANIC GARDENS (see SIGHTS). As at the
Sheraton and Hilton, the facilities are
very much geared to the executive.

SHERATON BRISBANE AND TOWERS

249 Turbot St., Brisbane, Qld, 4000 ☎*835
3535* ✉*44944* ℻*835 4960. Map 7C2*
▥ *503 rms* ⊷ ⇒ AE ⊙ ⊚ ▨ ⇔ &
⇎ 🖂 ∵ ☞ �

*Location: Above the old Central rail
station in the downtown shopping and
business district.* This is a truly luxurious and elegant Sheraton. The trend
toward two-class accommodations is
represented by the **Towers** section, located in the three top stories, which
offers club-like seclusion with its own
check-in desk and lounge, and other
additional luxuries. To be thus
cocooned from the hoi polloi costs
around 40 percent more than the standard rate. Top-of-the-world dining at
Denisons restaurant on the 30th floor.

TOWER MILL MOTOR INN

239 Wickham Terrace, Brisbane, Qld, 4000
☎*832 1421* ✉*40382. Map 7C2* ▥ *70
rms* ⊷ ⇒ AE ⊙ ⊚ ▨ 🖂 ∵ �
Location: Overlooking city center. A
quality motel-style inn with rooftop restaurant, bar and a few efficiency (self-catering) units.

Dining out

Restaurant standards have not kept pace with the great strides made in improving Brisbane's accommodations in recent years. Given the quality of local ingredients, seafood, beef and tropical produce, there is little excuse for this. Visitors staying at one of the better hotels may find the in-house restaurant offers better dining than many city eateries. The following, however, can be recommended.

BARRIER REEF SEAFOOD RESTAURANT ♣

138 Albert St. ☎221 9366. Map 7D2 ▥ ▢ ↤ AE ◉ ◎ ▨ *Closed Sat lunch; Sun.*
The unpretentious surroundings will not be favored by diners seeking stylish presentation, but fresh seafood, simply and well prepared, and quite reasonable prices add up to good value. Try the barramundi, a meaty Queensland game fish, which, if fresh, is a genuine treat.

DAVID'S

157 Elizabeth St. (upstairs) ☎229 9033. Map 7D2 ▥ ▢ Y AE ◉ ◎ ▨ *Last orders 11pm. Closed Sun except for private functions.*
Most of Brisbane's restaurants seem to be named after men. (As well as David's and Michael's, there are Aldo's and Jann's.) The cuisine here is actually Chinese-based (Cantonese) but with international variations.

THE DRAWING ROOM ♣

Brisbane City TraveLodge, Roma St. ☎238 2288. Map 7D2 ▥ ▢ ↴ Y ↤ AE ◉ ◎ ▨

Surprisingly good dining is offered in the restaurant of the BRISBANE CITY TRAVELODGE (SEE WHERE TO STAY). Unambitious though it may be, The Drawing Room is nevertheless satisfying; it provides a sensible menu, carefully prepared, simple cuisine, and pleasing surroundings and service.

MICHAEL'S

Riverside Centre 123 Eagle St. ☎832 5522. Map 7D3 ▥ ▢ ↴ Y AE ◉ ◎ ▨ *Closed Sun.*
One of the city's better eating spots, Michael's has won the American Express Award for the Best European-style Restaurant in Brisbane four times, most recently in 1991. Built partly on stilts over the Brisbane River, it enjoys first-class views, particularly at night. It has a stylish interior in keeping with fine dining. Local specialties include coral (sea) trout, mud crabs, lobster and the Moreton Bay bug, a flavorsome crustacean. Its extensive cellar offers a choice of around 600 wines. Attached to the restaurant is a more casual Italian-style bistro with its own kitchen, which offers an à la carte menu.

Entertainment

Like Queensland itself, Brisbane's nightlife is conservative. The main focus is the performing arts complex at the QUEENSLAND CULTURAL CENTRE (see SIGHTS, and below) for theater, opera and concerts, which has gone some way toward silencing the innumerable Sydney and Melbourne jokes about culture in Queensland.

Flashy discos and urban chic have never been Brisbane's style, but there are a few spots where you can bop until late. Visiting international artists now include Brisbane on their itinerary, which in the past was not always the case. Check current productions and shows in *This Week in*

Brisbane, a giveaway guide available at most hotels, and the daily *Courier Mail.*

QUEENSLAND CULTURAL CENTRE

South Bank, South Brisbane ☎information 840 7229, reservations 840 7478. Map 7E2 ✆ ⊒ 𝔸𝔼 ⊕ ⊙ 𝑣𝑖𝑠𝑎

The performing arts complex has transformed the cultural life of the city, bringing under one roof the **Lyric Theatre**, which has become the principal venue for stage shows, and the **Concert Hall**. It can cost less to see a visiting artist here than in, say, Sydney. Otherwise, for drama productions, the **Brisbane Arts Theatre** *(210 Petrie Terrace ☎369 2344)* remains an important venue.

SIBYL'S NIGHTCLUB

383 Adelaide St. ☎839 2355. Map 7C3 ✆ ⊙ ⊒ ⊟ 𝔸𝔼 ⊕ ⊙ 𝑣𝑖𝑠𝑎 Open Wed-Sat 7pm-3am; Sun 7pm-midnight. Casual dining until 11.30pm.

This disco-cum-nightclub is Brisbane's most popular young spot. The two-floor establishment includes a casual dining area, open until 11.30pm. The promotion says Sibyl's is open until 3am, but there are actually times when not enough young Brisbanites bop on to warrant staying open very much beyond midnight.

Where to shop

Brisbane might not offer the variety of Sydney or Melbourne, but shopping here can be less hectic, with the odd chance, in antiques particularly, of a good buy. Like other centers with international airports, Brisbane's duty-free shops can produce real bargains.

Late-night shopping in the city is on Friday until 9pm, but on Saturday shops are open only until noon. The main concentration of shops, including the modern Queen St. Mall, is roughly between George St. and Edward St., and Ann St. and Elizabeth St.

ABORIGINAL ART

Considering that more Aborigines live in Queensland than any other state in Australia, one might have expected to find a good selection of Aboriginal artifacts on sale in Brisbane's shops. Unfortunately this is not the case.

QUEENSLAND ABORIGINAL CREATIONS

135 George St. ☎224 5730. Open Mon-Fri 8.30 am-4.30pm. Map 7D2 & 𝔸𝔼 ⊕ ⊙ 𝑣𝑖𝑠𝑎
This is the curio section of the Department of Aboriginal and Islanders Advancement, and is worth visiting. On sale are the predictable boomerangs, T-shirts and bark paintings for the tourists, but also work with more soul.

ANTIQUES

There is no single hub of the antique trade, rather a few centers with many small stalls under one roof.

CORDELIA STREET ANTIQUE CENTRE

Corner of Cordelia St. and Glenelg St., South Brisbane ☎44 8514. Map 7E2. Open Wed-Sun 10am-5pm 𝔸𝔼 ⊕ ⊙ 𝑣𝑖𝑠𝑎

Housed in an old church, this center specializes in quality pieces rather than bric-a-brac.

PADDINGTON ANTIQUE CENTRE
167 Latrobe Terrace, Paddington ☎*369 8458. Open every day 10am-5pm* 🆎 🔵 🔵 💳
Collectors of objects from the 1940s and 1950s will delight in this center, open seven days from 10am-5pm. Another attraction hereabouts is the **Paddington Circle**, a specialty shopping area in the old suburb to the w of the city on the way to MT. COOT-THA (see SIGHTS, page 157). The shops are in restored Queensland bungalows in Given Terrace and Latrobe Terrace.

ARCADES AND DEPARTMENT STORES
There are a number of modern shopping arcades, including the large **Wintergarden** on the Queen St. Mall, and the **City Plaza** next to the City Hall. But if it is style and old-world charm you seek, ROWES ARCADE is the first choice. There are the usual department stores, including **Myer** and **David Jones**.

ROWES ARCADE
235 Edward St. Map 7D2 🔲 🆎 🔵 💳
Restoration skills have transformed a rather nondescript 1950s shopping arcade, in a late-19thC building, into what it might have been: a grand Victorian structure with vaulted ceilings and Australian red-cedar columns. It houses about 20 boutiques, and has a glassed-in terrace area, where you can have lunch.

Excursions

There are a number of things to be done with a spare day in the environs of Brisbane. Drive w, for example, toward **Mt. Nebo**, 35km (22 miles) into the **Brisbane Forest Park**, which has many pleasant picnic spots, and fine views from the **D'Aguilar Range**. Or take the road N a similar distance to **Redcliffe**, now a rather run-down resort, but actually the first European settlement in Queensland, which had to be abandoned because of fierce opposition from local Aborigines.

Unfortunately, the beaches in the vicinity of Brisbane are not up to Queensland's high standards, and for good swimming you must travel farther afield. The excursions described below offer the same basic features: vast stretches of white beach, superb surf and almost continuous sunshine. Choice of destination will be dictated by what sort of environment you prefer. The distinction, it should be stressed, is an important one. As always in Australia, the distances make it preferable to set aside at least 2 days, and a car is essential.

THE GOLD COAST
Round trip of 210km (131 miles) to Coolangatta, southern limit of the coast, but allow for an overnight stop.
This is, by a long way, Australia's most popular resort area, and offers very much what you might expect of a local version of the Costa del

Sol or Miami, with similar advantages and drawbacks. The beachfront is a solid 30km (19 miles) of high-rises, neon, motels, fast-food outlets and nightspots. At its worst, the Gold Coast is tawdry and over-crowded. On the credit side, there is a great deal to do, particularly for families and younger vacationers, and keen competition has given local services, and prices, the sort of edge it would be good to find elsewhere in Australia. The beach everywhere is splendid.

Leave Brisbane via Ann St., following the signs to the South East Freeway, which becomes Route 1, the Pacific Highway. The turn-off for Southport — the start of the Gold Coast — is 62km (39 miles) to the s of the city.

From here the resorts run one into the other: **Main Beach**, **Surfers Paradise**, **Broadbeach**, **Mermaid Beach**, **Burleigh Heads**, **Palm Beach**, **Currumbin**, **Tugun**, **Bilinga** and **Coolangatta**. Most populous of all these is Surfers Paradise, where the skyscraper jungle blots out the sun from the beach in the late afternoon. Generally speaking, the farther s you go, the less crowded the resorts become.

There are several off-beach attractions along the way. **Dreamworld** *(open 10am-5pm* ☎ *(075)53 1133)*, a Disneyland imitation on the Pacific Highway 4km (2½ miles) before the Southport turn-off, is recommended for children young and old, but is pricey. **Sea World** *(open 10am-5pm* ☎ *(075)32 5131)*, a marine showland at Main Beach, features dolphins and sea lions and has an amusement park; as at Dreamworld, a hefty entrance fee gets you admission to all shows and rides. The **Warner Bros. Movie World Theme Park** *(* ☎ *(075) 7399)*, on the Pacific Highway at Oxenford on the Gold Coast, is based on a successful US concept. For a hefty entrance fee, you can see a fully operational movie studio with behind-the-scenes action, comedy and stunts. Fun for the children — if you can afford it.

☞ The range of accommodations on the Gold Coast is so vast — literally hundreds of motels, hotels and efficiency (self-catering) apartments — that to offer more than a few pointers is impossible. At the height of the season you may be lucky to find a bed on short notice at all; at other times you can take your pick, and even negotiate a rate. Bear in mind that catering standards are variable: self-con-tained units can mean that you eat better, as well as save money.

The **Conrad International Hotel and Jupiters Casino** *(Southport* ☎ *(075) 92 1133* ▥ *to* ▥*)* offers Hilton-style accommodations and the chance to lose your shirt 24 hours a day. The **Ramada** *(Surfers Paradise* ☎ *(075) 59 3400* ▥*)* is another 5-star establishment. The **Greenmount Inn** *(Coolangatta* ☎ *(075) 36 1222* ▥*)* is comfortable and located in a comparatively quiet resort.

THE SUNSHINE COAST

Caloundra, nearest point on the Sunshine Coast to Brisbane, is a round trip of 220km (138 miles). Noosa Heads, the farthest, is 320km (200 miles) N.

Another sun-drenched stretch of perfect beach, roughly the same dis-tance N of Brisbane as the Gold Coast is s, the Sunshine Coast is, however, much less a resort. The beaches are splendid, the weather just as good, the environment less gaudy, but there are not the distractions of, say, Surfers Paradise. Most travelers are apt to prefer this less commercial development. If your idea of heaven is basking with a good book, and swimming (the surf is good here too), this could be your favorite spot in Australia.

To get there, take Turbot St. going N out of Brisbane and follow signs for Route 1, the Bruce Highway. The Caloundra turn-off is about 10km (6 miles) beyond Landsborough. From Caloundra the road runs N along the coast for 60km (38 miles) or so to the attractive development of **Noosa Heads** before swinging back inland to the Bruce Highway. Resorts along the Sunshine Coast include **Maroochydore**, **Marcoola Beach**, **Coolum Beach** and **Peregian Beach**. These are all pleasant spots with excellent surf and swimming, and preferences are a matter for the individual. However, Coolum can be particularly recommended for its beach, placid pace and comfortable accommodations at reasonable rates; Noosa offers plenty of diversion and some fine accommodations.

But the Sunshine Coast has a few attractions besides the beach. At Maroochydore there is a two-thirds-scale replica of **Cook's ship**, HM *Endeavour Bark (open 10am-4pm ☎ (074) 48 4488)*. The headland overlooking the Pacific at Noosa is a national park where this splendid coastline is preserved, and offers 10km (6 miles) of walking tracks around the headland, with fine views and good picnicking.

✎   There is no shortage of hotels and motels along the Sunshine Coast, as well as numerous efficiency (self-catering) apartments (although these are usually for a minimum of 2 days). Agencies such as **Accom Noosa** *(Hastings St., Noosa Heads, Qld, 4567 ☎ (074) 47 3444 ⓣ 43494)* will make reservations and give advice.

The following all have efficiency units as well as restaurants: the **Noosa International** *(Noosa Heads ☎ (071) 47 4822 ▥ to▥)*, a luxurious resort with 65 units, two swimming pools, bars and conference facilities; and the **Stewarts Coolum Hotel/Motel** *(Coolum Beach ☎ (074) 46 1899 ▢)*, an excellent-value, comfortable motel.

•   See also ROUTE 5 and map in TOURS on pages 74-5.

The Great Barrier Reef and islands

When all is said and done, Queensland has one unique natural resource that transcends all others. The beaches in New South Wales may be almost as good. Tasmania is probably prettier. Victoria is undoubtedly more stimulating. What finally makes Queensland worth visiting is the Great Barrier Reef.

So what, in fact, is the Great Barrier Reef? Quite simply, it is the world's largest complex of coral reefs — more than 2,600 in all — which follow, roughly, the coast for about 2,000km (1,250 miles), incorporate some 300 islands, and — as any self-respecting Queenslander will tell you, with a fondness for dimension that is a local characteristic — also constitute the largest creation of living creatures in the world.

More to the point, the reef is the infrastructure for a breathtaking variety of marine fauna. Here, at depths in some cases of no more than a couple of feet, are literally hundreds of coral forms in different colors, thousands of shellfish varieties, and, most dazzling of all, the many fish species: vivid parrot fish, angelfish, rays and sharks, which glide through these turquoise waters like visions of a fantasy underwater world glimpsed by most people only on film.

You need not be an experienced underwater diver either with scuba or snorkel to enter this world. The wonders of the Great Barrier Reef can be seen as readily from a glass-bottom boat, although skindiving offers profounder pleasure, and can be accomplished by ordinary swimmers.

There are other reasons for visiting the islands. They offer splendid isolation in the sort of Pacific setting represented by exotic advertising campaigns. It is all quite genuine: this is an idyllic, tropical Australia of coconut palms and astonishingly blue seas.

GETTING THERE

One myth has to be dispelled, and that is the idea that having arrived in Queensland, you will find coral reefs lying off the beach. This is not the Red Sea, where you step straight into a brilliantly colored subaqueous world. The Great Barrier Reef does not start until you are around 450km (280 miles) N of Brisbane, and the southern section is more than 100km (60 miles) out to sea. Generally speaking, the farther N you go, the closer the reef comes to the mainland, but there is no one point at which they meet.

To get to the reef, therefore, involves cruising from the islands as well as the mainland. Some tour operators unfortunately tend to perpetuate the common misconception that the islands are located on coral reefs. In fact, of the 20 or so islands that have been commercially developed as resorts, only three — **Green Island**, **Heron Island** and **Lady Elliott Island** — are genuine coral cays. Others may have fringing reef close by, but to see the Great Barrier Reef in its full splendor you will still need to join a cruise ship or one of the high-speed catamarans operating along the coast.

A word of warning, however. Most of the islands have just one, often extravagantly expensive, resort, and if you have reserved an extended

166

stay and find you dislike it, there is little to be done. Quite a number of guests come away from an island with a feeling that what the system needs is an injection of old-fashioned competition. When all fares, accommodations and extras are paid, an excursion to the islands and reef is not going to be cheap, so find out as much as you can in advance. (It is worth asking about stand-by offers available at most island resorts out of season, which provide cut-rate accommodations on short notice.)

Cautionary advice should not be regarded as a deterrent. The reef is arguably Australia's greatest natural wonder, with its hundreds of varieties of coral encrusting the seabed, from large mushroom formations to delicate fan shapes. It should leave a memory to cherish.

But, at the risk of laboring a point, avoidable disappointments do occur. You may, for example, go out for a day's sailing on one of the numerous charter yachts in the **Whitsundays**, a cluster of islands off the coast near **Mackay**. You will be told that the vessel will be calling at a number of islands, and that during the day you will be able to dive at the reef. Now the chance to island-hop on a graceful 40-foot yacht is another of Queensland's attractions. These cruises can be great fun, and they do indeed offer an opportunity to do some snorkeling. But they are decidedly not specialized reef visits, and often what you get to see gives no idea of the wonders of the coral world. Broadly speaking, the visitor who has a week or so to explore the Queensland coast should keep skindiving and sailing apart. That way, neither is likely to be a disappointment.

It is for these reasons that this section has been divided into two main parts. The reef is closest to the mainland and thus most accessible in the far N of the state, and much of the section under the heading CAIRNS TO TOWNSVILLE deals with ways of visiting the reef from here. The central coast, on the other hand, is the cruise capital of Queensland, and the emphasis in the section MACKAY AND THE WHITSUNDAYS is on sailing and island resorts.

For further information, contact the **Great Barrier Reef Marine Park Authority** *(P.O. Box 1379, Townsville, Qld, 4810 ☎(077) 81 8811),* which has produced an excellent series of pamphlets on corals and marine life.

Cairns to Townsville

This section, which covers the Far North, is presented in the form of an extended excursion. The distance involved, around 650km (400 miles) with side trips, is not great in Australian terms, but 4 days is a minimum time-framework; the region is full of variety, and even a week would not be too long.

Cairns has an international airport, which makes it possible to start, or end, your Australian visit here. Most travelers will want to see CAIRNS, the main center for visiting the reef. The point of the 370km (231-mile) drive s along the coastal road is that it affords access to a number of islands off the usual track, and ends in TOWNSVILLE, which is one of Queensland's few unheralded pleasures. Cars rented in Cairns can be returned in Townsville, which connects by air with Brisbane and Sydney, as well as other centers. If you were departing Australia from Cairns, the excursion could be done in reverse, starting at Townsville. Either way, much of what is best in Queensland can be found in this relatively small section of the Far North.

CAIRNS

1,840km (1,150 miles) NW of Brisbane ☎*STD (area) code: 070. Airport* ☎*50 5222; Ansett* ☎*50 2211; Australian* ☎*50 3711. Rail station: McLeod St.* ☎*51 1111. Car rental: Avis* ☎*51 5911; Budget* ☎*51 9222; Hertz* ☎*51 6399.*

Despite the enormous commercial development that Cairns has undergone in the past 15 years, it retains a flavor of the tropics that makes it not quite Australian, rather of the South Pacific. The **wharf**, once called the Barbary Coast, the palm trees, the ethnic blend, which includes Torres Strait islanders: all these seem to belong more in the pages of William Somerset Maugham than in the songs of Banjo Patterson.

Still, the impact on the town flowing from the tourism boom of the past 15 years or so has been immense. Cairns has become a major game-fishing center, the **black marlin** being the lure for big-spending sportsmen. The other main attraction, of course, is the Great Barrier Reef. Because of the reef's proximity to Cairns and the little town of **Port Douglas**, about 60km (38 miles) N, these are the best points on the Queensland coast from which to explore the reef.

For the visitor, this is Cairns' main significance. The town has little of intrinsic interest, being more a launching pad for its environs, which include not only the reef, but the splendid tropical **Daintree rainforest**, and, to the W, the **Atherton Tablelands**.

Just what you can accomplish will depend on how much time you have. The advised minimum for a stay in the Cairns area would be 2 days, allowing a day for a visit to the reef and a day for a side trip to the rainforest. An additional day could be spent on a side trip to the Atherton Tablelands, or on the beach.

Odd though it may sound, it is worth considering whether you actually need to stay in Cairns at all. There is no beach to speak of in town, and if you want to spend your 2-3 days here alongside a fine palm-fringed beach it is necessary to drive N. From **Holloways Beach**, about 12km (7½ miles) from Cairns, there is a string of splendid beaches with good accommodations. Some of these are mentioned below, under the heading NORTH TO PORT DOUGLAS AND DAINTREE.

What follows is a series of options that could be fitted into a stay in the Cairns region. Additional information is available from the centrally located **Visitor Information Centre** *(27 Shield St.* ☎*51 7366* 🅴🅰*31 3318, open 8am-6pm).*

☜   The **Hilton** *(* ☎*52 1599* 🅴🅰*52 1370* ▥*)* is the best Cairns has to offer. Situated on Wharf St., it is close to the city's business and tourist center with views across Trinity Bay, the mountains and the Pacific. The **Pacific International**

(☎ 51 7888 ☒ 48352 Fx 51 0210 Ⅲ) is the Hilton's main rival for the well-heeled, and is ideally placed on the esplanade. The **Lyons** *(☎ 51 2311 Fx 31 1294 ☒ 48415 Ⅲ)*, also on the seafront, is comfortable and good value. A block from the esplanade is **Coral Cay Villas** *(☎ 31 2377 Fx 31 2703)*, typical of the good-quality, reasonably priced holiday apartments that abound in Cairns. It has 42 units, some of which are family-sized.

SEEING THE REEF

There are two main commercial cruise operators to the reef, **Great Adventures** of Cairns *(☎ (070) 51 5644)* and **Quicksilver and Connections** of Port Douglas *(☎ (070) 99 5500)*. Both offer a range of cruises to the nearby islands and to the outer reef.

GREEN ISLAND

Great Adventures runs cruises to this popular resort off Cairns. The *cognoscenti* tend to be contemptuous of Green Island, which hosts a stream of day-trippers and which, far from being a secluded Pacific hideaway, can on a busy day seem more like England's Brighton. It remains, however, a genuine coral cay, and is the easiest and cheapest way of seeing the reef. There are fast and slow (and less expensive) services daily from the Great Adventures wharf, which include lunch and a spin round the reef in a glass-bottom boat. The coral here suffered quite severely from the voracious crown-of-thorns starfish, but has regenerated to some extent.

THE LOW ISLES

The Low Isles are also coral cays, but without a resort — indeed, the isles are uninhabited except for a lighthouse keeper. They are served by the highly professional Quicksilver and Low Isles Cruises from Port Douglas, with bus connections possible from Cairns and various points in-between. A day's outing, departing 10.30am and returning 4.30pm, includes a good lunch, instruction on and use of snorkeling gear, a diving platform, and glass-bottom-boat viewing. The reef here has more varied coral than Green Island, and this excursion arguably offers better value.

THE OUTER REEF

The same operators also run cruises to the outer reef. What, it may be asked, does the outer reef offer that is not found elsewhere? The short answer is visibility. Sediment from the seabed is stirred far less than on the inner reef, so that the clarity and colors of coral life and fish are greatly enhanced. The cost of the outer-reef one-day excursion is high, but well worth considering as a once-in-a-lifetime experience. If you are only ever going to make one trip out to the Great Barrier Reef, this should be it.

The high-speed catamaran *Quicksilver* moors at a diving platform off **Agincourt Reef**. Snorkeling equipment, glass-bottom boat viewing and lunch are included. Optional extras are guided snorkeling with a marine biologist, and for those with recognized certificates, two 40-minute dives.

Great Adventures also cruises to the outer reef, from Cairns, with a stop at Green Island to pick up guests at the resort; but less time is spent

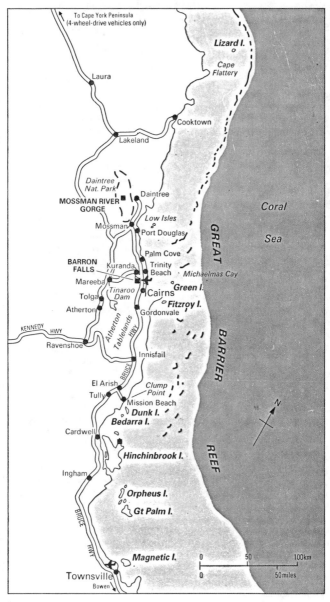

at the outer reef. Another Great Adventures service, also calling at Green Island, runs to **Michaelmas Cay**, a protected breeding ground for seabirds.

OTHER OPTIONS

Cairns offers access to two other island resorts on the reef. One is **Lizard Island**, possibly Australia's most exclusive getaway, apparently favored by celebrities and with prices to match. Lizard is reachable only by air, from Cairns.

    Fitzroy Island is a happy medium between Green and Lizard islands. This is an attractive spot with good beaches, some walking opportunities and a fast catamaran service to the outer reef.

    Other pointers for seeing the reef from Cairns: the **Deep Sea Divers Den** (☎ *(070) 31 2223)* offers scuba-diving instruction; **Down Under Aquatics** (☎ *(070) 31 1588)* runs daily diving trips for experienced and novice scuba users. Even snorkellers are welcome.

✥   **Green Island** *(inquiries for day trips* ☎*(070) 51 4644* ▥*)*. **Fitzroy Island** accommodations: in lodges *(inquiries and reservations* ☎*(070) 51 9588* ▥*)*.

NORTH TO PORT DOUGLAS AND DAINTREE

Over a distance of only 80km (50 miles) or so, the road N of Cairns runs by some of the loveliest, most unspoiled beaches in Australia, passing the delightful settlement of Port Douglas and the rainforests of Daintree. If at all possible, it really ought not to be missed.

    Follow Route 1, the Cook Highway, N of Cairns. There are turnoffs to beach resorts until at **Palm Cove** the road joins the coast, and from here to Mossman is a glorious drive. There are accommodations at **Holloways Beach**, 12km (7½ miles) from Cairns, **Trinity Beach**, 24km (15 miles) and **Clifton Beach**, 26km (16 miles). At **Palm Cove**, 30km (19 miles) N of Cairns, is the **Ramada Reef Resort**, a most attractive and comfortable development. Also at Palm Cove is **Wild World** (☎ *(070) 55 3669 for feeding times)*, which has a few specimens of the estuarine saltwater crocodile found in these parts. Up to 20 feet long and responsible for all of the recent crocodile attacks on humans, this is the world's largest and most fearsome reptile.

    Port Douglas, although 60km (38 miles) N of Cairns, could serve just as well as your base for N Queensland. This charming little fishing port has as its main attraction the magnificent **Four Mile Beach**, and is the center of operations for Quicksilver and Low Isles Cruises. Local folk are starting to regret, however, that their sleepy hollow is becoming an exclusive international destination. The **Port Douglas Sheraton Mirage** (☎ *070 99 5888)*, a 5-star resort with 300 rooms, a golf course and a swimming pool covering 1.6ha (4 acres), was completed in 1987 and has had a considerable impact on what was once a backwater.

    The **Daintree National Park**, one of Australia's great, but diminishing, tropical rainforests, stretches almost 57,000ha (140,000 acres), but its southern end is within 20km (12½ miles) of Port Douglas. To get there, continue N on the Cook Highway to **Mossman**, a small farming town, and follow the turnoff on the left to **Mossman River Gorge**, a lovely unspoiled wilderness where you can picnic and swim in a large fresh-water pool at the bottom of some rapids (no danger of crocodiles). **Platypuses**, rarely seen in the wild, can sometimes be spotted surfacing on quiet stretches of the river, and there is grand walking in the rainforest.

There is no shortage of attractions N of Cairns, and if you have only a day to spare after seeing the reef you could spend it well here. **Daintree Rain Forest Walkabout** *(☎(070) 34 1110)* runs day tours of the Daintree and Cape Tribulation in 4-wheel-drive vehicles.

✆   Two alternatives to staying in Cairns are the **Clifton Sands** *(right on Clifton Beach ☎(070) 55 3355 ☒(070)55 3902)*, secluded, with efficiency (self-catering) units, and the **Ramada Reef Resort** *(Palm Cove ☎(070) 55 3999 ☒(070) 55 3902 ▥ to ▥)*.

Perhaps the best value in Port Douglas is the **Island Point Motel** *(☎(070) 98 5126 ▢)*: superb sea views, and a short walk to the beach. Also comfortable is the **Rusty Pelican Inn** *(☎(070) 98 5266 ▢)*.

Accommodations overlooking Mossman River Gorge are available at the **Silky Oaks Colonial Lodge** *(☎(070) 98 1666 ▥)*.

▭   In Port Douglas, dine at **Danny's** *(☎(070) 98 5187 ▥)*, at the waterside, a restaurant of a quality unusual in N Queensland that serves good bouillabaisse.

ATHERTON TABLELANDS

These highlands, at an altitude of 700m (2,300 feet), are a popular weekend trip among Cairns residents looking to escape the coastal humidity. A round trip taking in all points along the way is about 185km (115 miles), but although the attractive scenery includes water-falls, lakes and rainforests, the foreign visitor pressed for time will not miss a great deal by doing only part of the circuit.

An off-beat excursion of obvious interest to rail buffs is offered by Queensland Railways. The **Cairns-Kuranda line**, opened in 1891 and an engineering wonder in its time, is still in service: tourist specials depart from Cairns station twice daily *(8.30am, 9am ☎(070) 51 0531 for reservations)*. It stops at the **Barron Falls**, a spectacular sight when in spate, and terminates at the picturesque old station of **Kuranda**.

For drivers, the route to the Atherton Tablelands is clearly signposted from Cairns. Kuranda is 27km (17 miles) by road, and the Barron Falls are passed *en route.* The road continues through **Mareeba**, but a turnoff at Tolga for **Tinaroo Dam** cuts out the town of Atherton, which is of no particular interest. At **Kairi** on Tinaroo Dam it is worth taking the dirt road that rounds the dam to the N and passes through tropical rainforest, where there is a giant old tree known as the **Cathedral Fig**. The road rejoins a tarmac road to **Gordonvale** and Cairns. A short detour, back toward Atherton, leads to **Lake Barrine**, an extinct volcano.

OTHER TRIPS FROM CAIRNS

Cape York Peninsula, the great prong of northern Queensland jutting out into the Coral Sea, is a truly awesome wilderness with access limited strictly to 4-wheel-drive vehicles. Such trips are more in the nature of expeditions of 2 weeks and more, and are confined to the dry season, from June to December. **Queensland Government Travel Centres** can help with information.

Reef Air (☎ *537 936)* offers three scenic flights from Cairns, ranging from 35 minutes to three hours. **Going Places** *(☎ (070) 51 4055* [Fx] *(070) 31 4405),* runs 7- to 14-day camping trips to Cape Yorke.

THE ROAD TO TOWNSVILLE
The road s, around 370km (230 miles) in length, and some distance from the coast, is unremarkable scenically. But it takes in lovely **Mission Beach**, and is the stepping-off point to three islands, **Dunk**, **Bedarra** and **Hinchinbrook**.

Leave Cairns heading s by Route 1, the Bruce Highway. **Innisfail**, 88km (55 miles) away, is an unremarkable commercial center, but at **El Arish**, about 40km (25 miles) farther, there is a turnoff to **Mission Beach**. A few kilometers away is **Clump Point**, the starting point for trips out to **Dunk Island** and the reef.

Three operators run crossings to Dunk, and fares are consequently competitive. The *Quick Cat,* a high-speed catamaran, is one of these, and cruises on from Dunk Island to the Great Barrier Reef; the reef fare includes lunch, snorkeling equipment and glass-bottom-boat viewing.

Dunk Island is lush and unspoiled, but the tariff puts the sole resort, owned by Australian Airlines, in the luxury category *(air transfers from Cairns or Townsville* ☎ *(070) 68 8199 for inquiries and reservations).* Nearby **Bedarra Island**, which is reachable from Dunk, has two resorts, the **Hideaway**, closed for refurbishment, and the **Bedarra Bay**, which has 16 private villas surrounding a bay. Bedarra Bay resort is one of Queensland's most exclusive and expensive. Small wonder that Queensland's islands are rapidly becoming inaccessible to all but wealthy travelers.

From Mission Beach the road is signposted to **Tully,** where you rejoin the Bruce Highway. **Cardwell**, about 50km (30 miles) farther s, is the terminus for ferries to **Hinchinbrook Island**. Having an area of 642sq.km (248sq. miles), this is the largest of the islands, and it has one of the smallest and most luxurious resorts. But you can also **camp** on Hinchinbrook, with permission from the **National Parks Office** in Cardwell.

The remaining distance to Townsville is about 160km (100 miles).

✎ At Mission Beach a new resort, **Castaways** *(☎ (070) 68 7444* [Fx] *(070) 687 429* ▥**□**), is secluded and tasteful and, compared with the adjacent islands, not expensive. For Dunk Island, contact Australian Airlines *(☎ (070) 68 8199* ▥). Hinchinbrook Island's exclusive resort *(☎ (070) 66 8585* [Tx] *148971* ▥) accommodates just 30 people in great luxury.

TOWNSVILLE
1,470km (919 miles) NW of Brisbane ☎*STD (area) code: 077. Airport* ☎*81 1211; Ansett* ☎*27 3666; Australian* ☎*81 6211. Rail station: 502 Flinders St.*

☎ *72 8211. Car rental: Avis* ☎ *75 2888; Budget* ☎ *25 2344; Hertz* ☎ *71 6033.*

There are few more pleasant urban centers in Queensland than this place of 86,000 souls. Townsville is described as a city — indeed, the second largest in the state — but in most terms it is a charming, leafy town nestling at the foot of a 290m (951-foot) peak, **Castle Hill**, overlooking the Pacific. Civic heads have been far more circumspect in allowing new development than their fellows elsewhere in the state, and apart from a **Sheraton** hotel-casino down at the port, high-rise building has been confined to the small city-center. The suburb of **North Ward**, below Castle Hill, consists largely of stylish old colonial homes with wide verandas.

The city's sights can be easily fitted into a half-day. The lookout at the top of Castle Hill offers a great panorama on either side: out to the Pacific, and back to the hinterland. Down on the park-lined waterfront of **The Strand** are two superb 19thC colonial buildings, the **Customs House** and **NQ Television Centre**, formerly the Queens Hotel. Neither is open for public inspection, but the exteriors alone are worth going to see. At the eastern end of The Strand is the wharf on **Ross Creek** where the ferries leave for **Magnetic Island**, and where the **Great Barrier Reef Wonderland**, an attractive concept combining scientific research and entertainment, opened in 1987.

For information on the Townsville region, contact **Townsville Enterprises Ltd.** *(3 The Strand, Townsville* ☎ *71 2724).*

✍ Townsville has only gained quality hotels quite recently. The **Sheraton Breakwater Casino-Hotel** *(*☎ *222 333* ⊡ *47999* ▥ *)* is a high-rise that opened in 1986. There is also the **Ambassador** *(The Strand* ☎ *72 4255* ⊠ *21 1316* ▥ *).* The budget-conscious should consider the **Townsville Reef International** *(The Strand* ☎ *21 1777* ⊠ *211 779* ▥ *),* good value and on the waterfront.

⊟ Recommended for eating out: **Café Veneto** *(Flinders St. East* ☎ *71 3111* ▥ *),* for Mediterranean-style cuisine, an open-air setting, and dinner from Tuesday to Sunday.

ISLANDS AND THE REEF

Two islands are served by transportation from Townsville: **Magnetic Island** and **Orpheus Island**. The latter is one of the most expensive of the luxury off-coast Queensland resorts — with astronomic rates per night and similar developments proliferating, it may be wondered where all the guests are coming from.

Magnetic Island, 35 minutes' ferry ride away (Great Adventures departs from the wharf roughly on the hour) is far from exclusive. It has a resident population, five resorts and more than a dozen sets of vacation units. But because it is one of the largest islands, being more than 10km (6 miles) across, it still has quiet beaches and coves: **Arcadia**, for example, is a quieter spot than **Picnic Bay**. Island transportation is by bus or rented Moke.

One of the new generation of fast catamarans, the *Reef Link,* runs from the Townsville wharf, via Picnic Bay on Magnetic Island, to a diving platform on the Great Barrier Reef. The fare covers lunch and snorkeling at the reef (☎ *(077) 21 2109 for reservations)*. It should be mentioned, however, that the coral around Townsville was ravaged by the crown-of-thorns starfish, and if possible it is better to take one of the reef cruises that start in Port Douglas or Cairns.

If you end this excursion in Townsville, you can fly s to MACKAY AND THE WHITSUNDAYS, to Brisbane, Sydney or Melbourne, or overseas.

✎ For details of self-catering (efficiency) accommodations on Magnetic Island contact the Tourist Bureau at Nelly Bay (☎ *78 5596)*.

Mackay and the Whitsundays

This region, virtually unknown outside Queensland until around 15 years ago, is now the fastest growing in terms of tourism. The attraction is the island group known as the **Whitsundays**, so named in 1770 by Captain James Cook on his epic *Endeavour* voyage. Of the 74 islands, eight have been developed as resorts, a concentration that offers the widest choice of island accommodations along the Queensland coast. Moreover, the shelter provided by the island chain makes the **Whitsunday Passage** a favorite all-year sailing ground, with opportunities for even the inexperienced and relatively impecunious to get the feel of a wooden deck under sail.

Once again, the object of this section is to offer a few options to the visitor who has limited time but intends to make full use of it. The approach is necessarily a subjective one, because of the great choice of resorts and cruises. Allowing for transfers, 3 days would be the minimum necessary for anyone wanting to stay on an island and do some sailing. The more specialized sailing packages are generally for 5-7 days.

For more detailed information before setting out, write to the **Whitsunday Tourism Association** *(P.O. Box 83, Airlie Beach, Qld, 4802* ☎ *(079) 46 6673* Ⓕ*46 7387)* for their unusually helpful guides.

WHERE TO START
Begin at **Mackay**, capital of the sugar-growing region, a pleasant and unhurried town roughly halfway up the Queensland coast. It can be reached by air from Sydney, Melbourne or Brisbane. Or extend the previous excursion from TOWNSVILLE, about 5 hours away by road — or do it in reverse, flying one-way to Mackay, renting a car, then driving N to Townsville and Cairns, a total distance of about 740km (460 miles).

In this part of the country a car comes in even more handy than usual, because the logistics of getting to the Whitsundays are complicated. Mackay is the main regional center, but it is still more than 150km (94 miles) s of **Shute Harbour**, center for island departures (and the busiest yachting marina outside Sydney). Island guests usually take another flight for the short hop to **Proserpine**, but the independent traveler is better off renting a car in Mackay, where it is unnecessary to linger, and heading N on Route 1, the **Bruce Highway**.

175

Proserpine is about 120km (75 miles) from Mackay. Just to the N of the town is the exit to **Airlie Beach** and Shute Harbour, another 35km (22 miles) away. Airlie Beach is the principal mainland resort of the Whitsundays, and as accommodations at Shute Harbour are extremely limited most visitors use this as their base. Many of the accommodations are undistinguished, but in season Airlie Beach gets crammed: reservations are necessary.

At Airlie Beach you can make your plans for cruising and visiting the islands. The resorts can supply a bewildering array of brochures on cruising and other entertainment. The **Whitsunday Tourism Association** (☎ *(079) 46 6673)* is good for advice. Island accommodations can be reserved in town.

☞ Recommended at Airlie Beach: you can sleep in attractive Polynesian-style huts at the **Club Magnums** (☎ *(079) 46 6266* ℻*(079) 46 5980* ▯*);* just out of town, the **Reef Oceania Village** (☎ *(079) 46 6137* ℻*46 6846*▯*)* is good value for a mainly young clientele.

SAILING IN THE WHITSUNDAYS

The readiest way to get a taste of sailing is on a one-day trip from Airlie or Shute. A number of vessels cruise daily and offer a similar package: a cruise, usually with up to 30 passengers, taking in two or three islands and stopping for snorkeling, windsurfing and lunch (all included in the package price).

Two recommended examples are the *Gretel,* a 67-foot sloop that challenged for the America's Cup, and the *Tri Tingira,* a spacious 45-foot trimaran, which would be more suitable for families, and good value. For snorkeling most vessels cruise to a reef known as **Langford**, but although it is still pleasant to dive here, it should not be imagined that this is the Great Barrier Reef at anything like its best. The first of the large coral reefs, **Hook Reef**, is another 40km (25 miles) or so farther out.

More serious sailing is also more expensive. There are two options for those interested in longer cruises: crewed charters, in which you are a guest on board, with all meals and services provided; or what are known as bareboat charters, where you rent a yacht and sail it yourself. Obviously the latter requires some competence, but courses can be arranged on short notice, for which inexperience is not necessarily looked upon as a disqualification.

Crewed charter options include *Cygnus,* a 55-foot ketch, which takes 18 passengers on a one-week cruise, anchoring each evening to camp on an island, and the *Golden Plover,* a square-rigged brigantine, which makes excellent-value 5-day cruises with 40 passengers on a similar basis. Details from **Coral Sea Line** *(P.O. Box 497, Airlie Beach, Qld, 4802* ☎*(079) 46 6049).*

Bareboat charter operators include **Queensland Yacht Charters** *(P.O. Box 293, Airlie Beach, Qld, 4802* ☎*(079) 46 7400)* and **Whitsunday Rent-a-Yacht** *(PMB 25, Mackay, Qld, 4741* ☎*(079) 46 9232).*

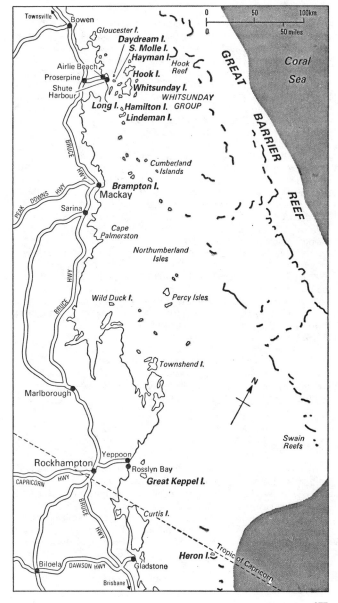

THE ISLANDS

The trend on the islands is increasingly toward exclusive, high-tariff resorts for a pampered few. Of the eight commercial islands in the Whitsundays, for example, two — **Lindeman** and **Hayman** — have undergone major refurbishment, with a consequent price hike. Lindeman has been bought by the French Club Mediterranée and reopens in the Club Med guise in September 1992. After an A$250 million rebuild, Hayman Island is now a member of the Leading Resorts and Hotels of the World organization, but has now widened its appeal to cover families. Another, **Hamilton Island**, has been developed, with a budget of around A$200m, to take around 1,000 guests, with flights from state capitals.

Rates of less than A$100 per person per day are exceptional, but remember that stand-by rates apply when the resort has vacancies, and these can involve big savings. For example, at **The Island**, one of the more reasonably priced resorts, on **Long Island**, the daily rate is reduced by 35 percent on stand-by. Some choices:

Daydream Island   A tiny island that is just about all resort. Windsurfing, waterskiing, canoeing, tennis, and access by launch to the reef for snorkeling and scuba diving *(☎(079) 46 9200 ℻(079) 48 8499).*

South Molle Island   A resort for the young, with plenty of nighttime activity. All the usual watersports, launch to reef, tennis, golf; 400ha (990 acres) of national park walks *(☎(079) 46 9433 ℻(079) 46 9580 ℡48132).*

Long Island   In addition to the **Whitsunday 100** resort mentioned above *(☎(079) 46 9400),* Long Island has a remarkably cheap resort, **Palm Bay**, with self-catering cabins *(☎(079) 46 9233).*

Hook Island   This large island of unspoiled beauty does not have a resort. What it does have to make the 90-minute launch-ride out from Shute Harbour worthwhile is an **underwater observatory**, a viewing platform 9m (30 feet) below the surface that is an obvious attraction for the elderly, for children, and for anyone unable to view the reef as a swimmer.

Other islands

For the overseas visitor there are two other islands in Queensland that are remote and do not fit into a convenient excursion-type framework, but nevertheless have specific attractions. One of the islands, **Heron**, is a true coral cay — in other words, it is actually part of the reef, with coral growing up to the beach. The other is **Great Keppel Island**, where the emphasis is on entertainment and a fairly hectic nightlife. Both are at the bottom end of the Great Barrier Reef, between Rockhampton and Gladstone. In general terms, the cost of getting there is such that it is only worthwhile if you intend staying some time, and it would be advisable to think in terms of a package, which includes air transfers.

GREAT KEPPEL ISLAND

The island is directly off the coast from **Rockhampton**, capital of the Queensland cattle-farming region and a town of some interest to students of colonial architecture. If only more hotels were like the 19thC **Criterion** *(Quay St, Rockhampton* ☎ *(079) 22 1225* Ⓔⓧ *(079) 22 1226* ▢ *):* not only splendid to look at, but providing quite acceptable accommodations at exceptional value.

For those not on a fly-in package, Great Keppel is accessible by launch from **Rosslyn Bay**, a rather seedy little port that is itself a 40km (25-mile) bus ride from Rockhampton.

Great Keppel is billed as being all about up-tempo fun: a resort where the music never stops, but where as well as a **Wreck Bar Disco**, there is a **Keppel Kids Klub** (so middle-aged ravers with kids are welcome as well). It is a large island of some 1,400ha (3,500 acres) and with more than a dozen beaches. There are accommodations for 320 guests. **Australian Airlines**, which owns the resort, has a range of Keppel packages.

HERON ISLAND

This is for people who can't get enough of the reef, with living coral virtually at the water's edge. Heron is not a large island, but the diversity of its sea life has been a lure for skindivers for years. Scuba equipment is available for rent, along with diving courses. The island is also a seasonal base for migratory birds and nesting turtles.

Rates for accommodations are quite reasonable by island standards. Transportation, however, is awkward and expensive: departures are from Gladstone, an isolated town 107km (67 miles) s of Rockhampton, by helicopter. All inquiries to **Heron Island Reservations** *(10th Floor, 60 Edward St., Brisbane, Qld, 4007* ☎ *(07) 210 0497).*

South Australia

Vast scorched deserts to the north, golden surfing beaches to the south... and in between, South Australia embraces luscious green vineyards, red and rugged mountain ranges, and sweeping plains on which forests, wheat farms and kangaroos all thrive. It is a place of great and vivid contrasts.

The scenic grandeur has made tourism an important part of South Australia's economy. Despite the recession, the tourist industry had a turnover of A$1.6 billion in 1990 and expects this to rise to A$2 billion by the end of the century. About A$300 million worth of new tourism projects were in development at the end of 1991.

In the early '90s, South Australia looked closely at its economic base and, as a result, went out of its way to court high technology companies. The state now leads in bio-technology genetic research (which has led to agricultural improvements that include grain yield and livestock size), medical research, laser technology, defense research and silicon chip design.

This prosperous, proud state is home for 1.4 million Australians. About one million of them live in its elegant capital, Adelaide, with the remaining 400,000 scattered through land about one and a half times the size of Texas: 984,377 square kilometers (380,071 square miles).

HISTORY

Adelaide, the fourth largest urban center in the country, covering 1,854 square kilometers (716 square miles), was founded on December 28, 1836. It was designed by the Surveyor General of the time, Colonel William Light, and named after Queen Adelaide, consort to Britain's King William IV. Understated wealth, style and charm have always featured prominently in the topography of this pleasant, leisurely city.

The first exploration of South Australia by Europeans was recorded as early as 1627 when the Dutch explorer Peter Nuyts charted part of the coastline. In 1801 Lieutenant James Grant sailed the *Lady Nelson* along the southeastern coast, claiming and naming land sighted on his journey. Soon after this the famous British navigator Matthew Flinders explored the coastline near present-day Adelaide, aboard HMS *Investigator*. On that journey he met Napoleon Bonaparte's naval explorer and cartographer, Nicolas Baudin, anchored off South Australia. Flinders named the waters where the two met Encounter Bay (and 100 years later at Rosetta Head, near Victor Harbour, a tablet was erected to commemorate their meeting).

180

Sealers established settlements on islands off South Australia at the beginning of the 19th century, but it was not until Colonel Light selected his site for Adelaide, on the banks of the Torrens River, that the first settlers put down their roots in the new land. No convicts were transported to South Australia; it is the only state that was settled entirely by free settlers. Perhaps as a result, SA has bred a distinct elite: families that cling onto their ancestral and social connections in a way that is seen nowhere else in the country.

The lack of cheap convict labor did little to help those struggling to establish themselves. But the discovery of copper in 1842 helped solve the problems of the early South Australians, raising finance and attracting hopeful and skilled newcomers to what was by now a crown colony. Adelaide swiftly developed into an agricultural center, processing and transporting wheat, wool and fruit. From Europe came Lutheran refugees. They brought with them the wine-making talents of their native lands and settled in the Barossa Valley, establishing what were to become the foundations of the Australian wine industry.

In 1856 a legislative assembly was elected and the colony attained self-government. (From 1863 until 1911 its administrators were also responsible for the Northern Territory.) Then in 1901 South Australia became a State of the Commonwealth of Australia.

FERTILE VINEYARDS, LUNAR LANDSCAPES

Most of South Australia is less than 300 meters (1,000 feet) above sea level, although there is a series of "hills" in the northwest that rise to 1,440 meters (4,725 feet). But that is remote and inhospitable country. More accessible is the Flinders Ranges, 430km (270 miles) northeast of Adelaide, a ribbon of majestic peaks and gorges that abounds in scenic delights and wildlife. Wedge-tailed eagles, frilled lizards, cockatoos, emus and wallabies... they, along with artists, photographers and other visitors, all lay claim to territory in this dramatically beautiful national park.

The Outback can be as astonishing as it is unique. This really is the land of the last frontier. Unforgettable for those who venture into the desert country is Andamooka and the lunar landscape of the underground city of Coober Pedy. From these two comes 75 percent of the world's opal, gouged from the yellow earth by fortune-seeking miners from all over the world. Coober Pedy is like no other place; the diggers have carved intricate dug-outs from the rock, creating surprisingly elegant underground homes that enjoy "natural air conditioning" in the desert heat.

South Australia, of course, is the center of the Australian wine industry, producing between 60 and 75 percent of its wine, making the finest of the best-known Australian wine styles, and winning the majority of the country's wine show awards. Many of the vineyards are close to Adelaide. The state's major wine areas are the Adelaide Hills, Adelaide Plains, Barossa Valley, Clare Valley, Coonawarra, Padthaway-Keppoch, Langhorne Creek, McLaren Vale and Riverland.

The most fertile area is in the southeast where the mighty Murray River makes its way from Renmark through to the Southern Ocean at Lake

181

Alexandrina. The Murray itself, which flows through three states, offers visitors to South Australia hundreds of kilometers of picturesque, navigable waters to chug along. There are luxury cruisers, with every conceivable gadget for the would-be pampered, as well as paddle-wheel houseboats that allow independent boatsmen or women to explore the great river at a leisurely pace. Some of these self-drive rental-boats have two-way radios to allow their crews to call for "room service" from base; a speedy courtesy boat delivers whatever is required when the fish are not biting.

The state also has 3,700 kilometers (2,300 miles) of coastline, from long, secluded, sandy beaches to 100-meter (330-foot) sheer-drop cliffs that are battered by huge seas, the haunting cries of the albatross and, in winter, chilling Antarctic winds. The more hospitable parts of this coast, however, are a delight for swimmers, sailors and fishermen, or those who simply crave a place to walk in solitude.

There are more than 100 islands off South Australia. The biggest, Kangaroo Island, 145 kilometers by 50 kilometers (90 by 31 miles), is easily reached by air or ferry from Adelaide. American sealers established a base here as far back as 1803. Kangaroo Island, which provides some of the most rewarding fishing in Australia, is unspoiled and fascinating. Teeming with accessible wildlife, it is a favorite attraction for visitors. Seals play on its beaches, and a tour through its national park will quickly reveal why it was given its name.

The boot-shaped Yorke Peninsula, to the west of Adelaide, has become known as *Little Cornwall*. For when copper was discovered there, it attracted Cornishmen from halfway round the world, and although the copper is now exhausted, the Cornish heritage lives on in towns such as Moonta.

Still farther to the west is the Eyre Peninsula, enjoying some of the state's most rugged coastal scenery. Its main center, Port Lincoln, is the focal point for the tuna- and lobster-fishing industries. A popular coastal resort, it was once considered as the possible capital for South Australia.

To the southeast of Adelaide, stretching toward the Victorian border, is the flat, almost mysterious Coorong, the lagoon country protected from the open sea by the Younghusband Peninsula. This land of islands, inlets and lakes is the nesting place for thousands upon thousands of pelicans. The Australian movie *Storm Boy,* about a youngster who befriends a pelican, was shot here.

South Australia has large deposits of iron ore and natural gas. There are important engineering plants, and chemical processing and oil refining take place in and around Adelaide. The state has also been a center for the automobile industry in Australia. From the 1950s, it has attracted to its assembly lines many immigrants, a big percentage of them British car workers, who, riding waves of hope and recession, have made their mark on Adelaide and its satellite city, Elizabeth.

To the northwest of Adelaide is Whyalla, which, with a population of 30,000, is the second largest city in the state. It holds the third biggest steelworks in Australia. The country's largest shipbuilding plant was also here until recession brought closure in 1978.

ADELAIDE — THE FESTIVAL CITY

Adelaide, a city nestling calm and distinguished between the Mount Lofty Ranges and the waters of St Vincent Gulf, was designed for those who want to live well without living dangerously. The air is clean, the pace relaxed; the streets and the parkland are inviting to walkers, the driving free of choking traffic jams. Thanks to the foresight of its planner, Colonel William Light, the city is wrapped in an unbroken, winding green belt of parks and recreation areas.

But Adelaide is a lively city. The Australian Grand Prix, a magnet for the country's enthusiastic band of auto-racing followers, is run here, enhanced by a week of frantic state, civic and private celebrations. Certainly, Adelaide enjoys its partying; nightlife — discos, piano bars, cabarets, rock and jazz clubs — thrives here. A focal point for the city's entertainment is the Adelaide Casino, elegantly housed in a splendidly restored old Adelaide railway station building on North Terrace.

Above all, though, Adelaide is *the* festival city. The first biennial Festival of Arts was staged in 1960 and has grown to become Australia's premier occasion for the performing and visual arts. The Adelaide Festival is held mainly in and around the Festival Centre complex on the bank of the Torrens.

This is a place of fine architecture: "the city of churches," it has been called. From central Victoria Sq., you can walk in any direction and appreciate eye-catching examples of colonial building at its finest. There are the impressive spires of St Peter's Cathedral, the elaborate face of Edmund Wright House on King William St., Ayers House, the lacework verandas of old hotels, mansions, and carefully restored bluestone villas and cottages.

Adelaide's grid-system of streets and squares encourages the pedestrian, making the city particularly easy to get around. One stroll that is a must for the shopper is along Rundle Mall, Australia's most concentrated shopping mall. Department stores, boutiques, arcades, fast-food stores, fruit and flower stalls, and street musicians... they elbow one another for space in this street cut off from the traffic. But if that becomes too crowded, then Adelaide's tranquil green belt is only a stroll away.

It can be deceptive to the first-time tourist. The beat appears to be a touch slower than in most of Australia's major cities, yet there is always something going on, always something to see. It is a beautiful, charming and generally relaxing place to visit.

Adelaide enjoys a warm, temperate "Mediterranean-style" climate: a short, generally mild winter and a long, dry summer. Summer (December to February) is warm to hot, with an average maximum of 29˚C (87˚F); winter (June to August) has an average maximum of 17˚C (62˚F). For other parts of South Australia, the climate varies greatly.

The city throws itself into a celebratory frenzy for two big events: the annual Australian Grand Prix (Formula One auto-racing) and the biennial Adelaide Arts Festival. When these take place there is no shortage of things to see and do; but even when Adelaide life is a lot quieter there is much to discover and explore. Be warned: the broad, long streets encourage you to stroll farther than you would in lesser cities.

Adelaide

ORIENTATION

Adelaide holds a central position on Australia's southern coast. The city lies on a coastal plain, between the Mount Lofty Ranges in the E and the beaches of Gulf St Vincent to the w. Although there has been some growth in the N and the s, most people still live within 15km (10 miles) of the city center.

The city's central business district, in keeping with Colonel Light's original plans, occupies 1sq. mile. A grid pattern of streets, with five squares transposed upon it, makes it easy to explore. Framing this pattern of streets are North, East, South and West terraces. Treelined North Terrace is considered one of the city's most elegant avenues; on it stands Parliament House, the Holy Trinity Church, the State Library, the South Australian Museum, the Art Gallery, Government House and the University of Adelaide.

A kilometer or so N along King William Rd., separated from the main part of the city by the Torrens River and the ubiquitous parklands, are the bluestone cottages, old mansions and quaint hotels of splendidly restored North Adelaide.

Adelaide airport is about 6km (4 miles) w of the city. Port Adelaide, 10km (6 miles) NW, has a container terminal as well as one for modern international cruise ships. Railways link Adelaide with Sydney, Melbourne, Perth and Alice Springs.

PRACTICAL INFORMATION

Maps 8-9 on pages 184-5

☎**STD (area) code**   08

Airport   ☎352 9304; Ansett ☎233 3322; Australian ☎217 3333

Rail stations   For country and interstate services, Passenger Rail Terminal, Keswick ☎217 1111; for suburban services, Adelaide rail station, North Terrace ☎210 1000.

Car rental   Avis ☎354 0444; Budget ☎223 1400; Hertz ☎231 2856

South Australian Government Travel Centre   18 King William St., Adelaide, SA, 5000 ☎212 1505, map **8D3**

American Express Travel Service   13 Grenfell St., Adelaide, SA, 5000 ☎212 7099, map **8D3**

Royal Automobile Association of South Australia (RAA)   41 Hindmarsh Sq., Adelaide, SA, 5000 ☎223 4555, map **8D3**

SEEING THE CITY

Do make sure you have a comfortable pair of walking shoes when you visit Adelaide, since there is no better way to explore the city than on foot. Its main streets are broad and lined with a blend of impressive 19thC and modern architecture, with many sights of interest close at hand. In the fierce heat of February, of course, walking can be something to restrict to early morning or late evening, although the shade of trees and the relief offered by cool shopping arcades or hotels is never too far away.

The hub of the city, its central point, is **Victoria Sq.** There is much to see, in whatever direction you travel. A stroll N along King William St., however, will take you beyond the insurance offices and banks, across North Terrace, and down to the **Adelaide Festival Centre**, where you can wander along the grassy banks of the Torrens River. It is a perfect place for a picnic. On the river itself are the small paddle boats and motor cruisers of the so-called "Popeye fleet," all of which can be rented.

The **Zoo** is a little to the E along the river; the really energetic may care to continue N, past **Adelaide Oval**, where Test cricket is played, into **North Adelaide**. Boutiques, art galleries and restaurants are among the many extra attractions in this area.

For those who have walked too far, Adelaide's public transportation system is there to offer relief. It brings most places of interest within easy reach, and is generally inexpensive. For disabled travelers there is a free information service, the **Disability Information and Resource Centre** *(195 Gillies St.* ☎ *223 7522, map 9 E4).*

BUSES

Adelaide and its suburbs are well catered to by clean and efficiently run **State Transport Authority (STA)** buses. There are various designated departure points within the city, while elsewhere the pick-up and set-down points are clearly signposted. The buses run 6am-11.30pm from Monday to Saturday and 9am-10.30pm on Sunday. A route map and timetables are available at the **STA Centre** *(79 King William St.* ☎ *210 1000, map 8 D3).* The center will also provide information on the **Circle Line** bus. This operates around Adelaide every 15 minutes, linking outbound bus, train and tram services. It runs 7am-6pm from Monday to Friday, and 8am-noon on Saturday.

Adelaide also has its free bus services. The **Beeline** and **City Loop** buses circle the main shopping area 8am-6pm from Monday to Thursday, 8am-9pm Friday, and 8am-noon on Saturday.

THE ADELAIDE EXPLORER

This tourist bus, somewhat eccentrically decorated as an old Adelaide tram, takes visitors around some of the city's major attractions — Adelaide Casino, HMS *Buffalo,* the Old Parliament House and Adelaide Zoo among them. Passengers may board or alight as many times as they wish. The Adelaide Explorer starts its circular journeys at the **South Australian Government Travel Centre** *(18 King William St., map 8 D3)* Further information: **Adelaide Sightseeing** *(101 Franklin St.* ☎ *231 4144, map 8 D2).*

TRAMS

Adelaide's only electric tram route runs between Victoria Sq. in the city's center to the seaside suburb of **Glenelg**, where the first colonists landed. The trams operate 6am-11.30pm from Monday to Saturday, and 9am-10.30pm on Sunday. The journey takes about 25 minutes. Further information can be obtained from the **STA Centre** *(* ☎ *210 1000).*

RAILWAYS

Suburban trains operate from Adelaide rail station on North Terrace to Bridgewater, Noarlunga, Outer Harbour, Grange and Gawler from 6am-11.30pm on weekdays, with reduced services on weekends and public holidays. Tickets may be bought at the major stations or on trains, and can be used, within a two-hour time limit, on the STA tram and buses as well. Further information: **STA Centre** *(☎210 1000)*.

TAXIS

As in other Australian state capitals, meter-operated taxis are to be found at hotels, transportation terminals and taxi stands around the city. Or you can simply hail them in the street. Vacant cabs have an illuminated sign on the roof. Where multiple renting occurs (and the first customer makes the decision on this) only 75 percent of the metered fare is payable. The main taxi companies include **Amalgamated** *(☎223 3333)*, **Suburban** *(☎211 8888)* and **United Yellow** *(☎223 3111)*.

BUS TOURS

Adelaide has an excellent selection of half-day and full-day sightseeing bus tours covering the sights in and around the city. For details, contact the **South Australian Government Travel Centre**.

Sights and places of interest

ADELAIDE FESTIVAL CENTRE

King William Rd. ☎*216 8600. Map 8C3* ⎹ *Open for guided tours ( ) on the hour Mon-Fri 10am-4pm; Sat at 10.30am, 11.30am, 12.30pm (check day before* ☎*216 8600).*

The Adelaide Festival Centre's peaceful location on the bank of the Torrens River, overlooking parkland, tends to remind English visitors of Stratford-on-Avon. It both welcomes and relaxes those who wish to stroll, rest or think within its gaze.

The architecture may be somewhat geometrical to inspire great passion, but it is neither too grand nor intimidating. Adelaide's performing arts complex suggests an easy intimacy. It is very egalitarian, very much a place for all the people, certainly not elitist.

This popular center, which was built within 3 years and completed in 1973, contains a main 2,000-seat auditorium, a remarkably versatile drama theater (612 seats), and an experimental theater (360 seats). Outside there is an open-air amphitheater, framed by vine-covered fences and a backdrop of trees and shrubs.

Adelaide has its own symphony orchestra, chamber music group, theater, opera and dance companies, and the theaters are kept well lit throughout the year. There are restaurants, bars and 1.2ha (3 acres) of open plaza and terrace that make the complex one of the city's favorite meeting places.

ART GALLERY OF SOUTH AUSTRALIA

North Terrace ☎*223 7200. Map 8C3* ⎹ *Open 10am-5pm. Closed Christmas Day, Good Friday.*

The focal point for South Australian art-lovers, this has impressive collections of Australian, English and European paintings, intriguing historical material from the early days of South Australia, and a comprehensive display of prints. Among the gallery's most prized exhibits are its Thai, Annamese and Chinese ceramics.

For the gallery's guide service, contact its education section (☎ *223 7200).* There is a bookstore in the foyer, and meals and refreshments are available in the coffee shop, which is located on the gallery's basement level.

AYERS HOUSE

288 North Terrace ☎ *233 1655. Map 9D4* 🚋 ✗ *by appointment (* ☎ *223 1655). Open Tues-Fri 10am-4pm; Sat, Sun 2-4pm.*

An elegant bluestone mansion, once the home of a former state premier, Sir Henry Ayers, and today the headquarters of the South Australian National Trust, Ayers House was designed by Sir George Kingston and took almost 30 years to build. Its central one-storied section was completed in 1846; Sir Henry later added to it the bow window dining and drawing rooms. Now completely restored, the present building contains two restaurants. It is a favored choice of students of early colonial architecture.

BOTANIC GARDENS ★

North Terrace ☎ *228 2311. Map 9C4* 📷 � & ✗ *on Tues and Fri at 10.30am from the kiosk* ⇜ *Open Mon-Fri 7am-sunset; Sat, Sun, hols 9am-sunset.*

Choose a cool, sunny morning or a fine late afternoon, a few hours before sunset. Dress comfortably, casually... and walk quietly through the verdant arch of the Botanic Gardens. Then feast your eyes on 16ha (40 acres) of Australian and exotic trees, shrubs and flowers, among them fine displays of lilies and lotuses, cacti and succulents. The greenhouses and hothouses also contain many spectacular and rare plants. The glass **Palm House** was made in Germany in 1871.

HMS BUFFALO ★

Patawalonga Boat Haven, Adelphi Terrace, Glenelg North ☎ *294 7000* 🚋 & ✾ ⬅ *Open Mon-Fri 9am-noon and 2.30pm-5pm; Sat, Sun, hols 10am-5pm.*

Forget your qualms. This full-scale replica of the *Buffalo,* the ship that brought Governor Hindmarsh and the state's first colonists to Glenelg in 1836, is far from maritime kitsch for the tourists. It contains old seafaring artifacts, fascinating extracts from the captain's log, and personal diaries of the original immigrants. These, together with illustrations and photographs, recall the voyage from Portsmouth, England, in July 1836 to Holdfast Bay on December 28, 1836. The ship, constructed from the original 1813 Admiralty plans at a cost of A$1.5 million in 1980, also holds a restaurant and bar and a small aquarium.

CONSTITUTIONAL MUSEUM (Old Parliament House) ★

North Terrace ☎ *212 6881. Map 8D3* & 💻 🚋 *for audiovisual show. Open Mon-Fri 10am-5pm; Sat-Sun noon-5pm. Closed Christmas Day, Good Friday.*

One of Adelaide's more unlikely star attractions, the Old Parliament House, built in 1855 as South Australia's original Legislative Council

Chamber, is now Australia's only museum of political history. As well as the curios and recollections of the pioneers, there is a well-produced audiovisual show, *Bound For South Australia,* which depicts the story of the state from its Aboriginal beginnings to the present day.

LIGHT'S VISION
Corner of Pennington Terrace and Montefiore Rd., North Adelaide. Map 8B2 ▣
♣ ➡ ◁ε

At the peak of Montefiore Hill, this is an appropriate tribute to Colonel William Light, the man who planned the layout of the city that lies below. The lookout provides excellent views across parklands and the Torrens River, across the city of Adelaide and onto a backdrop of the Adelaide Hills.

Col. Light is also commemorated once a year with a toast in South Australian wine by the Mayor at Adelaide Town Hall. A silver bowl was presented to the city by some of the colony's original founders for just this purpose.

ST PETER'S CATHEDRAL
Pennington Terrace, North Adelaide. Map 8B3 ▣ ✗ *at 3pm on second Sun of each month.*

The building of St Peter's, the Anglican pride of the "city of churches", began in 1869 and was completed in 1876. Its towers and spires were built and consecrated in 1902. The cathedral has the heaviest and finest bells in the southern hemisphere.

SOUTH AUSTRALIAN MUSEUM
North Terrace ☎ *223 8911/223 8863. Map 8C3* ▣ ♿ *Open daily 10am-5pm; Anzac Day 1-5pm. Closed Christmas Day, Good Friday.*

This museum holds the largest and most carefully researched collection of Aboriginal artifacts in the world. It also boasts a comprehensive Melanesian collection and a fine display of New Guinea amphibia. The **Natural History Museum** contains the world's largest collection of australites (small pieces of dark, glassy meteorite of unknown origin, found only in Australia).

ZOOLOGICAL GARDENS
Frome Rd. ☎ *267 3255. Map 9B4-C4* ▣ ♿ ✗ 🖪 ♣ ➡ *Open 9.30am-5pm. Closed Christmas Day.*

The Zoo, like so many of the appealing tourist spots in Adelaide, is close to the city center. This and its attractive park-like setting rightly puts it at the top of most sightseeing lists.

The Zoo enjoys a particularly high reputation in Australia and abroad both for its outstanding collection of Australian birds and for its skills in breeding rare species of animals in captivity. Among its treasured exhibits are sloths, ring-tailed lemurs, agoutis, coatis, giant anteaters, squirrel and spider monkeys, and polar bears. There is also a special "children's zoo" in which youngsters are encouraged to meet tame animals at close range.

Where to stay

Adelaide provides the full range of accommodations, from first-class international hotels to small motels, private hotels and efficiency (self-catering) apartments. Generally, prices are a little cheaper than in Sydney, Melbourne and Perth, although there are signs that this is changing. Extras in larger hotels, as in other cities, range from courtesy buses to valet parking, from a daily bowl of fresh fruit or flowers in the room to in-house video movies, or from free drinks to tickets for a disco.

As well as the hotels listed below, there are homestay and farm vacations available for visitors to South Australia. These can be organized through the **South Australian Government Travel Centre** *(18 King William St., Adelaide, SA, 5000* ☎ *212 1505, map 8 D3)*.

ADELAIDE PARKROYAL

226 South Terrace, Adelaide, SA, 5000
☎ *223 4355* ▨ 🖷*82156* 🖷*232 0769*.
Map *8E3* ▥ *95 rms* 🛏 ⚡ 🛎 AE ⊙
⊙ VISA ≋ 🔳 ▽ ⌖ ☵

Location: At southern end of city. This peaceful hotel provides superb views of the Adelaide Hills as well as access to a jogger's paradise in the nearby parks. The management have obviously gone out of their way to attract visiting business executives, with secretarial services, and a lounge-cum-private bar for guests only. There is 24-hour room service and, for insomniacs, in-house movies. The **Christies** restaurant offers an "international" *à la carte* menu.

THE TERRACE ADELAIDE

150 North Terrace, Adelaide, SA, 5000
☎ *217 7552* ▨ 🖷*88325* 🖷*231 7572*.
Map *8D3* ▥ *313 rms* 🛏 ⚡ AE ⊙ ⊙
VISA ♿ ≋ 🔳 ▽ ⌖ ☵ ☵

Location: Close to the Festival Theatre, opposite the Casino. This favorite choice of the interstate arts festival crowd is within a glance of the most important buildings in the city. The Terrace offers fine French cuisine in its elegant, modern **Crystal Room** restaurant, and there is a , stylish sidewalk café overlooking busy North Terrace. The piano cocktail lounge is a popular place for young players to meet.

GROSVENOR ♣

125 North Terrace, Adelaide, SA, 5000
☎ *231 2961* ▨ 🖷*82634* 🖷*231 0765*.

Map *8D3* ▥ *289 rms* 🛏 ⚡ AE ⊙ ⊙
VISA 🔳 ▽ ⌖ ☵ ☵

Location: Directly opposite Adelaide rail station. A comfortable Edwardian establishment with an admirable two-tiered system of accommodations: budget rates are available for those prepared to accept rooms a little less luxurious than the standard fare. Within the hotel are a gift store, hairdresser and gymnasium. Four large rooms are reserved for conventions.

HILTON INTERNATIONAL ADELAIDE ♣

233 Victoria Sq., Adelaide, SA, 5000
☎ *217 0711* ▨ 🖷*87173* 🖷*231 0158*.
Map *8E3* ▥ *387 rms* 🛏 ⚡ AE ⊙ ⊙
VISA ♿ ≋ 🔳 ▽ ⌖ ⁀ ⌖ ☵ ☵

Location: Centrally placed in leafy and graceful Victoria Sq. Since its opening in 1982, the Hilton has maintained a position as one of Adelaide's most distinguished luxury hotels. Among its attractions is **The Grange**, arguably the city's finest restaurant. A more comfortably priced family eating place is the **Market Place Café**. One of several special features of this unusually good hotel is a "nonsmokers floor"; another is a floor of 19 rooms specially equipped for handicapped guests. The Hilton also offers comprehensive secretarial services for the international executive.

HOTEL ADELAIDE

62 Brougham Pl., North Adelaide, SA, 5006
☎ *267 3444* ▨ 🖷*82174* 🖷*239 0189*.

Map *8B3* ▥ *146 rms* ⇌ AE ⊕ ⊙ ▥ ⓑ ⇌ ▣ ⓨ

Location: Overlooks central Adelaide from one of the oldest parts of the city. This North Adelaide hotel offers panoramic views across the main business and shopping district. Management is smart and helpful. Two main restaurants serve international dishes. Try to ensure that you get a room overlooking the parklands and the Adelaide Festival Theatre.

HYATT REGENCY

North Terrace, Adelaide, SA, 5000 ☎*231 1234* ▥ ✆*88582* ✉*231 1120. Map 8D3* ▥ *369 rms* ⇌ ⇌ AE ⊕ ⊙ ▥ ⓑ ⇌ ▣ ⓨ ⓧ ⓦ ⛳ ⚓ ♪

Location: Centrally placed, overlooking Torrens River and adjacent to Adelaide Casino. Adelaide's newest five-star hotel offers the luxury one would expect of the Hyatt chain — and more. Its business center includes translation and interpreting services and a satellite broadcast facility for international teleconferencing. The hotel's restaurants include the new **Blake's** restaurant, the **Riverside** buffet restaurant, and the award-winning **Shiki**, which specializes in Japanese *teppanyaki* and *tempura* cuisine.

OLD ADELAIDE INN

Corner of O'Connell St. and Gover St., North Adelaide, SA, 5006 ☎*267 5066*

✆*89271* ✉*267 2946. Map 8A2* ▥ *63 rms* ⇌ ⇌ AE ⊕ ⊙ ▥ ⓑ ⇌ ▣ ⓨ ⓦ ⛳ ⚓ ♨

Location: Right in the bluestone heart of swanky North Adelaide. A hotel that prides itself on its "old-world charm." Built in the early 1980s, it is a perfect base for exploring the mansions of North Adelaide.

PATAWALONGA MOTOR INN

13 Adelphi Terrace, Glenelg North, SA, 5045 ☎*294 2122* ▥ ✆*82824* ✉*295 7331* ▥ *56 rms* ⇌ ⇌ AE ⊕ ⊙ ▥ ⓑ ⇌ ⚓ ▣ ⓨ ✦/ ⛳ ⚓ ♨

Location: Close to the sea, within walking distance of popular Glenelg beach. Ideal for families with children, this clean, well-run, unpretentious motel-style establishment faces a yacht-filled boat haven. It incorporates a pleasant, reliable restaurant, the **Adelphi**, whose menu often betrays the Hong Kong origins of its chef.

RICHMOND

128 Rundle Mall, Adelaide, SA, 5000 ☎*223 4044* ▥ ✆*86330* ✉*232 2290. Map 8D3* ▥ *31 rms* ⇌ ⇌ AE ⊕ ⊙ ▥ ⓑ ▣ ⓨ

Location: A unique position within Adelaide's pedestrians-only shopping mall. This is a small, sensible, older-style city hotel, modernized a few years ago, with three restaurants. Valet parking is available.

Dining out

Adelaide may have neither the number nor the variety of restaurants found in Sydney or Melbourne, but there are establishments here that can delight the tastebuds as well as, if not better than, any of their kind around the world.

Not surprisingly, with the sea lapping at the door, seafood is a local specialty. Lobsters, prawns and (in particular) King George whiting are among the local delights. The wines of South Australia, of course, are not to be missed.

Licensing laws are more liberal in South Australia, and Adelaide does not have the BYO restaurants that are found elsewhere. The advantage of this is that wine is readily available at most restaurants; the disadvantage is that they do not sell them at "bottle shop" prices.

Adelaide caters to all tastes. Indian and Pakistani restaurants are more prevalent in this part of Australia, and there are also Chinese, Lebanese, Italian and German restaurants.

A fast-food specialty that may not be to all tastes, but is peculiarly South Australian, is the "pie floater." This delicacy, served from one of the pie carts outside Adelaide's rail station or post office late at night, comprises a hearty meat pie floating in a thick soup of peas. You will never be offered that at Maxim's!

BANGKOK ✿
1st floor, 217 Rundle St. ☎223 5406. Map **9**D4 ▯ ▭ ≡ AE ⦶ ◉ VISA *Last orders 9.30pm. Closed Sat lunch; Sun.*
Busy and unpretentious, this centrally located Thai restaurant has flourished under the careful eye of Peter Thanissorn. Its Asian chefs specialize in *satays,* noodles and curries. The green curry (spiced with green chillies) is an excellent choice, but if you want to taste something sensational, then try the *tom yum* soup.

BLAKE'S
Hyatt Regency, North Terrace ☎238 2381. Map **8**D3 ▯ ▭ ≡ Y ▰ AE ⦶ ◉ VISA *Open lunch Fri noon-2pm; dinner Mon-Sat 6pm-10pm.*
A fine hotel-restaurant that has replaced the superb but recession-prone **Fleurieu**. This delightful Mediterranean-style establishment is a little more casual and less expensive than its predecessor. (See HYATT REGENCY in WHERE TO STAY.)

HMS BUFFALO RESTAURANT
Patawalonga Boat Haven, Adelphi Terrace, Glenelg North ☎294 7000 ▯ ▭ ≡ Y ▰ ≪ AE ⦶ ◉ VISA *Last orders 9pm. Closed Sat lunch; Christmas Day, Good Friday.*
Distinctly G & S rather than Royal Navy, but the rich, warm, natural timbers and relaxing views across the boat haven make the *Buffalo* easy sailing for the fussiest of landlubbers. Seafood, of course, is the specialty of the galley, and "authentic" pewter dishes are used. (See SIGHTS.)

THE FEATHERS
516 Glynburn Rd., Burnside ☎332 6133 ▯ ▭ ■ ≡ Y ▰ AE ⦶ ◉ VISA *Last orders 11.30pm. Closed Sat lunch; Sun dinner.*
The Feathers is modeled on the hotel of the same name in Shropshire, England: the decor of the three rooms — the Doulton, Alfresco and Georgian — is aggressively Olde English, but the food, wines and service, fortunately, are warmly Australian. The menu is straightforwardly "European," with a smørgasbørd-carvery on Sunday. Desserts include superb freshly cooked donuts.

THE GRANGE ✿

Hilton International, 233 Victoria Sq. ☎*217 0711. Map 8E3* ▦ ▭ ▬ ♈ ➟ ▣ ◉ ◉ ▥ *Last orders 11.15pm. Closed lunch; Sun.*

The Grange is one of Adelaide's grandest restaurants, with food, wine and service of the highest quality. Named after South Australia's renowned Grange Hermitage wine, it features a walk-in cellar where, on polished brass racks, are displayed limited-release wines. The Grange stocks more than 400 Australian labels and a remarkable selection of overseas wine. Under the guidance of its young Singaporean executive chef, Gerard Taye, The Grange has gained a reputation for innovative "Australian" variations to a European-styled menu. Among the specialties are delicious preparations of kangaroo. The fresh poached salmon is also worth sampling when available.

JARMER'S RESTAURANT ✿

297 Kensington Rd., Kensington Park ☎*332 2080. Map 9E5* ▥ ▭ ▬ ♈ ▣ ◉ ◉ ▥ *Dinner Mon-Sat from 6.30pm; last orders 2.30am.*

A fashionable favorite, just 5-10 minutes away from the city by taxi, Jarmer's is located in an elegant old villa, with the main dining room overlooking a pleasant courtyard and fountain. Peter and Kathy Jarmer describe their menu as "creative French"; it includes venison, buffalo, veal, pork and seafood dishes (the Morton Bay bugs are notoriously delicious). There is a large cellar of predominantly South Australian wines.

MANDARIN DUCK BISTRO ✿

110 Flinders St. ☎*223 2370. Map 8D3* ▥ ▭ ▬ ♈ ▣ ◉ ▥ *Open lunch Tues-Fri noon-2.30pm; dinner Tues-Sat 6pm-10.30pm.*

A bustling restaurant with an exciting French-Chinese menu, the inspiration of the Vietnamese-born chef Cedric Eu. Among the more exotic examples of "fusion cuisine" is his stir-fried kangaroo with Sichuan brown-bean paste, chillies and eggplant. The service is fast and efficient.

NEDIZ TU

170 Hutt St. ☎*223 2618. Map 9E4* ▥ ▭ ▭ ▬ ♈ ◉ ▥ *Open dinner Tues-Sat 6.30pm-10pm.*

Nediz Tu is possibly the best example in the country of the exciting, innovative Australian cuisine that has come from mixing the tastes of the East with those of the West. The chef, Le Tu Thai, a refugee from Vietnam, is equally at home with stir-fried chili squid and tender kangaroo fillets. A mallee-root fire adds warmth to the simple decor in winter.

PETALUMA'S BRIDGEWATER MILL

Mt. Barker Rd., Bridgewater ☎*339 4227* ▦ ▭ ▭ ♈ ▬ ♈ ➟ ▣ ◉ ◉ ▥ *Lunch Wed-Mon; closed Tues.*

Well worth the drive into the Adelaide Hills, this fine restaurant, located within the old Bridgewater Mill, combines stylishness with friendliness. The menu has a creative, Asian influence. Among the dishes you may discover are kangaroo fillets with an oyster, ginger, soya and chili sauce and Vietnamese chicken salad. For dessert try the mango-and-passionfruit soft meringue layer cake. There is outside dining on a balcony adjacent to the mill's revolving water wheel. Wine-tasting and cellar sales seven days a week. (See ADELAIDE HILLS in EXCURSIONS.)

PHEASANT FARM ✿

Samuel Rd., near Nuriootpa ☎*(085) 62 1286* ▥ ▭ ▬ ➟ ♈ ◉ ▥ *Open Wed-Sun for lunch 12.30pm-2pm; Sat for dinner 7-8.30pm.*

Colin and Maggie Beer's Barossa Valley restaurant was once the ill-kept secret of local gourmets with a taste for game. Now early reservations are essential. Pheasant Farm, with its timberlined walls and warm furnishings, is on the edge of a trout-filled dam and in the middle of a vineyard. The views are magnificent. Chef Maggie Beer's specialties include warm salad of quail, roast breast of pheasant, scrambled guinea fowl eggs and rainbow trout. The wine list is exclusively from the Barossa Valley.

Entertainment

Adelaide was once the most staid of Australian cities, conservative and "wowser-ish," a place where the nightlife went little further than even-song on Sundays, or putting out the cat. In the past 30 years that has all changed dramatically.

Today, largely because of the immense cultural impact of the **Adelaide Arts Festival**, a forward-thinking state government, the clamor of a new generation, and the influence of immigrants, it is a progressive city whose residents enjoy going out to be entertained. What's more, South Australia produces some of the world's finest wines — and Adelaide has no qualms about celebrating that proud fact.

For music, opera, ballet and drama, the A\$20 million ADELAIDE FESTIVAL CENTRE (see SIGHTS) is the venue that the visitor should investigate first. The top international and local classical, jazz and popular music performers appear here, as well as all the major Australian companies.

The theater also has a major presence in central Adelaide: the **Adelaide Repertory Theatre** *(53 Angas St.* ☎ *212 5777, map 9D5)*, the **Royalty Theatre** *(65 Angas St.* ☎ *223 5765, map 9D5)*, the **State Opera Theatre** in Grote St., **Union Hall** and the **Little Theatre** in the University of Adelaide. Reservations can be made through the relevant box offices or the **Bass Bookings Agencies** *(*☎ *information 213 4788, reservations 213 4777).*

Adelaide's hotels offer a great deal of entertainment, ranging from rough 'n' ready rock bands to comedy and sophisticated modern jazz. Performances are advertised daily in the local newspapers.

Discos and night clubs are studded around the city — **Le Rox** *(9 Light Sq.* ☎ *231 3234, map 8D2)*, **Jules's** *(94 Hindley St.* ☎ *51 3023, map 8D2)*, and **Regines** *(69 Light Sq.* ☎ *212 6044, map 8D2)* are leading contenders — and there are movie theaters and adults-only clubs, mixed with good restaurants and cafés, around Hindley St.

For the past decade a company called **Ace Promotions** has been operating a reasonably priced Mystery Disco Bus Tour on Friday and Sat nights, taking visitors and locals around the city's major discos by bus *(*AE *accepted)*, and including a complimentary drink on board the bus. The tours set off from the Newmarket Hotel on the corner of North and West terraces *(reservations and further information* ☎ *337 3399).*

ADELAIDE CASINO
North Terrace ☎ *212 2811. Map 8C3* ☎
☰ *Open Mon-Thurs 11am-4am; continuous Fri 11am-Mon 4am. Closed Christmas Day, Good Friday.*

The vast Adelaide Casino, which occupies the northern half of the old Adelaide rail station, uses the Gothic grandeur of that building (there are 1,000sq.m of pink and green marble in the Great Hall) to re-create the elegant opulence of Europe's finer gaming palaces. In looks, at least, it is Monte Carlo-plus, and has an astonishing 2.5 million visitors annually. For weekend players, there are few better places in Adelaide for Sunday brunch than the casino's superb 300-seat **Pullman** restaurant (AE ◘ ◙ VISA); it serves up its winners at 11.30am.

ADELAIDE GREYHOUND RACING CLUB
Days Rd., Angle Park ☎ *45 8574/268 1923* ☎ ☰ *Open Mon and Thurs nights.*

On a fine evening Adelaide likes nothing better than going to the dogs. To capture a different flavor of the city, look up the race times in the local newspapers and set off to lose a few dollars at the Angle Park dog track. Popular, too, are Australian Rules football (April to September) and cricket (October to March) under the floodlights at **Adelaide Oval** *(King William Rd., map 8C2-3)* There is also often late-night international tennis at **Memorial Drive Tennis Club** *(corner of War Memorial Drive and Montefiore Rd., map 8C2)*. Check the newspaper sports pages.

BOGART'S
151 Melbourne St., North Adelaide ☎ *267 3018. Map 9B4* ♈ ◐ ▣ ▭ *Open about 6pm-2am or later.*

This North Adelaide wine bar/restaurant/disco has contrived to become a magnet for the trendies of the city without losing any of its original good-natured atmosphere. The bar prices are inexpensive, the music is loud, the dancing is near impossible, the food is actually edible... Bogart's is sheer blissful torture!

TIVOLI HOTEL
261 Pirie St. ☎ *223 2388. Map 9D4* ♈ ▭ *Open till late; rock evenings Tues-Thurs 8pm-3am.*

The Tiv offers rock bands from Tuesday to Thursday and comedy on Friday and Saturday nights, with an obligatory meal (▭).

Where to shop

The busiest shopping area in South Australia is Adelaide's **Rundle Mall**, a tightly packed, brick-paved, pedestrians-only street that contains the city's leading department stores (**David Jones**, **Myer** and **John Martin**), boutiques, cafés, restaurants and intriguing arcades. The Mall, with its fruit and flower stalls, newspaper stands and open-air cafés, provides the shopper with the greatest temptation in the most pleasant of surroundings.

But for bargains, for the rare or unusual, and for surprises, it pays, of course, to wander. Browse around the southern suburb of **Unley**, and through **Melbourne St.** in North Adelaide. The city's well-known best-buys include locally mined opals, wine, leather goods, jewelry, pottery, paintings and sports goods. Normal shopping hours are Saturday 8.30am-midday. City shops are open late on Friday night up to 9pm; in the suburbs late-night shopping is on Thursday night.

ABORIGINAL ART
Most state capitals have reputable outlets for Aboriginal artifacts, but occasionally the unwary or simply inexpert visitor can be tricked by dealers cashing in on the increasing popularity of native crafts. One place where you can feel at ease is the ADELLA GALLERY.

ADELLA GALLERY
27-29 Gilbert Pl. ☎ *212 3600. Map 8D3* ▣ ◉
Authentic Aboriginal art and traditional and modern artifacts can be bought here. There is a fine collection of didjeridus, boomerangs, bark paintings, emu-egg carvings, and basketry.

BOOKS

Adelaide has won a reputation as one of the country's most literary cities. Several well-known writers live here and some of Australia's most controversial literary disputes have their roots among local authors. Naturally, there are many fine bookstores to be found here.

EUROPA BOOKSHOP

16 Pulteney St. ☎ *223 2289. Map 8D3* 🆎 💳 💳 💳

The Europa specializes in foreign-language texts. As well as novels, nonfiction works, newspapers and magazines from around the world, it has a wide selection of dictionaries, phrase books, maps, and language courses on record and cassette.

FABLES BOOKSTORE

21 Chesser St. ☎ *232 0766. Map 8D3* 💳 💳

A good selection of unusual Australian and art books can be found here.

FASHION

In keeping with Adelaide's culturally progressive image, its fashion houses are among the leaders in Australia. You will find the young alternative designer stores in **Rundle Mall**.

SHOUZ

144 King William Rd., Hyde Park ☎ *272 1270* 🆎 💳 💳 💳

This high-fashion shoe boutique for women has a large selection of imported and local shoes, from casual to dressy. Shouz also stocks handbagz.

TOFFS FASHION HOUSE

167-171 King William Rd., Hyde Park ☎ *271 3711/274 1030* 🆎 💳 💳 💳

This stylish shop carries an extensive range of designer labels and accessories from Australia and overseas. Among the women's fashions are the works of Harry Who and George Gross.

JEWELRY

About 80 percent of the world's opal is mined in Australia, with most coming from the rugged wilderness in remote parts of this state. When buying, look for the depth of color in this "blue fire stone."

ADELAIDE GEM CENTRE.

27-29 Gilbert Pl. ☎ *212 3600. Map 8D3* 🆎 💳 💳 💳

Opals — black, boulder, solids, triplets and rough opals — are the gems this company trades in. They mine them, cut them and sell them. Free courtesy car service for visitors, and for serious buyers after-hours appointments can be arranged.

COWELL JADE PTY LTD

52 King William St. ☎ *231 1007. Map 8D3* 🆎 💳 💳 💳

Cowell jade, mined in South Australia, comes in beautiful shades of green through to black. The rare black jade is recognized by experts for its high quality. The Nephrite jade deposits were discovered by a local farmer in 1965 and are among the largest in the world. Jade from the mine has been fashioned into jewelry and carvings.

OPAL FIELD GEMS
Ground and 3rd floors, 29 King William St. ☎*212 5300. Map 8D3* 🆎 💳 💳 💳
This is the largest opal-cutting factory in Australia: 100,000 carats of solid opal and 750,000 triplet opals a year. Visitors can see the gems being cut and polished on the 3rd floor. There is a 30 percent sales tax exemption for overseas visitors who show a passport and travel ticket.

MARKETS AND SHOPPING MALLS
Australians love a bustling market, and Adelaide's are excellent. They provide everything from bric-a-brac to rare antiques, fresh fruit to gourmet delicatessen fare. The ambience and aromas alone make these markets worth adding to your itinerary; the bargains are simply a bonus.

BRICKWORKS MARKETS
South Rd., Thebarton ☎*352 4822* 🔥 💳 🔥
This complex, to the NW of the city, is a combined market and family-entertainment center. It has more than 200 stalls, shops, a beer garden, mini-golf, bumper boats, kiddie cars and other novelty rides. The Markets are open Friday to Sunday 9am-5pm, with access to the leisure park in school vacations.

CENTRAL MARKET
Grote St. Map 8E2 🔥 💳 *Open Tues 7am-5.30pm; Thurs 11am-5.30pm; Fri 7am-9pm; Sat 7am-1pm.*
Well worth a visit. The stalls in this colorful, comprehensive market sell fruit, vegetables, fish, meat, delicatessen food, craft work and jewelry... almost anything.

GALLERIE SHOPPING CENTRE
20 Gawler Pl. through to 200 North Terrace ☎*223 1699. Map 8D3* 🔥 💳
Three floors of 60 shops that include the **R. M. Williams** (Australian bushmen's clothing) store and the **Australian Broadcasting Corporation Shop** (records, books and posters). There are also 14 international food outlets (dine-in or takeout).

SPORTS GOODS
Sporting-equipment stores are something of an Adelaide specialty. This is, after all, the city of that legendary cricketer Sir Don Bradman. There is nothing quite like ROWE AND JARMAN for the young cricket fan, however. Here you will see Australia's dreamers browsing and buying alongside their sporting heroes.

ROWE AND JARMAN SPORTS STORE
104 Grenfell St. ☎*223 5666. Map 8D3* 🆎 💳 💳 💳
An excellent shop for sporting equipment and clothing, known around the world for its cricketing supplies. Other sports are also well catered to, with a good selection of tennis gear.

Excursions

Many of Adelaide's attractions begin at the edge of the city: the wine valleys, the beach resorts, towns with a flavor of the past, and the bushland reserves among them. The following excursions are within relatively easy reach of Adelaide. Parts of South Australia are described on pages 201-4, and in ROUTE 2 in TOURS on pages 71-3.

The **Royal Automobile Association of South Australia** *(41 Hindmarsh Sq.* ☎ *223 4555, map 8 D3-9 D4)* offers reciprocal membership to members of affiliated automobile clubs. Visitors should bring along their overseas membership card. The RAA offers touring advice, maps and travel agency services. It has also published a particularly useful book for visitors, *Tours From Adelaide,* which details more than 20 excellent round trips from the city.

Day and half-day bus tours to most of the region's points of interest are available from **Adelaide Sightseeing** *(101 Franklin St.* ☎ *231 4144* ⁅Fx⁆ *212 6275, map 8 D3).* **Ansett Pioneer** *(111 Franklin St.* ☎ *51 2075/216 5452, map 8 D2)* also offers similar air-conditioned bus tours.

Details and reservations for extended tours to all parts of the state can be obtained through the **South Australian Government Travel Centre** *(18 King William St.* ☎ *212 1644, map 8 D3).*

Excursions (1): Environs of Adelaide

ADELAIDE HILLS

Few cities can have such a magnificent backdrop as the Adelaide Hills, part of the tree-clad **Mount Lofty Range** and just 20 minutes from the center of Adelaide itself.

There are many ways to explore their charms, but one leading to many delights is the drive that begins by traveling SE from Adelaide onto the Glen Osmond Rd. Follow this through to **Mt. Barker Rd.**, where, preserved in the median strip, there is an old tollhouse and gate used more than a century ago.

Climb on past the **Eagle-on-the-Hill**, once an old staging post and now a hotel, up to the small town of **Crafers**. David Crafer opened the **Sawyer's Arms Hotel** here in 1839; it was reputedly used by bushrangers who held up travelers in the hills.

Drive on to the 711m (2,333-foot) summit of **Mt. Lofty** for a dramatic view over Adelaide and the coast. Then enjoy a short detour into the **Cleland Conservation Park** *(* ☎ *339 2572* ⊠ ✳ ← ⇚ *open 9.30am-5pm),* one of Adelaide's favorite picnic spots. This vast reserve has koalas (handling and viewing 2-4pm), kangaroos, emus, wombats, dingoes, wallabies and native birds. From here you can travel on to **Norton Summit** to meet up with the **Montacute Scenic Route** that will wind you back into Adelaide.

But the Adelaide Hills call for detours. Take them to find the **Birdwood Mill**, an old flour mill converted into a museum, with an excellent collection of old cars and motorcycles. Find the lane that leads into **Bridgewater**, and visit **Gumeracha** and see the biggest rocking horse in the world, 18.3m (21½ feet) high, at **The Toy Factory** *(Mannum Rd.)* The Hills hold many surprises for the dogged explorer.

THE BAROSSA VALLEY

The Barossa was named in 1837 by Adelaide's founder, Colonel William Light, after a valley he knew in Spain. It became home for immigrants from Silesia and Prussia in the 1840s, who quickly realized its potential for farming and winemaking. Their heritage is evident today in the Lutheran churches, the stone restaurants, the bakeries and, of course, the names of the winemakers.

The Barossa Valley, which is Australia's most famous wine-making district, is only 55km (34 miles) NE of Adelaide. It is a broad, shallow valley with more than 40 wineries scattered across it, many of them open daily for wine-tasting and sales.

To drive to it take the Main North Rd. from Adelaide up to **Gawler**, turn right at the Barossa Valley Highway sign and drive on to **Rosedale**. From here you follow a circular route that takes in the towns of **Tanunda**, **Angaston**, **Nuriootpa** and **Seppeltsfield**.

• Around Easter every odd-numbered year the **Barossa Valley Vintage Festival** is celebrated, a week-long carnival of wine, folk-dancing and German brass-band music.

A little farther to the N is the **Clare Valley**, another great wine-making area and, like the Barossa, well worth imbibing.

HAHNDORF

28km (18 miles) SE. By car, via South Eastern Freeway, then turn off N.

The fascinating town of Hahndorf, a little bit of old Germany in the Australian bush, is well worth a visit. Hahndorf was settled by Germans fleeing from Silesia in 1839 and named after Captain Dirk Hahn, the man who commanded the ship that brought the immigrants to their new land. The original stone cottages are still in use. The visitor walks by such buildings as the **Hahndorf Academy**, **Hahndorf Inn**, the **German Arms Hotel** and the **Lutheran Church**. It is touristy, but charming. The German-style beer, food and folk-dancing festival of Schutzenfest is celebrated in the town each January.

🍽 **Hahndorf Bavarian** *(145a Main St. ☎(08) 388 7921 ▥).*

VICTOR HARBOUR

84km (52 miles) s. By car, via Main South Rd. to Old Noarlunga, the McLaren Vale, Willunga and Mt. Compass, and across the Hindmarsh River. Bicycle rental: Causeway Kiosk, Victor Harbour ☎(085) 52 1838.

Victor Harbour is one of South Australia's most fascinating coastal resorts and is the largest town on the Fleurieu Peninsula. Linked to it by a long causeway is **Granite Island**, which provides fine views of Encounter Bay. Victor Harbour offers a superb base for fishermen, safe beaches for swimmers, and some exciting waves for surfers.

The island, a wildlife sanctuary, is reached either by an energetic stroll or by a horse-drawn tram, which operates daily 10am-4pm. On one side of the island are fairy penguins and many species of sea bird; at the top of the island the careful visitor can enjoy the company of the shy rock wallabies. Dusk is the best time to view the penguins, when they waddle in from the sea to the rookeries.

Victor Harbour's other prominent landmark is **The Bluff** at Rosetta Head. This 100m-high (328-foot) rock formation, which dominates the skyline to the w of the town, was used as a lookout for the Encounter Bay Whaling Station in the 1830s. When a whale was sighted a flag was raised.

➴   Two possibilities for overnight stops in Victor Harbour are the **Apollon Motor Inn** *(Hindmarsh Rd. Victor Harbour, SA, 5211* ☎ *(085) 52 1755* ▨*)* and the **Victor** *(Albert Pl., Victor Harbour, SA, 5211* ☎ *52 1288* ▨*)*, which faces the bay.

➾   The **Glacier Rock** *(13km/8 miles from Victor Harbour on Inman Valley Rd.* ☎ *(085) 58 8202* ▨*)* has excellent views.

WEST BEACH
Directly to the w of the city, along Burbridge Rd.
The West Beach Reserve is a playground that contains many playing fields, two golf courses, a boating lake, a boat ramp and sailing club. There is fine, safe swimming here and its nearness to the city makes it one of the great targets for those escaping offices on the hottest days. To the n is **West Lakes**, where the enthusiast can take part in sailing, canoeing, sailboarding and swimming. West Lakes is also the location of **Football Park**, home of the SA Football League.

Excursions (2): Farther afield

COOBER PEDY AND THE OUTBACK
960km (600 miles) nw. By car, via Stuart Highway.
Much of the northern part of South Australia is semidesert. It is made up of stony plains, salt pans and sandhills, and the terrain is extremely harsh. This, of course, is still pioneering country; rugged, inhospitable, deadly... and yet often uncannily beautiful.

Although the Outback is an intriguing place for the adventurer, it can also be hazardous to visitors unused to the extremes found here. Before driving or venturing into this country, seek specialist advice in Adelaide. Better still, travel with one of the well-known safari tour operators who know the territory and its rules.

Coober Pedy is *Mad Max* territory — a grim and dusty moonscape of sandy ridges, famous for its fine opals and for the fact that the majority of its inhabitants live underground. The miners' cave-like homes, often luxurious and magnificently furnished, keep naturally cool although temperatures above ground may be unbearable. The town's name is taken from the Aboriginal *Kupa* (white person) and *Piti* (burrow) — hence *Kupa Piti:* white man's burrow.

Opal Air (☎ *352 3337)* has 3-hour flights from Adelaide to Coober Pedy as well as 2-to-3-day air-and-motel-accommodations tours. **Treckabout Safaris** *(30 Berryman Drive, Modbury* ☎ *(08) 264 3770)* offers tours into the Outback. Transportation from Adelaide is by air-conditioned 4-wheel-drive vehicle; at night you camp out under the stars. All meals are included, and the equipment is first class. For tours from Coober Pedy, contact **Coober Pedy Tours** *(Main St.* ☎ *(086) 72 5333).*

✎ Two subterranean possibilities for those who wish to stay in Coober Pedy are the **Underground Motel** *(P.O. Box 375, Coober Pedy, SA, 5273* ☎ *(086) 72 5324* ▧ *)* and the **Opal Inn** *(Hutchison St., Coober Pedy, SA, 5273* ☎ *(086) 72 5054* ▣ *(086) 72 5501* ▧ *).*

THE EYRE PENINSULA

This is part of the "West Coast Country", the first land in South Australia ever seen by European eyes. The Dutch explorer Peter Nuyts sailed just this far before returning W in 1627.

The Eyre Peninsula itself was named after the explorer Edward John Eyre, who was the first to cross Australia overland from E to W. The major centers on the peninsula are **Whyalla**, which rejoices in approximately 300 days of sunshine per year, and **Port Lincoln**, a tuna-fishing port overlooking Boston Bay, and there are many small coastal resorts. Together with the bush country and rich wheatlands, they make this a fine place for a quiet get-away.

Kendall Airlines *(150 North Terrace* ☎ *233 3322)* offers 2-day air tours to Port Lincoln, including motel accommodations. Useful addresses are **Whyalla Tourist Centre** *(3 Patterson St., City Plaza, Whyalla, SA, 5600* ☎ *(086) 45 7428)* and **Port Lincoln Tourist Office** *(Civic Hall, Tasman Terrace, Port Lincoln, SA, 5606* ☎ *(086) 82 3255* ▨ *80493).*

THE FLINDERS RANGES

The route to the Flinders Ranges follows the footsteps of the pioneers, through hard, exhilaratingly spectacular country. This was where the first Europeans came, unprepared, abandoning homes and often hope as the fierce droughts and unforgiving land made their lives a misery.

The Ranges, some 350km (220 miles) N of Adelaide, are dramatic peaks beloved of movie-makers, artists and bushwalkers. Native birds and animals abound here, and in some locations there are Aboriginal rock paintings to be appreciated.

Treckabout Safaris *(30 Berryman Drive, Modbury* ☎ *(08) 264 3770)* provide a 4-day minibus tour, including meals and motel accommodations, from Adelaide to the Flinders Ranges. It includes a visit to **Wilpena Pound**, **Leigh Creek**, **Gammon Ranges** and **Arkaroola**.

KANGAROO ISLAND

There are more than 100 islands off the South Australian coast. Kangaroo Island, a peaceful resort some 113km (71 miles) sw of Adelaide, is,
at 145km long by 50km wide (91 by 31 miles), the biggest of them all.

The main town is **Kingscote**. There is some farming, but a large part
of the island is taken up by the **Flinders Chase National Park**. There
are camping sites and bushwalking tracks aplenty, and the island beaches
are a delight to swimmers, surfers and fishermen. The island is a wildlife
paradise: seals cavorting on its surf-splashed rocks, fairy penguins,
abundant kangaroos, koalas, goannas, and emus "drumming" you away
from their territory.

A **vehicle ferry** sails from Port Adelaide to Kangaroo Island every
weekday, but the journey takes more than six hours. Perhaps a better
idea would be to take the 40-minute air trip. **Air Kangaroo Island** *(James
Scofield Drive, Adelaide Airport* ☎ *234 4177)* runs several flights from
7.30am daily to Kingscote and three other centers.

THE MURRAY RIVER

Australia's greatest river, the Murray, completes its last 650km (400
miles) through South Australia. Once it was a major trading route to the
interior; today its main purpose seems to be recreational.

The Murray is there for all to enjoy... fisherman, poet, artist or swimmer. Explorers can rent one of the self-drive houseboats from the fleets
based at **Murray Bridge** or **Mannum**, or elsewhere along this majestic
river. They are easy to pilot, well maintained, comfortable, and you can
tie up at night wherever you wish.

For those who would have it easier, there is a paddle-wheeler cruise
from Murray Bridge aboard the *Proud Mary,* her passengers living in
luxury as she steams upriver past huge gums, willows and river cliffs.
Nothing can be quite so relaxing.

Cruises on the Murray River can be booked through the **South
Australian Government Travel Centre** *(18 King William St.* ☎ *212
1644).*

MT. GAMBIER

455km (284 miles) SE. By car, via Princes Highway.

Mt. Gambier, the bustling and prosperous halfway point between Adelaide and Melbourne, is famous for its lakes and, in particular, its unusually vivid **Blue Lake**. The city is built on the slopes of an extinct
volcano, which has three craters; in the main one lies the Blue Lake. Its
average depth is 77m (253 feet), but in parts it sinks to about 200m
(655 feet). The lake is used as Mt. Gambier's main water supply.

THE YORKE PENINSULA

The Yorke Peninsula, with its distinctive "leg" shape, was originally
settled by the Narungga people, who took advantage of its abundant

sea foods. In 1859 copper was discovered near the present town of Kadina, and in came the Cornish miners.

Today the peninsula is largely devoted to cereal crops and sheep-farming. The biggest attraction, however, is "Australia's Little Cornwall," the three towns of **Moonta**, **Kadina** and **Wallaroo**. Every second May (on odd years) the region holds a biennial festival, the Kernewek Lowender, to celebrate its Cornish heritage.

- See also ROUTE 2 and map in TOURS on pages 71-3.

Tasmania

The visitor to Tasmania might well feel that the island is no part of Australia, such is the contrast with the mainland. There are many similarities to the British Isles, and the early settlers must have had the same impression, judging by the names of towns: Richmond, Kingston, New Norfolk, Devonport, Perth, Swansea, Derwent, Cambridge... Much of the island resembles England, but parts are reminiscent of Scotland, and others could be nowhere else on earth.

Tasmania crams great scenic variety into what is, by Australian standards, a relatively small area, from soft, gentle fields, some with hedgerows of hawthorn (may) around Launceston, to the savage and untamed beauty — for once the cliché is accurate — of the Gordon River, in the state's northwestern World Heritage-listed region.

TASMANIANS
Tasmanians, while friendly, betray that insularity often seen in island people. To be fair, they have rather been neglected by the rest of Australia and in many ways pay the penalty for being a small and isolated state in a federal system. Since World War II Tasmania has seen far fewer changes than the rest of Australia.

There is a faint suspicion therefore that Tasmanians distrust "mainlanders" and somehow prefer to keep themselves to themselves. Some hoary old jokes persist on the mainland about inbreeding among Tasmanians, who have a reputation for extreme parochialism — no mean achievement in a nation that still, despite the increasing ethnic diversity of its population, embraces the parochial.

Yet Tasmanians patently welcome overseas tourists. The island is far more tourist-oriented than any other part of Australia. The economy relies heavily on the tourist dollar, partly because Tasmania did not share significantly in the postwar industrialization that transformed the mainland.

THE ISLAND
More than 40 percent of the island is covered in forest, and forestry plays a major part in the economy. Mining — mainly zinc, aluminum, iron ore, copper and tin — and basic mineral-processing such as smelting, are also major industries. There are few large manufacturing plants, and the lack of a substantial industrial base has led to higher-than-average unemployment in recent years, enhancing, if anything, the importance of tourism.

205

Much of the island is extremely isolated, and transportation and communications can be difficult. The southwest is true wilderness, with few, if any, roads through the heavily timbered, mountainous country. Tasmania tends to divide along a north-south line, the two major centers of population, Hobart and Launceston, being at opposite ends of the island. The north coast, which faces Bass Strait and the mainland of Australia, is quite densely populated and has several towns, including Devonport (where the ferry *Abel Tasman* docks with cars and passengers from Melbourne after its overnight journey), Burnie, Wynyard and Ulverstone. Inland, Launceston, on the Tamar River estuary, dominates the region.

In the south, Hobart, the capital, is one of the world's most picturesque cities. It is set against a backdrop of Mt. Wellington, snow-covered for two, sometimes three, months of the year, and the Derwent Estuary — which, as yachting enthusiasts are quick to point out, has more sailable area than Sydney Harbour. It is also, of course, the most southerly Australian city, and on winter days when the wind roars in from the Antarctic one is keenly aware of that fact — although summers are often superb.

Hobart, which was the second site of European settlement in Australia (in 1803), is fortunate in having largely escaped the ravages of the developers, and has retained more of its heritage than any other major Australian city. Some parts, such as Battery Point, have changed little in more than 150 years. Yet while it retains a strong sense of its distinctive place in Australia's short history, Hobart has been unafraid to take risks. The decision by the state government to sanction Australia's first legal casino, which opened in 1973 at the Wrest Point Hotel overlooking the Derwent River, was considered highly daring at the time. Hobart is also one of the few cities in the world where the largest ships are able to tie up within a few hundred meters of the main shopping center. It has a pleasing sense of intimacy that makes it quite unlike any other Australian state capital.

Launceston, Tasmania's second city, is "English" in both appearance and atmosphere. Situated in the valleys formed by the South and North Esk Rivers, which join to become the Tamar River, Launceston is surrounded by rolling hills, small fields divided up by hedgerows, and numerous villages, many with Georgian and Regency mansions. There are also extensive public and private gardens that enhance the rural setting. The Launceston Country Club-Casino has helped to attract increasing numbers of visitors from the mainland, particularly from Melbourne.

TASMANIA'S BRUTAL PAST

It is sad to reflect that such a beautiful island had such an inauspicious beginning. Tasmania, the site of some of the most tyrannical penal settlements that Britain ever ruled, had a record of brutality rarely equaled in Australia. One settlement, Port Arthur, in fact quite enlightened by the standards of its day, is now Australia's most important historical site.

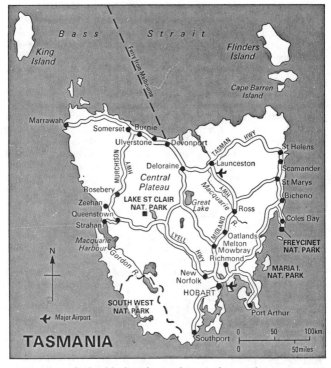

TASMANIA

Even more deplorable than the cruelty meted out to the convicts was the attitude of the early British settlers to local Aborigines, a very different people from their mainland cousins. After a mere 70 years' contact with Europeans the Tasmanian Aborigines were extinct, victims of disease and of avaricious settlers who hunted, shot and poisoned them in their hundreds, seeing them as vermin and competition for the available land. Today there are few traces of Tasmania's savage past, other than several ruins and some horrific stories.

The huge scale of the mainland states demands a focused approach to planning by the visitor, but in contrast Tasmania's relative compactness permits a more comfortable approach. It is possible to plan a trip of reasonable duration that can take in all or most of the island, and this chapter is geared to a state-wide overview. Introductory essays discuss practical matters: how to get to Tasmania, getting around the island, accommodations, eating out, nightlife and shopping. A special feature spotlights Tasmanian wildlife.

There are city gazetteers for both Hobart and Launceston, followed by a selection of excursions that quarter the island.

The chapter ends with suggested tours and tour operators.

GETTING THERE

A pleasant way to reach the island is to take the ferry from Melbourne to the northern port of **Devonport**, an industrial town of 21,000 people. Devonport is situated at the southern end of the **Cradle Mountain/Lake St Clair National Park**, a favorite with bushwalkers and wilderness lovers. Recommended below are a convenient hotel and the popular **Impressions Gallery**.

The *Abel Tasman*, a 19,200-tonne (21,150 US tons) ferry, plies between the mainland and Tasmania three times a week in each direction, carrying 440 cars and 850 passengers in mini-liner comfort. It has three restaurants, a large bar, a disco, children's playroom and coffee shop. Accommodations are all-cabin for the overnight journey. The boat leaves Melbourne and Devonport at 6pm and arrives at its destination at 8.30am the following morning. It sails from Melbourne to Devonport on Monday, Wednesday and Friday, and from Devonport to Melbourne on Sunday, Tuesday and Thursday. Reserve well ahead for the busy December to April period. A new, larger vessel with capacity for 1,500 passengers and 550 cars is due to come into service in mid-1993.

The wave-piercing catamaran *Seacat Tasmania* operates daily services for passengers and cars from Port Welshpool (160km/100 miles E of Melbourne) to Georgetown, Tasmania. The journey takes $4\frac{1}{2}$ hours. The *Seacat Tasmania* can carry more than 350 passengers and 84 cars.

The major airlines, **Ansett** and **Australian Airlines**, **East-West Airlines** and **Kendell**, fly to Tasmania from both Melbourne and Sydney. Ansett flies to Hobart, Launceston, Wynyard and Devonport; Australian to Launceston and Hobart; East-West to Hobart, Devonport, Burnie/Wynyard; and Kendell to Burnie/Wynyard and Devonport.

☙ GATEWAY INN

16 Fenton St., Devonport, Tas., 7310 ☎*(004) 24 4922* 🔟🔟 🏧*59187* 🏧 *64 rms* 🛏 🍽
🆎 🔳 🔳 🔳 & 🔳 🍸 🎿

Location: Near town center. A medium-sized motor inn, the Gateway, like scores of good-quality motor inns or motels in Australia, offers acceptable self-contained accommodations and a licensed dining room. It is convenient for an overnight stop.

IMPRESSIONS GALLERY

5 Best St., Devonport, Tas., 7310 ☎*(004) 24 1287* 🆎 🔳 🔳 🔳 *Open daily 9am-5pm.*
A large selection of Tasmanian souvenirs, with particular emphasis on wood, including items in Huon Pine, Sassafras, Blackwood, Myrtle and minor species. The gallery also sells Tasmanian pottery, jewelry, and leather. Helpful, enthusiastic staff.

GETTING AROUND

The tourist trade in Tasmania is very much geared to the **car-rental** concept, and many vacation packages include a rented car in the price. **Campervans** are a popular alternative to cars: camping and trailer (caravan) sites are of a good standard, and in some places it is possible to camp out in the bush. All the major **car rental companies** are represented in Tasmania, which has a good network of main roads between major centers.

Tasmania now has no passenger rail services, the last line having closed in the 1970s, but there are good **bus services**. A regular daily service links **Hobart** with **Launceston** via the Midland Highway, and then continues along the N coast to **Smithton**, stopping at Devonport, Burnie and Wynyard. An alternative service links Hobart and Launceston, traveling along the E coast, and another service connects Hobart with Burnie via the W coast. A Tassie Pass, available from **Tasmania Redline Coaches** *(96 Harrington St., Hobart* ☎ *(002) 34 4577)*, gives 7, 14 and 21 days' unlimited travel.

Light aircraft can be chartered for sightseeing and other journeys, in Launceston, Hobart (at Cambridge aerodrome, near Hobart's main aerodrome), Evandale, Devonport, Wynyard and Queenstown. In addition, **Airlines of Tasmania** operates scheduled services between Hobart and Launceston, Queenstown, Strahan, Devonport, Wynyard, Flinders Island and King Island.

ACCOMMODATIONS
Tasmania can offer the traveler a greater variety of accommodations than any other part of Australia, ranging from top-class hotels and casinos to traditional English-style bed-and-breakfast guesthouses, with ample choice in the medium-price range. Several hotel/motel chains, such as the **Four Seasons** group, have state-wide networks. There is also a scheme called **Host Farms**, which involves "living in" with a family.

Colonial Accommodation is a term used for private bed-and-breakfast accommodations, in anything from an old cottage to a stately country home. Look for signs outside saying "Colonial Accommodation." An example is **Prospect House** in RICHMOND (see HOBART SIGHTS), a beautifully proportioned Georgian house built c.1830 and classified by the National Trust, which has ten double rooms for guests, in a convict-built barn set in the courtyard, among 12ha (30 acres) of ground. A full or continental breakfast is served, and, unusually for this kind of accommodations, there is a licensed restaurant, specializing in game dishes.

Twenty-seven houses involved in the scheme have formed themselves into the **Colonial Accommodation Association**. Reservations can be made through any branch of the Tasmanian Government Tourist Bureau, through Ansett and East-West Airlines, or directly.

Ordinary public houses throughout Tasmania offer good, clean accommodations, although in most cases without private facilities. However, prices are low and often include a hearty breakfast. Another increasingly popular class of low-budget accommodations is the efficiency (self-catering) vacation, which usually means renting a self-contained house or cabin, sometimes on a farm.

The **Host Farm** scheme involves staying as the guest of a farming family, either in the main home or in a cabin on the property. Guests can join in farm activities. A booklet explaining the idea and listing the farms is published by the **Country Accommodation Association of Tasmania**, available through branches of the Tasmanian Government Tourist Bureau, who can also take reservations.

Most trailer (caravan) sites have on-site trailers to rent on a per-night or longer-term basis, for really economical accommodations.

DINING OUT IN TASMANIA

Tasmania is fish country. It provides a chance to eat the finest scallops, lobsters, tuna and fresh trout to be found in Australia or, as some islanders insist, in the world. For they are surrounded by some of the best fisheries imaginable and by some of the finest trout rivers and lakes in Australia.

Supplementing this natural wealth, there is a fish farm for Atlantic salmon, which delivers fresh salmon to restaurants on the island and to selected outlets in Sydney and Melbourne. Reportedly its produce compares well with the best Scottish or Canadian salmon.

For a small state, Tasmania has some excellent restaurants, particularly in Hobart and Launceston. In rural areas standards can most charitably be described as patchy.

ENTERTAINMENT

With the notable exception of Hobart's **Wrest Point Hotel-Casino** and the **Country Club-Casino** near Launceston, nightlife in Tasmania centers largely on the home and on such simple pleasures as dining out.

There are, it is true, discos in both main cities, usually attached to public houses, which open and close and change names with the usual frequency. Consult the *Hobart Mercury* or *Launceston Examiner* newspapers for the latest picture.

The **Wrest Point Hotel-Casino** in Hobart has several nightspots within the hotel complex. The **Riviera Room** has a program of live entertainment, music and dancing in a traditional cabaret setting. **Regines** is a more relaxed disco-style nightspot, with live bands every night. There is a resident pianist in the **Birdcage** bar, and jazz on Sunday in the **Riverview** lounge.

The **Country Club-Casino** near Launceston offers pretty much the same format, but on a smaller scale. The **Mount Pleasant Room** features cabaret, with guest artists, live music, and dancing Tuesday to Saturday; **Regines** has disco music, with some live music Wednesday to Sunday; and in the **Lanai** bar a resident pianist plays nightly.

Try to catch the excellent **Tasmanian Symphony Orchestra**, which has a touring program around the state.

SHOPPING

Shopping in Tasmania has one major disadvantage: prices are anything up to 10 percent more expensive than on the mainland because most goods have to be transported across Bass Strait.

However, despite its population of only 500,000, Tasmania boasts a large number of craft stores and galleries, and is building a reputation for the quality of its **crafts**, particularly in **woodworking** media. **Woolen goods** manufactured on the island are excellent, both in quality and value. And items made from local woods, particularly the rare **Huon pine**, make unusual gifts and souvenirs.

Tasmania can be a happy hunting ground for **antique collectors**. There are many old country homes, and by Australian standards the island has a long history. Antique dealers are licensed by the state government, but shoppers still need to know what they are looking at and for. Dealers can arrange transportation of antiques either to the mainland or overseas.

Shopping hours conform with those in the rest of Australia.

TASMANIAN WILDLIFE

Because of its isolation from the mainland, Tasmania's flora and fauna are distinctive and sometimes unique. Keep your eyes peeled, for there is much of interest. Some highlights are described briefly below.

TASMANIAN DEVIL   A small, smelly, dark-brown-to-black, nocturnal creature, reputed to have the most powerful jaws of any beast of its size. Unpredictable and vicious when cornered.

TASMANIAN TIGER   Probably extinct, but may still survive in some remote parts. A marsupial, about the size of a large dog, striped across the length of its body. At the point where the tail joins the body, has a strong resemblance to a kangaroo. If you see anything resembling this description, report it to the **National Parks and Wildlife Service** (look in the telephone book).

FISH   The island is famed for its fishing, in particular for freshwater **trout**, **bream** in the river estuaries, and **tuna** offshore. Superb **Atlantic salmon** are bred in a fish-farm.

TREES   Several unique species give Tasmania its special look and feel. The **Huon pine**, found in only a few areas, mainly the NW and SW, grows extremely slowly — about 120mm (4.7 inches) a century. Other species include the **celery-top pine**, **Tasmanian blackwood**, **King Billy pine**, **sassafras** and **wattle**.

HONEY   Tasmania is a major producer, and **leatherwood honey**, from the W, is unique. White beehives are everywhere. Leatherwood trees have white waxy flowers from December to March.

Hobart

PRACTICAL INFORMATION
☎STD (area) code   002.
Airport   ☎48 5279; Ansett ☎38 0800; Australian ☎38 3333; East-
west ☎312 943/131711 (toll-free numbers).
Car rental   Avis ☎34 4222; Budget ☎34 5222; Hertz ☎34 5555.
Tourism Tasmania   80 Elizabeth St., Hobart, Tas., 7000 ☎30 0250.
American Express Travel Service   Websters Travel, 124 Liverpool
St., Hobart, Tas., 7000 ☎31 2955 Ⓕₓ23 7642.
Royal Automobile Club of Tasmania (RACT)   Corner of Patrick
St. and Murray St., Hobart, Tas., 7000 ☎38 2200.

Tourism Tasmania can provide information about hotels, sights and
tours, and publishes an excellent, free series of leaflets, *Let's Talk
About...,* covering attractions in the city and environs. The **National
Trust** too has leaflets listing its properties region-by-region, and the
Department of Tourism publishes a very full twice-yearly calendar
of events.

Sights and places of interest

ANGLESEA BARRACKS ★
Davey St. ☎*21 2205* ▣ ✗ *compulsory. Open Tues: tours start 11am.*
The headquarters of the Australian Military Forces in Tasmania, Angle-
sea Barracks is the oldest military establishment in Australia still occupied by the army. Many of the original Georgian buildings have been
preserved and restored. Free guided tours of the barracks take in the
guardhouse, hospital, military jail, the original officers' mess, the old
drill hall dating back to the early 19thC, and barracks for the other
ranks.

BATTERY POINT ★ ◁€
One of the best-preserved areas of any Australian city and the oldest
part of Hobart, Battery Point is a lived-in, vital area that has largely
escaped being "restored," or overwhelmed by souvenir stores. It was
first settled in 1804, and takes its name from the battery of guns established in 1818 on the promontory of land overlooking the Derwent
Estuary.

Battery Point's architecture is nearly all Georgian and early Victorian,
many buildings dating back to the 1830s and '40s. The oldest is the **signal
station** used to relay messages to Mt. Nelson near the mouth of the river,
mainly announcing the arrival of ships. Old taverns and inns lend the area
an almost Dickensian atmosphere. Many of them have been converted
into art galleries, antique stores and restaurants. Among the finest streetscapes is **Arthur's Circus**, a perfectly preserved group of single-story
cottages around a central grassed traffic circle (roundabout). **St George's
Anglican Church** (built 1836-37) in Cromwell St., a fine example of

Georgian church architecture, is known as the "Mariners' Church" and has some fine boxed pews.

This is very much walking territory, for its charm lies in discovering little nooks and crannies that you would miss on four wheels.

BOTANIC GARDENS ★

Domain Rd. ☎*34 6299* ▣ ⧖ ✗ ♣ ▣ ⇀ ⇐ *Open Nov-Mar 8am-6.30pm; Apr, Sept-Oct 8am-5.30pm; May-Aug 8am-4.45pm.*

Established in 1818 and situated on 13ha (32 acres) of high ground overlooking the Derwent, Hobart's gardens are small compared to most mainland equivalents, but therein lies their special charm. The gardens have several world-class features, such as a fine **tropical greenhouse**, a **cactus house**, a **fuchsia house** and a **herb garden**. The **conservatory**, with its magnificent floral display, changed four times a year, should not be missed. Look out too for the **floral clock**, the **rose garden**, and numerous fountains and water features. There is an easy-access area for disabled people.

CONSTITUTION DOCK

Davey St. ⇀

This is the finishing point for the annual classic blue-water **ocean yacht race**, the Sydney-to-Hobart, which starts from the mainland on Boxing Day (December 26). Following the end of the race it is the scene of much revelry, but at other times it is a quiet place where fishing boats and private sailing craft tie up. Constitution Dock is within a few hundred meters of the **Elizabeth Street Pier**, where large ships dock, and **Brooke Street Pier**, where ferries leave for the eastern shore and pleasure craft depart for cruises in the Derwent Estuary.

LADY FRANKLIN GALLERY

Lenah Valley Rd., Lenah ☎*28 0076* ▣ ✗ ⇀ *Open Sat, Sun 2-4.30pm. Closed Mon-Fri.*

The gallery, home of the Art Society of Tasmania, is housed in a Greek-revival building constructed in sandstone in 1842, under the sponsorship of Lady Franklin, the Governor's wife. Today it houses a display of paintings by members of the society, many of them Tasmania's leading artists, and a library of art books.

LIBRARY AND MUSEUM OF FINE ARTS

91 Murray St. ☎*30 7484* ▣ ⧖ *Open 9.30am-5pm. Closed Sat, Sun.*

Housed in the State Library, the museum and library have a collection of fine and rare books, a large collection of paintings and prints, and a collection of antique furniture, ceramics, glass and silver.

MARITIME MUSEUM OF AUSTRALIA ★

Secheron House, Secheron Rd., Battery Point ☎*23 5082* ▣ *Children under 15 free. Open Mon-Fri, Sun 1-4.30pm; Sat 10am-4.30pm.*

Hidden away down a cul-de-sac in Battery Point, the Maritime Museum is a fascinating collection of models, paintings, artifacts and memorabi-

213

lia from Tasmania's maritime past. The museum is in **Secheron House**, overlooking the Derwent Estuary.

PARLIAMENT HOUSE ★

Morrison St. 🔲 *Public access but no guided tours.*

Tasmania's Parliament House is one of the oldest buildings in Hobart, built between 1836-41 to a design by John Lee Archer in a style described as colonial Regency. Its situation at the end of Murray St., opposite the wharves, betrays the origins of the building: it started life as the Customs House, and its cellars, which still show the broad, arrowed bricks in the vaulted ceiling, used to be the bond store. It became the home of the State Parliament in 1856. The building is fronted by a spacious **garden** planted with trees, and colorful flowerbeds in summer, well patronized on fine days by office workers eating their lunch.

PORT ARTHUR HISTORIC SITE ★

About 100km (63 miles) SE ☎*50 2363* 🔲 *(*✉*museum only)* ✗*at 9.30am, then hourly to 3.30pm* 🚌 ➤ ◄◄ *Site open at all times. Museum open 9am-5pm. Guided bus tours leave Tourism Tasmania, 80 Elizabeth St.* ☎*300250 for details. Ghost tours Dec 1-Easter every evening 9.30pm; Easter-Nov 30 Fri-Sat 9.30pm.*

This is probably the single most significant historical site in Australia. Port Arthur, established in 1830, was once the major penal settlement of Van Diemen's Land, as Tasmania was originally called, and operated until 1877 when it was abandoned and the remaining convicts were sent to jail in Hobart. More than 12,000 convicts passed through the settlement. The regime was extremely strict and harsh — witness the so-called model prison, based on rules of solitary confinement and silence, with its tiny one-man cells and a chapel where prisoners could not see one another.

The major points of interest are the **chapel**, never consecrated; the **model prison**; the **asylum**, with its visitor reception center, video display tracing the history of Port Arthur, and museum; the **penitentiary**, **hospital**, **guardhouse** and **magazine**; and the **government cottages** where visitors were accommodated. The penitentiary, the largest building in the settlement, started life as a flour mill before being converted to house convicts.

Much of Port Arthur was damaged in bushfires during 1897, but the extensive remaining ruins give a vivid outline of what prison life was like 150 or more years ago.

NATIONAL POSTAL AND TELECOMMUNICATIONS MUSEUM

19-21 Castray Esplanade ☎*23 3492* ✉ *Open Mon-Fri 9am-5pm; Sat 9am-1pm. Closed for lunch 12.30-1.30pm and Sun.*

An extensive display traces the history and development of postal and telegraphic services in Tasmania. A visit to the museum can easily be combined with a walk around to SALAMANCA PLACE, 100m (110 yards) away.

RICHMOND ★

26km (16 miles) NE.

This is the site of the oldest **bridge** still standing in Australia, built by convicts in 1823-25. Richmond and its bridge were important in the 19thC. They enabled heavy horse traffic to travel faster between Hobart and the E coast, and later to PORT ARTHUR. Today the bridge is still used to cross the Coal River. There are alarming bows in its structure, but you can rest assured that it is quite sound, much work having been done to ensure its survival.

Richmond, a classified historical town, has much else to offer. It claims the country's oldest Roman Catholic church, **St John's** (1836). A Catholic school has operated in Richmond since 1843, and the restored old **school room** is behind the church. **Richmond Gaol** *(open to visitors)* predates Port Arthur, construction having started in 1825.

There are more than 40 buildings of historical interest, including many fine private houses in classic Georgian style. Most noteworthy are the **Courthouse** (1825); the **Granary**, now home to an art gallery and a boutique selling mohair; the **Old Post Office and General Store** (started in 1826), which served as the local post office from 1832-1973 and is the oldest surviving postal building in Australia; **St Luke's Church of England** (1834); and **James Gordon's House** (1831), a fine colonial Georgian house built by Captain James Gordon, the district magistrate, who gave his name to the Gordon River on the W coast of Tasmania.

RISDON COVE HISTORIC SITE ★

Bowen Park Grasstree Hill Rd., East Risdon ☎338399 ♿ Barbecue facilities Open 9.30am-4.30pm.

This is the site, on the eastern shores of Hobart, of the first recognized European settlement in Tasmania, in September 1803. It was abandoned in 1804 in favor of Sullivans Cove, which is the present site of Hobart. Risdon Cove consists of ruins in varying states of decay, some being mere outlines of foundations, dotted around the cove area. The whole site has been landscaped, and there is an impressive visitors' center.

Risdon Cove is significant in the overall picture of Tasmania's development. Study the models in the visitors' center for an excellent idea of what the area looked like more than 180 years ago.

RUNNYMEDE HOUSE ★

61 Bay Rd., New Town ☎28 1269 Open 10am-4.30pm. Closed Christmas Day; Good Friday; July. Ring bell at front door to gain admission.

A beautifully proportioned and preserved house in the suburb of New Town, Runnymede was built in 1844 by the lawyer and reformer Robert Pitcairn, a leading advocate of the abolition of penal transportation. It is a single-story house in the late-Georgian style, set in an English-style garden. The house was occupied until the late 1970s, when the National Trust took it over, and much of the furnishing is original. At one time the house stood on the shore of New Town, but the land in front has since been reclaimed from the sea.

SALAMANCA PLACE ★

Every Georgian warehouse in this superbly preserved row, dating from the late 1830s, is still in use. Some survive as warehouses; others have become cafés, restaurants, art galleries or shops. Today there is grass where once there would have been cargo stacked from ships unloading on the waterfront opposite. Saturday is market day, and people come from miles around to sell and buy anything from fruit and vegetables to handcrafted leather work and bric-a-brac. Street musicians (sometimes the Tasmanian Police pipe and drum band) perform, adding a festive note to the activities.

Salamanca Place is virtually an extension of BATTERY POINT, and the two areas can be visited together.

SHOT TOWER ★

Channel Highway, Taroona ☎*27 8885* 🚋 🖥 🚗 ⫷ *Open 9am-5pm.*
The tower offers unsurpassed views across the Derwent Estuary. It was built in 1870 and was used to make musket balls and shot. Extensively restored, the 60m-tall (197 feet) tower is now a museum and souvenir and craft outlet. A short continuously-running video explains its history.

TASMANIAN MUSEUM AND ART GALLERY ★

5 Argyle St. ☎*23 1422* 🖭 ♿ *Open 10am-5pm. Closed Christmas Day; Anzac Day; Good Friday.*
The museum possesses a good collection of stuffed native animals including the Tasmanian Devil and the now almost certainly extinct Tasmanian Tiger. Elsewhere the emphasis is on Tasmanian Aborigines and early colonial life.

The art gallery has six galleries devoted to the permanent collection, plus a series of special exhibitions throughout the year. The permanent exhibition has works mainly by Australian and prominent Tasmanian artists, and by early convict painters and colonial painters (those not born in Australia but who did much work there). The permanent collection features such noted Australian artists as William Dobell, Sidney Nolan and Frederick McCubbin.

TASMANIAN TRANSPORT MUSEUM

Anfield St., Glenorchy ☎*49 2403* 🚋 ♣ *Open Sat, Sun and public holidays 1-5pm. Closed Mon-Fri.*
A must for bus, train and tram buffs. The museum, complete with a tram and a rail station, is crammed with memorabilia from an earlier transportation era. Train rides are available on the first Sunday of every month.

THEATRE ROYAL

29 Campbell St. ☎*34 6266. Open for performances: see press.*
Australia's oldest surviving theater, Hobart's Theatre Royal celebrated its 150th anniversary in 1987. The external walls and the stage are largely original. The theater's acoustics are excellent and the Regency

decor adds charm and intimacy to the small auditorium. Visitors are welcome when no performance is scheduled.

VAN DIEMEN'S LAND FOLK MUSEUM
Narryna, 103 Hampden Rd., Battery Point ☎ *34 2791* 🚗 ⬛ ✗ *by arrangement. Open Mon-Fri 10am-5pm; Sat 11am-5pm; Sun, hols 2-5pm. Closed Christmas Day; ANZAC Day; Good Friday and all July.*

Housed in **Narryna**, one of Hobart's oldest houses, built c.1836, the museum, the oldest of its type in Australia, has a fine collection of furniture, china, silver, paintings and other articles from the early days of the colony.

Where to stay

FOUNTAINSIDE MOTOR INN ✿
40 Brooker Ave., Hobart, Tas., 7000 ☎ *34 2911* 📠 *57017* 📶 *42 rms* 🟰 *AE* 🔄 💳 📷 ⬅ 💺 ✗

Location: Convenient for the city. Situated on a busy road intersection, this hotel can be noisy at times, but offers reasonably priced, centrally located accommodations. A restaurant on the top floor has excellent views across Hobart and the Derwent.

HOBART PACIFIC MOTOR INN
Kirby Court, West Hobart, Tas., 7000 ☎ *34 6733* 📠 *31 1197* 📶 *60 rms* *AE* 🔄 💳 📷 🟰 🛏 💺 ⬅ 💺 ✗

Location: 2km (1 mile) from center. A good, average motor inn, part of the Flag Inn chain, the Hobart Pacific provides decent, clean accommodations.

LENNA MOTOR INN OF HOBART
20 Runnymede St., Battery Point, Hobart, Tas., 7000 ☎ *23 2911* 📠 *24 0112* 📶 *50 rms* ⬅ 🟰 *AE* 🔄 💳 💳 💳 ⬅ 💺 ✗

Location: Ideal for exploring Battery Point. This is a two-story 19thC mansion, to which 50 rooms have been added, tastefully and entirely in keeping. The surroundings may be old-world, but the service and facilities are decidedly not.

SHERATON HOBART
1 Davey St., Hobart, Tas, 7000 ☎ *35 4535* 📠 *58037* 📶 *234 rms* ⬅ 🟰 *AE* 🔄 💳 💳 ✈ 🍴 ⬅ 💺 ✗

Location: Prime waterfront position on Sullivans Cove in central Hobart, with view of Constitution Dock. The finishing place for the Sydney-Hobart Blue Water Classic, the **Sheraton** offers the sort of accommodations one would expect from a five-star hotel. All guest rooms have unrivaled views either across the Derwent River or toward Mt. Wellington. **The Cove Restaurant** offers a relaxed style of dining, specializing in seafood.

WESTSIDE
150 Bathurst St., Hobart, Tas., 7000 ☎ *34 6255* 📠 *58228* 📶 *139 rms* ⬅ 🟰 *AE* 🔄 💳 💳 ⬅ 💺 ✗

Location: Western edge of city. In the best style of modern motor inns, the **Westside** offers good-quality, unpretentious accommodations in generous sized rooms with all the usual services. It has two nonsmoking floors. The **Silver Skillet** (SEE DINING OUT) and an excellent, inexpensive bistro provide a choice of food and price.

WREST POINT HOTEL-CASINO
410 Sandy Bay Rd., Sandy Bay, Tas., 7000 ☎ *25 0112* 📠 *58115* 📠 *25 3909* 📶 *278 rms* ⬅ 🟰 *AE* 🔄 💳 💳 📷 ⬅ 💺 ✗ 🍴 ⛳ 🏊 ⛵ 💺 ⚓

Location: On a small promontory jutting out into the Derwent River. This was Australia's first legal casino. Its unmatched location provides superb views from rooms in the 17-story tower

217

— but note that the two other wings do not share the view, and only the tower is air conditioned, a strange omission. Otherwise, the standard throughout is superb. The **casino** is suitably exciting and glamorous, but like the hotel man-

ages to retain a sense of intimacy. **The Point Revolving Restaurant** (see DINING OUT) can be recommended. There is also a restaurant serving a variety of Asian food and a coffee shop, which is open 24 hours a day.

Dining out

DEAR FRIENDS
8 Brooke St., The Waterfront ☎ *23 2646* ▥ ▭ ▰ 🄰🄴 ⊙ 🄳 🅅🅂🄰 *Last orders about 10pm. Open for dinner Mon-Sat from 7pm. Lunch Thurs and Fri only.*
A sense of style pervades this refurbished flour mill, built in 1863. Waiters are dressed in long green aprons. The food is *nouvelle cuisine* adapted to local conditions, with a strong leaning toward Tasmanian fish.

MILAN'S SEAFOOD RESTAURANT
7 Beach Rd., Sandy Bay ☎ *25 2180* ▥ ▭ ▰ 🍷 ⇍ ⟨€ 🄰🄴 ⊙ 🄳 🅅🅂🄰 *Last orders about 10pm. Closed Sun.*
Housed in an elegant old mansion in Hobart's premier suburb of Sandy Bay, Milan's offers a huge range of delicious local seafood, including locally caught lobster.

MR WOOBY'S ✿
Rear of 65 Salamanca Pl. ☎ *34 3466* ▥ ▭ ⇍ *Last orders 11pm. Closed Sun.*
Mr Wooby's is ideal for a light lunch or dinner and a cup of coffee, but the menu caters to all tastes from German to Italian and uses Tasmanian produce. Dishes include homemade soups (recommended), savory crepes, schnitzel, steaks, lasagne, and a mixed Lebanese platter. It is far from elegant, but genuinely friendly.

MURES FISH CENTRE
Victoria Dock ☎ *31 2121* ▥ ▭ ▰ 🍷 ⊙ 🅅🅂🄰 *Last orders 10pm. Open 7 days.*
If you don't like fish, forget Mures. This Hobart institution has vacated its former Georgian home in Battery Point and moved to purpose-built, two-level premises by the wharf. It has, however,

managed to maintain its reputation as one of Australia's finest fish restaurants. Mures' new home has a fishmonger, a bakery, an ice cream parlor, a sushi bar and a travel agent on ground level, and the **Upper Deck** restaurant on the first floor, which offers a wide range of freshly caught fish. While many bemoan the move from the Battery Point premises, Mures has maintained its following.

THE POINT REVOLVING RESTAURANT
Wrest Point Hotel-Casino, 410 Sandy Bay Rd., Sandy Bay ☎ *25 0112* ▥ ▭ ▰ ▰ 🍷 ⇍ ⟨€ 🄰🄴 ⊙ 🄳 🅅🅂🄰 *Last orders 9.30pm.*
From the top of the tower at the WREST POINT (see WHERE TO STAY), The Point offers unrivaled views across Hobart and the Derwent: the moon reflected on the water on a calm evening should bring out the poet in even the hardest heart. Fortunately both food and service match the view. The menu may be unadventurous, but the dishes are all impeccably prepared, some at the table. The restaurant revolves at a sedate pace that does not threaten the digestion, about once an hour.

SAKURA JAPANESE RESTAURANT
85 Salamanca Pl. ☎ *23 4773* ▥ ▭ ▰ 🍷 🄰🄴 ⊙ 🄳 🅅🅂🄰 *Last orders 11.30pm. Closed lunch.*
Highly recommended by Japanese visitors and businessmen, this restaurant is housed in one of the old warehouses on SALAMANCA PLACE (see SIGHTS). It is part of the Japanese Seamens' Club opened in 1974 to cater to visiting tuna-fishing fleets from Japan, and is now open to the public.

SILVER SKILLET

Westside, 156 Bathurst St. ☎ *34 6255* ▦
▢ ≡ ▾ ⚊ ﾑﾑ ▣ ◐ ◑ ﾜﾑ *Last orders
9.30pm. Closed lunch; Sun.*

Impeccable Silver Service plus a "traditional" menu is what is on offer here — the Silver Skillet succeeds admirably in its deliberate appeal to long-valued standards. It is part of the Westside hotel.

LA SUPREMA PASTA HOUSE

255 Liverpool St. ☎ *31 0770* ▦ ▢ *Last orders 10-10.30pm. Closed Sat-Tues lunch. BYO license.*

Indulge in some fine homemade pasta in this casual, busy restaurant. The *fettuccine* with *fegatini* (chicken livers) sauce is recommended; there are good veal dishes too. It's essential to reserve ahead.

Where to shop

Distinctively Tasmanian crafts, jewelry, locally-made clothes... the following is a representative cross-section of the best shops in Hobart. The main shopping area is bounded by Liverpool, Murray, Elizabeth and Collins Streets; at its center is the modern **Cat and Fiddle Arcade and Square**.

ASPECT DESIGN

79 Salamanca Pl. ☎ *23 2642* ⚬ ✳ ﾑﾑ
◐ ﾜﾑ

In an old warehouse in SALAMANCA PLACE (see SIGHTS), resident craftspeople can be seen at work: a goldsmith, a silversmith and a glassblower. Also displayed for sale is the work of some 90 artists and craftspeople. A good place in which to find an interesting souvenir of your stay in Tasmania.

HUON PINE SHOP

18 Criterion St. ☎ *34 5171* ◐ ◑ ﾜﾑ

A wide range of gifts made from Tasmania's unique Huon pine and other local woods. The pine's light weight and color make it an ideal wood for working, and some first-class, imaginative gifts can be purchased. Special orders are taken.

SHEEPSKIN AND OPAL WORLD

35 Morrison St. ☎ *34 8142/34 9523* ﾑﾑ
◐ ◑ ﾜﾑ

A wide selection of opals from triplets to the expensive black opals gives this shop one of the best ranges in the state. There is also a vast selection of sheepskin and kangaroo-skin products, from rugs to coats and boots. There's knitwear too, and souvenirs of Tasmania.

MOSTLY MOHAIR

*Bridge Inne Mews (The Courtyard),
Richmond, Tas., 7075* ☎ *62 2492* ﾑﾑ ◐
◑ ﾜﾑ *Open 7 days 9.30am-5pm.*

An award-winning shop, situated in the historic town of Richmond, just 26km NE of Hobart and a leisurely $\frac{1}{2}$-hour drive, Mostly Mohair specializes in exclusive knitted and woven fashion garments, with the accent on mohair.

Launceston

PRACTICAL INFORMATION

☎STD (area) code   003.

Airport   ☎91 8699; Ansett ☎325101; Australian ☎32 9911.

Car rental   Avis ☎91 8314; Budget ☎34 0099; Hertz ☎91 8388.

Tourism Tasmania   Corner of St John St. and Paterson St., Launceston, Tas., 7250 ☎373 111.

American Express Travel Service   Service available only from Hobart office — no representation in Launceston.

Royal Automobile Club of Tasmania (RACT)   Corner of York St. and George St., Launceston, Tas., 7250 ☎31 3166.

   Tourism Tasmania publishes a useful series of leaflets entitled *Let's Talk About...*, available from any Tasbureau outlet. One of the best is *Let's Talk About the Cataract Gorge and Cliff Grounds Reserve*. The **National Trust** also has a helpful guide to its properties in the Launceston region.

Sights and places of interest

CATARACT GORGE ★

Gorge Rd. ☎31 5915 🚠 for chair lift ══ 🄿 🛶 ⟨⟨⟨ Chair lift operates mid-Aug to mid-June 9am-4.30pm; mid-June to mid-Aug Sat, Sun only 9am-4.30pm.

The gorge, situated on the western edge of Launceston, is carved out of softer rock by the South Esk River and provides spectacular views, floral walks and hiking tracks. The chair lift across the gorge is said to have the longest central span in the world, at 308m (1,010 feet); the crossing takes about 6 minutes.

   A large area, the **First Basin**, worn away by the river before it rushes down the cataract to feed into the Tamar River, is Launceston's favorite picnic spot and recreational area. Facilities include swimming and paddling pools. Overlooking the First Basin is the dramatically located GORGE RESTAURANT (see DINING OUT). A visitors' information center, occupying a former bandstand, provides background information on the gorge and exhibits local flora and fauna.

   The city end of the gorge is sometimes floodlit; good views can be obtained from Kings Bridge or Cataract Walk. For times of floodlighting contact the **Town Hall** *(John St.)* or the **Tasmanian Government Tourist Bureau**.

CLARENDON HOUSE ★

Clarendon, near Nile, 28km (18 miles) s ☎98 6220 🄿 🛶 ✦ Open Sept-May 10am-5pm; June-Aug 10am-4pm. Closed Christmas Day; Good Friday.

Among the finest examples of colonial Georgian architecture in Australia, Clarendon is a large 3-story house of fine proportions, built 1836-38, situated in a parkland setting with an English-style garden and kitchen garden enclosed by a wall. The house has been restored and furnished in the style of the 1830s and '40s, and is maintained by the National Trust.

Clarendon was built by the Englishman James Cox, a merchant who amassed a fortune from wool, meat and grain. He lived, in effect, the life of an English country squire, founding the village of Lymington, now renamed Nile, and endowing its church. He died in 1866 and was buried in the family vault in St Andrew's Church at EVANDALE.

ENTALLY HOUSE ★

Bass Highway, Hadspen, 15km (9 miles) SW ☎*93 6201* 📷 ♿ *on ground floor* 🚌 *Open 10am-12.30pm, 1-5pm. Closed Christmas Day.*

Entally House, built c.1820, is possibly the most gracious of Tasmania's 19thC mansions. Situated on the outskirts of the historic town of Hadspen, it was built by Thomas Reibey II, who played a leading part in the development of Tasmania. His son, the first Archdeacon of the Church of England at Launceston, later left the Church and became for a short period Premier of Tasmania. Entally House contains some fine and valuable antiques. The gardens, like the house itself, are beautifully maintained.

EVANDALE VILLAGE ★

20km (12 miles) S.

Evandale is classified as an historic town and is as nearly as perfect a Georgian village as you are likely to see in Australia. Many of the buildings have remained astonishingly untouched, forming some perfectly preserved 19thC streetscapes.

At **Nile**, 8km (5 miles) beyond Evandale, there are two remarkable Georgian buildings, **St Andrew's Church of England** and CLARENDON HOUSE.

FRANKLIN HOUSE

Franklin Village, 6km (4 miles) S ☎*44 7824* 📷 🍴🍽 🚌 *Open Sept-May 9am-5pm; June-Aug 9am-4pm. Closed Christmas Day; Good Friday.*

This is another charming colonial Georgian house, the first house purchased by the Tasmanian National Trust. It was built in 1838 for Britton Jones, an early Launceston brewer, with two stories and an attractive porch. The interior timberwork is noteworthy in consisting entirely of New South Wales cedarwood. Tearooms attached to the house are open for lunch and for morning and afternoon teas.

PENNY ROYAL WORLD ★

147 Paterson St. ☎*31 6699* 📷 🍽🍴 🚌 *Open 9am-4.30pm. (Gunpowder Mill closed 29 July-9 Aug.)*

Situated on the western edge of Launceston, this imaginative attraction combines re-creations of 19thC industries: a gunpowder mill, a cannon foundry, an arsenal, a watermill, a windmill and a corn mill. A canal system and a lake have been created inside the complex, plied by large-scale model sailing ships, big enough to carry real passengers. A model sloop, the *Sandpiper,* fires its cannons daily. A full-size paddle steamer, the *Lady Stelfox,* built of Huon pine, cruises up the Tamar River, sailing on the hour from 10am-5pm.

Other attractions include a millwright's store, a wheelwright and a blacksmith. A gift store sells English pottery, Welsh woolen goods and bags of stoneground wholewheat flour produced on the premises.

WAVERLEY WOOLEN MILLS ★

Waverley Rd., Waverley ☎*39 1106* 🖼 & ✗ 🖳 ⬅ *Tours Mon-Fri 9am-4pm. Showrooms open 9am-5pm.*

One of several woolen mills in Launceston, the Waverley Mills were established in 1874 and still process wool from fleece to finished product, much of the work being carried out on old-fashioned machinery. A showroom attached to the mills features a range of quality garments. They are situated in Waverley, about 4km ($2\frac{1}{2}$ miles) E of the center.

Where to stay

COLONIAL MOTOR INN ♻

31 Elizabeth St., Launceston, Tas., 7250 ☎*31 6588* Ⓕⓧ*34 2765* Ⅷ *64 rms* ⬅ ⥋ 𝔸𝔼 ⊕ ⊙ Ⅷ & ▣ ☿ 𝓳

Location: Convenient, although not central. A first-class motor inn, offering a wide range of facilities at a competitive price.

COUNTRY CLUB-CASINO

Country Club Ave., Prospect Vale, Tas., 7250 ☎*44 8855* Ⅷ Ⓣⓧ*58600* Ⓕⓧ*43 1880* Ⅷ *104 rms* ⬅ ⥋ 𝔸𝔼 ⊕ ⊙ Ⅷ & ⇝ ▣ ☿ ❧ ⚬ ⚓ 𝓳

Location: Set in its own extensive grounds, 8km (5 miles) sw. This is built in the style of a Deep South mansion in the US. Somehow it lacks the style of its Hobart sister establishment, Wrest Point, yet the accommodations are excellent and all facilities are first-class. The setting, among English-style lawns and formal gardens, with a water spout and a bridge across an artificial creek, is nicely designed and laid out. If you aspire to nothing higher than a good meal, a flutter at the tables and a comfortable bed for the night, this hotel will suit you admirably.

GREAT NORTHERN

3 Earl St., Launceston, Tas., 7250 ☎*31 9999* Ⓕⓧ*31 3712* Ⅷ *114 rms* ⥋ 𝔸𝔼 ⊕ ⊙ Ⅷ & ▣ ☿ 𝓳

Location: Handily placed for the main attractions. The Great Northern is a comfortable establishment with two restaurants, and courteous and attentive staff.

LAUNCESTON INTERNATIONAL TRAVELODGE

29 Cameron St., Launceston, Tas., 7250 ☎*34 3434* Ⅷ Ⓣⓧ*58888* Ⓕⓧ*31 7347* Ⅷ *165 rms* ⬅ ⥋ 𝔸𝔼 ⊕ ⊙ Ⅷ & 𝓳 ⥋ ▢ ☿ ❧ ▣

Location: In the central business district of Launceston. The **International** has been built in the style of the old Pullman hotels of America, but with ultramodern facilities. It adjoins Yorktown Square, an imaginative development of stalls, shops and restaurants around a cobbled square, access to which can be gained through the hotel. The hotel has contrived to achieve an intimate atmosphere without sacrificing first-class service. It has a coffee shop-style café and two bars.

Dining out

BURGUNDYS
O'Keefes Hotel, 124 George St. ☎31
5422 ▥ ■ ≡ ⅄ ⇍ AE ⬦ CB VISA *Last orders 8pm.*
Burgundy's is worth a visit just to see the splendid genuine Tasmanian antiques, but the food, chosen from a blackboard menu, is good and hearty too.

GORGE RESTAURANT
Cataract Gorge Cliff Grounds, Gorge Rd.
☎31 3330 ▥ ▢ ≡ ⅄ ⇍ ⇇ AE ⬦ CB VISA
Last orders about 9.30-10pm. Closed Sun night and all day Mon.
Excellent food in a splendid location, among the lawns and trees of the spectacular CATARACT GORGE grounds (see SIGHTS). The menu is strong on local seafood and game, and the atmosphere is warm and intimate.

QUILL AND CANE
Colonial Motor Inn, 31 Elizabeth St. ☎31
6588 ▥ ▢ ≡ ⅄ ⇍ AE ⬦ CB VISA *Last orders 10pm. Closed Sat-Wed lunch.*
Attached to the COLONIAL MOTOR INN (see WHERE TO STAY on page 222), this is, by the normal, fairly bland standards of motel dining, a surprisingly imaginative restaurant.

SHRIMPS
72 George St. ☎34 0584 ▥ ▢ ≡ ⇍
AE ⬦ CB VISA *Last orders about 9pm.*
Closed Sat lunch; Sun.
Seafood, naturally, is the specialty here, prepared with some style. Shrimps also serves Tasmanian wines, for some obscure reason hard to find in most restaurants on the island. It is housed in a National Trust-classified Georgian building in the heart of Launceston.

TERRACE RESTAURANT
Country Club-Casino, Country Club Ave., Prospect Vale ☎44 8855 ▥ ▢ ≡ ⅄
⇍ ⇇ AE ⬦ CB VISA *Last orders 9.30pm.*
The main restaurant at the COUNTRY CLUB-CASINO (see WHERE TO STAY), the elegant Terrace, all wood paneling and brass light fixtures, aspires to high standards, matched by the excellent food but rather let down by the patchy service. However, the wine list is nicely balanced and the view, across well-manicured lawns and formal gardens, relaxing.

Where to shop

The central mall and surrounding streets comprise the major shopping area. But a number of arts and crafts stores are spread throughout the city. The three that follow are leading examples.

EMMA'S ARTS
78 George St. ☎31 5630 ✿ AE CB VISA
Emma's Arts stocks only work by Tasmanian craftspeople and artists, and carries a wide range of handcrafted gifts with a particular emphasis on local woods. There is also a selection of oils and watercolors painted by well-known local artists.

THE SHEEP'S BACK
53 George St. ☎31 2539
An extensive range of sheepskin and woolen goods; some Tasmanian handknits.

PETIT POINT
57 George St. ☎31 2021
A huge range of goods for the keen needleworker, including Danish cross stitch, tapestry, ribbons, quilting, fabric and books.

Tasmania excursions

Touring Tasmania is relatively easy, partly because there are few options. Basically, you can choose to travel from Launceston to Hobart or vice versa, depending on your city of arrival, via either the w coast, the E coast or through the heartland. Although limited in number, however, these routes offer a breathtaking variety of scenery, from dramatic mountains and expanses of unspoiled wilderness to panoramic vistas of the ocean.

For speed and good highway conditions the best route is through the center, using the Midland Highway, which is mostly a first-class road. The route also offers several side trips, such as a visit to Evandale, near Launceston.

The route along the w coast passes through stretches of spectacular wilderness country, such as the **Lake St Clair National Park**, with the option of an excursion to STRAHAN (see below) and a boat trip up the Gordon River.

The E coast route, which goes through towns such as **St Helens**, **Scamander** and **St Marys**, follows the coast closely for much of the journey, providing some spectacular sea views. It also passes close to the **Freycinet National Park**, famed for its red granite outcrops and excellent bushwalking, combined with swimming and sunbathing on some fine, uncluttered beaches. This route is described in PLANNING — see ROUTE 4, page 73.

The two following excursions are ideal for drivers. The **Royal Automobile Club of Tasmania** *(corner of Murray St. and Patrick St., Hobart* ☎ *(002) 38 2200; corner of York St. and George St., Launceston* ☎ *(003) 31 3166)* sells maps and can recommend routes. For a map of Tasmania, see page 207.

THE MIDLAND HIGHWAY

This is the easiest route, skipping most of the mountainous areas. It is an excellent road, well surfaced, with gentle bends, and has several opportunities for side trips.

Leaving Launceston heading toward the s the first detour is to the historic town of EVANDALE (see LAUNCESTON SIGHTS), to the E of the main highway. The turn-off is at Breadalbane, about 13km (8 miles) from Launceston. The detour rejoins the Midland Highway about 10km (6 miles) farther along.

The next 60km (38 miles) or so pass through rich farmland and rolling countryside, until the road nears the town of **Ross**, which is worth a short detour. Built on the banks of the Macquarie River, the town used to be an important stopping place for stagecoaches on the Hobart-Launceston route. The **bridge** at Ross, built in 1836 by convict labor, has **carvings** by the convict artist Daniel Herbert, which were so much admired that they earned him a pardon. **Church St**. has many notable buildings including **Scotch Thistle Inn**, now a restaurant, but first granted a license in 1830.

Next the highway passes through the village of **Oatlands**, on the shore of Lake Dulverton. Historic buildings of note include the courthouse, jail, flour mill and several churches.

Melton Mowbray, at the junction of the Midland and Lake Highways, was named in 1843 after the English town of the same name. In the immediate area are several homesteads that are more than 100 years old. The highway then passes through Kempton, Bagdad, Mangalore and Brighton, crossing the Derwent at **Bridgewater Junction**, to the N of Hobart.

THE WEST COAST ROUTE

Between Hobart and Launceston the w coast route encounters some of the most spectacular scenery on the island.

Leaving Hobart NW on the Lyell Highway, the road follows the Derwent for about 20km (12½ miles).

New Norfolk, the first largish town on the route, was settled in 1807 by convicts brought from Norfolk Island, off the Queensland coast. It is notable for Australia's oldest church building, **St Matthew's Church of England**, and for one of the oldest continuously licensed pubs in the country, the **Bush Inn**, which dates back to 1815.

The road next crosses the **Mt. Field National Park**, a popular skiing area, which covers 16,000ha (39,500 acres). The scenery is spectacular: rugged mountains, an area of alpine plateau, and lakes in the lower regions.

The highway takes a sharp turn due w at the small township of **Bronte**, as it heads toward **Queenstown**, a mining town since the 1880s, surrounded by a moonlike landscape caused by copper smelting, now stopped, which killed all the vegetation. The huge open-cut **copper mine** can be visited.

Here the road detours to STRAHAN (see below), a distance of 42km (26 miles), which is the gateway to the Gordon River.

From Strahan, you can either retrace the route to Queenstown and then take the Zeehan Highway to **Zeehan**, or take the minor road to Zeehan that follows the coast for a number of kilometers before striking inland.

From Zeehan the Murchison Highway passes through **Rosebery**, a mining town. At **Williamsford**, 7km (4½ miles) s, zinc is extracted.

The road then passes through fairly mountainous country before reaching the coast at **Somerset**. From there, travel E, following the coast. By Tasmanian standards, the road becomes busy as it passes through a series of coastal towns such as Burnie, Penguin, Ulverstone and the ferry port of Devonport, before heading inland to Launceston.

STRAHAN AND THE GORDON RIVER

On **Macquarie Harbour**, into which flows the **Gordon River**, lies **Strahan**, the only town on Tasmania's rugged w coast. The entrance to the Harbour, known as **Hell's Gates**, was so named by convicts who in the 19thC helped carve out something from nothing on this inhospitable coast.

A pleasant if isolated community, Strahan has manifestly benefited from the worldwide interest aroused by the Hydro Electricity Commission of Tasmania's proposal some years ago to dam the Gordon River. The environmentalists' blockade of the river and the ensuing arrests, including that of the British botanist David Bellamy, forced the Commonwealth Government to intervene in 1982. The area was added to the World Heritage List, allowing Canberra to treat the matter as a foreign-affairs issue.

The area has many attractions. Strahan has some magnificent beaches, and there are impressive sand dunes on the ocean beach; good surfing and surf-fishing can also be found near the harbor entrance. Macquarie Harbour itself offers good sailboarding, sailing and waterskiing.

And then there is the Gordon River, which, although perhaps thrust into the limelight in recent years, has actually been a popular tourist attraction since the late 19thC. Three jet-powered boats and a seaplane are based at Strahan to take tourists up the Gordon River. Keeping up his family tradition, boat operator Rex Kearney today runs two of the three boats (details are given on page 224), just as in the 1890s his grandfather guided tourists up the river.

Navigable, although not for very large craft, for 42km (26 miles) from its mouth in Macquarie Harbour, the river is a true wilderness. Trees grow down to and actually into the water, and on all sides it is virtually untouched by man. In places the riverbed reaches a depth of more than 42m (138 feet), punctuated by cataracts and towering cliffs. No effort should be spared to see this great spectacle.

At the mouth of the Gordon River is **Sarah Island**, a few hectares of land with no fresh water, used as a penal settlement for the worst prisoners until it was abandoned in 1833 for the model prison conditions of PORT ARTHUR (SEE HOBART SIGHTS). The outlines of some of the buildings erected by the inmates can still be seen. The structures failed the test of time, for the brackish water used in the mortar ate away the lime. Most Gordon River cruises include a short stop at the island.

Along the banks of the Gordon River are some of the few remaining stands of Huon pine, found only in Tasmania. Extremely slow-growing, its value to woodworkers was soon recognized by early settlers, who cut the trees down in large numbers, so that today few survive. Some of the Huon pines along the river's banks started growing before the birth of Christ.

GORDON RIVER CRUISES

Cruises on the jet-powered boats *James Kelly II, Wilderness Seeker* and *Gordon Explorer* depart daily at 9am, returning at approximately 1.30pm. At most times reservations are advisable, from **Scenic Gordon and Hell's Gates Charters** *(P.O. Box 40, Strahan, Tas., 7468 ☎ (004) 71 7187/71 7281)*. All three boats are fully licensed and serve tea and coffee and light refreshments.

FROM THE AIR

Wilderness Air *(Strahan Wharf, Strahan, Tas., 7468 ☎ (004) 71 7280)* operates a single-engined floatplane, based at Strahan, across the wilderness region — one of the best ways of seeing the Gordon and surrounding area. River height and weather permitting, the plane lands on the river. There is no scheduled service, and flights are by previous arrangement only.

✎ STRAHAN MOTOR INN

Jolly St., Strahan, Tas., 7468 ☎*(004) 71 7160* 🖾*(004) 71 7372* 🔲 *50 rms* 🛏 ⇝ 𝔸𝔼
🔲 ◎ 📠 ⅋ ⊟ 𝚈 👥

Location: On high ground overlooking Strahan's harbor. This motel has a basic rustic charm, with a theme of Tasmanian wood used throughout. The restaurant is no more than average — the choice in Strahan is limited, so there is little incentive to improve. But there are excellent views from most of the self-contained suites.

Tasmanian tours and tour operators

Much of Tasmania is wilderness country, and a number of companies specialize in tours of the remote regions by 4-wheel-drive vehicle and on foot. There are also, of course, conventional tours of a more sedate nature by bus.

Some words of warning are in order about Tasmania's wilderness regions, which are subject to extremely heavy rainfall. Weather conditions can change so suddenly and dramatically that in the highland regions people have died of exposure, even in summer. Sensible clothing should always be worn; reputable tour operators working in the wilderness areas will recommend what to wear. It is also inadvisable for tourists unfamiliar with the bush to venture alone into some of the more remote, untamed areas, where it is easy to get lost.

Those caveats apart, a trip into one of the wilderness regions under the eye of an experienced guide can be most rewarding.

Below are given a selection of tour operators. The **Tasmanian Government Tourist Offices** (or **Tasbureaux**, as they are also known) can offer guidance on the best sort of tour to suit particular needs and can arrange reservations with most tour operators. Main addresses are given under HOBART and LAUNCESTON.

For 4-wheel-drive tours, **Bushventures 4 WD Tours** *(199 Davey St., South Hobart, Tas., 7004* ☎ *(002) 23 6910)* — tours to wilderness areas and to the World Heritage-listed Franklin River region. **Tas Trek** *(11 Edward St., Perth, Tas., 7018* ☎ *(003) 34 1787)* offers a range of 4-wheel-drive vacations to the West Highlands and West Coast, as well as fishing trips. Vacations are from three to 11 days.

For hiking tours, **Craclair Tours** *(P.O. Box 516, PO Devonport, Tas., 7310* ☎ *(004) 24 7833)* — escorted hiking tours of up to 8 days visiting wilderness regions, such as Cradle Mountain.

For cruises, **MV Commodore** and **Derwent Explorer** *(inquiries* ☎ *(002) 34 9294/25 2794)* — runs trips around Hobart harbor, lasting 2 hours, usually with morning and afternoon departures.

For bus tours, **Tasmanian Redline Coaches** *(Hobart terminal* ☎ *(002) 34 4577; Launceston terminal* ☎ *(003) 31 9177)* — scheduled passenger services, and tours and charters. The company has terminals

TASMANIAN TOURS AND TOUR OPERATORS

in all major towns and cities. Reservations can also be made through Tasmanian Tourist Offices.

For scenic flights, **Par Avion** of Cambridge aerodrome near Hobart *(P.O. Box 324, Rosny Park, Tas., 7018 ☎ (002) 48 5390)* offers a range of scenic flights and in season has a daily flight, weather permitting, to the SW wilderness area. It also runs scenic flights to the SE. Special flights can be tailored to requirements. All flights are on demand and require a minimum of two people. There are also scenic flights to PORT ARTHUR (see HOBART SIGHTS).

Victoria

Victoria's compactness — it is the smallest of the mainland states, with a land area of 227,600 square kilometers (84,884 square miles), only 3 percent of the Australian total — means that its major attractions are readily accessible. Yet there is greater variety here than anywhere else on the continent. For example, a motoring trip down the Murray River (which forms the border between Victoria and New South Wales), from, say, Mildura to Albury, would provide an excellent and representative cross-section of the state.

Victoria manages to cram into a compact area the broadest possible variety of scenery, ranging from snowfields in the north and north-east to some of the world's finest surf beaches just beyond Geelong and within an easy drive of Melbourne; from orange and lemon groves in the semi-arid region of the far north-west to the cool vineyards of the Yarra Valley, just north of Melbourne.

The wheatfields of the north-west contrast sharply with the majestic forests of Gippsland in the south-east, which contain some of the tallest hardwood trees in the world, while the coastal scenery of the Great Ocean Road (see EXCURSIONS) is unmatched in its grandeur. The Murray River, which forms the border between Victoria and New South Wales, for much of its length cutting a majestic, tree-lined swathe through the rich countryside, is, with its paddle steamers and legacy of river trade, reminiscent of the Mississippi.

Victoria's climate, like its scenery, also offers something for everyone, from Mildura in the far north-west, with temperatures often soaring to 45°C, to the high country of the Australian Alps where temperatures often plummet to minus 10°C.

CRADLE OF THE RULING CLASS

Victoria, and particularly Melbourne, is where the ruling elite of Australia makes its home. Don't take too seriously all those stories about this being a completely classless society: a short stroll down Melbourne's Collins St., or a visit to Toorak, Australia's most exclusive suburb, soon dispels any such myth. Victorians have a superior air, and the "squattocracy" — descendants of the early settlers who squatted on the land and then lobbied the authorities to recognize their claims — has a code of conduct as rigid as that of any upper-class group in the world.

Much of Victoria's early wealth was based on land, and many large estates remain in the hands of descendants of those pioneers who claimed the land more than 120 years ago. Such families consider themselves the cream of society, much like their counterparts elsewhere, and they have provided some of the nation's leading politicians and entrepreneurs.

Melbourne very much reflects this sense of continuity and adheres to many of those old-fashioned virtues beloved by conservatives everywhere: church, school and family (although not necessarily in that order). An old cliché — that in Sydney people ask you the size of your bank balance, in Adelaide what church you attend, in Brisbane whether you'd like a beer, and in Melbourne what school you went to — reflects pretty fairly on the values of Melbournians and Victorians. The most prestigious private schools in the country are in Victoria, and Geelong Grammar counts the Prince of Wales among its old boys.

MELBOURNE VS. SYDNEY
And yet, despite this innate sense of superiority, Victoria feels acutely that in the postwar period it has lagged behind the brasher New South Wales and its, to Victorian eyes, rather vulgar capital, Sydney. Melbourne was the federal capital from 1901-27, and its current second-rank status is not readily accepted. Yet somehow all efforts to emulate Sydney's style belie Victoria's solidly respectable image. Melbourne never quite achieves Perth's laid-back feel or Sydney's fast-lane vibrancy; and unlike Sydney, Melbourne still seems to be influenced more by London than by Los Angeles, although today that is changing.

Victoria forms the base for many large companies in long-established sectors such as engineering, mining and industrial farming. Newer hi-tech enterprises almost exclusively choose Sydney, as do most of the new wave of overseas banks. If anything this sectoral split emphasizes differences between Victoria and its arch rival to the north. Melbourne continues its traditional role as Australia's financial capital, and its reliance on the traditional industries of banking, insurance and stockbroking reinforces the city's conservative image, and fosters in its citizens an air of gravity and reserve.

Victoria abounds in contradictions. Conservative in all other respects, it has a reputation for radical politics. It numbers more than 50 nationalities among its population, which in June, 1990 stood at 4,379,940, although in many of its attitudes — for example, its intense preoccupation with Australian Rules football and almost total disregard of the nationally more popular soccer — the state is remarkably insular. Melbourne feels itself superior to Sydney, but worries disproportionately about what its rival is up to. Such rivalry is not easy for outsiders to understand, for it is intense and sometimes bitter.

FROM GOLD RUSH TO CONSERVATIVE CHIC
During the gold rush of the 1850s and 1860s, Melbourne was the fastest-growing city in the British Empire. Then it probably boasted more public houses and bordellos per head of population than any other English-speaking city. It was quite common to see drunken miners light Havana cigars with banknotes and marry prostitutes they had met only a few hours before.

There followed, inevitably, a moral reaction, compounded by a disastrous slump in land prices. From this catastrophe grew an urge for respectability, giving rise to the temperance, and kindred, movements, who achieved so much power that the city soon acquired the reputation of being the home of "wowsers," or killjoys.

Money from the gold rush fueled a huge building boom and underpinned the growth of great landed families, who made their fortunes out of feeding the miners who flooded into the colony. These families built substantial mansions that still adorn inner suburbs such as South Yarra, Toorak and St Kilda.

Much of Melbourne's elegance stems from its physical layout and a tradition of genuine municipal pride. The central city area is laid out on a grid pattern with main thoroughfares running straight and wide. Narrower one-way streets, bearing the diminutive of the major street (e.g., Bourke St. and Little Bourke St.) run parallel. Many of the major streets are linked by arcades of chic shops.

But although Melbourne is a fine city it can also be incredibly stuffy and pompous. Older men are still inclined to wear three-piece suits in winter, complete with London-made overcoats. Until recently, women were not allowed into such places as the members' stands at most horse-racing tracks. The city also has the most hidebound gentleman's club in the country, the Melbourne Club. One British knight recently remarked that such clubs no longer existed even in London.

Rural Victorians are conservative in their attire and politics, like the majority of their city cousins. The annual Royal Melbourne Show, held in September, sees the moleskin-attired farmers, all with compulsory hat, and their sensibly-dressed wives descend for their annual encounter with city life.

The arcades, the green-and-gold trams (the newer ones sport a sort of municipal orange), coupled with a large Mediterranean immigrant population, contribute to the distinctly European flavor. Melbourne has one of the country's largest Italian communities, and is the third-largest Greek-speaking city in the world.

Above all, it is a city of parks and gardens. One-fifth of the central area is made up of parkland — one of the largest ratios of open space to built-up area of any city of comparable size in the world. There is a sense of spaciousness, mitigating the impact of the high-rise buildings of recent years. And if Melbourne lacks the stunning beauty of Sydney's harbor or Perth's handsome Swan River, it possesses a sense of quiet, unassuming style that other world cities find hard to match.

Melbourne

ORIENTATION

Melbourne, the most southerly of Australia's mainland capital cities, lies largely around the saucerlike rim of Port Phillip Bay. To the s it stretches for 60km (38 miles) through a series of beachside suburbs such as Brighton, Hampton, Black Rock and Beaumaris, the urban sprawl petering out at Frankston, at the end of the suburban railway line. To the E — residentially popular and generally the more expensive side — the Dandenong Ranges more or less mark the physical limit of the built-up area. And to the w, flat and comparatively cheap land encourages continuing industrial development.

Melbourne has been slowly reaching out along the western fringe of Port Phillip Bay toward the town of Geelong, a process accelerated by the opening in 1978 of the West Gate Bridge across the Yarra River, making that side of the bay much more accessible.

The northern part has escaped most of the burgeoning postwar development that swallowed up orchards and small farmsteads in the eastern and southern areas, and mostly dates back to the early 20thC or even before.

PRACTICAL INFORMATION

See Melbourne city maps (maps **10** and **11**) on pages 236-237 and Melbourne environs maps (maps **12** and **13**) on pages 262-263.

☎**STD (area) code**   03.

Airport   Tullamarine ☎339 1600.

Rail stations   For country services and reservations ☎619 5000, map **10**C2; for suburban services ☎617 0900, map **10**C3.

Car rental   Avis ☎663 6366; Budget ☎320 6333; Hertz ☎698 2555.

Royal Automobile Club of Victoria (RACV)   123 Queen St., Melbourne, Vic., 3000 ☎607 2211, map **10**C3.

RACV Travel Centre, formerly Victorian Government Travel Centre   230 Collins St., Melbourne, Vic., 3000 ☎650 1522, map **10**C3.

American Express Travel Service   105 Elizabeth St., Melbourne, Vic., 3000 ☎608 0333, map **10**C3.

SEEING THE CITY

Melbourne is an easy city to negotiate. The center has wide, pleasant, tree-lined main thoroughfares, and most of the postwar suburbs have wide, straight main roads.

The **RACV Travel Centre** *(230 Collins St. ☎650 1522, map **10** C3)* can answer most questions about Melbourne and Victoria. The **Melbourne Tourism Authority** *(Level 1, 114 Flinders St. ☎654 2288, map **11** C4),* a free-enterprise organization funded by city business, is a valuable source of information about the state capital. There is also an information booth on the Collins St. side of the City Square, which can help with general information.

Melbourne has an extensive and efficient tram system, convenient for journeys up to about 10km (6 miles). There is also a well-developed suburban rail system.

The **Metropolitan Transit Authority** (popularly styled the "Met"), which runs the trams, trains and buses and coordinates most of the privately owned bus lines, issues free maps showing the city transportation network, available from main rail stations, tram depots and bus garages. There is a 24-hour transportation information service *(☎617 0900)* for train and tram times.

After several attempts at finding a satisfactory ticketing system for the metropolitan transportation system, the Met has settled on 3 metropolitan **fare zones** spreading out in rings from the center of the city. Ticket prices vary between zones, and tickets that traverse two zones are more expensive than single zone tickets. There are also 3-hour and daily tickets that allow unlimited travel on trains, trams and buses. In addition there are City Saver tickets, Short Trip tickets for use within Zone 1, Family tickets and Off Peak Saver tickets. Weekly and monthly season tickets are also available. When in doubt, ask the tram conductor or station assistant for the best sort of ticket to buy. A useful guide is *Melways Street Directory,* which shows tram routes and stop numbers, as well as rail stations.

TRAMS
Melbourne's trams, once objects of scorn when every other city was converting to buses, are now a source of pride. Quiet and pollution-free, they set Melbourne apart from Australia's other major cities.

Tram **tours** depart from the intersection of Collins St. and Exhibition St. every Tuesday and Thursday at 11.30am. The trip lasts 3 hours and includes all the major sights on the tram routes. *(Tickets ☎654 8629, or through any branch of the RACV.)*

BUSES
The **City Explorer Bus** leaves on the hour from outside Flinders Street station on the Swanston St. side every day at 10am and 4pm. The red double-decker bus offers a first-class tour of the city's sights, and you can disembark where you wish.

Melbourne Sightseeing *(☎670 9706)* runs a series of day- and half-day tours that include: visits to Phillip Island to see the penguins come ashore, the Dandenongs, Sovereign Hill at Ballarat, as well as Melbourne by Night, City Sights and Chinatown. Tours depart from the Melbourne Coach Terminal outside Spencer Street Railway Station. Hotel pick-up can also be arranged.

CYCLING
Melbourne has more than 100km (over 60 miles) of designated bicycle paths. Cycling is easy in this fairly flat city, particularly in the cooler spring and fall seasons. On weekends bicycles can be rented on the Yarra Bank on Alexandra Ave., opposite the Botanic Gardens. Rental is from noon to dusk on Saturday, and from 10am to dusk on Sunday. Many suburban bicycle stores also rent out bicycles.

A book, *Melbourne Bike Tours,* describing 20 cycle tours, is published by the State Bicycle Committee and is sold at larger newsstands and camping stores.

For the indulgent, **Pedicabs** (☎ *555 1393)* will give you a city tour in a pedal-powered two-person modern version of a rickshaw on Friday and Saturday nights only. Tours depart from the Bourke St. Mall.

ON FOOT

Melbourne is also a good city for walkers. **Melbourne Heritage Walks** (☎ *827 1085)* has a choice of six guided walks lasting about 1½ hours that explore historic Melbourne. Tailor-made walks can be organized.

RIVER AND BAY CRUISES

The Yarra River, which runs through the center of Melbourne, provides fascinating views of the city. **City River Cruises** (☎ *650 2214)* leave from Princes Bridge near Flinders Street station five times a day. The trips take in the port area, pass under West Gate Bridge (the longest in the southern hemisphere), and go past the Botanic Gardens and Como Island in the Yarra. **Melbourne Cruisers** (☎ *614 1215)* offer similar cruises, with special theme trips, such as Aboriginal Dreamtime on the Yarra, tracing the history of Aboriginals in the Melbourne region. Boats depart from Princess Bridge.

Sights and places of interest

BEACHES

Melbourne, situated as it is on **Port Phillip Bay**, is blessed with fine, sheltered, sandy and safe beaches within easy reach of the city — in many cases just a tram-ride away. There are also some fine surf beaches within comfortable driving distance, on the ocean side of the **Mornington Peninsula**, to the s of the city. From the eastern side the closest surf beach is **Point Leo**; from the southern suburbs **Rye** ocean beach offers the easiest-to-reach surf.

Because of the way the Mornington Peninsula narrows close to the entrance to Port Phillip Bay, the best of both worlds can be found at such beachside towns as **Rye**, **Sorrento** and **Portsea**. All these have safe bay beaches on one side and open-ocean surf beaches only a 10-minute drive away on the other side of the narrow strip of land. Melbournians call the bayside beaches "front" beaches and the ocean ones "back" beaches. So if someone says they are going to Portsea back beach, they mean the ocean.

Close to the city, about 5km (3 miles) from the center, **St Kilda** beach (which was much maligned by the Prince of Wales after a swim there some years ago) has long been popular, as has **Elwood** beach, about 3km (2 miles) farther s. St Kilda is easily accessible by train or tram and is a favorite place for city workers rushing to grab a lunchtime or after-work swim. Although a decade ago it probably deserved its reputation as a dirty beach, great strides have since been made toward cleaning up all Melbourne's inner-city beaches. Throughout summer the Environment Protection Authority publishes regular press reports on the condition of the beaches.

BOURKE STREET MALL
*Bourke St. Map **10**C3.*

Melbourne's attempt to introduce a European flavor to the city, the Bourke Street Mall is reminiscent of Amsterdam, an impression reinforced by the trams that run along the center of the pedestrian mall. It runs for one block from Elizabeth St. to Swanston St.

After a shaky beginning — no one believed it would work with trams running down the center — the mall is now an established favorite with Melbournians and visitors. There are several rest areas, with seating and enormous potted plants. The entire surface of the mall has been leveled and laid in herringbone-pattern brickwork. On most days, street entertainers regale shoppers with music, from Bach to U2.

CAPTAIN COOK'S COTTAGE
*Fitzroy Gardens, off Wellington Parade, East Melbourne. Map **11**C4* ▨ ✦ *Open 9am-5pm.*

In 1934, to mark Melbourne's centenary, a private citizen, Sir Russell Grimwade, financed the transportation of this cottage from the village of Great Ayton, Yorkshire, England, and its re-erection in the FITZROY GARDENS. The ivy covering the cottage was grown from a cutting taken at Great Ayton. Cook, however, never lived in the cottage: it was merely the home of his parents.

CARLTON
*Map **10**A3.*

The inner suburb of Carlton, Melbourne's substantial Italian quarter, is one of the most entertaining and stimulating areas of the city, particularly on Sunday morning when Lygon St., 3km (2 miles) N of the city, turns into a fashion parade as the locals sport their best finery, some on foot, others cruising in their cars. It is all very crowded, noisy, and immensely enjoyable. Carlton is lively at nighttime too, for it has one of the largest concentrations of restaurants and cafés in Melbourne.

The best way to soak in the atmosphere and excitement is on foot. Start at the beginning of **Lygon St.**, where it extends from Russell St. in the city center, and walk N past the **Downtowner Motel** on the right. This is the Italian heart of Carlton, alive with bistros and cafés (the scenes when Italy won the World Cup soccer championship in 1982 had to be seen to be believed). Each November the Italian community of Carlton holds a street festival, the **Lygon Street Festa**, lasting a week and including street theater, folk dancing, music and general Italian-style carnival fun.

But the area has more than just a strong Italian identity, and has become increasingly popular among young business executives and students as a place to live. As a result prices have soared. Carlton was built in the 1860s-'80s and has some fine examples of Victorian colonial architecture. Try to detour down **Grattan St.** and **Elgin St.**, which both cross Lygon St., and along some of the minor streets off these two main thoroughfares. Here you will find some architectural gems: single-fronted Victorian cottages of one and two stories with ornate lace balcony

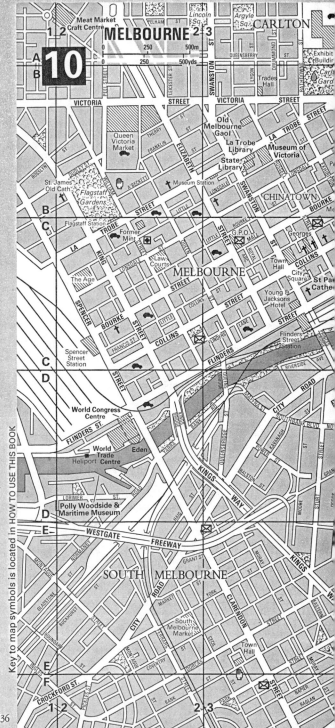

Key to map symbols is located in HOW TO USE THIS BOOK

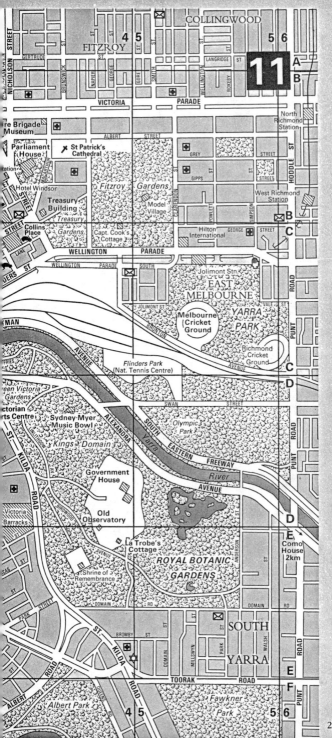

ironwork, most of them lovingly restored in the 1960s to their original condition. **Drummond St.**, running parallel to Lygon St. a block to the E, is arguably the best-preserved 19thC street in Melbourne and must not be missed; one block E are **Carlton Gardens** (see GARDENS, page 240) and the EXHIBITION BUILDINGS.

The campus of Melbourne University, two blocks to the w of Lygon St., is a mix of building styles and periods and has some neo-Gothic buildings of merit. The campus grounds are crisscrossed by pedestrian streets.

Lygon St. crosses Princes St. at **Melbourne General Cemetery**, worth a stroll for fascinating insights into the hardships of early colonial life: note the many graves of children. Adjacent is **Princes Park**. Then turn right into Princes St. and walk four blocks to Nicholson St. for a tram to the center.

CHINATOWN ★
Little Bourke St. Map 10B3 ✿
A somewhat strained attempt was made in the mid-1970s to create a tourist-type Chinatown in a short section of Little Bourke St., a narrow one-way street, by adding a couple of kitsch Chinese-style arches and generally upgrading the area.

At first the district was a source of cheap lodgings for the Chinese who in the 1850s flocked to Victoria during the gold rush; but gradually the boarding houses were replaced by Chinese businesses. Today the area houses some of Australia's finest Chinese restaurants, the MUSEUM OF CHINESE AUSTRALIAN HISTORY, a Chinese Methodist Church, the Chinese Masonic Society and numerous Chinese stores, emporiums and businesses.

CITY SQUARE ★
Map 10C3.
This earnest attempt by the city fathers to give Melbourne a focal point has proved successful up to a point, although only time will reveal the true value of such an expensively created piece of open space. The City Square has been the subject of more plans and proposals than any other comparable piece of real estate in Melbourne. At present it comprises a mix of water races and waterfalls, glass canopies, trees and conversation alcoves; a graffiti wall is provided for would-be artists. Yet despite the good intentions, the City Square seems to lack heart, although it is becoming the focal point for rallies, demonstrations and marches.

COMO HOUSE ★
Como Ave., South Yarra. Map 12D2 🖼 ✿ *Open 10am-5pm.*
This is the headquarters of the National Trust. Designed by Arthur Johnson, the two-story mansion, with a wide colonial veranda, is one of the finest surviving examples of early colonial architecture designed on the grand scale. All the rooms opened to the public are furnished in the Victorian style of the house's heyday. The oldest part, dating from

1847, is the kitchen wing, which has staff quarters, a laundry and stables. Highlight of the interior is the white and gold **ballroom**, the focal point for social life in Melbourne in the Victorian and Edwardian eras.

Como House is set in a landscaped garden, distinguished by several enormous magnolia trees. The garden was developed with advice from the botanist Baron Ferdinand von Mueller, who was responsible also for planning Melbourne's ROYAL BOTANIC GARDENS.

EXHIBITION BUILDINGS ★

Nicholson St., Carlton ☎*663 5000. Map* **10**A3 *(Nicholson St. entrance best)* *Open: depending on exhibition.*

A magnificent example of Victorian architecture, reflecting all the confidence of the era, the Exhibition Buildings were erected by David Mitchell (father of Dame Nellie Melba, the world-famous soprano) for the vast 1880 International Exhibition. Here, on May 9, 1901, Australia's first Federal Parliament was opened by Prince George, the future King George V. The occasion was marked by the celebrated proposal by Australia's first prime minister, Sir Edmund Barton: "A continent for a nation and a nation for a continent."

The **Western Annex** of the Exhibition Buildings provided housing for the Victorian State Parliament from 1901-27, after it gave up its magnificent Spring St. home for the use of the Federal Parliament while the design for the new Federal Parliament House was selected and built in Canberra.

Situated in **Carlton Gardens**, the Exhibition Buildings are flanked by gardens and an ornamental pond on the s side, and are still used today for conferences, exhibitions and trade fairs. Because of their timber construction, they have the unfortunate reputation of being one of Melbourne's worst fire risks.

FITZROY GARDENS

Off Wellington Parade. Map **11**B4-5

Among Melbourne's glorious gardens, the Fitzroy Gardens, laid out in 1850, are deservedly popular. Children enjoy the model **Tudor village** and, nearby, an old tree whose trunk was carved with tiny fantasy creatures by the late Australian sculptress, Ola Cohn. CAPTAIN COOK'S

COTTAGE is also located here. Together with other city parks, the gardens play host in summer to a program of free entertainment that ranges from open-air theater to pop concerts and is claimed to be the largest entertainment scheme of its kind in the world.

GARDENS

Melbourne's gardens are its greatest treasure. No other state capital has them in such quantity or variety, and few world cities have such a high proportion of open space.

Brightest of its jewels are the ROYAL BOTANIC GARDENS, 2km ($1\frac{1}{4}$ miles) s of the city center and easily accessible by tram. They are situated in the middle of the **King's Domain Gardens**, which unlike the Botanic Gardens are not enclosed. In the center of the King's Domain is LA TROBE'S COTTAGE, the state's first Government House.

Closer to the center are the FITZROY GARDENS, 1km ($\frac{1}{2}$ mile) away to the E, which date back to 1850. Adjoining them are the **Treasury Gardens**, handily placed for politicians seeking respite from the affairs of state: the Victorian PARLIAMENT HOUSE is a short walk away. The gardens are bounded by Spring St., Treasury Place and Lansdowne St.

Oldest of Melbourne's gardens are the **Flagstaff Gardens** on the NW fringe of the city proper, bounded by King St., William St. and La Trobe St. They rise gently from La Trobe St., and are terraced down to King St. Paths wind through stands of lovely elms and oaks.

Carlton Gardens, on the NE fringe of the city center, have as their centerpiece the EXHIBITION BUILDINGS. The gardens, which have some very fine oaks and elms, make a striking sight in fall when the leaves change color.

Royal Park, N of the city, has part of its area given over to the ROYAL MELBOURNE ZOO. Much of the remaining space is used for sports playing areas. The park was the departure point for the ill-fated Burke and Wills expedition in 1860: a cairn marks the spot, off The Avenue. Farther afield is the **Yarra Bend Park** in the suburb of Kew, about 5km (3 miles) E of the city, an extensive natural bushland park beside the Yarra River. Rowboats and canoes can be rented, and the area is ideal for picnics and barbecues.

LA TROBE'S COTTAGE ★

King's Domain Gardens, Birdwood Ave. ☎*654 5528. Map **11E4*** ▩ &.*by prior arrangement with curator* ⚘ *Open 11am-4.30pm. Closed Fri.*
This cottage was prefabricated in England and brought to Australia by Charles La Trobe, who was appointed Lieutenant-Governor of Victoria in 1851, a post he held for 3 years. In effect it was Victoria's first Government House. The cottage has been restored and furnished in the style of the period and still contains many of its original furnishings. It is a National Trust property.

LAW COURTS AND SUPREME COURT LIBRARY

Lonsdale St. ☎*603 6111. Map **10C2*** ▣ ✗ *in court. Open to public during sitting of courts, commencing 10am.*

Grouped around a cobbled courtyard, these Classical buildings, dating from 1885, are a fine example of Victorian civic architecture. A noteworthy feature is a rotunda, and the central library is topped by a vaulted dome. The Law Courts are open to the public during most trials.

MEAT MARKET CRAFT CENTRE

Corner of Courtney St. and Blackwood St., North Melbourne ☎*329 9966. Map 10A2* ☒ & ☑ ✳ *Open Tues-Sun 10am-5pm.*

Formerly one of Melbourne's meat markets, the center houses craftspeople, including potters, fabric printers, weavers, silversmiths and others. It was set up by the Victorian Ministry for the Arts to form the center for crafts in the state. The program of exhibitions and demonstrations changes regularly, and there are craft stores, workshops and a resource and information center. Most work shown is available for sale. The building itself is an excellent example of a Victorian produce market, now tastefully and imaginatively refurbished for its new role. At its rear is the **State Craft Collection**.

MELBOURNE CRICKET GROUND ★

Batman Ave. Match-day inquiries ☎*657 8888. Map 11C5* ☒ & ✗ *of ground, library, gallery and museum (2 hours) every Wed at 10am* ☑ ✳ ☛ *Ground open for viewing if no match in progress Mon-Fri 9am-5pm.*

In size the greatest cricket ground in the world, the Melbourne Cricket Ground (MCG) has witnessed many famous epic struggles. Here was staged the first international cricket match in 1862 and the first test match between England and Australia in 1877. In 1956 it was the main stadium for the Olympic Games.

The MCG was established on its present site in 1853. Today it has a capacity of just over 100,000 and holds the world record for attendance at a one-day cricket match (78,000 in 1982 for Australia v. West Indies), as well as the highest attendance for a single day of a full test match (90,800 in 1961, again for Australia v. West Indies).

It is also the home of Australian Rules Football, that spectacular hybrid of rugby and Gaelic football. It is common to see crowds of 50-60,000 for club games at the MCG, and every September the Grand Final attracts 120,000 spectators here.

Since 1985 the MCG has been floodlit, allowing football and cricket matches to be played at night, and in 1992 the Great Southern Stand was added, providing seating for 41,000 spectators.

The **Australian Gallery of Sports and Olympic Museum** *(at main entrance to MCG* ☎*654 8922* ☒ *open 7 days 10am-4pm),* opened in 1986, contains a display of Australian sports memorabilia.

MONTSALVAT

Hillcrest Ave., Eltham ☎*439 7712. Map 12B3* ☒ & ☑ *(weekends)* ✳ ☛ *Open 7 days 9am-5pm.*

In 1934 architect and philosopher Justuf Jorgensen, whose defiantly Bohemian life-style once outraged conservative Melbourne, started an artists' colony at Eltham, then virgin bushland but now an outer suburb of Melbourne, about 18km (11 miles) NE of the city center. All the buildings were designed by Justuf, in a style described by his son Sigmund Jorgensen as Provincial French Gothic. They comprise the **Great Hall**, **chapel** and **living quarters**. The floor of the Great Hall and some other parts of the complex are made of Welsh slate slabs once used by sailing ships as ballast on the voyage from Britain. Some of the windows were recovered from buildings being demolished in Melbourne.

Today Montsalvat is operated as a trust and is home to some 20 artists. Their work is available for purchase. Occasional varied concerts are held in the Great Hall and include supper with wine. Look in *The Age* newspaper for details.

MUSEUM OF CHINESE AUSTRALIAN HISTORY
22 Cohen Pl. ☎662 2888. Map 10B3 ▨ ✿ Open Sun-Thurs 12pm-5pm.
A replica of Ling Xing Gate facing Heaven Palace in Nanjing, in China's Jiangsu Province, forms the entrance to this CHINATOWN museum. Exhibits and audiovisual aids outline the history of the Chinese in Australia and their contribution to the nation's culture and development, and the museum houses the **Sun Loong** (dragon) of the Melbourne Chinese community. There is no attempt to gloss over the early bitter resentment felt toward the Chinese in Australia, nor some of the vicious racism practiced against the Chinese community.

MUSEUM OF VICTORIA AND STATE LIBRARY ★
328 Swanston St. (entry also from Russell St.) ☎669 9888. Map 10B3 ▨
& access via La Trobe St. entrance, then through library to museum ▣ ✿
Museum open 10am-5pm. Children's Museum open 11am-5pm every day. Library
open Mon 1pm-9pm; Tues 10am-6pm; Wed 10am-9pm; every other day
10am-6pm including public holidays.
An amalgamation of the **National Museum of Victoria** and the **Science Museum**, this new hybrid is clearly a success. As befits a nation of sports lovers, a highly popular exhibit (in the former National Museum) is the racehorse **Phar Lap**, world-famous and the subject of a movie, who died in the US in the 1930s after winning countless races in Australia.

The science section of the museum moved to a new home early in 1992 in the western suburb of Spotswood. Now known as **Scienceworks** *(Booker St, Spotswood, map 12D1),* its new home is a converted sewage pumping station beside the Yarra River that is itself a building of some interest and merit. It was built in 1896, and some of the machinery, dating from 1911, is still in place. The building has been earmarked for World Heritage listing. The science section includes Australia's first aircraft and car and many working models, with much emphasis laid on education.

The separate **Children's Museum** is designed to appeal to children between the ages of five and 12. A major attraction is the opportunity offered for "hands-on" experience. The museum puts on theme exhibitions that stay in place for two to three years. Its latest offering is on water — its importance to life, and problems associated with its conservation and pollution.

OLD MELBOURNE GAOL
Russell St. ☎*663 7228. Map **10B3*** ▦ *Open 9.30am-4.30pm.*
This finely preserved bluestone building of 1845 is a ghouls' delight, notably for its collection of death masks of executed prisoners. Here the renowned bushranger Ned Kelly was hanged in 1880, making his departure from this world with the laconically immortal words, "Such is life." The gallows where Kelly was hanged still remain. A triangle to which prisoners were strapped for floggings and numerous other items of prisoner paraphernalia have also survived. Several cells are laid out in the fashion of the Victorian era, complete with dummy prisoners clad in arrow-marked garb.

PARLIAMENT HOUSE ★
Spring St. ☎*651 8911. Map **11B4*** ▣ *✗compulsory ♣ ◄€ ₺ Tours lasting half an hour start Mon-Fri at 10am, 10.30am, 11am, 11.30am, 12.00pm, 12.30pm, 2pm, 2.30pm, 3pm, 3.30pm, 3.45pm, when State Parliament not in session.*
Before Parliament House was opened in Canberra in 1927, this was the meeting place for the Federal Parliament. Today it houses Victoria's Legislative Assembly and the Legislative Council (the upper house).

Described by the late Sir John Betjeman as one of the finest examples of Victorian architecture, the Neoclassical structure is superbly sited looking down Bourke St. The plans called for "a magnificent classic design for a building of colossal proportions surmounted by a tower 256 feet high." The original design included a dome and N and S wings, although these are unlikely ever to be completed. The Parliamentary Library was completed in 1860, Queen's Hall and the Vestibule in 1879, and the W facade, with a grand flight of steps and a colonnade, in 1892.

The outer walls and foundations are made of stone from the Grampians mountain range (about 240km/150 miles to the W of Melbourne). **Queen's Hall** was intended to be as nearly as possible the length and width of the House of Commons in London. The **Council chamber** has fine gold-leaf decoration covering a vaulted ceiling; the red benches and carpet again echo the style and character of the Parliament in Westminster. The **Assembly chamber**, more utilitarian, is still imposing, and the grand **Parliamentary Library** has a splendid glass chandelier.

POLLY WOODSIDE AND MARITIME PARK ★
Corner of Normanby Rd. and Phayer St., South Melbourne ☎*699 9760. Map **10D2*** ▦ ₺ ✗ ▣ ♣ ⇌ *Open Mon-Fri 10am-4pm; Sat, Sun 10am-5pm.*
The 648-ton restored barque *Polly Woodside*, built in Ireland in 1885, had by 1897 rounded Cape Horn no fewer than 16 times on the England to South America run. Later she was sold to a New Zealand concern and renamed *Rona*, plying the Tasman Sea between Australia and New Zealand and later working the passage through the Pacific to the US. By 1962 she was the only survivor of the 120 sailing ships that as

243

recently as 1930 still carried coal around the coast of Australia. She was saved from an ignominious end by enthusiasts who in 1972 started restoring the old ship.

Today the *Polly Woodside* is run by the National Trust and is the only full-rigged ship still afloat in Australia. She forms part of a maritime display housed in buildings beside the barque, which is moored in an old water-filled dry dock. The display includes a good collection of relics, photographs and other memorabilia of the days of sail.

RIPPONLEA ★

192 Hotham St., Elsternwick ☎ *523 9150. Map 12D2* 🚩 *Open 10am-5pm.*

Designed in the Romanesque style by Joseph Reed for the wealthy businessman Frederick Sargood, using intricate polychromatic brick-work, the house (see illustration on page 24) originally contained 15 rooms, which over a period of 20 years or more grew to today's total of 33.

Despite the architectural significance of the house, the landscaped gardens are the outstanding attraction of this National Trust property, built between the late 1860s and 1887. The 6ha (15 acres) feature an ornamental lake with a series of bridges, a fernery, a grotto, ranks of English elms and other European trees, and vast expanses of sweeping lawns — a fine example of the early colonists' urge to re-create the style and ambience of the English country gentleman. Ripponlea was given to the National Trust in 1963.

ROYAL BOTANIC GARDENS ★

Birdwood Ave., South Yarra ☎ *63 9424. Map 11E5* 🔲 ♿ 🖵 ♣ ◁€ *Open Mon-Sat 7am-sunset; Sun, hols 8.30am-sunset.*

One of the great gardens of the world, yielding first place only to London's Kew Gardens, covering 35ha (88 acres), the Royal Botanic Gardens contain examples of more than 12,000 species of native and non-native plants.

The site beside the Yarra River was selected by Governor Charles La Trobe in 1845, and the gardens as they look today were shaped by Dr Ferdinand von Mueller (later Baron Sir Ferdinand von Mueller, ap-pointed Government Botanist in 1852) and the landscape artist W. R. Guilfoyle.

Today they form a tranquil setting for a picnic or walk, with acres of sweeping lawns, flowerbeds, specimen trees and an ornamental lake (home to families of ducks, moorhens and black swans), all within an easy 10-minute tram ride from the city center. The lake is popular with children, who enjoy feeding the birds and spotting eels swarming in its waters. The **Tennyson lawn** features four English elms more than 120 years old. Adjoining it is the **National Herbarium** (not open to the public), a research center housing a vast collection of herbs and other plants.

A special explanatory leaflet, which indicates walks around the gar-dens, is produced each year and is usually available at most of the major gates.

ROYAL MELBOURNE ZOO ★

Elliott Ave., Parkville ☎285 9300. *Map* **12C2** 🚻 ♿ 𝄢 *(free)* 🖵 🚻 🚗 *Open 9am-5pm.*

Among the oldest zoos in the world, housing more than 3,000 animals, Melbourne Zoo has been substantially upgraded with a number of walk-through compounds that provide a first-class view of the animals. The **enclosure for big cats** is spanned by a bridge that gives the spectator the feeling of being physically in with the animals: an interesting sensation at feeding time... Another, less pulse-quickening highlight is the walk-through **butterfly enclosure**. There are excellent displays of wombats, emus, kangaroos, platypuses, echidnas and reptiles. The zoo has also carried out some pioneering work in the artificial insemination of rare species: the gorilla Mzuri, born by artificial insemination, is a major attraction. Free strollers are provided for visitors with small children.

ST JAMES OLD CATHEDRAL ★

King St. (at corner of Batman St.) ☎329 6133. *Map* **10B2**.

Work on the construction of this, Melbourne's oldest church, started in 1839. Designed by Robert Russell, Melbourne's first City Architect, it was originally sited at the corner of William St. and Little Collins St., but in 1913-14 was moved stone by stone to its present site.

The building, which was built from sandstone and bluestone, is a charming example of early colonial workmanship. The main entrance has a display of old prints and photographs. Note the old enclosed box pews, and a font from the London church of St Katharine Cree.

ST KILDA UPPER ESPLANADE ★

St Kilda. Map **12D2**.

The Upper Esplanade has become a traditional Sunday favorite among local craft lovers and bargain hunters. Most of the work displayed on the stalls that line the esplanade is in ceramic, leather or wax; woodwork and paintings also stand out. In any case, it is worth a visit just to see the characters who make up the Sunday morning scene, who are often a form of entertainment in their own right.

ST PATRICK'S CATHEDRAL ★

Albert St. ☎662 2233. *Map* **11B4** ♿ *(ramps for the disabled in Cathedral Pl.). Open 6am-6pm.*
The tallest church in Australia, William Wardell's St Patrick's Cathedral is a massive bluestone building surmounted by a spire 104m (340 feet) high. Its grandeur

245

is a reflection of Melbourne's strong connection with Irish Roman Catholicism.

ST PAUL'S CATHEDRAL ★
Flinders Lane ☎*63 3791. Map 10C3. Open 7am-6pm.*
Melbourne's fine Gothic-style Anglican cathedral, built in 1891, is regrettably hemmed in by modern city buildings, although it provides a fine landmark from across the Yarra River. The water cascade and modern glass-canopied shopping arcade of the CITY SQUARE adjoin the cathedral close, the square's pond pleasingly reflecting the traditional cathedral.

SHRINE OF REMEMBRANCE ★
St Kilda Rd. Map 11E4 🖾 ⤶ *Open Mon-Sat 10am-5pm; Sun 2-5pm.*
The shrine, approached from St Kilda Rd., Domain Rd. or Birdwood Ave., is the most imposing war memorial in the country. The foundation stone was laid on Armistice Day 1927, and St Kilda Rd. was realigned to give a continuous line s through from Swanston St. Inside, each year, at the 11th hour on November 11, sunlight strikes the **Stone of Remembrance**.

Public subscription financed the construction of the shrine, as the enormity of Australia's losses in World War I dawned — of an all-volunteer army of 400,000, Australia had suffered casualties totaling nearly 200,000 either killed or wounded, one of the highest per capita of any of the combatant countries. Today the shrine forms the focus of Melbourne's Anzac Day commemorations.

SIDNEY MYER MUSIC BOWL
Alexandra Ave. ☎*617 8211, 617 8332. Map 11D4* ♿
The Bowl, as it is affectionately known, is a huge sound-shell, able to seat 2,000 people under cover and up to 100,000 on the surrounding lawns of the **Kings Domain**. The bowl can be approached through the gardens from either St Kilda Rd. or Alexandra Ave. In winter, part of the stage is frozen over for public ice-skating, and it is the home of the annual Christmas Eve "Carols by Candlelight" show.

Contact the ARTS CENTRE for reservations and details of performances, ranging from pops to classics, or look in the metropolitan press.

TREASURY BUILDING ★
Corner of Spring St. and Treasury Pl. Map 11B4.
A Neoclassical structure of fine proportions, built in 1857, the Treasury Building is situated in Spring St., a block away from PARLIAMENT HOUSE. Adjacent are the **Treasury Gardens**, a quiet oasis in a busy part of the city, and the small open space of the **Gordon Reserve**, with its statue of the defender of Khartoum, General Charles Gordon.

VICTORIA RACING MUSEUM
Gate 22, Caulfield Racecourse, Station St., Caulfield ☎*572 1111. Map 12D3* 🖾 ⬤ *Open Tues, Thurs 10am-4pm. Closed Fri-Mon, Wed.*

A must for all who love the sport of kings, the Victoria Racing Museum is dedicated to preserving the history of horse racing in Australia. The museum, the only one of its kind in the country, was opened in 1981 by Queen Elizabeth II. Statues of winning jockeys welcome visitors.

VICTORIAN ARTS CENTRE ★

*100 St Kilda Rd. ☎617 8211. Map **10D3** ➦ ▨ & ✗ of concert halls and theaters by arrangement (ask at the center) ▣ ➦ National Gallery ☎618 0222, open 10am-5pm. Performing Arts Museum open Mon-Sat 11am-6pm; Sun noon-6pm.*

Three large buildings on tree-lined St Kilda Rd. beside the Yarra River form the focal point for the arts in Melbourne. They house the **National Gallery of Victoria**, the **Melbourne Concert Hall**, three theaters, the **Performing Arts Museum** and several restaurants, all linked by lawns, gardens and walkways.

Designed by the late Australian architect, Sir Roy Grounds, and completed in 1968, the **National Gallery** is constructed in local bluestone,

with a moat lapping the sides of the building echoed by water running between two sheets of glass at the entrance. The gallery, built around three courtyards, houses an extensive collection of **Australian paintings** by, among others, Tom Roberts, Frederick McCubbin, Russell Drysdale, Sidney Nolan, Arthur Streeton, and more recent figures such as Jeffrey Smart and Jon Balsaitis. Sculptures exhibited in the courtyards include Sir Henry Moore's *Seated Figure.* Among the fine European collection are Picasso's *Weeping Woman,* works by Turner, Tiepolo's *Banquet of Cleopatra* (one of the center's highlights), engravings by Dürer and watercolors by Blake.

The much newer **Concert Hall** can seat 2,677 (considerably more than the Sydney Opera House) and is designed primarily for symphonic performances; it is equipped with highly advanced acoustic facilities. An outstanding feature of the stunning interior design is Sir Sidney Nolan's monumental *Paradise Garden,* comprising 1,320 individual paintings in 220 panels.

The theater building is topped by a metal spire, a poor-man's Eiffel Tower, considerably foreshortened by cuts in the building budget. It is divided into three theaters: the 2,000-seat **State**, home of the **Australian Opera**, the **Victorian State Opera** and the **Australian Ballet**; the 880-seat **Playhouse**, used for much of the year by the **Melbourne**

247

Theatre Company; and the multipurpose 420-seat **Studio**, a center for experimental theater.

The **Performing Arts Museum** houses a fascinating and exhaustive collection of theater memorabilia. Tours of the concert hall and theaters leave at 10.30am and 4pm and last about one hour, and on Sunday there are $1\frac{1}{2}$-hour backstage tours.

WILLIAMSTOWN
Map 12D2.

Williamstown has been a backwater for several decades, chiefly because until the opening in 1978 of the West Gate Bridge across the Yarra River it was a roundabout journey from the city by road (although there is a good train service). This comparative isolation has enabled the area to escape much of the postwar development that transformed other inner suburbs of Melbourne.

To catch the atmosphere of Williamstown — the whiff of the sea, the comings and goings of the boating fraternity who inhabit the area — it is essential to explore it on foot.

The best way to get there is to take a train from Melbourne to Williamstown Pier station, then start walking w down Nelson Parade. To your right is the **Royal Australian Naval Dockyard**, which has built several of the RAN's destroyers. The dockyard building itself, dating from 1874, is a fine example of local bluestone industrial architecture. Opposite the dockyard is the **Prince of Wales Hotel**, an imposing building with fine cast-iron balcony decorations, built in the 1850s.

Farther along is the **Gem Pier**, to which is moored a World War II **minesweeper**, HMAS *Castlemaine (open Sat, Sun 10am-6pm),* now a maritime museum. The **Customs House** (1874), with its twin porticos, is a fine example of civic building. On the reserve — an area of lawn in front of Gem Pier — is the **Tide Gauge House** (built 1869), formerly an automatic device for gauging the tide.

Continuing past Gem Pier, you come to the continuation of Nelson Parade, which here changes its name to The Strand. Here too is the **Williamstown Yacht Club jetty** and a ramp for launching boats. Retrace your steps to Williamstown Pier station and take a train two stops to North Williamstown. This is the home of the **Williamstown Railway Museum**, which has an extensive collection of steam engines, carriages and rolling stock *(open Sat, Sun, hols 2-5pm).*

Williamstown also has a **historical museum**, on the corner of Melbourne Rd. and Electra St. *(open Sun 2-5pm).* Reach it by walking up Parker St., which turns off Nelson Parade and crosses Electra St. It has a good collection of old model ships, and pictures from Williamstown's 19thC heyday.

YOUNG AND JACKSON'S HOTEL
Corner of Swanston St. and Flinders St. ☎*650 3884. Map **10**C3* ▣ *Open normal pub hours. Restaurant open Mon-Sat lunch and dinner.*

One of the most famous public houses in Australia, Young and Jackson's occupies a special place in the hearts of Melbournians. It is situated on a corner opposite Flinders Street rail station, Melbourne's main commuter terminus, and ST PAUL'S CATHEDRAL. During World War II Australian soldiers from Melbourne promised to meet here for a drink if they made it back alive, and its central location makes it still a popular meeting place.

Why Young and Jackson's should command so much affection is a mystery. Inside, the pub is largely nondescript, apart from a large oil painting of a nude, *Chloe,* of dubious merit and the subject of much moral outrage over the years. Many efforts have been made to have her removed; but she still reigns supreme.

Where to stay

Melbourne has seen a boom in hotel building since the mid-1970s, transforming it from an accommodations desert with only a handful of first-class hotels into a city offering world-standard accommodations supplemented by a good selection of inexpensive hotels and motels.

As in all cities, location very much governs price. Many of the major new hotel developments of the last decade have been located in the central area. The HYATT, MENZIES AT RIALTO, REGENT, THE SEBEL OF MELBOURNE and REGENCY are all notable additions to the city proper. However, a number of more modest hotels and motels have also sprung up on the fringes of the city, offering excellent accommodations at an economical price.

Those wanting first-class accommodations of international standard naturally will look for a city-center hotel. More budget-conscious travelers can achieve substantial savings by moving 4 or 5km (2-3 miles) out of the center; but as most areas are served by trams the distance is unlikely to present a problem. Two inexpensive areas are **Carlton** and **St Kilda Rd.**, both near the center and with frequent tram services.

Reservations are advisable at most times, and are essential during busy periods such as Easter, Christmas and the week of the Melbourne Cup horse race, run on the first Tuesday of November.

Most larger hotels ask guests for a charge- or credit-card imprint.

THE BRYSON ✿
186 Exhibition St., Melbourne, Vic., 3000
☎*662 0511* [DC] [TX]*32779* [FX]*663 6988.*
Map 10B3 [III] *363 rms* ⊒ [AE] [⊕] [◎] [VISA]
& ⇌ ▣ ☿ ⇴ ⛟
Location: At eastern end of center, a block away from Parliament House. The Bryson occupies a modern 23-story building that has recently undergone a multi-million dollar total refurbishment. It is ideally positioned in an exciting part of the city with easy access to entertainment. Theaters and cinemas are

within easy walking distance, and CHINATOWN (SEE SIGHTS) is just around the corner. The standard is good and the hotel is quietly restrained, apart from its theme restaurant **Barney McGee**, which features singing waiters and other gimmicks. Not the place for a quiet meal but good fun if you are in the mood.

HILTON INTERNATIONAL
192 Wellington Parade, East Melbourne, Vic., 3002 ☎*419 3311* [DC] [TX]*33057*

249

[Fx]419 5630. Map **11C5** [IIII] 406 rms ⚓ ≡ [AE] [⊙] [◎] [VISA] ⅋ ⇜ ▣ ♈ ♈ ♈ ♈ ♤ ♨ ♪

Location: Beside Fitzroy Gardens, opposite Jolimont rail station. The Hilton has the best outlook of any hotel in Melbourne, and is only a 5-minute stroll from elegant Collins St. In its showpiece **Cliveden Room** restaurant (see DINING OUT), the Hilton has retained a link with the elegant old mansion it displaced, furnishing it with a fine selection of antiques. **Juliana's** nightclub has a fashionable clientele and features top international acts (see ENTERTAINMENT), and the **Tapestry Lounge** has a resident pianist to accompany cocktails.

HYATT ON COLLINS

123 Collins St., Melbourne, Vic., 3000
☎657 1234 [IDD] [Tx]38796 [Fx]680 3491.
Map **10C3** [IIII]580 rms ⚓ ≡ [AE] [⊙] [◎] [VISA] ⅋ ⇜ ▣ ♈ ♈ ♈ ♨ ♪

Location: Near Parliament House, at top end of Collins St. Built in 1986, the Hyatt has a classic facade, a 34-story tower rising up behind, and a striking exterior of gold glazing. Inside, marble is much in evidence. The exclusive **Regency Club** occupies the top four floors, with personalized service, a lounge, complimentary breakfasts and a serviced bar. There is also a fully equipped business center. A fashionable food court, **Collins Chase**, with eight food outlets and two bars, provides a wide choice of meals from 7.30am.

JOHN SPENCER HOTEL ✿

44 Spencer St., Melbourne, Vic., 3000
☎629 6991 [IDD] [Tx]37544 [Fx]614 7963.
Map **10C2** [▢] 160 rms ⚓ ≡ [AE] [⊙] [◎] [VISA] ▣

Location: Almost opposite Spencer Street station. At the unfashionable end of town, the Spencer offers good, basic budget accommodations in a convenient location. There are no frills, but then the price is remarkably modest.

MENZIES AT RIALTO

495 Collins St., Melbourne, Vic., 3000
☎620 9111 [IDD] [Tx]136189 [Fx]614 1219

ext. 1646. Map **10C2** [IIII]243 rms ⚓ ≡ [AE] [⊙] [◎] [VISA] ⅋ ⇜ ▣ ♈ ♈ ♈ ♤ ♨

Location: At western end of city, just over a block away from Spencer Street rail station. The Menzies is part of the twin-tower Rialto complex, at 242m (794 feet) one of Australia's tallest buildings. The hotel is built around a courtyard with twin wings of nine and five stories respectively; the base was built in 1890. Mixing the old and the new, it still offers all the facilities of a top-class hotel. The rooms are of a generous size, and the hotel is well placed for the **World Trade Centre** in Spencer St.

OLD MELBOURNE ✿

5 Flemington Rd., North Melbourne, Vic., 3051 ☎329 9344 [IDD] [Tx]32057 [Fx]328 4870. Map **12C2** [IIII]212 rms ⚓ ≡ [AE] [⊙] [◎] [VISA] ⇜ ▣ ♈ ♈ ♨

Location: In North Melbourne. The image is of an old English coaching inn: outside lighting, decor and balconied rooms, overlooking a paved central courtyard, echo this theme. Convenient for Melbourne University campus, Royal Park, and the Italianate suburb of CARLTON (see SIGHTS) — and on the way to the airport.

PARKROYAL

562 St Kilda Rd., Melbourne, Vic., 3004
☎529 8888 [IDD] [Tx]152242 [Fx]525 1242.
Map **11E4** [IIII]219 rms ⚓ ≡ [AE] [⊙] [◎] [VISA] ⇜ ▣ ♈ ♈ ♈ ♨ ♪

Location: Halfway along St Kilda Rd. traveling s from city. The outlook — onto a wide, tree-lined road, lined with gardens, some decent office buildings and a few remaining old mansions — suits those not needing to be in the heart of the city. The Parkroyal is a stark white building, but a canopied entrance offers a warm welcome, and there is attentive service for arriving guests. Only a short walk away are the **Albert Park** public golf course and lake, where sailboats can be rented. The hotel can arrange tennis at a nearby public court.

RADISSON PRESIDENT MELBOURNE

65 Queens Rd., Melbourne, Vic., 3004
☎529 4300 [IDD] [Tx]30987 [Fx]521 3111.

Map **11F4** ▥ 375 rms ⇨ ⇄ AE ⊙ ⊚
VISA & ▭ ▽ ☂ ♥ ⚓ 🛆

Location: Opposite Albert Park Lake.
This popular business hotel, with a
superb view across parkland, has recently been greatly enlarged and refurbished. A public golf course is nearby,
and the hotel is a 10-minute tram ride
from the center. Standards are high
without being too lavish.

REGENT

25 Collins St., Melbourne, Vic., 3000
☎653 0000 ▣ ✆37724 ℻650 4261.
Map **11C4** ▥ 363 rms ⇨ ⇄ AE ⊙ ⊚
VISA & ▭ ▽ 🛆

*Location: Near Parliament House, at
top end — the "Paris end" — of Collins
St.* A hotel on the grand scale, the Regent occupies 16 stories of the 50-story
Collins Tower building. The pan-
oramas across Port Phillip Bay, the city
and Melbourne's generous parklands
are superb, and there are good views of
Government House, the MELBOURNE
CRICKET GROUND (see SIGHTS) and many
other landmarks. The hotel lobby is at
ground level, function rooms are on the
first floor, and rooms on floors 34-50 are
reached by a glass elevator in a trans-
parent shaft. The building, among the
most imaginative of Melbourne's modern structures, is created around a central space, surrounded by shops facing
into the center; choirs and carol singers
perform here. Service is always impeccable.

ROCKMANS REGENCY

*Corner of Lonsdale St. and Exhibition St.,
Melbourne, Vic., 3000* ☎662 3900 ▣
✆38890 ℻663 4297. Map **10B3** ▥
183 rms ⇨ ⇄ AE ⊙ ⊚ VISA & ≋ ▭ ▽
♥ ⚓

*Location: Eastern end of center, a block
away from Little Bourke St. and Chinatown.* This small boutique hotel, the
brainchild of Irvine Rockman, has a genuinely friendly, intimate and very individual atmosphere. Rockman persisted
when warned that people did not want
smaller hotels and that this was quite
the wrong part of town, but the
Regency now has occupancy rates that

are the envy of many larger hotels. The
hotel is a tribute to Rockman, who
supervises in person.

THE SEBEL OF MELBOURNE

321 Flinders Lane, Melbourne, Vic, 3000
☎629 4088 ℻629 4066. Map **10C3** ▥
59 rms ⇨ & ☂ 🛆 ⇄ ⇆ AE ⊙ ⊚ VISA
*Location: Centrally located in Mel-
bourne's central business district and a
block away from the Bourke Street mall.*
The Sebel is a true boutique hotel, offering a high level of service while retaining a personalized atmosphere only
possible with a hotel of this small size.
The Melbourne Sebel follows the successful formula of its sister property in
Sydney.

SOUTHERN CROSS

131 Exhibition St., Melbourne, Vic., 3000
☎653 0221 ▣ ✆30193 ℻650 2119.
Map **10B3** ▥ 426 rms ⇨ ⇄ AE ⊙ ⊚
VISA & ≋ ▭ ▽ ♥ 𝑃 ⚓ 🛆

*Location: Eastern end of center, a block
from Parliament House.* Opened in
1962, the Southern Cross was one of
Melbourne's original first-class hotels.
Its 1960s exterior now looks somewhat
dated, but major renovation and upgrading has helped it maintain its position in the marketplace. The hotel has
first-class facilities for conventions (a
specialty) and hosts many long-established functions and balls. Set in pleasant surroundings, it has an excellent
shopping arcade, part of the street-level
entry area.

WINDSOR

103 Spring St., Melbourne, Vic., 3000
☎653 0653 ▣ ✆30437 ℻654 5183.
Map **11B4** ▥ 190 rms ⇨ ⇄ ▭ AE
⊙ ⊚ VISA & ▭ ▽ 🛆

Location: Opposite Parliament House.
Melbourne's (indeed, Australia's) last
remaining "Grand" hotel is listed by the
National Trust. Always a favorite with
politicians and Victoria's wealthy rural
landholders, it feels like a very traditional, elegant British hotel. Excellent
meals are served in the impressive
Grand Dining Room (see DINING OUT).
The Windsor is housed in an elegant,

251

tall Victorian building built in 1883, which was extensively modernized after its purchase by the state government. It has since been purchased by the Oberoi Hotel Group. 19thC furnishings and color schemes were retained, with gold-leaf work on ceilings and black marble fireplaces.

Dining out

Melbourne has the greatest selection and some of the finest restaurants in Australia. A bold statement, perhaps, but one repeatedly borne out by awards and by plaudits from food writers and gastronomic experts.

An indication of the number of eating establishments in Melbourne can be gained from the fact that the Melbourne *Yellow Pages* (1992 edition) has 34 pages of restaurants, the majority of which are licensed to Bring Your Own liquor (BYO) — a sign you will see everywhere. This is a license that allows restaurant patrons to drink with their meal without the costs usually associated with a fully licensed establishment. The rules governing such matters as the ratio of WCs to customers, air conditioning and parking are far stricter for a fully licensed restaurant than for a BYO and greatly increase business costs. The hygiene rules governing both categories are the same, though, and strict.

The eating-out selection in Melbourne ranges from international-class cuisine to a simple dish in a Chinese restaurant in Little Bourke St., in the Chinatown district. In between it is possible to eat virtually every sort of cuisine, including Russian, Vietnamese, Lebanese, Afghan, Japanese, Nepalese and Greek. In Melbourne, you name it, and you can probably eat it.

Most restaurants in Melbourne, whether humble or prestigious, are usually full on Friday and Saturday nights, so it might be wise to reserve ahead.

AMARETTO ✿
209 Victoria Parade, Fitzroy ☎*417 5169. Map 11B4* ▥ ▭ ▨ ◉ ◎ *Closed Sun. BYO license.*

Owned and run by Sicilian-born Jo Alagona, Amaretto is a lively and entertaining place to eat. It offers a fine selection of traditional Italian dishes. Diners are greeted with a plate of pickled vegetables and a home-made loaf. Daily specials are written up on a blackboard. Joe Alagona is a former singer with the Victorian State Opera and can sometimes be pressed to sing in a fine tenor voice. The waiters are friendly and fun. Amaretto is a popular place with Melbourne's radio and TV people. Perhaps despite that fact, the prices are more than reasonable.

BROWNS RESTAURANT
1097-1111 High St., Armadale ☎*822 3188. Map 12D3* ▥ ▨ ◉ ◎ *Restaurant open Mon-Sat 12.30pm-2pm; Fri 7pm-10pm. Bistro Mon-Sun 12am-2.30pm; 6pm-10.30pm. Restaurant* ▥ *bistro* ▥.

Set amid the antique stores of High St., Browns has risen virtually from nowhere to vying for number one spot as Melbourne's finest restaurant. This has been achieved by meticulous attention to detail and innovation by owner Greg Brown. Browns is two eating establishments in one, with a classic restaurant situated at the rear of a casual but smart bistro. Greg Brown's credentials are impeccable and include a stint with the Roux Brothers at London's Le Gavroche and The Waterside Inn, Bray,

England. Imaginative treatment of seafood is one of Brown's specialties.

CLIVEDEN ROOM
Corner of Wellington Parade and Clarendon St., East Melbourne ☎*412 3054. Map 11C5* ▥ ⃞ ≟ ⃤ ▦ ◉ ◎ ▨ *Last orders 11pm. Closed Sun, Mon.*

The Cliveden Room at the HILTON (see WHERE TO STAY) is widely acknowledged to be one of Melbourne's best hotel dining rooms. The decor, imaginative and tasteful, features some fine antiques. The menu is cautious but interesting, with a good selection of traditional dishes. A specialty is superb smoked salmon, sliced at the table. The ideal place for a special night out.

DOWNSTAIRS AT ERIC'S
149 Toorak Rd., South Yarra ☎*820 3804. Map 11F5* ▥ ⃞ ≟ ▦ ◉ ◎ ▨ *Last orders 12.30am. Open Tues-Sat for dinner Sun lunch only.*

One of Melbourne's few restaurant/jazz clubs, **Downstairs at Eric's** is, as you would image, a cellar complete with low ceiling, low lights and tons of atmosphere. There is live jazz on two or three nights a week, which vary, so it is best to check first. The menu is French-based and of a good standard. Predominantly a place for those in their 20s and 30s, but don't be put off if you love jazz and don't fall into that age group. Occupies premises that were once the home of one of Melbourne's best-loved restaurants, Two Faces.

EMPRESS OF CHINA ♥
120 Little Bourke St. ☎*663 1883. Map 10B3* ▥ ⃞ ▦ ◉ ◎ ▨ *BYO license.*

Melbourne is blessed with a large number of excellent Chinese restaurants, particularly in the Little Bourke St. area. This popular Cantonese restaurant gives good service, prices are reasonable and the menu is extensive. Seafood is their specialty: try the crystal prawns.

FLORENTINO ♥
80 Bourke St. ☎*662 1811. Map 10B3* ▥ ⃞ ≟ ▦ ◉ ◎ ▨ *Last orders 10.30pm. Closed Sun.*

Florentino maintains a thoroughly traditional approach, and the Italian food, served with panache by black-tied waiters with long white aprons, is consistently good. The restaurant can get crowded, so it is advisable to reserve.

GLENCOE
766 Whitehorse Rd., Mont Albert ☎*898 5188* ▥ ⃞ ▦ ◉ ◎ ▨ *Last orders 10pm. Open Mon-Fri for lunch; Mon-Sat for dinner. BYO license.*

Located 18km ($10\frac{1}{2}$ miles) from the city, Glencoe is one of a number of new restaurants bringing good food to the suburbs. Despite the Scottish name, it is owned and run by Argentinian-born Jo Majetko. It offers a fixed-price lunch menu and à la carte in the evenings. Cuisine is best described as international with French overtones. Situated in a large house built in 1912, Glencoe's decor reflects its Edwardian setting; so do the waiters, who dress the part in black.

GRAND DINING ROOM AT THE WINDSOR
115 Spring St. ☎*653 0653. Map 11B4* ▥ ⃞ ▩ ≟ ▦ ◉ ◎ ▨ *Last orders 10pm. Closed Sun.*

The WINDSOR (see WHERE TO STAY) is the last of the great traditional hotels. Its restaurant, the Grand Dining Room, oozes tradition, with silver service, white table linen, first-class staff and an excellent menu that changes with the seasons. A fixed-price "menu gastronomique" has been introduced of three, four or five courses including wine, featuring such tempting dishes as red mullet on artichokes, coral trout fillets, and chicken filled with oyster mushrooms — excellent value. A carvery-style meal is available at lunchtimes, usually with at least two roasts and poultry, an extensive cheese table and some deliciously tempting desserts. Unmissable.

MIETTA'S
7 Alfred Place ☎*654 2366. Map 10E3* ▥ ⃞ ▩ ▦ ◉ ◎ ▨ *Last orders 9.45pm. Downstairs lounge last orders 1am; Fri, Sat 2am.*

253

Mietta's serves some of the most imaginative food in Melbourne, in the somewhat cavernous former Naval and Military Club building. The owner, Mietta O'Donnell, has built a formidable reputation here for good food. Downstairs there is a lounge where coffee and liqueurs, light meals and lunches are served. The formal restaurant is upstairs in what used to be the ballroom; here, chef Jacques Reymond shows his talents best. Sauces are his specialty.

POTTER'S COTTAGE ✿

Jumping Creek Rd. (near Ringwood Rd.), Warrandyte ☎ *844 2270. Map 13B4*
□□▩�& ⬤ ⬛ ㎍ ⬛ ⬛ ㎉ ⬛ ♙
Closed dinner Sun-Wed. Open for lunch Tues-Sun.

Although it is some way out of town, this restaurant is handy for several of the day trips suggested in ENVIRONS OF MELBOURNE. Charmingly situated beside the Yarra River at Warrandyte, Potter's Cottage is part of a craft center (see ENVIRONS OF MELBOURNE). The building, long and low with a wide veranda and slate floors, has a homey atmosphere. The menu changes constantly: choose from hearty dishes such as individual beef casserole, or lighter ones such as quail salad and smoked trout mousse. Local ingredients are used wherever possible and a good selection of Yarra Valley wines is featured. There's usually live music — pianist, trio or guitarist — on Friday and Saturday nights: be sure to reserve.

ROSATI ✿

95 Flinders Lane ☎ *654 7772. Map 10C3*
□□☿⬛⬤⬛㎉ *Last orders midnight. Open Mon-Fri 10-1am; Sat-Sun 4pm-1am.*

Handy for people exploring the city center, this vast establishment seats 500. The menu is predictable but the food is well presented and the service first-class. The emphasis is Italian, but there is also steak, chicken and so on. It's a

good place too for morning coffee breaks or afternoon tea. The decor is impressive: the name set in mosaic in Venetian glass over the entrance, a bright, airy atmosphere inside and, as a centerpiece, a large bar.

STEPHANIE'S

405 Tooronga Rd., East Hawthorn ☎ *20 8944* □ ▩ ➔ ⬛ ⬤ ⬛ *Last orders 9pm. Closed Sun.*

Stephanie's is one of the grandest restaurants in Melbourne, and certainly rates as one of the finest, the service and attention to details such as table settings being unsurpassed. It is housed in an ornate former mansion in the suburb of East Hawthorn. Much of Stephanie Alexander's food is simple but prepared with a flair that raises it above the mundane. The menu is mostly French Provincial.

THE LATIN

55 Lonsdale St., Melbourne ☎ *662 1985. Map 10B3* ㎍ □ ➔ ☿ ⬛ ⬤ ⬛ ㎉ *Last orders 10.30pm. Open 7 days for lunch and dinner.*

Elegant surroundings and first-class food make The Latin, also known as Marchetti's Latin, a delight for lovers of Italian food. Their gnocchi and spaghetti marinara are particularly recommended. Attentive waiters in black with white aprons, a good selection of Italian wines and great coffee combine to create the impression that one is in Rome or Florence rather than the center of Melbourne.

THE WILLOWS

462 St Kilda Rd. ☎ *867 5252. Map 11F5*
㎍ □ ☿ ⬛ ⬤ ⬛ *Last orders midnight. Closed Sun.*

Housed in a National Trust-classified building on St Kilda Rd., one of the best settings in Melbourne, The Willows offers first-class service, crisp table linen, classic pink-and-white decor and a sense of space. The cuisine is traditional French; game and beef are specialties.

Entertainment

In Melbourne the arts flourish, bolstered by an excellent symphony orchestra, ten mainstream theaters, scores of smaller fringe theaters, the open-air SIDNEY MYER MUSIC BOWL (see SIGHTS), the **Sports and Entertainment Centre** in Richmond, for ice shows, pop concerts and so on, and the **Festival Hall** in West Melbourne, which also stages pop concerts.

Since 1986 the city has staged the annual springtime **Melbourne International Festival of the Arts**. The program includes opera, dance and ballet, music, drama and arts exhibitions.

Melbourne Summer Music, which is held in January, is run by the Victorian Arts Centre and offers a wide selection of concerts, musical events and plays to cater to most tastes. It usually features a number of visiting performers. Recent participants have been English music writer Mike Batt and French concert pianist Jean Bernard Pommier.

Melbourne's reputation as a place where nothing happened after 9pm has been shattered in recent years as the city wholeheartedly embraced the disco, nightclub and theater-restaurant. Now there are more than 40 **discos and nightclubs**, ranging from local pub discos playing well-worn records to the sophisticated JULIANA'S at the Hilton.

The nightclub and disco scene is fluid and fast-moving, and it is advisable to check out the rise and fall of various establishments and which ones are considered trendy at any given time. If you lack local contacts, your hotel desk and concierge should help.

For computerized theater and concert reservations contact **BASS (Best Available Seating Service)** (☎ *11500, or at branches of Myer department store).* The best daily guide to arts and entertainments is *The Age* and its weekly liftout guide called *EG,* published on Thursday.

CAROUSEL

Aughtie Dve., Albert Park ☎*696 2777* ◄≡
≡ 🍷 ⊘ AE ⊙ VISA *Open Tues-Sun 7pm-2am (restaurant kitchen closes at 11pm).*

A cabaret restaurant, popular with pop groups such as INXS. Live music Thursday to Sunday. The Carousel has splendid views across Albert Park Lake and, with fountains playing, is ideal for a romantic evening. Reservations are a must.

CHASERS

386 Chapel St., South Yarra ☎*827 6615*
🍷 ⊘ ▣ ⚭ AE ⊙ ⊙ VISA *Open Wed-Sun. Licensed until 7am.*

Currently Melbourne's hippest nightspot, Chasers is the place for the young seeking the latest in music and fashion trends. There are pool tables upstairs for when the music gets too much. Built on three levels with five bars, Chasers is situated in fashionable South Yarra.

CHEVRON

519 St Kilda Rd., South Yarra ☎*510 1281*
🍷 ⊘ ⚭ AE ⊙ ⊙ VISA *Closed Mon.*

Established for 25 years, the Chevron underwent a \$1 million facelift in 1989 and is now one of Melbourne's favorite discos, with up to 2,000 people passing through its doors on a Saturday night. It is licensed until 7am and has three bars and the ear-splitting music you would expect. As evenings tend to be geared toward a particular sort of music, check to ensure your sound is playing.

CRAZY HOUSE

169 Exhibition St. ☎*663 1754. Map* **10***B3*
🍷 ≡ ⊘ AE ⊙ ⊙ VISA *Open Tues-Sat 6.30pm-1am.*

Among Melbourne's flourishing

theater-restaurants, this has become an institution. There's reasonable food, and the entertainment, comedy and sketches, can be fun. As Friday and Saturday evenings are usually reserved months in advance, it may be easier to go during the week.

INFLATION

60 King St. ☎*614 6122. Map 10C2* ☨ ◉
☲ 🄰🄴 ⬧ ◉ 🆅🆂🄰 *Open Wed-Mon 9pm-4 or 5am.*

Inflation, is aimed at the younger set, with a hard-rock disco, a video bar, a restaurant, a cocktail bar and an attractive rooftop garden.

JULIANA'S

Hilton Hotel, 192 Wellington Parade, East Melbourne ☎*419 3311. Map 11C5* ☨ ◉
🄹 🄰🄴 ⬧ ◉ 🆅🆂🄰 *Open Tues-Sat 7pm-3am.*

Very classy nightspot, part of the HILTON (see WHERE TO STAY), with live bands and disco as well as visiting international entertainers. First-class restaurant.

THE LAST LAUGH THEATRE RESTAURANT

64 Smith St., Collingwood ☎*419 8600. Map 11B5* ☨ ☲ ◉ 🄰🄴 ⬧ ◉ 🆅🆂🄰 *Open Wed-Sat, dinner 7.30-9.30pm, show starts 9.30pm (weekends), 9pm weekdays. Licensed until 3am.*

Zany, irreverent and unique, this is one of the best-known, longest-established Australian theater-restaurants, for 25 years a nursery for scores of successful entertainers. Here you will see original Australian humor, perhaps a future star.

THE PALACE

Lower Esplanade, St Kilda ☎*534 0655. Map 12D2* ☲ ☨ ◉ 🄹 🄽 🆅 🄰🄴 ⬧ ◉
🆅🆂🄰

The Palace caters for all tastes in a three-room complex. Among the attractions are a gay night on Saturdays; the Baseline Club in the back room, Caesars bar and café, which features live music Mon-Thurs, a Sunday afternoon disco club (4pm-8pm), and a variety of big-name bands.

21ST CENTURY DANCE CLUB

1 Davey St., Frankston ☎*783 7311* ☨ ◉
☲ 🄰🄴 ⬧ ◉ 🆅🆂🄰 *Open Wed-Sat 8pm-3am.*

Situated in a beachside dormitory town well s of Melbourne, the trip here is worthwhile for the sheer assault on the senses. The plush, spacious interior reflects the fortune spent by owner John Finch in converting a former bowling alley into a top-class entertainment center; the computer-controlled lighting system alone cost A$800,000. It has room for 1,000 people, but there is always a line at the door on weekends.

THE METRO

20-30 Bourke St., Melbourne ☎*663 4288. Map 11B4* ☨ ◉ 🄹 🄽 🆅 ☲ 🄰🄴 ⬧ ◉
🆅🆂🄰 *Open Wed-Sat. Licensed until 7am.*

Probably Melbourne's most popular nightspot, the Metro has eight bars, and occupies three levels, each with its own dance floor. There is live music on most Wednesday nights and disco music on the other evenings. A restaurant is also part of the complex.

VICTORIAN ARTS CENTRE

100 St Kilda Rd. ☎*information 11 566, reservations 11 500. Map 11D4* ☨ 🄰🄴 ⬧
◉ 🆅🆂🄰

Focal point for the arts in the city (see SIGHTS), the Arts Centre is home or host to some of Australia's leading performance companies. The **Melbourne Symphony Orchestra** plays at the **Concert Hall** during the "Red Series" season, from April to October. The **State** theater hosts the **Australian Ballet Company** from June to July and October to November, the **Australian Opera Company** from March to May, and the **Victorian State Opera** from July to August and November to December. The **Melbourne Theatre Company**, more or less the city's repertory company, performs at the **Playhouse**, and also at the **Athenaeum** *(188 Collins St.* ☎*650 1500, map 10C3)* and the **Russell Street Theatre** *(19 Russell St.* ☎*654 4000, map 10C3).* Melbourne's **Playbox Theatre Company** performs in its new home, the two-theater **Malthouse** *(113 Sturt St., s Melbourne, map 10D3).*

Where to shop

Often called the shopping capital of Australia, Melbourne has some of Australia's finest department stores, as well as a number of specialty shops of high standing.

The real power in Melbourne retailing lies with the department stores — and one, MYER, stands alone. The old slogan, "Myer is Melbourne," is in many ways still true. In 1985 Myer was taken over by G. J. Coles, the Melbourne-based supermarket-and-variety-store chain. The new group now accounts for about 20 cents in every retail dollar spent in Australia and is the fifth-largest retailer in the world. Myer's major city store is in Melbourne's shopping heart, the BOURKE STREET MALL (see SIGHTS). There are also Myer stores at the major regional shopping centers that dot the outer suburbs.

The central shopping area declined as the suburban sprawl, fueled by the postwar immigration program, grew apace, encouraging major retailers to concentrate on shops located in huge suburban shopping malls. These offer complete one-stop shopping and easy parking. But the central area has fought back. The **Bourke Street Mall** was one successful answer. Friday-night late shopping, introduced in the 1970s, has also helped regenerate the city center.

One of the joys of shopping in Melbourne is a browse through the arcades that crisscross the center. The major ones are **Block Arcade**, which runs off Collins St. and is renowned for its smart boutiques; **Royal Arcade,** between Bourke St. and Little Collins St.; **Australia Arcade**, running between Collins St. and Little Collins St. and with several coffee lounges and light-snack outlets; and **Centrepoint Mall** and **The Walk**, both in the Bourke Street Mall.

There are some excellent conventional, high-street-style shopping centers in the inner suburbs, notably at **South Yarra**, **Toorak Village, Prahran**, **High St.** in **Armadale** and **Smith St.** in **Collingwood**.

The **High St.** in **Armadale** is renowned for antiques. Scores of shops are concentrated into one length of street, many importing antiques direct from Great Britain and Europe. There are also several exclusive dress and menswear stores.

Shopping hours are Monday to Thursday 9am-5.30pm, Friday 9am-9pm and Saturday 9am-noon.

AUSTRALIANA
Antipodes *(22 Toorak Rd., South Yarra* ☎ *866 5749* AE Φ CD VISA, *map 11 F5)* has a big selection of Australian souvenirs. At the **Australiana General Store** *(1227 High St., Armadale* ☎ *822 2324* AE Φ CD VISA, *map 12 D3)* there's kitchenware, giant soft-toy kangaroos and rocking horses.

BEAUTY PARLORS AND HAIRDRESSERS
The major department stores have excellent salons in their city branches. Long-established is **Frederic Muller Hairdressing** *(100 Collins St.* ☎ *650 4173* CD VISA *map 10 C3),* very exclusive but very

257

good. **Edward Beale** *(428 Toorak Rd., Toorak, 3142* ☎*826 1706* ▣ ▣ *map 12 C2)* appeals more to the younger set.

BOOKS AND RECORDS
Kenneth Hince *(485 High St., Prahran, 3181* ☎*525 1649* ▣ ▣ ▣ *map 12 C2)* has a fine selection of antique and hard-to-find books. **Collins Booksellers** *(city shops: 86 Bourke St., 115 Elizabeth St., map 10 C3 and 401 Swanston St., map 10 B3* ☎*654 3144 for all three branches* ▣ ▣*)*, with three city shops and 11 suburban outlets, is hard to beat for everyday book needs. **Brashs** *(108 Elizabeth St.* ☎*654 6544, map 10 C3* ▣ ▣ ▣ ▣*)* has a wide selection of tapes and records, with 24 branches and an outlet at almost every major shopping center.

DEPARTMENT STORES
Melbourne has some of the largest department stores in Australia: MYER in Bourke St. claims to be the biggest in the country.

DAIMARU
211 La Trobe St. ☎*660 6666. Map 10 B3*
ᵭ ⇍ ⇌ ▣ ▣ ▣ ▣ ▣

The first entry into Australian retailing by the Japanese-owned group, Daimaru has had a big impact on Melbourne shopping with its uncluttered, wide-aisled store. Daimaru specializes in fashion, stocking leading imported and Australian brands such as Burberry, Hugo Boss, Ralph Lauren, Anne Klein, Miriam Haskell, Country Road and Sportscraft for Men. It also carries many leading furniture and homeware brands from around the world. There are eight food and beverage outlets at the store, which is on six levels and forms part of the Melbourne Central complex. Included in the eating spots is the very upmarket **Paul Bocuse** restaurant. Well worth a visit for the eye-catching displays, if for nothing else.

DAVID JONES
310 Bourke St. (entrance in Bourke Street Mall) ☎*669 8200. Map 10 C3* ᵭ ▣ ▣ ▣ ▣ ▣

Very upscale, David Jones is renowned for its imaginative displays, using fresh flowers and even a pianist. It carries top brand names, especially in men's and women's fashions.

GEORGES
162 Collins St. ☎*283 5555. Map 10 C3*
ᵭ ▣ ▣ ▣ ▣

An unashamedly elite shop with the best international designer names, Georges is renowned for children's clothes and window displays. It also stocks fine china, glassware and kitchen accessories.

MYER MELBOURNE LTD.
314 Bourke St. and 295 Lonsdale St.
☎*66111. Map 10 C3, 10 B3* ᵭ ▣ ▣ ▣
▣ ▣

It is almost impossible to avoid shopping at Myer when in Melbourne: the store dominates the center and advertises everywhere. This classic store, solid and reliable, sells nearly everything and has an outstanding food hall. There is a Myer store in nearly every major regional shopping mall around the city and in the larger country towns.

FASHION
Australian women are highly fashion-conscious. Melbourne has good representatives in every sector of the market. Although boutiques and fashion chain-stores have made inroads, large stores such as DAVID JONES and GEORGES have also held their own.

COUNTRY ROAD
281 Bourke St. ☎*654 8231. Map 10C3*
& ⛺ ☯ ☯ VISA
Country Road specializes in excellent-quality, fashionable clothes aimed at the upper end of the mass market. There are 14 suburban branches, nearly all for both men and women.

HEMDEN TAILORED SHIRTS
1024 High St., Armadale ☎*509 0933. Map 12D3* AE ☯ ☯
As well as handmade shirts in exclusive fabrics, Hemden sells classically designed women's clothing. It is expensive, but the workmanship is likely to be unsurpassed.

HENRY BUCK
320 Collins St. ☎*670 9951. 476 Toorak Rd, Toorak* ☎*826 1225 Map 10C3, 12D2* AE ☯ ☯ VISA
Outfitters to the professions, Henry Buck stocks well-known names such as Daks, Aquascutum, Van Heusen and Church's Shoes, and the best European, American and Australian brands.

KATIES
284 Bourke St. ☎*663 2711. Map 10C3* AE ☯ ☯ VISA
Another big chain offering inexpensive clothes for women on a tight budget. There are more than 20 suburban branches.

SPORTSGIRL
234 Collins St. ☎*650 6755. Map 10C3* & ⛺ AE ☯ ☯ VISA
Top-quality but conservative women's clothes aimed at the top end of the mass market, plus accessories such as handbags, stockings, jewelry and shoes. Window displays are imaginative and eye-catching. Sportsgirl has 17 suburban branches.

SUSSAN
Walk Arcade, Bourke St. ☎*650 2744. Map 10C3* ☯ VISA
Inexpensive clothes for the working girl, with more than 30 suburban branches. Shops are bright and cheery. Good-value clothes, and nothing too avant-garde.

JEWELERS
There are several good chain jewelers such as **Proud** and **Edment**, who in addition to city shops have extensive networks of suburban branches selling affordable jewelry and silverware. Better-class jewelers tend to have only one or two branches: HARDY BROTHERS is a good example.

HARDY BROTHERS
338 Collins St. ☎*670 0435. Map 10C3* AE ☯ ☯
Melbourne's most exclusive jewelers and silversmiths stock the best in jewelry, porcelain and glassware, including Waterford, Royal Worcester, Orrefors and Caran d'Ache, plus fine antique silverware and jewelry.

PAMAMULL'S JEWELERS
Shops 47 and 44, Lower Plaza, Southern Cross Hotel, Exhibition St. ☎*650 5906/654 7535. Map 10B3* AE ☯ ☯ VISA
A wide selection of loose opals such as solid blacks, reds and greens, rough-cut and specimen stones, as well as opal jewelry. (Australia has 90 percent of the world's opals.)

MARKETS
One of the joys of living in Melbourne is the proliferation of markets both in the city and suburbs. They have proved so popular that several suburban markets have been enlarged or completely rebuilt in recent years. Price competition is intense and real bargains can be had — but be on your guard, for some of the goods are cheap... and nasty.

PRAHRAN
Commercial Rd., Prahran.
Mainly fruit and vegetables, but there are some fish and meat outlets and other stalls selling cosmetics, sunglasses and such.

QUEEN VICTORIA
Corner of Peel St. and Victoria St., North Melbourne. Map 10B2.
One of the largest markets (under one roof) in the world, where you can buy virtually every exotic and ethnic food, from Camembert to rollmops and kiwi fruit to custard apples, plus a vast range of other goods. Especially popular on Sunday, when take-away refreshment stalls offer anything from hot dogs to dim sims (a kind of Australianized Chinese meat roll eaten with soy sauce).

SOUTH MELBOURNE
Corner of Cecil St. and Coventry St., South Melbourne. Map 10E2.
Essentially a food market, but other items are also sold. Rooftop parking.

SHOPPING MALLS
Melbourne is ringed with suburban shopping malls afloat in seas of parked cars. Most are first-rate and offer virtually all the facilities and services available in the city. They are, however, geared almost exclusively to the car, and a shopping trip can be an unpleasant experience if you try to get by with public transportation.

Doncaster Shoppingtown, one of the largest in the eastern suburbs, has a branch of **Myer** department store, a large supermarket, more than 100 specialty shops on two floors, and a twin-screen movie theater. **Box Hill Central** and **White Horse Plaza**, built over Box Hill rail station, is one of the few shopping malls connected to public transportation. **The New Chadstone** is a spectacular addition to Melbourne's shopping, its 80-shop extension now making it the largest mall in Australia, with a total of more than 350 shops. The extension is a two-story glass-roofed extravaganza complete with 60-foot palm trees, white grand piano and French-style café. Many of the designer label shops have taken space, making it a mecca for the smart set.

JAM FACTORY
500 Chapel St., South Yarra ☎826 0537.
The former Henry Jones IXL jam factory has been imaginatively converted into a modern 50-shop mall, selling mainly women's fashions. Constructed around a central courtyard area, with a glass roof. Coffee lounges serve snacks, and browsing is fun.

Excursions (1): Environs of Melbourne

Not all Melbourne's many attractions are in the immediate city area. The DANDENONG RANGES to the E, for example, make an ideal spot for a picnic or barbecue, with some magnificent scenery and lovely bush walks. To the W, WERRIBEE PARK is another popular picnic spot, with extensive grounds and tennis and golf nearby.

This section offers highlights that are easily reachable in a half-day's drive there and back. A chat with your hotel porter will probably uncover more options.

DANDENONG RANGES ★
50km (31 miles) SE of Melbourne. Map 13E4 ♣ ◁⋲ By car, via Burwood Highway; by train, to Belgrave; also bus tours from Melbourne.

The range of densely forested hills known as the Dandenongs (or sometimes as the Blue Dandenongs) may be compared to the Vienna Woods or the Bois de Boulogne, in being a favored recreation area for Melbournians. In large part they are a National Park, having a mix of native bushland and private garden, and they are home to some of the world's largest **hardwood trees**, such as the mountain ash. Spectacular **tree ferns** grow there to prodigious sizes, fed by heavy rainfall nearly double that of Melbourne.

The highest point is **Mt. Dandenong**, 471m (1,545 feet) high, which has a panoramic view of Melbourne and Port Phillip Bay, with a restaurant at the summit and extensive viewing areas equipped with telescopes. Numerous craft- and art-galleries are to be found among the hills, which over the years have developed a reputation as an artists' haven.

There are many points of interest in "the Hills," as Melbournians are apt to call the Dandenongs. The **William Ricketts Sanctuary**, near Mt. Dandenong, is administered by the Forests Commission and exhibits open-air works by the eponymous sculptor, whose art uses Aboriginal themes. The **National Rhododendron Gardens**, near **Olinda**, have a first-class display of rhododendrons and other specialized plants. Tulip farms, a joy in spring, abound around the **Silvan** area. Between **Belgrave** and **Emerald Lake**, a narrow-gauge steam train, **Puffing Billy**, runs on weekends and during school vacations; a timetable is available from the **Metropolitan Transit Authority**, or at most rail stations.

The hills are rich in exotic birdlife — even, sometimes, the elusive **lyrebird**, famed for its spectacular tail. The year-round popularity of the hills for picnics and barbecues leads to many of the birds, such as **galahs** and **parrots**, being tame enough to eat out of your hand. If possible, visit the hills during the week, for the narrow roads get busy on weekends.

GULF STATION ★
Yea Rd., Yarra Glen, 50km (31 miles) NE of Melbourne ☎730 1286 ▥ ♣ ⇌ Open Wed-Sun 10am-4pm. By car, through Lilydale, then look for Yarra Glen turnoff on left, 5km (3 miles) on.

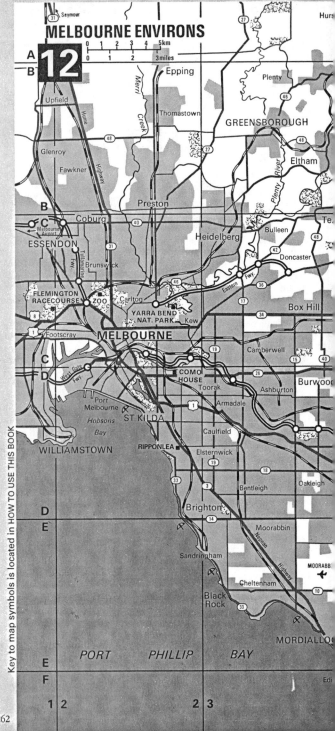

MELBOURNE ENVIRONS

12

0 1 2 3 4 5km
0 1 2 3miles

Seymour

Hurs

Epping

Plenty

Upfield

Thomastown

GREENSBOROUGH

Glenroy

Fawkner

Eltham

Merri Creek

Hume Highway

Preston

Plenty River

Coburg

Te.

Bulleen

Heidelberg

ESSENDON

Melbourne Airport

Brunswick

Doncaster

Tullamarine Fwy

FLEMINGTON RACECOURSE

ZOO

Carlton

YARRA BEND NAT. PARK

Kew

Eastern Fwy

Box Hill

Footscray

MELBOURNE

Camberwell

West Gate Fwy

COMO HOUSE

Toorak

Ashburton

Burwoo

Port Melbourne

Armadale

ST KILDA

Hobsons Bay

Caulfield

WILLIAMSTOWN

RIPPONLEA

Elsternwick

Bentleigh

Oakleigh

Brighton

Moorabbin

Sandringham

Nepean Highway

MOORABB

Cheltenham

Black Rock

MORDIALLO

PORT   PHILLIP   BAY

Edi

262

A B B C C D D E E F

1 2 2 3

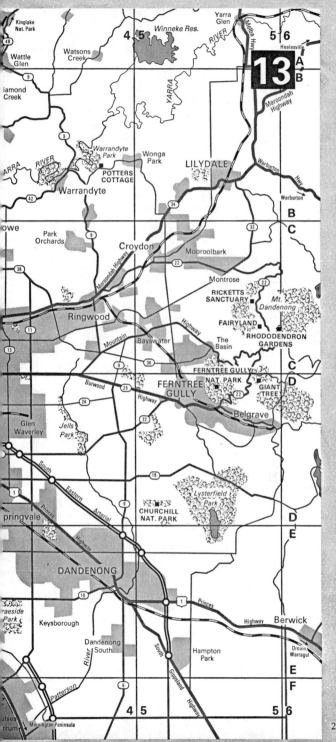

Gulf Station provides a rare taste of life as it must have been for the early colonists. The Bell family settled on this land during the 1850s and established a prosperous farm. When the last of the Bells died in the 1950s the farm was still run very much as a 19thC enterprise. The National Trust then assumed responsibility for the property, and has since restored it to its 19thC condition. The **farmhouse** is built of vertical slabs of local timber, as are the farm buildings, which include a milking shed, barn, butcher's shop, slaughterhouse and woolshed. There is also a **schoolhouse** where the Bell children were taught.

HANGING ROCK AND WOODEND ★

80km (50 miles) NW of Melbourne ◁€ By car, via Calder Highway to Mt. Macedon or Woodend; by train, to Woodend, then taxi to Hanging Rock.

This is familiar as the setting for the movie *Picnic at Hanging Rock,* about a party of young girls who mysteriously disappear while on a school picnic. The rock and surrounding region has been a popular destination since the 1870s. In the 1880s many large houses were built on the slopes of **Mt. Macedon**, many of them sadly destroyed in the 1983 Ash Wednesday bushfires, which devastated much of the mountain. So resilient is the Australian bush that most of the Ash Wednesday scars have since vanished.

Hanging Rock itself is a strange, massive outcrop of volcanic origin, quite easily climbed, although the track should be noted carefully. There are **barbecue facilities** with a refreshment kiosk and WCs at the base.

Nearby **Woodend** nowadays is a quiet country community, but in the gold-rush era it marked an important stopping point on the way to the Bendigo goldfield. The stone bridge across **Five Mile Creek**, built in 1862, is noteworthy, as are the BENTINCK HOTEL (see below) and the bluestone Anglican church.

🐾 ☛ **Bentinck Hotel** *(Carlisle St., Woodend* ☎ *(054) 27 2330* ▥ *)* was once a large country house. The open log fires in winter give the feel of an old-fashioned English country house. Advance reservation essential. Fully licensed dining room.

HEALESVILLE SANCTUARY (Sir Colin Mackenzie Sanctuary)

Badger Creek Rd., Healesville, 65km (41 miles) NE of Melbourne ☎ (059) 62 4022 ▣ ♿ ▤ ✳ ↝ *Open 9am-5pm. By car, via Maroondah Highway; by train, to Healesville, then taxi.*

One of the "must see" sights around Melbourne, the sanctuary, situated 5km (3 miles) SE of the town of Healesville, houses one of the finest collections of Australian wildlife in the country. The sanctuary was founded in the 1920s by Sir Colin MacKenzie, an expert on Australian fauna. In 1944 it became the first place in the world to breed the **duck-billed platypus** in captivity.

Most of the sanctuary is open-plan. Kangaroos and wallabies live in free-range enclosures, allowing visitors to get near to the animals and even to touch them. Emus wander around freely, stealing brazenly from picnic tables. All the enormous **aviaries** are of the walk-through variety, which allows the birds to live in an environment as near as possible to their natural habitat. There are excellent displays of **nocturnal animals**, and at certain times it is possible to see the **duck-billed platypus** swimming in a glass-sided tank. There is also an extensive collection of snakes, koalas, wombats, cassowaries and water birds.

PHILLIP ISLAND

Situated in Westernport Bay, the island is a popular vacation destination for Melbourne residents. Its greatest claim to fame are the **Fairy Penguins**, who leave the water and parade up the beach every night to their burrows in the sand dunes. The nightly parade is Australia's second largest tourist attraction and is particularly loved by Japanese visitors. A number of tour operators run trips from Melbourne.

POTTER'S COTTAGE

Jumping Creek Rd. (near Ringwood Rd.), Warrandyte, 30km (18 miles) NE of Melbourne ☎844 3078. *Map 13B4* ☒ ☴ ✳ ☛ *Gallery open 7 days 10am-5pm. By car, via Eastern Freeway — take Thompsons Rd. exit, following signs to Templestowe; Thompsons Rd. becomes Parker St., then Andersons Rd., then Warrandyte Rd.*

Opened in 1958 by a group of potters to promote Australian studio pottery, Potter's Cottage has since developed into a popular weekend destination for locals and visitors. The gallery, where the potters' work is exhibited and sold, stands beside the Yarra River in an attractive bush setting at **Warrandyte**. Both gallery and restaurant (see DINING OUT) are timber-built.

Several other arts and crafts galleries can be found in Warrandyte itself, which is surrounded by **Warrandyte State Park**. Here, on **Anderson's Creek**, gold was first discovered in Victoria in 1851: a cairn marks the spot.

The State Park borders the Yarra River and is heavily timbered bushland. It is made up of three separate reserves. One of these, the **Pound Bend Reserve**, w of Warrandyte, has a tunnel hacked through the river valley's side by goldminers in the 19thC, intending to divert the river so that the dry riverbed could be sluiced for gold.

WERRIBEE PARK ★

K Rd., Werribee, 35km (22 miles) w of Melbourne ☎741 2444 ☒ *grounds* ☒ *mansion* ♿ ☛ ☛ ≫° *Grounds open 10am-8pm (summer); 10am-5pm (winter). Mansion open 10am-3.45pm (weekdays in winter); 10am-4.45pm (summer, winter weekends). By car, via Princes Highway; by train, to Werribee, then taxi.*

Werribee Park is an impressive estate whose centerpiece is a large, 60-room mansion, **Chirnside**, built in the 1870s in Italianate style for the Chirnside brothers, who established a pastoral empire to the w of Melbourne. A two-story building of local bluestone, Chirnside was designed by London architect James Henry Fox. No expense was spared, and the mansion is resplendent with gold leaf, mosaic floors and fine ornamentation.

The garden of Werribee Park was laid out by the curator of the ROYAL BOTANIC GARDENS (see SIGHTS); a lake surrounds an island, which features a grotto. Outbuildings contemporary with the mansion, such as shepherds' huts, a dairy and woolsheds, still survive.

Excursions (2): Farther afield

For driving tourists Victoria could hardly be easier. Distances are fairly manageable, and much of interest and beauty lies between the major centers. The following excursions are selected from the best the Garden State has to offer. For more ideas and maps, see ROUTES 1 and 2 in TOURS on pages 68-71.

THE MORNINGTON PENINSULA
240km (150-mile) round trip. Allow 2 days. Recommended stop: Sorrento.
The Mornington Peninsula is often called Melbourne's playground. A southern extension of the city's bayside suburbs, it divides Port Phillip Bay from Westernport Bay, to the E. An overnight stop is recommended, for although it can be seen in one long day, some of the best sights would have to be missed. Traffic jams are likely along the coastal roads during summer vacations and on weekends.

Driving s through St Kilda junction, take the Nepean Highway, following signs for Frankston. The highway passes through **Brighton**, one of the most expensive suburbs; take a detour w just to glimpse the scale and opulence of some of the houses.

Just past Brighton, at a place called **Half Moon Bay**, look out for HMAS *Cerberus*, the hulk of an ironclad battleship, flagship of the Victorian navy in the late 19thC and thought to be the only surviving ironclad.

Frankston, back on the Nepean Highway, is a dormitory town at the end of the rail line, 41km (26 miles) s of the city, with an excellent shopping mall and a pleasant beach, good for fishing. Continue through **Mornington**, home base for many competitors in the Sydney-Hobart blue-water and Melbourne-Devonport w coast classics. Take time to walk along the pier to see these fine yachts.

Several bayside towns, such as **Mt. Martha** and **Safety Beach**, follow. At **Dromana**, with its backdrop of **Arthur's Seat**, a high point rising steeply from the coast to 305m (1,000 feet), a chair lift up Arthur's Seat affords a spectacular view of the bay as far as Melbourne. More small resorts, such as **McCrae**, **Rosebud**, **Rye**, **Blairgowrie** and **Sorrento**, lead to **Portsea** at the end of the peninsula.

Sorrento, a lovely old town with many well-preserved buildings and a small museum, is the site of the first European settlement in Victoria, in

1803. There is a memorial to the leader, Colonel Collins. Overlooking **Sullivan's Bay** are several graves of early settlers. Near the pier is an excellent **aquarium** *(open every day in summer)*.

Portsea is the playground for Melbourne's rich, who live close to the beach in large, secluded houses. On the s side of the peninsula is **London Bridge**, a rocky part of the cliff, worn away and separated, with a hole straight through the center that resembles a bridge — hence the name. The **surf beach** at Portsea is one of the best within easy reach of Melbourne; but beware of the strong riptide (in summer the beach is patrolled by lifeguards).

The extreme end of the peninsula, which is controlled by the federal government, encompasses a quarantine station and an army officers' training college. The quarantine station has been in existence since the 19thC, when many of the early immigrant vessels buried their dead there.

Return from Portsea on the Old Melbourne Rd., which runs parallel to the Nepean Highway and passes through some lovely coastal bushland, rejoining the Nepean Highway at **Rye**. Continue to **Rosebud West**, then turn right onto Boneo Rd. toward Flinders. The road passes near **Cape Schanck**, 4km (2½ miles) s, a most spectacular point looking across **Bass Strait**, with a **lighthouse** that can be visited most weekends at certain times. A walk E along **Cape Schanck Coastal Park** to **Bushrangers Bay** repays the effort.

Flinders is a charming fishing village on Westernport Bay, opposite **Phillip Island**, with one licensed hotel, a motel, a trailer (caravan) park and a few shops. Sample the fine bread from **Flinders Bakery** in the main street, which uses a wood-fired 19thC oven.

The main road back to Melbourne passes **Point Leo**, about 8km (5 miles) on, which has an excellent surf beach that is patrolled. The road bypasses Hastings and feeds into the Mulgrave Freeway, via Dandenong back into Melbourne.

☞ Sorrento has several hotels and motels. Among them is the **Koonya** *(Nepean Highway* ☎ *(059) 84 2281* ▢ *)*, offering comfortable accommodations and an excellent restaurant (see below). Nearby is the **Oceanic** *(Ocean Beach Rd., 1.5km (1 mile) from Sorrento* ☎ *(059) 84 1417* ▢ *)*, a 20-unit motel.

⇶ The restaurant at the **Koonya** *(see hotel above)* serves delicious locally caught fish. In Flinders, the **Bakery Restaurant** *(in front of Flinders Bakery, in the main street* ☎ *(059) 89 0291* ▥ *)* provides superb home-cooked food.

THE GREAT OCEAN ROAD, PORTLAND AND HAMILTON
725km (450-mile) round trip. Allow at least 2 days. Recommended stops: Port Fairy, Hamilton.

The Great Ocean Road, which starts just outside Torquay, 23km (14 miles) s of Geelong, is about 180km (112 miles) long and presents some of the most spectacular coastal scenery in Australia. Built during the Great Depression as a make-work scheme, the road demanded great engineering skill, frequently having to be carved out of almost sheer cliffs.

Take the Princes Highway to the port of **Geelong**, 74km (46 miles) SW. This is Victoria's second largest city (population 125,279), important for grain export and major oil refineries. Beyond Geelong look for the sign to **Torquay** and the Great Ocean Road. Torquay and nearby **Bells Beach** have some of the finest surf in Australia.

The road follows the coast through several picturesque villages such as **Aireys Inlet** and **Fairhaven** until it reaches attractive **Lorne**, with its backdrop of the **Otway Ranges**, a popular watering place since the 19thC. The 1983 Ash Wednesday bushfire licked the outskirts of Lorne and the population had to be evacuated to the beach for several hours.

From Lorne the road continues along the coast for 45km (28 miles) until **Apollo Bay**, a pleasant resort town, then turns inland and meanders through the **Otway National Park**, rejoining the coast again at **Princetown**.

Some magnificent views open up on the ocean-hugging stretch to **Port Campbell**. From Port Campbell to Warrnambool the coast is the graveyard of scores of sailing vessels, wrecked as they sailed down Bass Strait. Just before Port Campbell is **Loch Ard Gorge**, a tiny inlet where the sailing ship *Loch Ard* was wrecked in 1878 with the loss of 50 lives; there were only two survivors. A sad little cemetery overlooks the gorge, which can be viewed from specially constructed platforms. Some days after the shipwreck a packing case washed up in the gorge was found to contain a life-sized **Minton pottery peacock**, destined for the Melbourne Great Exhibition of 1880.

In **Warrnambool**, a city of 21,414 people, the main attraction is the **Flagstaff Hill Maritime Museum** *(open 9.30am-4.30pm),* a faithful re-creation of a 19thC seaport similar to many that dotted the coast before large vessels concentrated trade into a few centers. The museum is based on an old lighthouse and on fortifications erected in 1887 against a putative Russian invasion; 60-pounder muzzle-loading guns remain in place. The *Loch Ard* Minton peacock is displayed here.

Stay on the Princes Highway for Portland, stopping at **Port Fairy**, a well-preserved fishing village, settled by sealers in the 1820s. Some of the oldest houses in Victoria, dating back to the 1840s, are open for viewing. At the **mutton bird rookery**, near the mouth of the Moyne River, watch the nightly return of the huge flocks, each bird unerringly finding its own nest — a hole in the ground — in the dark.

From Port Fairy head for **Portland**, said to be the site of the first permanent settlement in Victoria, in 1834. (Port Fairy also claims that title: the argument revolves around the word "permanent.") Modern Portland's landmark is its huge aluminum smelter.

Now turn inland, heading northward 76km (48 miles) on the Henty Highway toward **Hamilton**, an important rural center that styles itself the "Wool Capital of the World." Hamilton's fine **art gallery** *(Brown St., open Tues-Fri 10am-5pm; Sat 10am-noon, 2-5pm; Sun, hols 2-5pm)* started with a local farmer's donation of an extensive collection of **Mediterranean pottery**, **antique porcelain** and **silver,** now housed in the downstairs Shaw Gallery. There are also fine **Chinese ceramics** from the Sung, Ming, Ching and Tang dynasties covering a period of about 1,600 years from AD95, and several good examples of Chinese lacquer work. Upstairs is an important collection of **Tibetan**, **Indian**, **Nepalese**, **Chinese** and **Indian artifacts**, mostly dating from the 16th-18thC, though some go back to the 13thC. There are works by Australian artists, and etchings and watercolors by English artist Paul Sandby.

From Hamilton, take the Hamilton Highway to Geelong (passing through some of the best sheep-rearing country in the world), then on to Melbourne.

✍⁼⁼ The **Lady Julia Percy Motel** *(54 Sackville St., Port Fairy ☎(055) 68 1800 ▭)* is comfortable and has a BYO restaurant with à la carte menu (not always open out of season, so check beforehand). The **Caledonian Motel** *(Thompson St., Hamilton ☎(055) 72 1055 ▭)* is simple, welcoming and has a restaurant.

THE MURRAY VALLEY

1,350km (850-mile) round trip, including short side trips from Mildura. Allow at least 3 days, preferably 4. Recommended stops: Echuca, Mildura, St Arnaud.

The Murray River (the "Mighty Murray"), a vital lifeline for Victoria, New South Wales and South Australia, forms, with the Darling River, the largest river system in Australia. The Murray Valley is also an important resort area.

Head NW on the Calder Highway toward **Bendigo**, then NE toward Echuca on the Midland Highway, which after 47km (30 miles) joins the Northern Highway at **Elmore**.

Echuca is a well-preserved town at the junction of the Murray, Campaspe and Goulburn Rivers. Once Australia's largest inland port, Echuca collected vast amounts of wool from sheep stations strung out along the Murray and its tributaries. Echuca's river boats helped open up large areas of the Outback, and by 1895 there were 105 steamers and 110 barges and boats registered.

The **Port of Echuca** *(open 9.15am-5pm)* has been restored to its former glory. The **Star Hotel** (built 1867) acts as the port information center, where you can buy tickets to visit the wharf and the **Bridge Hotel** (1858), where travelers quenched their thirst while waiting for the pontoon ferry. Obtain tickets here too for the Star Hotel itself, which has an underground bar to provide a cool resting place out of the sun; the hotel was delicensed in 1897, and a **tunnel** from the bar is believed to have been used as an escape route by illegal drinkers. The **wharf**, built in 1864 out of red gumwood, was at one time nearly 1km (over half a mile) long, and is constructed on three levels to accommodate the massive rise and fall of the Murray. A visit to the wharf includes a continuous 10-minute audiovisual explanation of the river trade and of the history of Echuca and the surrounding area. Also part of the display are the paddle steamers *Pevensey* and *Adelaide;* cruises can be taken on another paddle steamer, *Canberra (☎(054) 82 2141 for bookings and information).*

Other attractions include the **Bond Store** *(open 9am-5pm),* built in 1859, where goods were stored awaiting payment of customs duty to the three states along the Murray River; the **Echuca Historical Society Museum** *(open Sat, Sun, hols, school hols 1-4pm),* formerly the police station and lockup (built 1867), which displays original charts of the river and numerous old photographs of Echuca; and the **Coach House Carriage Collection** *(open 9.30am-5pm)*, housing 35 restored horse-drawn coaches from all over the world.

Just outside Echuca, off the Murray Valley Highway, to the SE, is the excellent **Tisdall winery** *(14 Cornelia Creek Rd., open for cellar-door sales Mon-Sat 10am-5pm; Sun noon-5pm)*. Qantas chose Tisdall wines in 1986 for serving in-flight.

From Echuca, you should head NW along the Murray Valley Highway, approximately following the river toward Swan Hill, about 160km (100 miles) away. On the way is **Kerang**, the center of a rich farming area. Several lakes are skirted, including **Lake Charm** and **Lake Boga**, both good for watersports. At Lake Boga is **Best's winery** *(open for cellar-door sales)*.

Swan Hill was a busy river port in the 19thC and, like Echuca, is now a major resort, with excellent fishing and boating facilities. The big attraction is the **Pioneer Settlement** *(open 8.30am-5pm; nightly light-and-sound tour)*, a re-creation of a river town, tracing the story of the riverland pioneers from 1830. The old paddle steamer *Gem* marks the entrance to the center; another one, *Pyap,* takes visitors on 1-hour river cruises *(depart 10.30am, 2.30pm)*. Swan Hill also has a reputable **military museum** *(open 9am-5pm; hols, school hols 8.30am-5.30pm)*.

The Murray Valley Highway follows the river NW until **Lake Powell**, then heads NW to join the Sunraysia Highway at **Hattah**. Alternatively the Murray can be crossed at **Robinvale** and the Stuart Highway taken in New South Wales, crossing back into Victoria at Mildura — the more direct route.

Mildura (population 15,763) is the center of the **Sunset Country**, famed for red soil, brilliantly blue skies and magnificent sunsets. Try to spend two days there, for the area has much to offer. Mildura's importance began when two brothers, George and William Chaffey, introduced irrigation to the region, following their success with similar projects in California. Today it is the center for a prosperous dried-fruit industry and for wine-making.

Several **paddle steamers** work out of Mildura. The *Rothbury, Avoca* and *Melbourne* offer day trips from Mildura wharf, and the *Coonawarra* and the *Murray Explorer,* a modern luxury craft, offer extended cruises lasting up to five days.

There are numerous other places of interest. The **Mildura Arts Centre** *(open Mon-Fri 9am-4.30pm; Sat, Sun 2-4.30pm)* comprises an art gallery and a theater; the gallery is housed in **Rio Vista**, formerly home of William Chaffey. In its collection, based on the R. D. Elliott collection of works by British and Australian painters, is Sir Jacob Epstein's *Eve Dervich,* executed in 1924. At the **Mildura Co-operative Fruit Company Limited** *(open 9am-noon, 1-4pm; closed Sat, Sun)* you can watch citrus grown in the area being handled at the packing-shed door. And **Merbein**, 15km (9 miles) W of Mildura, is the home of **Mildara Wines**, one of the largest Australian producers *(self-guided tours Mon-Fri 8-11.15am, 1-4.15pm; open for cellar-door sales Mon-Fri 9am-5pm)*.

The route back to Melbourne follows the Sunraysia Highway. At first this passes through the **Mallee** country, an arid, semidesert region famous for spectacular sunsets and home of the strange mallee fowl, which can be seen at the **Wathe Fauna Reserve** in **Lascelles**. After Lascelles the countryside rolls with vast wheat fields.

From Ballarat, take the Midland Highway to Melbourne. The complete journey from Mildura, a distance of 557km (348 miles) can be managed in one day. Alternatively, stop in **St Arnaud**, an old gold-mining town containing several buildings with fine cast-iron lacework decoration: the **Botanical Hotel** is an excellent example. There is good fishing near St Arnaud in the **Avoca River** and **Teddington Reservoir**.

☎ In Echuca, the **Steam Packet** *(corner of Leslie St. and Murray Esplanade* ☎*(054) 82 3411* ▢*)* is handy for all the attractions: old-fashioned charm in a National Trust-classified building. On the Northern Highway, 4km/2½ miles s, is the **Red Carpet Inn** *(* ☎*(054) 82 4244* ▢*)*, a good motel.

In Mildura, **The Grand** *(Seventh St.* ☎*(050) 23 0511* ▥*)* is a comfortable, well-appointed old-world hotel with excellent facilities. In St Arnaud, try the **St Arnaud Motel** *(5 Ballarat Rd.* ☎*(054) 95 1755* ▢*)*.

🍽 Echuca has several first-class restaurants. **The Bridge Hotel** *(High St.* ☎*(054) 82 2247* ▥*)* has a seasonally changing à la carte menu. The **Steam Packet** *(see hotel above* ☎*(054) 82 3411*▥*)* specializes in steaks; BYO license. **The Cock 'n' Bull** *(17-21 Warren St.* ☎*(054) 82 4287*▥*)*, in an idyllic setting beside the Campaspe River, also serves steaks; BYO license.

In Mildura, **The Grand** *(see hotel above)* has **Stefano's Cantina**, a bistro where the chef, the first-class food and the manager are Italian. In St Arnaud, the **St Arnaud Motel** *(see hotel above* ▥*)* has a BYO-licensed restaurant.

THE GOLDEN TRIANGLE: BALLARAT AND BENDIGO

Round trip of about 330km (206 miles). Allow at least 2 days. Recommended stops: Ballarat, Bendigo.

Victoria's "golden cities," **Ballarat** and **Bendigo**, were the foundation of Victoria's — and Australia's — wealth in the 19thC. Between them they claim some of the finest Victorian buildings in Australia; you should go out of your way to visit both cities if you hope to understand how the modern Australia was forged.

For **Ballarat**, take the Western Highway, passing through the suburbs of Deer Park and heading w (via Bacchus Marsh). The city, Victoria's largest inland conurbation, has a population of 62,000. Its vital part in Australia's development into a democracy centers upon the 1854 **Eureka Stockade rebellion**, a short-lived uprising against an oppressive administration and the gold-mining licencing system.

Gold was first discovered in the **Clunes** region near Ballarat in 1851. Within 3 months some 8,000 people were on the diggings between Ballarat and **Buninyong**; 4 years later the influx had swelled to 100,000, turning the area into a lunar landscape in the frantic hunt for gold. This gold rush led to an alarming reduction in the population of Melbourne, and immigrants poured in from the US, Britain and elsewhere.

A shuttlebus (with commentary) takes 1 hour to view the major attractions. Take a ride too on the remaining old public tramway system

271

(operated by enthusiasts on weekends and during school hols), which circles **Lake Wendouree**, site of the rowing contests in the 1956 Olympics. The adjoining **Botanic Gardens** contain an avenue of busts of every prime minister since Federation.

Sovereign Hill *(☎ (053) 31 1944 for bookings and information on on-site accommodations; open 9.30am-5pm)* is an accurate working re-creation of a mid-19thC gold township, located on the site of the Sovereign Quartz Mining Company. Near the summit, the company sank a shaft, which still survives, to a depth of 216m (709 feet). Here you can pan for gold and be guaranteed to find a speck, ride an authentic Cobb and Co. stagecoach, visit the town's shops, see a live music hall and watch a smithy at work.

The **Eureka Stockade** is marked by a memorial of the uprising; a diorama explains the events leading up to it. Opposite is an exhibition *(open 9am-5pm)* with a moving tableau of the dramatic events of 1854. The **Gold Museum** *(open Sat-Thurs 10am-5pm, Fri noon-5pm)* recounts gold's effects on society since prehistory.

Ballarat Fine Art Gallery *(open 10.30am-4.30pm, closed Mon)* has one of the finest collections of Australian paintings, including work by Eugene von Guerard, Walter Wither, Lionel Lindsay, E. Phillips Fox, William Dobell, Sidney Nolan, Aaron Sherritt, Russell Drysdale and Fred Williams.

A walk through the city reveals several outstanding Victorian buildings, lovingly maintained and renovated. When the mighty McDonald's hamburger chain sought to open a branch here, the city council eventually persuaded the company to restore rather than demolish the old building on its site and to develop it in keeping with its surroundings — the first time McDonald's had ever departed from their universal format.

Leaving Ballarat, take the Midland Highway N to **Castlemaine**, another old gold-mining town with a fine Classical **market** *(open for viewing 10am-5pm)* that resembles a church basilica, built in 1862. Then continue to Bendigo, about 40km (25 miles) N on the Midland Highway.

Bendigo (population 52,700) is the other great regional gold-field town. Gold was discovered here in the same year (1851) as at Ballarat. The gold fields became known as the Bendigo Diggings, and the town that grew up nearby was known as Sandhurst, changed to Bendigo in the 1890s. During the gold rush thousands of Chinese flooded into the Bendigo Diggings, causing severe racial tension. Bendigo today retains its long association with the Chinese, and a major attraction is the **Joss House** *(open 10am-5pm),* constructed of handmade bricks in the 1860s. One of the finest Chinese dragons in the country parades annually through the city as part of the Chinese New Year celebrations.

Other attractions include a guided tour of the **Central Deborah Mine**, built in 1909 and closed in 1954, providing a view of operations above and below ground; the vintage **"Talking Tram"** *(departs hourly Sat, Sun 9.30am-5pm from Central Deborah Mine),* with a taped commentary on points of interest around the city; and **Bendigo Art Gallery** *(open Mon-Thurs 10am-5pm, Fri-Sun, hols 2-5pm),* built in 1887, an outstanding regional gallery with an important collection of Australian and European paintings.

From Bendigo the route s back to Melbourne along the Calder Highway passes through rich farming country. A detour w of about 17km (10½ miles) is worthwhile to visit **Maldon**, another gold-mining township that has recently developed into a center for crafts. The town has some outstanding streetscapes.

The Calder Highway continues through **Mt. Macedon**, which suffered badly during the 1983 Ash Wednesday bushfires (a side-trip to HANGING ROCK — see page 264 — and **Woodend** is possible here), and passes **Tullamarine airport** on the way back into Melbourne.

🕭🛏 **Ballarat** has some good hotels and motels. Recommended: the **Bell Tower** *(Western Highway, 6km / 4 miles w from city center* ☎*(053) 34 1600* 🏨*)*, with excellent facilities including swimming pool, sauna, spa, tennis courts and fully licensed restaurant.

In Bendigo, the **Shamrock** *(corner of Pall Mall St. and Williamson St.* ☎*(054) 43 0333* 🏨*)* combines comfort and history. The ornate building, built in 1897 and classified by the National Trust, counts among former guests singer Dame Nellie Melba and cricketer Sir Donald Bradman. There is a bistro restaurant.

Western Australia

Mountains of iron, fields of gold and diamonds, valleys of wine, the most intricate wild flowers, the hardiest of creatures, lush green pastures and wild scrub desert... Western Australia, the country's largest state, appears rich in all but population.

Only 1.6 million people live here, 1.1 million of them clustering around the handsome capital of Perth on the Swan River. The grandness of scale of the land itself is overpowering. Western Australia, which occupies almost a third of the continent, is three times the size of Texas or as large as Western Europe, and the 450,000 people who live outside Perth are scattered in small towns and remote settlements across an area of some 2.5 million square kilometers (965,000 square miles). Here native and visitor alike may grasp the vast size of Australia, the true experience of isolation, and feel something of what it is like to live in frontierland. Little quite shakes the soul so much as spending one day among the ebullient, zinc-creamed, sun-worshiping crowd on Perth's Cottesloe Beach, and the next in the emptiness of the red dust and spinifex wilderness outside Kalgoorlie.

The landscape of Western Australia is infinitely varied. The state's climate ranges from temperate in the southwest, through Mediterranean between Perth and Geraldton, to subtropical beyond the Pilbara. A large part of the interior, however, is arid wilderness, marked only by exotic rock formations, rugged red gorges and shimmering salt lakes.

MAKING A VIRTUE OF ISOLATION

Perth claims the title of "the most remote capital in the Western world." Its "neighbor," Adelaide, is 2,700 kilometers (1,700 miles) to the east; the Indonesian capital of Jakarta is closer than the Australian federal capital of Canberra. For Australians on the east coast, it can be cheaper to fly to Hawaii for a vacation than to Perth; for those in the west, Singapore or Bali may seem a more economical destination than the east coast. But Western Australians have turned their isolation into a challenging sort of virtue, looking with some condescension to the "Eastern States," as they somewhat disparagingly refer to them, and particularly to that mass of politicians in the Australian Capital Territory, "the Wise Men from the East." Sandgropers — the nickname they have happily accepted — believe they are blessed with the best and are determined, it seems, to prove it. In sports, entertainment and big business, Western Australians manifest an aggressive dynamism that others in Australia, and indeed the world, find hard to match.

EARLY SETTLERS

Evidently at first glance it did not appear a hospitable place in which to settle. The first Europeans known to have landed in Western Australia were 17th century Dutch seamen, blown off course by the Roaring Forties on their way from Holland to Batavia (present-day Jakarta). Englishman William Dampier, a pirate who became a Royal Navy officer, explored the coast of "New Holland" in 1688 and 1699, but his report to the British government was so unfavorable that the Colonial Office lost all interest.

It was only when the French began showing the flag in Australian waters, at the beginning of the 19th century, that the British felt that perhaps the time had come to act. So in 1826 Major Lockyer was sent from the east to establish the settlement of King George's Sound (now known as Albany). Then, 2 years later, the British decided to form a colony around the Swan River, which had been partly surveyed by the French in 1801. On May 2, 1829, Captain Charles Fremantle, commander of HMS *Challenger,* raised the British flag at the head of the Swan River and took possession of the territory. A month later, Captain James Stirling (later to become the first governor of Western Australia) arrived aboard the ship *Parmelia* with settlers; on August 12, 1829, he founded Perth in a simple ceremony near the city's present Town Hall.

EARTHY RICHES, SUBTLE PLEASURES

Today the state's financial wealth derives largely from its immense mineral deposits. Barely a week seems to pass without another vein of rare stone, yet another mountain of ore being discovered. The Hamersley Range of the Pilbara is among the world's largest sources of iron ore. Huge deposits of oil and natural gas have been found off the northwest coast. One of the world's richest diamond fields is in the Kimberleys. And gold, first discovered in the 1890s around Kalgoorlie and Coolgardie, is mined now throughout the state, as are silver, nickel, lead and zinc.

There is danger, of course, in simply daubing the vivid main features of this broad landscape. The picture is of earthy reds and browns — a huge quarry for the world — with tycoons, miners, oilmen, engineers, muscled sportsmen and obstinate adventurers appearing like so many Lowry stick-figures trapped in an unnatural sandy plain. But Western Australia is far from this caricature; and certainly not all its pleasures are crudely hedonistic. In frontierland such as this there is always room for subtleties, although it lies with the individual to seek out and paint in these other riches. They may take the form of a meeting with a green sea turtle in the Exmouth Gulf; an unexpected chat about poetry with a fisherman in a pub; a lonely wind whistling through abandoned, rusting goldmining equipment at Boulder; a sudden face-to-face with a frill-necked lizard; being dive-bombed by a frisky pelican; or finding yourself sailing nervously among dolphins. Every view is a different one — and you might suddenly find you are *truly* alone for the first time in your life.

The light, the colors are memorably vivid in Western Australia. In the west the sky truly seems a deeper blue, as though the more subtle shades had been reserved for the northern hemisphere alone. So it is all the more magical when the wild flowers here bloom and break the artist's rules, showing far more delicate shades of color. Western Australia claims to have the world's largest collection of native wild flowers — more than 6,500 species — and in spring, from about September 1 onward, they dramatically change the landscape.

Delicate the wild flowers may be in appearance, but they are all hardy survivors, well attuned to the harsh conditions of climate and territory. The most popular, attracting thousands of visitors to Western Australia each year, are kangaroo paws, distinctively shaped plants with bizarre plumes, of which there are 12 species in varying color combinations: red and yellow, green and black, and red and green, this last adopted as Western Australia's floral emblem. Most of the plush carpet of flowers spreads through the southwest of the state, in and around the forests and rolling grasslands. There are leschenaultias, delicately petaled in blue, violet, scarlet and yellow, and dampiera, named after the English buccaneer and appropriately colored in various shades of ocean blue. In the drier northern reaches, the visitor may witness the remarkable transformation of a sandy wilderness into vast, rich red-and-black fields of the Sturt desert pea.

But if the wild-flower season in Western Australia is one of Australia's better-kept secrets, her fine wines are fast becoming known throughout the country, and overseas. For many years the state's wineries were overshadowed by the excellent quality of the wines produced in the Hunter Valley in New South Wales, the Barossa Valley in South Australia and the north of Victoria. Only the white Burgundy produced in the Swan Valley, just 30 minutes' drive from Perth, received acclaim. In the past 15-20 years, however, there has been rapid growth in the number of vineyards in the state. The Margaret River winemakers, in the southwest, have produced Chardonnays and Cabernet Sauvignons to delight the most perceptive palate.

Western Australia itself is a blend of the raw and the sophisticated. Perth, one of the most attractive modern cities in the world, offers every facility and comfort a traveler might want. Yet within hours the true adventurer can escape to quite another world.

PERTH: STEEL AND GLASS WITH SOFT EDGES

Flanked by the Indian Ocean and the broad stretches of the Swan River, Perth to many eyes is Australia's most attractive city, probably its cleanest, and certainly the sunniest, with an average of eight hours of sunshine a day. In winter the average temperature is 18°C (65°F), in summer 29°C (84°F); everyday dress is generally light and casual. As the interior heats up each day in summer, it draws cool sea air from the Indian Ocean. This cooling sea breeze, usually from the southwest, is known by locals as the "Fremantle Doctor."

Perth is a city of modern steel-and-glass office towers, traffic-free shopping malls, uncluttered freeways, lakes and parks. Residential areas lie within minutes of the central city blocks, and half a dozen cars ahead of you at the traffic lights amounts to a traffic jam. Glorious, and remarkably clean ocean beaches fringe the city's western reaches, offering both exhilarating swimming and excellent sea-fishing from man-made groynes.

Although the capital has grown fast, it never seems overcrowded. The boom in construction work and the influx of big business that followed the America's Cup yachting trophy into the city in the mid-1980s led to financial journalists tagging it "Dallas Down Under." But the name doesn't quite ring true. Certainly wheeling and dealing go on in Perth, and in recent years the city has been rocked by political and financial scandals. But the place itself seems barely affected, and the delights of small-town life are still there for the taking. The people are warm, open, usually friendly, occasionally blunt; they are curious about visitors, eager to converse and happy to share. Theirs is a young city still growing into its clothes.

To capture one pleasing flavor of Perth, wander through Kings Park in spring. From this splendidly conserved bush-and-parkland you can enjoy a fine view across the Narrows Bridge and down the Swan River. Take advantage of the free city Clipper buses; take a ferry or a cruise boat on the Swan, a bus to Nedlands to sip a Swan beer or two in a beer garden, then a taxi home via riverfront Dalkeith to see how the country's moguls live... Perth's pleasures need not come expensively.

FREMANTLE AND BEYOND
In recent years the focus in Western Australia has switched somewhat away from the capital, down the road (or river) to the port of Fremantle. In 1983 businessman Alan Bond and The Royal Perth Yacht Club brought to Western Australia the America's Cup, the "Auld Mug" awarded in perhaps the greatest regatta of all, and in 1986-87 the challengers raced on the ocean off Fremantle. After months of tacking and talking, Dennis Connor and the San Diego Yacht Club regained the prized trophy for the US.

Before that, however, the port city had gone through a multimillion-dollar facelift that turned a somewhat sleepy arts-and-crafts and fishing harbor into a cosmopolitan center that truly bubbles with atmosphere. Fremantle, with new restaurants and boutiques peppering the sympathetically restored historic buildings, has emerged as Perth's recreation spot. There are old maritime streets to wander in, hundreds of craft stalls to browse over, and a place in the sun where you can watch the fishing boats jostle with the yachts. Young people flock in on summery evenings to eat pasta and drink *cappuccini* in terraced cafés... the influences are visibly, relaxingly Mediterranean.

Beyond Perth and Fremantle lies the sheer enormity of Western Australia. Visitors often find it difficult to understand just how far away those places are that seem to beckon on the map. What looks like a three-hour drive might turn out to take three days. One of the more remote and yet fascinating points on the coast is Broome, once the pearling capital of the world — 2,230 kilometers (1,394 miles) north of Perth! Sydney is 3,400 kilometers (2,125 miles) — or a 65-hour rail journey aboard the *Indian-Pacific* — away. From the north to the south of

Western Australia is roughly equivalent to the distance from Oslo in Norway to Madrid in Spain.

Simply, to those who go west in Australia, the advice is stark: plan your expedition with extreme care and expect to lament the lack of time...

Perth

ORIENTATION

Perth, the most isolated and arguably the most attractive of Australia's mainland capital cities, flanks the broad, final stretches of the Swan River, with its western suburbs licked by the surf of the Indian Ocean. The city is 19km (12 miles) inland from the seaport it embraces, Fremantle. Around the northern stretch of its riverfront are the luxurious palaces of the rich and famous. To the s, in suburbs such as Welshpool and Kwinana, its heavy industry is concentrated. To the w and n is the suburban sprawl, but also the clean ocean beaches that make this such a pleasant city in which to live. In the NE, 11km (7 miles) from the center of the city, is Perth Airport, and more suburban homes, stretching as far inland as the Darling Range.

The heart of downtown Perth is Hay St. It runs parallel to the other main business and shopping streets: Murray St. and Wellington St., and elegant St Georges Terrace, which runs from the w, following the Swan River, but becomes Adelaide Terrace as it moves E. Kings Park overlooks the city and the two main bridges, the Causeway, which is E of Barrack Street Jetty, and the Narrows, which is to the w.

PRACTICAL INFORMATION

Maps 14-15 (see pages 282-283).

☎**STD (area) code**   09.

Airport   ☎478 8888 (domestic), 478 8770 (international); Ansett ☎323 1111; Australian ☎323 8444.

Rail stations   For country services ☎326 2222; for suburban information ☎325 8511.

Car rental   Avis ☎325 7677/277 1729 (airport); Budget ☎322 1100/277 9277 (airport)/481 1004 (chauffeur drive); Hertz ☎321 7777.

Western Australian Holiday WA Centre   772 Hay St., Perth, WA, 6000 ☎322 2999, map **15**C4.

American Express Travel Service   10 William St., Perth, WA, 6000 ☎426 3777, map **15**C4.

Royal Automobile Club of Western Australia (RACWA)   228 Adelaide Terrace, Perth, WA, 6000 ☎421 4444, map **15**C5.

SEEING THE CITY

The center of Perth is easy for the walker to get around, although not quite so convenient for the unwary visiting driver. Signposts and street signs are good on the highways and underpasses around the city, but somewhat eccentric within the busy shopping area. Nevertheless, the state of the roads is generally excellent, and as long as you keep an eye out for the tricky one-way streets there should be no trouble at all. One great advantage that Perth does have over Sydney and Melbourne is that parking is cheap and never far away, and traffic snarls are a rarity.

Perth's public transportation system is clean, cheap and efficient and can put most of the sights of interest within easy reach.

CLIPPER BUSES

Among the most delightful surprises are the free city **Clipper buses** for shoppers. They circle the center of Perth and run every 10 minutes, on Monday to Friday from 7am to 5.30pm, on Saturday from 9 to 11.30am, from specially marked bus stops. **Red**, **Blue** and **Green** Clipper buses operate on other city routes and are also free.

FERRIES

Transperth Ferries operates ferry boats daily, from 6.45am-7.15pm, from Barrack St. jetty to Mends St., South Perth (convenient for those visiting the Zoo).

BUSES

The Perth central business district and suburban areas are well-connected by **Transperth** buses. The buses, which are comfortable and punctual, have designated departure points in the city, but elsewhere can be hailed at signposted stops. The passenger pays the bus driver; tickets are valid for two hours and can also be used on Transperth trains and ferries.

For further information on Transperth timetables or routes for Clippers, ferries or buses ☎221 1211 from 6am-9pm, or visit the **Transperth Information Office** *(Perth Central Bus Station, Wellington St., map 15 B4).*

TRAINS

Suburban trains operate from Perth to Fremantle, Midland and Armadale from 5.40am-11.30pm on weekdays, with reduced services at the weekends and on public holidays. Interstate and Kalgoorlie trains leave from Perth Railway Terminal, East Perth *(☎ 326 2222);* suburban and Bunbury trains from City station, Wellington St., Perth.

TAXIS

Meter-operated taxis are to be found at hotels, transportation terminals and taxi stands around the city. Or you can simply hail them in the street. Vacant cabs have an illuminated sign on the roof. Where multiple renting occurs (and the first customer makes the decision on this) only 75 percent of the metered fare is payable. The main taxi companies include **Black & White Taxis** *(☎ 328 8288),* **Swan Taxis** *(☎ 322 0111)* and **Green & Gold Taxis** *(☎ 328 3455).*

BUS TOURS

Perth offers a huge selection of half-day and full-day bus tours covering the sights in and around the city. Most of them depart from the Hay Street Coach Rank on the corner of William St. For details, contact the **WA Tourist Centre** *(772 Hay St. ☎ 322 2999, map 15 C4).*

RIVER CRUISES

Swan River sightseeing cruises are available from Barrack Street Jetty. There are several operators:

Boat Torque ☎325 6033
Captain Cook ☎325 3341/325 2041
Fremantle Harbour Tours ☎430 4037
PS Decoy ☎325 5269
Swan River Cruises ☎325 3793
Transperth Ferries ☎425 2525
WA Wine Cruises ☎325 6033
ON FOOT

Escorted walking tours of Perth and Fremantle are available, including personalized excursions for small groups or individuals. Details are obtainable from the **WA Tourist Centre** *(772 Hay St.* ☎*322 2999, or at Fremantle Town Hall Shop, Town Hall Ctr, St John's Sq., Fremantle* ☎ *335 2952).*

FOR DISABLED PEOPLE

Many of Perth's hotels, restaurants, movie theaters and shops have facilities for disabled people, although not all of them cater to severely handicapped people or to those in wheelchairs. The Australian Tourist Commission recommends that advance notice be given wherever possible to ensure the best possible assistance. A useful series of pamphlets, entitled *Accent On Access,* can be obtained from the **Department for Youth, Sport and Recreation** *(Perry Lakes Stadium, Wembley* ☎ *387 9700)* or from **ACROD Access And Mobility Committee** *(* ☎ *222 2961).*

Sights and places of interest

ALAN GREEN CONSERVATORY

Corner of William St. and The Esplanade. Map **15***C4* ▣ *Open Mon-Sat 10am-5pm; Sun, hols 2-6pm.*

For those inspired by Western Australia's wild flowers, this is something a little different. Here, a short walk from the main shopping arcades, is a rare and remarkable collection of exotic plants. These tropical flowers have been raised within the controlled environment of this small pyramid-shaped greenhouse on the lawns of The Esplanade.

ART GALLERY OF WESTERN AUSTRALIA ★

James St. ☎*328 7233. Map* **15***B4* ▣ Ġ 🖂 *(restricted to certain exhibits: ask at inquiries desk)* ✗ *Open 10am-5pm (including most hols); Anzac Day 1-5pm. Closed Christmas Day, Good Friday.*

The somewhat austere exterior of the building belies what is held within. The gallery was opened only in 1979, since when it has acquired a broad range of significant international and Australian works. In recent years there has been a renewed interest in early Australian art throughout the country, and Western Australia is fortunate to have particularly fine paintings by Frederick McCubbin, Tom Roberts and Arthur Streeton. Other Australians — Nolan, Boyd, Lindsay, Dobell, Drysdale and Blackman — are also well represented.

The gallery is proud of its collection of European sculpture, which includes works by Henry Moore, Rodin, Greco, Renoir and Hepworth. The Gallery's Aboriginal carvings and paintings, and its unique collection of works from Southeast Asia and the Indian Ocean, should not be missed.

BARRACKS ARCHWAY

*St Georges Terrace. Map **14C3** ◁€*

An odd architectural curiosity, this — a strange but fascinating brick monument, in front of PARLIAMENT HOUSE, left as a memorial to the early colonists of the state. The Archway was all that was retained when the headquarters of soldier-settlers of the enrolled Pensioner Forces was demolished in 1966. The Tudor-style edifice was built in the 1860s in Flemish bond brickwork to the design of Richard Roach Jewell, the Colonial Superintendent of Works.

GOVERNMENT HOUSE

*St Georges Terrace ☎ 325 3222. Map **15C4**. Gardens open several days each year: telephone for dates and times.*

This, the official residence of the Governor of Western Australia, was built between 1859-64 in the romantic Tudor-Gothic style of architecture that was much favored by nostalgic early settlers in the mid-19thC. The gardens may have occasioned further nostalgia in English occupants of the house, for they offer a unique Australian example of informal landscape design from the Old Country. In 1979 the **Western Australian Native Garden** was added as a permanent memorial to the state's 150th anniversary.

Government House, which was built with convict labor, caused a financial scandal, having cost the equivalent of A$30,000, double the original estimate. Today it is used to entertain members of the Royal Family and for state occasions. Both House and gardens have been classified by the National Trust of Australia.

GOVERNOR KENNEDY'S FOUNTAIN

*Mounts Bay Rd. Map **14C2**.*

Finding suitable fresh water was always a major problem for the early colonists. This small stone structure at the base of Mt. Eliza was built in 1861 to enclose a permanent spring in the park. The fountain provided Perth with its first public water supply.

KINGS PARK ★

*Kings Park Rd., West Perth ☎ 321 4801. Map **14C2** ▣ ♿ 𝕏 (free guided bush tours Apr-Oct) ▣ ✦ ➤ ◁€ Bicycles can be rented.*

Perth can thank its pioneers for their foresight in establishing this magnificent piece of land, so close to the city, as a recreation area. An energetic 20-minute walk up the hill from St Georges Terrace takes you to the park, and to the most spectacular views of both the city and the Swan River.

Today it encompasses 404ha (998 acres), much of which remains largely bushland. Locals tend to outdo one another on what wild crea-

Key to map symbols is located in HOW TO USE THIS BOOK

tures can be found here (raise an eyebrow if they start talking about bunyips), but you are quite likely to see skinks, lizards and a variety of birdlife... if not a few fellow trekkers.

Not all of the park has been left "native." There are broad expanses of lawn, avenues of trees, 12ha (30 acres) of botanic gardens, carefully cultivated flowerbeds and drifts of wild flowers. **Kings Park Restaurant** caters to diners, and there is a refreshment kiosk for those who want to have a picnic on the park's grassy slopes. A **lookout tower** provides panoramic views of Perth and the suburbs; but photographers seem to take many of their best shots near the park's **war memorial**, looking across the yacht-speckled Swan toward the mountains of the distant Darling Range.

LONDON COURT
Between Hay Street Mall and St Georges Terrace. Map 15C4 ♣

A kitschy shopping arcade whose decorative mock-Tudor facade never fails to fascinate photographers. London Court, best-known of Perth's many arcades, was built in 1937 by Claude de Bernales, an entrepreneur who made his fortune mining gold around Kalgoorlie. Its dubious attractions include statues of Sir Walter Raleigh and Dick Whittington and, at the Hay St. end of the Court, medieval knights who joust as the clock strikes the quarter-hour. At the terrace entrance St George and the Dragon perform similar battles with Time. The shops themselves, trapped in narrow and intricately carved woodwork, sell jewelry, T-shirts, souvenirs and refreshments.

MUSEUM OF CHILDHOOD ★
160 Hamersley Rd., Subiaco ☎*381 1103* 📧 ⑆ 🚹 ♣ 🚌 *Open Mon-Fri 10am-3pm; Sun 2-5pm. Closed Sat.*

This charming museum was created for children, but with adults in mind. It holds the treasure of many childhoods, and on display are wax and wooden dolls of the 19thC, clockwork toys from before World War I, and nursery furniture from the Victorian era. Director Brian Shepherd recommends a guided tour, but says that for all visitors "the emphasis is on hospitality."

Among the museum's exhibits are a large collection of traditional Japanese toys, Indian toys, and 150 items from the toy box of a local archbishop's children. Most prized, however, is the original manuscript for a child's alphabet, drawn up by William Makepeace Thackeray in 1833.

OCEAN BEACHES
The Perth metropolitan area is blessed with no fewer than 19 sandy ocean beaches, spreading from South Fremantle to Mullaloo in the northern suburbs. **Cottesloe**, **City Beach**, **Scarborough** and **Trigg Island** are among the most popular and, remarkably, the cleanest. All are close to the city and are patrolled by surf life-saving clubs. The beaches are generally safe for all swimmers, although there is often a small surf in which the unwary can be dumped. For surfers, Scarbo-

rough and Trigg hold the best waves. **Swanbourne**, between Cottesloe and City Beach, is for those who prefer swimming *au naturel*.
Don't forget the suntan lotion!

OLD GAOL AND COURTHOUSE
Francis St. ☎328 4411. Map 15B4 ▣ *Open Mon-Fri 10.30am-5pm; Sat-Sun
1-5pm. Closed Christmas Day, Good Friday.*
Behind the WESTERN AUSTRALIAN MUSEUM is a Georgian-style stone building, built in 1856, that served as Perth's original prison. The architect
was R. R. Jewell and the jail and courthouse, a fine example of early
colonial architecture, were constructed with convict labor. In April
1888 the last prisoner was removed from the Perth prison and put in
nearby Fremantle Gaol; in November that year the gallows were also
moved to Fremantle. It has been extensively restored, and the old cells
contain early dental and pharmacy equipment and intriguing reminders
of Perth's pioneering days.

OLD MILL
Narrows Bridge, South Perth. Map 14D3 ▣ ✿ *Open Sun, Mon, Wed, Thurs
1-5pm; Sat 1-4pm. Closed Tues, Fri.*
A modest "museum" in a spectacular location on the Swan River. This
flour mill was built in 1835 and, now restored, displays many relics
from the early days of settlement.

OLD PERTH BOYS' SCHOOL
139 St Georges Terrace ☎321 2754. Map 14C3 ▣ *Open Mon-Fri 9am-5pm.*
Convicts ferried the limestone up the Swan River from Rocky Bay, near
Fremantle, for the building of this quaint early school building. Pupils
from the Government school, founded in 1847, were able to move into
it from an old courthouse in 1854.

The school was designed by William Sandford, Colonial Secretary and
Director of Education, in a style that, with its long, narrow windows and
steeply pitched gables, was obviously influenced by the Gothic ecclesias-
tical architecture of the 19thC. Today it serves as the headquarters in
Western Australia of the National Trust.

PARLIAMENT HOUSE
Harvest Terrace, West Perth ☎222 7222. Map 14B3 ▣ ♿ ✿*in parts (ask
first)* ✗ ☞ *Open 8.30am-5pm. Closed Sat, Sun.*
Look w and past the BARRACKS ARCHWAY at the end of St Georges Terrace
and you will see the predictably impressive architecture of Parliament
House. Here the state's politicians gather to deal with Western Australian (rather than federal) legislation.

For individuals or small groups, 10-15-minute tours are available
throughout the week; for larger, organized groups there are one-hour
conducted tours of both Houses of Parliament. But tours depend on
Parliamentary sessions, so be sure to telephone and check for times.
Historical detail and explanations of parliamentary procedure are provided on the tours.

PERTH CONCERT HALL
St Georges Terrace ☎ *325 9944. Map 15C4* & ➡ *Open Mon-Sat for viewing when not in use.*

The Perth Concert Hall was opened on Australia Day (January 26) 1973, mainly as a performance venue for symphony concerts. However, successful performances of opera, chamber music and folk music have also been staged here, and art exhibitions are held in the rooms and corridors surrounding the main theater. The hall, whose somewhat austere exterior is transformed for concerts by artfully placed lights, also contains a restaurant, a tavern bar and cocktail lounge.

ROLLY TASKER'S AMERICA'S CUP MODEL ROOM
43 Swan St., North Fremantle ☎ *430 4323* 📷 *Open daily 9.30am-5pm.*

Rolly Tasker, one of Western Australia's most successful yachtsmen, toured the world to bring together a superb collection honoring the great competitors of America's Cup racing. After Alan Bond's brief but glorious triumph, it seemed that everyone in Perth was an expert on the event. Tasker's extensive private collection of America's Cup yachts, models and drawings are more than sufficient to keep deskbound yachtsmen enthralled.

ROUND HOUSE
Arthur Head (between Cliff St. and Fleet St.), Fremantle ☎ *335 9283* 📷 *Open daily 10am-5pm.*

The Round House, the oldest surviving public building in Western Australia, is in fact not round, but a 12-sided establishment that stands imposingly like a fortress over Fremantle Harbour. It was designed by the colony's first civil engineer, Henry Reveley, as a jail for minor offenders, and was completed in January 1831. Today its history is on display in paintings, photographs and documents, and visitors can see the cells where convicts were chained during the night.

ST GEORGES CATHEDRAL
St Georges Terrace. Map 15C4 &

The present Anglican cathedral was designed by Edmund Blacket and built on the site of an earlier cathedral. (In the 1840s this had replaced a wood-and-rushes church hurriedly erected by the first settlers in time to hold Christmas services in 1829.) The foundation stone was laid in 1880 and the church itself was consecrated in 1888, 5 years after the death of the architect. Notable interior features include an impressive wrought-iron **chancel screen**, erected as a memorial to the city's first two bishops.

STIRLING AND SUPREME COURT GARDENS
Corner of St Georges Terrace and Barrack St. Map 15C4 📷 ✿

These attractively laid-out gardens are a favorite lunchtime spot for Perth's city workers, who picnic beneath the huge Norfolk Island pines. The land on which they stand, close to where the city was founded, was set aside in 1829 for botanic gardens. In 1845 the area was officially proclaimed public gardens; in 1899 they were officially opened.

UNIVERSITY OF WESTERN AUSTRALIA
Crawley, 5km (3 miles) w ➡ ◄€
An international competition in the 1920s produced the distinctive Mediterranean style of architecture seen in the University of Western Australia. Few man-made structures merge so charmingly with the landscape as do these pleasing sandstone and orange-tiled buildings in the riverside suburb of Crawley.

Visitors may wander through much of the grounds, which stretch down toward the Swan River. During the Festival of Perth, the university's theaters (which include a small but charming stage in sunken gardens) are often open for public performances. Nearby is the headquarters of the **Royal Perth Yacht Club**, until early 1987 the home of the America's Cup.

WESTERN AUSTRALIAN MARITIME MUSEUM ★
Cliff St., Fremantle ☎ *335 8211* 🖭 *(but small donation requested)* ♿ ✗ ▣ ♣
Open Mon-Thurs 10.30am-5pm; Fri-Sun 1-5pm. Closed Christmas Day, Good Friday.
The maritime museum, an imposing 2-story building in the Georgian style, is among the finest of Fremantle's remarkably handsome restored buildings. But it also houses a wealth of Australian naval history, most notably a reconstruction of the stern of the 1629 Dutch wreck *Batavia.* An archway from the *Batavia,* as well as relics and pictorial displays from other ships wrecked off the coastline of Western Australia, is also on display. Suitably nautical gifts and souvenirs are available from the museum's shop.

WESTERN AUSTRALIAN MUSEUM
Francis St. ☎ *328 4411. Map* **15B4** 🖭 ♿ ▣ ♣ *Open Mon-Fri 10.30am-5pm; Sat-Sun, Anzac Day, Boxing Day 1-5pm; other hols 9.30-5pm.*
The museum includes a spectacular marine gallery that contains among its exhibits the 25m (82-foot) skeleton of a **blue whale**. Other attractions include Aboriginal artifacts and paintings; a very popular collection of veteran and vintage cars and motorcycles; and the 11-metric-tonne (12-US-ton) **Mundrabilla meteorite**.

ZOOLOGICAL GARDENS
Labouchere Rd., South Perth ☎ *367 7988. Map* **14F3** 🖾 ♿ ▣ ♣ ➡ *Open 10am-5pm. Ferry from Barrack St. to South Perth, or bus from city.*
In a relaxing park-like setting across the river, the zoo has an extensive collection of exotic and native animals and birds. Always popular are the koalas, and always fascinating are the **numbats**, the official fauna emblem of Western Australia.

Where to stay

Perth and Fremantle have an abundant supply of good, clean hotels, motels and other accommodations. Before the America's Cup returned to American hands, an enormous amount of building took place in anticipation of a boom in tourism.

For visitors seeking budget-style accommodations (from A$75 and below), the **WA Tourist Centre** *(772 Hay St., Perth, map 15 C4* ☎ *322 2999, and St John's Sq., Fremantle* ☎ *335 2952)* have useful accommodations listings. They also have details for those who would like to stay in a private home or on a working farm. The overseas offices of the **Australian Tourist Commission** can supply similar accommodations listings on request.

BURSWOOD RESORT HOTEL

Great Eastern Highway, Victoria Park, Perth, WA, 6100 ☎ *362 7777* 🏨 ☎ *197224* ☒ *470 2553* ▥ *410 rms* ◼ ⬛ AE ◯ ◉ ▦ & ⚹ ❦ ❧ ⚲ ♈ ☗ ✗ ⛷

Location: 3km E of central Perth. One of the latest additions to Perth's crowded hotel scene. The Burswood is part of the huge **Burswood Resort** — reputed to be the biggest casino-resort complex in the southern hemisphere. Bubble elevators service the 10 floors of luxuriously appointed rooms, and large picture windows provide superb views of skiing and boating activities on the Swan River. The resort boasts an impressive range of sports and exercise facilities: an 18-hole golf course, four tennis courts and a fully-equipped gymnasium.

CHATEAU COMMODORE

Corner of Victoria Ave. and Hay St., Perth, WA, 6000 ☎ *325 0461* 🏨 ☎ *92872* ☒ *221 2448. Map 15 C5* ▥ *133 rms* ◼ ⬛ AE ◯ ◉ ▦ ⚹ ◼ ♈ ⛷

Location: Only a short walk from main shopping center. A smartly efficient hotel with clean, spacious rooms, but be sure to ask for one with a reasonable view. The hotel's main dining room, **Isabella's**, has recently been upgraded, and **Stamina**, an Indonesian restaurant, offers alternative dining with a karaoke bar.

FREMANTLE ESPLANADE ❀

Marine Terrace, Fremantle, WA, 6160 ☎ *430 4000* 🏨 ☎ *96977* ☒ *430 4539* ▥ *141 rms* ◼ ⬛ AE ◯ ◉ ▦ & ⚹ ❦ ◼ ♈ ❧ ♈ ☗ ⛷

Location: Splendidly located near Fremantle's fishing harbor. This elegantly restored hotel, where the ambience is spacious, cool and peaceful, was a favorite of the well-heeled international yachties who attended the America's Cup races off Fremantle. Diners can choose from fine smørgasbørd meals in the **Atrium** on Friday, Saturday and Sunday and bistro-type meals in the **Esplanade Fish Café.** There is also a popular **Sidewalk Café** that takes advantage of Fremantle's pleasant climate.

HYATT REGENCY

99 Adelaide Terrace, Perth, WA, 6000 ☎ *225 1234* 🏨 ☎ *95823* ☒ *325 8899. Map 15 D6* ▥ *369 rms* ◼ ⬛ AE ◯ ◉ ▦ & ⚹ ◼ ♈ ❧ ❦ ❀ ⛷

Location: In the less crowded, eastern stretch of fashionable Adelaide Terrace. A luxurious and large, if slightly overpowering, hotel with friendly management and staff, and spacious rooms. The easy shopping clustered around the atrium compensates for the uncanny feeling of being a figure in an architect's drawing. But the Hyatt Regency has 24-hour room service and some useful extras (among them tennis and squash courts, and a fitness center for business executives). It has first-class restaurants: **Gershwin's** offers classic European dining; **Rama Thai** provides the finest in Royal Thai cuisine.

MISS MAUD ♻

97 Murray St., Perth, WA, 6000 ☎ *325 3900* Ⓓ ⓕ*93176* Ⓕ*221 3225. Map 15C4* Ⓘ*52 rms* ⚐ ⚞ Ⓐ Ⓕ Ⓒ ⓕ 🔲
Location: Usefully situated close to the busy heart of city shopping. Miss Maud Edmonston, the Swedish proprietor of this clean, friendly and unpretentious hotel, is famous for her coffee and pastry shops. The restaurant serves a particularly hearty smørgasbørd.

NEW ESPLANADE

18 The Esplanade, Perth, WA, 6000 ☎ *325 2000* Ⓓ ⓕ*93327* Ⓕ*221 2190. Map 15C4* Ⓘ *74 rms* ⚐ ⚞ Ⓐ Ⓕ Ⓒ Ⓤ 🔲 Ⓨ ☂ Ⓤ ⛵ ⛱
Location: Overlooking The Esplanade, with fine views across the Swan and Kings Park. This is a bright, modern and sensible hotel, superbly located. Its **Grand Palace** Chinese restaurant offers a restful dining spot overlooking the river.

OBSERVATION CITY RESORT HOTEL

The Esplanade, Scarborough, WA, 6019 ☎ *245 1000* Ⓓ ⓕ*95782* Ⓕ*245 1345* Ⓘ *336 rms* ⚐ ⚞ Ⓐ Ⓕ Ⓒ Ⓤ ⛱ 🔲 Ⓨ ☂ ♨ Ⓤ ⛵ ⛱
Location: On one of Perth's favored Indian Ocean beaches. An extraordinarily sited luxury hotel. Observation City boasts that this is "where golden sands meet silver service." Among its five restaurants, the **Ocean Room** specializes in fine dining with fresh local produce. Relaxed and friendly, the hotel offers, among other things, a convenient recreation room for families on vacation. There is late-night entertainment at **Nero's** and **Club Atlantis**. A courtesy coach links the hotel to Perth.

ORCHARD ♻

Corner of Milligan St. and Wellington St., Perth, WA, 6000 ☎ *327 7000* Ⓓ ⓕ*95050* Ⓕ*327 7017. Map 14B3* Ⓘ*279 rms* ⚐ ⚞ Ⓐ Ⓕ Ⓒ Ⓤ ⛱ 🔲 Ⓨ ☂ Ⓤ ⛵ ⛱
Location: Near Perth Entertainment Centre. The Huang family, who run this clean, modern and friendly hotel, have a similar establishment in San Francisco. Two restaurants are attached to the hotel, and there are a total of seven — Chinese, Japanese, Italian, seafood etc. — within the complex of shops and offices in which it stands. The **Brasserie** offers 24-hour service.

PERTH AMBASSADOR

196 Adelaide Terrace, Perth, WA, 6000 ☎ *325 1455* Ⓓ ⓕ*95799* Ⓕ*325 6317. Map 15C5* Ⓘ *171 rms* ⚐ ⚞ Ⓐ Ⓕ Ⓒ Ⓤ ⓕ 🔲 Ⓨ ☂ Ⓤ ⛵ ⛱
Location: Just an invigorating walk away from city center. A stylish hotel, decorated in soft, pastel colors. Service is congenial. Its restaurant, **Spices Delight**, features both European and Asian cuisine and competes with the finest in Perth.

THE PERTH INTERNATIONAL HOTEL

10 Irwin St., Perth, WA, 6000 ☎ *325 0481* Ⓓ ⓕ*92999* Ⓕ*323 2902. Map 15C4* Ⓘ *227 rms* ⚐ ⚞ Ⓐ Ⓕ Ⓒ Ⓤ ⛱ ♨ 🔲 Ⓨ ☂ Ⓤ ⛵ ⛱
Location: Conveniently central. This flourishing top-of-the-range luxury hotel, which has been modernized with great success since it changed its name from the Gateway several years ago, is just a few minutes' walk from the theaters, restaurants and art gallery. Its acclaimed restaurant is the **Number 10 Studio**. Young night owls can while away the small hours at **Brannigans** night club. Valet parking is provided for guests.

PERTH PARKROYAL

54 Terrace Rd., Perth, WA, 6000 ☎ *325 3811* Ⓓ ⓕ*92316* Ⓕ*221 1564. Map 15D5* Ⓘ*99 rms* ⚐ ⚞ Ⓐ Ⓕ Ⓒ Ⓤ ♨ 🔲 Ⓨ Ⓤ ⛵ ⛱
Location: Overlooking Langley Park. Every room in this intimate, immaculately clean hotel offers a fine view across the Swan. Its restaurant, **The Royal Palm**, presents monthly food promotions (New Orleans/Cajun, Scandinavian etc.).

PERTH PARMELIA HILTON ♻

Mill St., Perth, WA, 6000 ☎ *322 3622* Ⓓ ⓕ*92365* Ⓕ*481 0857. Map 14C3* Ⓘ

289

275 rms ⊷ ⇌ AE ⊙ ⊙ VISA ⅋ ⇌ ⊟ ☿
⌗ ⌲ ⛺

Location: In the heart of Perth's central business district. A first-class hotel offering the familiarity of a Hilton plus unexpected warmth in service from general manager George van Holst's efficient staff. The Parmelia has been a favorite of visiting interstate executives since the early 1970s. In 1979 it was taken over by Hilton International and has managed to hold its own against a barrage of newcomers. Rooms are spacious and well-equipped (at least two phones to a room, hair dryer, cocktail bar etc.) and relaxingly furnished. The hotel itself is decorated with a valuable collection of European *objets d'art.* The **Garden Restaurant**, under executive chef André Billon-Tirard, has an enviable reputation for its seafood.

QUALITY PRINCES

334 Murray St., Perth, WA, 6000 ☎*322 2844* IDD Fx *95000* Fx *321 6314. Map* **14**B3 ▥ *167 rms* ⊷ ⇌ AE ⊙ ⊙ VISA ⅋ ⊟ ☿ ⛺

Location: In a very competitive, busy part of the city center. A pleasant and efficient hotel. Its **Society** restaurant has won the coveted local Gold Plate Award for its European-style menu.

REGATTA

560 Hay St., Perth, WA, 6000 ☎*325 5155* Fx *325 4786. Map* **15**C4 ▥ *61 rms*

⊷ ⇌ AE ⊙ ⊙ VISA ☿

Location: Opposite Town Hall. An old-fashioned, well-worn Victorian-style establishment, and probably the most conveniently placed of Perth's budget-priced hotels. Bedrooms are compact, although they have high ceilings, fashionable before the days of air conditioning. As well as several bars, the Regatta has a dining room offering inexpensive, hearty dinners.

SHERATON PERTH

207 Adelaide Terrace, Perth, WA, 6000 ☎*325 0501* IDD Fx *92938* Fx *325 4032. Map* **15**C5 ▥ *396 rms* ⊷ ⇌ AE ⊙ ⊙ VISA ⅋ ⇌ ⊟ ☿ ⌗ ⌲ ⛺

Location: Overlooking the Swan River. Decorated in cool, restfully good taste, this sensitively run, well-managed hotel incorporates all the facilities travelers require.

TRANSIT INN

37 Pier St., Perth, WA, 6000 ☎*325 7655* IDD Fx *92739* Fx *325 7655. Map* **15**C4 ▥ *121 rms* ⊷ ⇌ AE ⊙ ⊙ VISA ⇌ ⊟ ☿ ⌲ ⛺

Location: Near to central business district. This pleasant hotel is another favorite among visiting executives. Its main restaurant, **Ruby's**, has a romantic, old-world atmosphere and is remarkably popular. For the energetic, it boasts Perth's largest ground-level hotel pool.

Dining out

There is no doubt that, for its size, Perth enjoys an extraordinary number of restaurants. There are more than 600 in and around the city, ranging from the woeful to the wonderful.

The food available to them is generally first-rate — with the **seafood** excelling. Dhufish, kingfish, crayfish (rock lobster), prawns and crabs are fresh and delicious. Well worth trying, if and when available, is the local delicacy, **marron**, a freshwater crayfish that is similar, albeit tastier, to the yabbies found in the eastern states. Fresh fruit and vegetables are plentiful and tasty.

Western Australia produces an excellent range of red and white table wines, with the **Margaret River** estates increasing in stature by the year. The state's local **beer**, Swan Lager, is crisp and invigorating and, arguably, rivals the Melbourne-based Fosters Lager as the country's tastiest brew.

Perth and Fremantle have good restaurants to cater to all tastes — French, Indonesian, Swiss, Spanish, Portuguese, Jewish, Yugoslav, Chinese, Thai, Japanese, Indian, Vietnamese, Greek, Dutch and Lebanese among them. The **Italian** restaurants, many of them situated in and around the Northbridge area of Perth (just across the rail line from the city center), are particularly fine.

Much of the improvement in Perth's dining-out scene has occurred since the early 1970s. Because there is such a demand for restaurant staff, the service in some restaurants is not always as smooth as that which you might find in, say, Sydney or Melbourne. But the situation is fast-changing. And for friendly service, the Western Australian waiters are second to none.

EMPEROR'S COURT

66 Lake St. ☎*328 8860. Map 15B4* ▥ ▢ ⅋ 🆎 🔾 🔾 ▨ *Closed Sat and Sun lunch.*

There are many above-average Chinese restaurants in Perth; quite possibly this is the best of the bunch. The Emperor's Court's menu offers a choice of Cantonese and hotter, spicier Szechuan dishes.

FAST EDDY'S

Corner of Murray St. and Milligan St. ☎*321 2552. Map 14B3* ▥ ▢ *BYO license.*

This burger restaurant is open 24 hours a day, seven days a week. As well as a full range of filling hamburgers, the menu at Fast Eddy's includes breakfasts, steaks, sandwiches and many other light meals. Fast Eddy's also serves ice-cream sundaes that are guaranteed to silence the noisier, younger members of the family.

HARBOUR LIGHTS (LOMBARDO'S)

Boat Harbour, Mews Rd., Fremantle ☎*430 4344* ▥ ▢ ➦ ⅋ ⫷ 🆎 🔾 🔾 ▨ *Last orders 10pm.*

An excellent place to watch the world sail by, this elegant seafood restaurant overlooks Fremantle's Mediterranean-style fishing harbor. Enjoy the crayfish (rock lobster), king prawns, dhufish and snapper and many, many other fruits of the sea.

JESSICA'S

Hyatt Regency Centre, 99 Adelaide Terrace, Perth, WA 6000 ☎*325 2511* ▥ ▢ ⅋ ➦ 🆎 🔾 🔾 ▨ *Open every day lunch and dinner.*

A splendidly light and airy restaurant that is particularly refreshing on one of Perth's dry summer days. The cheery green and white decor is an eye-catcher and there are no dark corners in this first-class establishment. The fish is a specialty, well worth considering. Jessica's also has a carefully stocked wine cellar.

MATILDA BAY ✿

3 Hackett Drive, Crawley ☎ *386 5425*
▥ ☐ ≞ ⵗ ➡ ⪦ 🖭 ⊕ ⊙ 🖾 *Last orders 10pm. Closed Sat lunch; Sun.*
The Matilda Bay is one of Perth's long-established favorites, situated only 10 minutes from the city and close to the University of Western Australia and the Royal Perth Yacht Club. It is a cool, airy, and elegant restaurant, serving excellent French-Californian cuisine. The views across the Swan River toward the city are spectacular. The service is first-class.

THE MEDITERRANEAN GARDEN RESTAURANT

414 Rokeby Rd., Subiaco ☎ *381 2188*
▥ ☐ ≞ ⵗ ⪩ 🖭 ⊕ ⊙ 🖾 *Lunch Mon-Fri; dinner Mon-Sat.*
Not surprisingly, this favorite of Perth's business set boasts a "Mediterranean" menu of seafood, veal and pasta. Diners enjoy comfortable seating around a circular open fireplace in winter. In spring and summer the terra cotta-tiled courtyard offers a more casual setting. The restaurant, a favorite of Alan Bond's flamboyant wife, Eileen, features the works of local artists.

ORD STREET CAFÉ ✿

27 Ord St., West Perth ☎ *321 6021. Map 14B2* ▥ ☐ ≞ ⪦ 🖭 ⊕ ⊙ 🖾 *Last orders 10.30pm. Closed Sun.*
With an ever-changing menu, this popular, youthful restaurant has become one of the busiest dining spots in the city. *The Bulletin* magazine presented it with a "best food in Perth" award. The pleasant garden is a bonus.

OYSTER BEDS

26 Riverside Rd., East Fremantle ☎ *339 1611* ▥ ☐ ≞ ⵗ ⪦ 🖭 ⊕ ⊙ 🖾 *Last orders 9.30pm. Open every day lunch and dinner.*

This river restaurant-on-stilts has for at least 15 years enjoyed the reputation of serving the area's finest seafood. The service may sometimes be a little sluggish, but the food is well worth waiting for, and the dhufish and crayfish are invariably excellent. On a balmy summer's evening you can dine outdoors and watch the tourist and fishing boats chug by.

PERUGINO

77 Outram St., West Perth ☎ *321 5420* ▥ ☐ ⵗ ≞ 🖭 ⊕ ⊙ 🖾 *Lunch Mon-Fri, dinner Mon-Sat.*
There are an extraordinary number of fine Italian restaurants in Perth and it is difficult to find a bad one. But this warm, cheerful establishment stands out with its devotion to the delightful traditional fare of Italy. It has a wine cellar that contains familiar and some rare European wines.

THE PLUM

47 Lake St., Northbridge ☎ *328 5920. Map 15B4* ▥ ☐ 🖭 ⊕ ⊙ 🖾 *Last orders 11.15pm. Lunch Mon-Fri; dinner Mon-Sat. BYO license.*
A Victorian-style restaurant whose four main burgundy-colored rooms are decorated with period art and memorabilia. Log fires (in winter), lace tablecloths and velvet drapes, soft lighting and music all add to the atmosphere. There's a choice of French and "international" dishes, with a set price for lunch.

PRIDEAU'S

Corner of Rockton St. and Stirling Highway, Claremont ☎ *386 8933* ▥ ☐ ≞ ⵗ 🖭 ⊕ ⊙ 🖾 *Last orders 10pm. Dinner Tues-Sat from 6pm.*
This is a stylish restaurant with an elegant, intimate ambience. The French menu from Parisian chef Frederic Poguet, formerly of the George-V hotel, includes a delightful variation of cray *thermidor.* Another attraction is the impressive cellar.

Entertainment

The city of Perth seems to go to sleep early, concentrating its entertainment and relaxation around the home. In the past the nightlife was indeed sparse. But the last decade has seen changes — more big international shows, more theater, more clubs — and, for the visitor who looks around, the city's nightlife is varied and offers something to suit most tastes.

For those who enjoy dancing until just before dawn, there are many discos in the city and the suburbs. Among the better known are **Margeaux**, part of the PERTH PARMELIA HILTON (see WHERE TO STAY) and **Clouds** *(207 Adelaide Terrace, map 15 C5 ☎325 0501),* part of the SHERATON PERTH complex (see WHERE TO STAY). For younger travelers, favorites include **Gobbles** *(613 Wellington St., map 14 B3 ☎322 1221)* and **Pinocchio's** *(393 Murray St., map 14 B3 ☎321 2521).*

A particularly lively area for both restaurants and nightclubs is **Northbridge**, a short walk from the city center, down William St. and across the railway bridge. Among the most popular nightclubs here are **The Berlin Club** *(89 Milligan St., map 14 C3 ☎328 9870)* and **The Ozone Bar** *(on the corner of James St. and Lake St., map 15 B4)*

The pubs and wine bars are always changing, but worth checking are the **Brewery Alehouse** *(149 Stirling Highway, Nedlands),* which sells beer from all across the world, as well as its own private brew, and the English pub-styled **Duck Inn** *(on the corner of Rowland St. and Barker St., Subiaco).*

BURSWOOD CASINO

Great Eastern Highway, Rivervale ☎362 7777 ✆ ⬛ Open 24hrs.

The Burswood Casino, on the other side of the causeway that leads into Perth, is the third largest in the world, with 140 gaming tables and facilities spread across an area of 6,975 sq.m. (75,000 square feet). Blackjack, baccarat, mini baccarat, roulette, big and small craps, keno, the Australian game two-up — all are played at Burswood. There are also restaurants (🆑 🔘 🔘 🆅), cocktail bars and a lounge-cabaret area. The casino is part of the **Burswood Resort**, which includes a 410-room hotel (see WHERE TO STAY), an entertainment and convention facility, a huge exhibition/sports complex, and an 18-hole golf course.

THE ENTERTAINMENT CENTRE

Wellington St. ☎information 322 4766, reservations 322 4766. Map 14 B3 ✆ 🆑 🔘 🔘 🆅

This is Perth's prime center for large-scale extravaganzas featuring the world's most popular entertainers. It seats 8,000, thus ensuring that the big stars who once bypassed the West Coast now include it in their schedules. Big attractions staged here have included the Miss Universe Contest, figure skaters Torvill and Dean, Disney on Parade, a major tennis tournament and the Bolshoi Ballet.

GLOUCESTER PARK

Nelson Crescent, East Perth ☎325 3555. Off map 15 C6 ✆ ⬛ Open for race meetings (see local newspapers for details), generally Fri nights.

The "Night Trots" offers a pleasant way to have a flutter or two on Western Australia's trotting or pacing horses. Under the lights on a balmy evening, Gloucester Park is a colorful delight. There are bars, on-course betting, and restaurants that range from fast-food to elegant.

HIS MAJESTY'S THEATRE

Corner of Hay St. and King St.
☎*information 322 2929, reservations 321 6288. Map 14C3* ☙ ⊒ 🆎 💷 💳 📟

"The Maj" offers theatergoers a glimpse into the past. This splendidly restored Edwardian theater retains the decor of the 1920s with the innovations of the 1990s. It is now the home of the **Western Australia Opera Company** and the **Western Australia Ballet Company**, but is also used for Gilbert and Sullivan productions and plays. Both Anna Pavlova and Dame Nellie Melba trod the boards here. Should you wish to follow in their footsteps, guided tours are available *(10am-4pm Mon-Fri)*.

HOLE IN THE WALL THEATRE

Hamersley Rd., Subiaco ☎*381 2733* ☙
This theater has gained an enviable reputation for its mix of modern and classical plays. Among the most popular productions are those by up-and-coming Australian writers.

PERTH CONCERT HALL

5 St Georges Terrace ☎*325 9944. Map 15C4* ☙ ⊒ 🆎 💷 💳 📟
The main hall for symphony concerts, this is the home of the **Western Australia Symphony Orchestra** and has seating for 1,900. The building includes a tavern called **Churchill's**, which serves pre-show cocktails and meals.

Where to shop

Probably the most novel aspect of Perth for visitors is the number of shopping arcades that wind through the city. They offer the banal with the intriguing, the curious with the kitsch. But look around, for there are bargains to be found. Modern department stores, such as **Myer** *(Forrest Pl., map 15 C4)* and **Aherns** *(between Hay St. and Murray St., near Barrack St., map 15 C4)* are efficient and well-stocked, but it is in the markets and off the beaten track that you will find the gifts or specialties that can only be found in Western Australia.

In Perth, you can buy a high-quality diamond that has been mined, cut and polished in Western Australia. These gems, which include unique pink diamonds, come from the Argyle Diamond Mine in the remote and rugged Kimberley region. There are also shops that specialize in that most beautiful of Australian stones, the opal. Other jewelers specialize in pearls retrieved from the waters off Broome in the far N of the state.

For shops specializing in jewelry, sports goods and folkcraft, a trip to the near-city suburb of **Claremont** is worthwhile. **Fremantle** — and particularly the attractive **Bannister Street Mall** — offers a range of shops dealing in everything from wool and leather goods to crafts and Aboriginal artifacts. There are also the excellent FREMANTLE MARKETS.

Most shops and arcades in Perth are in the area bounded by St Georges Terrace, William St., Murray St. and Barrack St. A favored starting point for any shopper's expedition is LONDON COURT (see SIGHTS), the arcade that links St Georges Terrace with the **Hay Street Mall**, right in the heart of the city's shopping district. The arcade itself offers mainly simple souvenirs and gifts, but it can be the start of a pleasant and profitable stroll. From here, you are only a browse or two away from **Piccadilly Arcade** *(between Hay Street Mall and Murray St., map 15 C4)* and the **City Arcade** *(between Hay St. and Murray St., map 15 C4)*, both of which are well worth visiting.

Shopping hours are 8.30am-5.30pm Monday to Friday and 8.30am-noon on Saturday. Late-night shopping is on Thursday.

Perth's main post office (and general delivery/poste restante) is the **GPO** *(3 Forrest Pl., map15 C4* ☎ *326 5211).* It is open Monday to Friday 8am-5pm. After-hours service (stamp sales only) is available Monday to Friday 5-7pm, Saturday 9am-noon and Sunday 9am-noon.

ABORIGINAL ART

If your purchase is old or of a sacred nature, it is advisable to inquire whether an export permit is needed.

ABORIGINAL ART GALLERY

242 St Georges Terrace. Map 14C3 ✳ AE ① ⓒ VISA

This is a Government-authorized marketing outlet for authentic items of Aboriginal culture. Among the items on sale here are bark paintings, boomerangs, spears and other weapons, carvings and basketware.

AUSTRALIANA

As well as the usual tourist knick-knacks, usually imported from Southeast Asia, which are widely available in shopping centers and department stores, Perth has a selection of quite individual shops selling authentic Australian artifacts.

PURELY AUSTRALIAN

London Court; Hay Street Mall; City Arcade, map 15C4; Perth Airport AE ① ⓒ VISA
Superb hand-knitted woolens with unique Australian designs, T-shirts and sweatshirts, blackboy wood and jarrah wood gifts, jewelry, stationery and books... and a fairly comprehensive selection of the sort of souvenirs that can be found throughout WA.

PURITAN MAN

343 Stirling Highway, Claremont (near Bayview Terrace) ☎ *384 3434* AE ① ⓒ VISA
An attractive shop that sells colonial and Oriental antiques, contemporary arts and crafts, and museum-quality folkcrafts.

TIMOTHY'S TOYS

Croke Lane, Fremantle ☎ *336 1982* ✳
Handcrafted wooden toys, designed and made in this Fremantle workshop, make ideal gifts for all ages.

FASHION

Shoes in Australia can be intimidatingly expensive or poorly made. One shop, however, where you can guarantee colorful and fashionable women's shoes is **Tamekas Footwear Boutique** *(1222 Hay St., West Perth, map 14B2* ☎ *321 7976* AE ① ⓒ VISA*).* For women's swimwear, casual clothes, evening and day wear (with specialist fittings and speedy alterations) there is **Thompsons** of West Perth *(1267 Hay St., West Perth, map 14B2* ☎ *321 8007* AE ① ⓒ VISA*).* And for men's clothes, formal, casual or practical, there are many fine outlets. Below are some examples.

JOHN BUZZA
Corner of Howard St. and St Georges Terrace ☎*325 8377. Map 15C4* 🆑 🔷 🔷 🔷

Classical men's outfitters, stocking a fine line of quality casual gear, both imported and Australian. Some excellent outfits for armchair sailors. First-class service.

COUNTRY LEATHER
75 Barrack St. ☎*325 4220. Map 15C4* 🔷 🔷 🔷 🔷

The place for sheepskin and lambskin wear, from jackets to boots, slippers to coats.

R. M. WILLIAMS
Carillon Centre, Hay Street Mall. Map 15C4 🔷 🔷 🔷 🔷

Akubra hats, moleskin strides, fine leather boots and all the other trappings to turn you into a dinki-di Aussie drover. This is the place where the Stock Exchange graziers go to get outfitted.

JEWELERS
Superb stones and jewelry are an Australian specialty. Western Australia itself is a prime source, making Perth a good place for purchasing jewelry. Below are two distinguished city outlets.

LINNEYS PEARL TRADERS
37 Rokeby Rd., Subiaco ☎*382 4077* 🔷 🔷 🔷 🔷

The pearls are from Broome in the N, the erstwhile "pearling capital of the world," most of them grown by marine biologist Bill Reed. Goldsmith Alan Linney uses them to make outstanding jewelry. Other specialties are Western Australian Argyle diamonds. Service here is particularly good.

OPAL CENTRE
Shop 1-6, St Martin's Arcade, off London Court ☎*325 8588. Map 15C4* 🔷 🔷 🔷 🔷

Opal, formed millions of years ago from a mixture of silica in water, is known as "the fire in the stone." Here it is easy to see why. The shop's brilliant collection of opals comes from Coober Pedy (South Australia) and Lightning Ride (New South Wales). There is normally a special discount for overseas visitors who can show an airline ticket and passport; ask for details. The staff here speak Japanese, Malay, French and German.

MARKETS AND FOOD CENTERS
Australians love a good, bustling market. FREMANTLE MARKETS is the best example in Perth and Fremantle. Look too at Perth's food centers, which are groups of kitchens sharing communal dining tables and chairs — a Singaporean idea.

FREMANTLE MARKETS
Corner of South Terrace and Henderson St., Fremantle ♿ 🔷 🔷

These excellent markets were originally built in 1897, but were remodeled and reopened in 1975 with 150 or so stalls. Here you can find jewelry, clothing, fresh fruit, pottery, leather, and homemade pickles... all you might need and a lot more. Open 9am-9pm Friday; 9am-5pm Saturday and 11am-5pm Sunday.

Excursions (1): Environs of Perth

The excursions described in this section cover places of interest within relatively easy reach of the city of Perth. Following them is a separate section on four main regions of Western Australia.

Details (and reservations) for extended tours to all parts of the state can be obtained through the **Holiday WA Centre** *(772 Hay St., map 14C3 ☎322 2999)*.

ARMADALE
One-day drive-yourself excursion. Tour operators offer trips that take in the highlights.
Take the Albany Highway SE toward Gosnells. Shortly before you reach the town, 20km (12½ miles) from Perth, turn off left to the **Cohunu Wildlife Park** *(Mills Rd. ☎ (09) 390 6090, open Mon-Fri 10am-5pm; Sat, Sun 10am-5.30pm)*, a sanctuary that has 16ha (40 acres) of bushland in which Australian birds and animals can thrive in natural settings. Cohunu has the biggest walk-through aviary in the southern hemisphere as well as a large collection of wild flowers.

Travel on toward Kelmscott and back onto the Albany Highway. Nearby, on Canns Rd., is the **Elizabethan Village**, a full-scale Tudor replica that includes a copy of Shakespeare's birthplace. At **Armadale** itself, the attraction is a village of another era. **Pioneer World** *(☎(09) 399 5322, open 10am-5pm)* celebrates the life of the country's settlers with its re-creation of an early Australian town. The focus is two 19thC streets, in which shop assistants in period costume go out of their way to provide a feeling of authenticity. Visitors can pan for gold, watch "traditional craftsmen" at work, buy opals and pearls, join in a sing-song in the pub, and play "two-up."

≡   If the Elizabethan Village (see above) isn't all too much for you, you can eat traditional olde English fare at the **Poet's Arbour Restaurant** *(☎(09) 399 3166 ▥)*.

AVON VALLEY
The three main towns, Toodyay, Northam and York, are all within 100km (63 miles) of Perth and ideal to explore either in a single day or over several one-day trips.
The "Valley For All Seasons" is a comfortable day's drive from Perth. Drive E through Guildford to Midland, then take the Great Northern Highway (Route 95) N for a few kilometers before turning right onto the Toodyay Rd.

Toodyay (pronounced Too-gee), 85km (53 miles) NE of Perth, was one of the first inland towns settled back in the colony's early days. Much of its history has been charmingly retained. It was in the rugged bushclad hills SW of Toodyay that Western Australia's most notorious bushranger, Moondyne Joe, roamed. The **Toodyay Tourist Centre** *(Connor's Mill, Stirling Terrace)* has a floor devoted to his life and times. In September this town of 800 commemorates his passing, in the **Moondyne Joe Festival**.

Follow the Avon River through the undulating farmland and bush country to **Northam**, 27km (17 miles) SE of Toodyay. Northam, the second largest *inland* town in WA with a population of only 8,500, is the commercial center for this rich agricultural district. It is also the home of what has become a classic white-water event for canoeists in Australia, the **Avon Descent**. Northam's less energetic attractions include stately white mute swans. These aristocratic birds, rare in Australia, can be seen from the pedestrian **Suspension Bridge**, near the town center.

Leaving the town, you can drive s direct to York on the main York Rd. Alternatively, take the scenic drive that follows the Avon through **Spencer's Brook**, 10km (6 miles) s of Northam, stopping for a drink at the 100 year-old **Spencer's Brook Tavern** before completing the final 25km (16 miles) to York. Once the Wild West town of the colony, **York** was a bustling center for the diggers in the gold rush of the 1890s. Today this picturesque town has been carefully renovated and restored to remind visitors of its wealthy past. A good example is the **York Town Hall**, once Western Australia's largest. For automobile enthusiasts, the **York Motor Museum** *(☎ (096) 411 288)* houses more than 150 classic and vintage cars, motorcycles and some horse-drawn vehicles. The **Perth-York Vintage Car Rally** is held over 2 days each November.

After York, it's a 97km (59-mile) journey w along the Great Southern and Great Eastern (Route 94) Highways back to Perth through fertile, restful countryside.

In Northam: the **Byfield House Restaurant** *(30 Gordon St.* ☎ *(096) 22 3380* ▥*)*, for Victorian elegance, or **The Colonial Restaurant** *(197 Duke St.* ☎ *(096) 22 1074* ▥*)*, for old-world charm (and Northam's only licensed restaurant). In York, the **Castle Hotel** *(Avon Terrace* ☎ *(096) 41 1007* ▢*)*, built in 1835 (and licensed since 1851), serves counter lunches.

THE GUMNUT FACTORY
30 Prindiville Drive, Wanneroo, WA, 6065 (outer northern suburb of Perth)
☎*409 6699. Open daily, 9am-5pm ✗ by appointment.*
Bizarre. That's the only word to describe the unique, kitschy creations of The Gumnut Factory. Here visitors can tour a model village entirely made from gumnuts, flowers and timber. (Gumnuts, from Australian eucalyptus trees and banksias, are often used to make little souvenirs.) There are more than 30 individually hand-crafted buildings, working model railways, roads, and many Gumnut people. The **Gumnut Street Museum** is a reproduction of a 1920s scene. Pottery, woodwork and local crafts are on sale here.

HILLARY'S BOAT HARBOUR
West Coast Drive, WA, 6025. 23km NW Perth. By car, via the West Coast Highway.

The leading attraction at this spectacular marina complex is **Underwater World** *(☎ 447 7500 ▨ open daily 9am-5pm)*, where you travel through a submerged acrylic tunnel and come face-to-face with sharks, giant rays, crustaceans and starfish. Also to be found within this area is **Microworld**, a hi-tech facility that allows you video close-ups of shellfish, seahorses and anemones, and the **Touch Pool**, which actually allows you to feel the creatures. The complex also contains souvenir shops, a restaurant, and an underwater café, with deep-sea views of the Indian Ocean.

THE HILLS

Explore the foothills of the Darling Range if you have a day to spare, and a car. The Hills run N-S, about 20km (12½ miles) E from Perth, and have some particularly pleasant picnic spots and lesser-known tourist attractions.

To get there, take the Guildford Rd. E from Perth through Guildford and Midland and drive onward along the Great Eastern Highway (Route 94). As you travel toward Mundaring, you will see on the left, about 26km (16 miles) from Perth, the entrance to the **John Forrest National Park**, the state's first national park. It contains an open eucalypt forest, good bushwalking, scenic views, spring wild flowers and a natural swimming pool for children.

Farther along the highway, on the right, is the **Old Mahogany Inn**, where you can enjoy morning tea. At **Mundaring**, stretch your legs again and explore one of the many trails that wind through the area's unique jarrah forest. Leave the highway here and drive along the Mundaring Weir Rd. until you get to the **weir** itself. In this wild bushland setting, you can prepare a picnic-barbecue or simply visit the splendidly restored **Mundaring Weir Pub**.

A little farther along the road from here is the **O'Connor Museum**, which records the history of the provision of water from this area to the Eastern Goldfields. From here, you should take a scenic drive along Mundaring Weir Rd. through the Hills to **Kalamunda**, then drive on to **Gooseberry Hill National Park** for spectacular, panoramic views of Perth to the W. Then follow the **Zig-Zag**, once an old railway line, down to the base of the hill.

To return to the city, you are faced with the choice of either turning back toward Midland and the Great Eastern Highway or working your way to the Albany Highway.

MANDURAH

74km (46 miles) s. By car, via Cockburn Rd. (Route 12) from Fremantle, then Mandurah-Fremantle Coast Rd.; by bus, from Fremantle rail station.

Life in Mandurah, one of Western Australia's favored resorts, revolves around the Murray and Serpentine Rivers, the attractive Peel Inlet and the Harvey Estuary. The magnificent waterways, rich in blue manna crabs, prawns and whiting, are a magnet to fishermen from all parts.

The sizeable town (population 16,500) also boasts 40km (25 miles) of clean, sandy Indian Ocean beaches, and caters to diving enthusiasts, windsurfers, surfers, waterskiers and canoeists... as well as family swimmers.

But really this is paradise for the amateur fisherman. Rent a boat with outboard motor and some tackle, buy some bait from the locals, and chug upriver to what seems a likely spot. A cast or two and the tailor fish will be lining up to get into the frying pan. Guide the boat around the estuary and you are likely to have a couple of dolphins as escorts, while a curious pelican swoops across the bows.

✆ For accommodations, contact the **Mandurah Tourist Bureau and Travel Centre** *(5 Pinjarra Rd., Mandurah, WA, 6210 ☎ (095) 35 1155).*

THE PINNACLES

260km (163 miles) N. By car, via Brand Highway, turning w to Cervantes a few kilometers s of Badgingarra; by tour bus, from Perth or Cervantes.
The Pinnacles, in the **Nambung National Park**, are limestone formations, the fossilized remains of an ancient forest. Today they stand as eerie windswept golden statues in a desert landscape.

The risk of sand drifts makes the road to the Pinnacles often unsuitable for conventional vehicles. Visitors are urged to join the 4-wheel-drive or air-conditioned bus tours that journey either from Perth or the fishing village of Cervantes into the park. In Perth, contact **Pinnacles Travel Centre** *(☎ 325 9455).*

ROTTNEST ISLAND

Off the coast, 20km (12 miles) w. By sea, Boat Torque Cruise Ferries ☎ 325 6033 (Perth)/335 7181 (Fremantle); by air, Rottnest Airlines ☎ 478 1322. General information: Rottnest Island Authority, Rottnest Island, WA, 6161 ☎ (09) 372 9729 ⊠ 372 9715.
Rottnest is the resort that Western Australians once tried to keep to themselves. No wonder! This delightfully relaxing island, carefully administered and kept as uncommercial as possible, seems to offer a cure for all the ills of boisterous city life.

There are no private landowners on Rottnest and no private motor vehicles. A small bus provides regular tours of the 11km by 5km (7 by 3 miles) island, but most visitors throw caution to the wind and, provoking muscles almost forgotten, rent a bicycle to get around *(☎ (09) 372 9729).*

Rottnest was named (in translation "Rats Nest") by the Dutch mariner William de Vlamingh in 1696 after he mistook for large rats the small rock wallabies that inhabit the island. These unique, endearing marsupials, known as quokkas, roam the island today, tame and well-fed by visitors.

A high-speed ferry takes about 40 minutes from Fremantle to reach the island; or it is a 10-minute flight from Perth Airport. Rottnest has a wide range of accommodations, but, over vacation periods and long weekends, it is generally heavily booked. So, if anything longer than a day trip is being considered, it is wise to ensure well in advance that you have a place to stay.

Relaxing it may be, but there is much that can be done on Rottnest. There are salt lakes to wallow in, pitted limestone cliffs to explore, picturesque bays with clear turquoise-blue water, and long, white, sandy beaches.

For swimmers, there are plenty of safe beaches, with no sharks or rip tides to worry about. Skin-diving gear is available for rent: on Rottnest you can explore some of the most southerly coral, or the numerous wrecks that can be found on the reef surrounding the island. There is exhilarating surfing, boating and fishing (the bold-hearted can catch crayfish on the reefs with their bare hands!)

Golf, tennis, bowls and volleyball are available for the energetic. For those less so, there are plenty of places in which to sunbake; the **Quokka Arms** will provide refreshingly chilled drinks in its beer garden overlooking Thomson Bay; and there are glass-bottom boats for a relaxing cruise over the coral.

✎ The **Rottnest Hotel** *(☎ (09) 292 5011 ▥)* has both hotel and motel rooms, with daily or weekly tariff; **The Rottnest Lodge Resort** *(☎ (09) 292 5161 ▥)* offers hotel or motel accommodations. Cottages, villas and tents, for those who wish to cater for themselves, are available through the **Rottnest Island Authority** *(☎ (09) 372 9729).*

SWAN VALLEY

20-30km (12-19 miles) NE. By car, via Guildford Rd., then Great Northern Highway; by bus or train, from Perth, Guildford or Midland; by boat, daily cruises from Barrack Street Jetty.

East of Perth, below the Darling Range, the Swan River winds its way through a maze of vineyards and small farms. This is the Swan Valley, which since the 1830s has been producing quality wines.

The Swan Valley covers an area of 104sq.kms (40 square miles). There are 30 commercial wine producers today. Many of the smaller, family vineyards produce under 90,000 liters per vintage, but the larger wineries, such as **Houghton's, Sandalford** and **Valencia**, produce up to 1.5 million liters.

A pleasant and economical way to see the valley is to take a river cruise from the Barrack Street jetty. The boats set off at about 9.45am on a 5-hour round trip that includes wine on board, a visit to a vineyard, the chance to sample and buy some of the best wines, lunch ashore, and a look at some of the more scenic reaches of the Swan.

Excursions (2): Farther afield

The **Holiday WA Centre** in Perth can provide details for a wide range of tours to the regions below and, indeed, to all places throughout Western Australia. Accommodations vary greatly and should be reserved well in advance wherever possible. Further suggestions and maps are given in TOURS — see ROUTES 6 AND 7 on pages 75-80.

THE KIMBERLEY

This is the northernmost part of the state, an expanse of land larger than California, three times the size of England, yet with a population of less than 10,000. It is rugged and spectacularly beautiful, one of the hottest places on earth, magnificently wild and, for the careless or unwary, ruthlessly unforgiving. The best time to visit is from April to November, when there are warm, sunny days and comfortable tropical evenings.

The **West Kimberley** is one of the oldest geological areas on earth, with rocks estimated at some 2,500 million years old. Time and the weather have carved out awesome gorges and mountain ranges; and crystal-clear pools that are sheltered by towering cliffs. This is awe-inspiring country.

The port of **Broome**, about 2,200km (1,375 miles) N of Perth, was once the center of the world's pearling industry. Settled in the 1800s, it is today the home of a polyglot community — a mixture of Malays, Filipinos, Japanese, Chinese, Aboriginals and white Australians. Well worth considering here is a **cruise** of the Kimberley coast aboard a restored **pearling lugger**. The cruises range from 2-hour trips to extended charters *(reservations and further details from Broome Tourist Bureau ☎ (091) 92 1176).*

Derby, 2,366km (1,479 miles) NE of Perth, is near the mouth of the Fitzroy River and, because of its location, has become the administrative center for the Kimberley. It has a population of just over 3,000. Tides in the adjoining **King Sound** rise twice daily to levels of up to 11.8m (39 feet)... an impressive feat of nature that can be observed from a 550m (600-yard) steel jetty. But, more important, Derby is the perfect starting point for visitors to explore the remarkable Gorge country of the Kimberley — **Geikie Gorge**, with its huge cliffs and waters abounding in freshwater crocodiles, barramundi, sharks, sawfish and stingrays, and **Windjana Gorge** and **Brooking Gorge**. Four-wheel-drive tours are available from Derby *(reservations and details: Derby Tourist Bureau ☎ (091) 91 1426).*

There is much to see in the East and West Kimberleys — including the second largest meteorite crater in the world at **Wolf Creek**, 1km (1,100 yards) in diameter and 49m (160 feet) deep; Australia's largest man-made lake, the **Ord River Dam**; the **Argyle Diamond Mines**; and the "lost world" of the **Bungle Bungle Mountains**. Though a popular tourist region, it is largely undeveloped, and much of it is still only being truly "discovered" today.

Ansett WA *(☎ (09) 478 9222)* offers 5-night fly-and-stay packages to Broome, Derby and Kununurra, which feature accommodations and return air travel from Perth. A rented Avis 4-wheel-drive Toyota Land Cruiser can be added to the package.

East Kimberley Tours *(Box 537, Kununurra, WA, 6743 ☎ (091) 68 2213/(091) 68 7882)* organize 7-day adventure safaris through the region. These include return airfare from Perth, an experienced bushman as a guide, a 4-wheel-drive vehicle, tent accommodations and all meals.

THE MIDWEST AND NORTHWEST

The Midwest, which occupies almost a quarter of the state's total area, extends from the Batavia Coast in the w to the Northern Territory border in the E. **Geraldton**, 424km (265 miles) N of Perth, is the main town, with a population of 18,000, and is an excellent base from which to explore. It is the center for the multimillion-dollar rock lobster (crayfish) industry.

Skywest *(☎ (09) 478 9898)* has day flights to Geraldton that include a local tour and meal. There are also weekly *Midwest Explorer* flights, which include a bus tour to the beach resort of **Kalbarri**, overnight accommodations, and a journey inland with refreshments on a farm property.

Farther N is the **Gascoyne Region**, with Carnarvon as its main center. Bananas, pineapples, beans, tomatoes and melons are grown here. Other important local industries are wool from the vast sheep stations and commercial fishing for prawns and scallops. This region, which takes in **Shark Bay**, **Exmouth**, **Monkey Mia** and **Coral Bay**, is tempting for the adventurous traveler. Off the coast, the dazzling blue sea abounds with mackerel, snapper, kingfish, tuna and, for game fishermen, sailfish and marlin. **VIP big-game fishing safaris** from Exmouth can be arranged through the Holiday WA Centre in Perth.

To the N of the Gascoyne region is the **Pilbara**, rich in massive iron and mineral deposits. **Port Hedland**, **Dampier**, **Onslow**, **Wittenoom** and **Marble Bar** (whose average daily maximum temperature is 35.67°C or 96.2°F) are its main centers. **East-West Airlines** *(☎ (09) 478 9888)* and **Amesz Adventure Charters** *(☎ (09) 271 2696)* can arrange week-long camping tours of the Pilbara.

THE SOUTHWEST

Rolling green hills, forests carpeted in wild flowers, meandering rivers, and a patchwork of orchards... the Southwest is indeed one of the most attractive and unspoiled parts of Australia. There are trout and marron (freshwater crayfish) in its streams, barely touched sandy beaches on its rim. The vineyards of Margaret River produce some of the country's finest wines — and where better for picnicking than among the karri trees, some soaring to 80m (262 feet)?

There are good roads throughout the region, and accommodations are mostly comfortable, clean and conveniently accessible. Many tours and excursions, by rail, bus or air, are available and can be organized from Perth. Examples:

Westrail (☎ *(09) 326 2811)*, the state's rail and bus service, offers a 3-day *Southern Highlights* tour taking in the forests, wineries and coastline, from Perth to Bunbury, Busselton, Margaret River, Bridgetown, Pemberton and Manjimup.

Parlorcars (☎ *(09) 325 5488)* runs a 3-day bus tour, *Margaret River Magic,* that takes in the ocean scenery, the tall timber, vineyards and a marron farm.

THE GOLDFIELDS

Some 600km (375 miles) E of Perth is **Kalgoorlie**, center of the Goldfields, a town almost as rich in history as it has been in gold. Paddy Hannan, an Irish-born prospector, first discovered gold here in 1893. His strike set off a gold rush and created the impetus for the development of Western Australia as a whole. Kalgoorlie, which has a population of 23,000, is still the center for mining and has a "frontier" feel to it even today. From "Kal" and **Boulder**, its twin town, the visitor can travel to the nearby "ghost towns" of **Coolgardie**, **Gwalia** and **Broad Arrow**, all deserted after the precious metal "cut out." Many air, rail and bus tours to the Goldfields can be arranged in Perth. Examples:

Skywest (☎ *(09) 478 9999)* offers a 3-day, 2-night *Diggers Delight* air package that includes gold-detecting, the game of "two-up," a tour of Kalgoorlie/Boulder and the ghost towns, and a visit to the **State Battery** (the gold treatment plant).

Westrail (☎ *(09) 326 2811)* provides a series of rail/bus tours that include transportation aboard WA's fastest train, *The Prospector.* "Goldrush Explorer," a 3-day, 2-night package, includes the rail trip and accommodations in Kalgoorlie.

- See also ROUTES 6 and 7 and maps on pages 75-80.

Index

Page numbers in **bold** type indicate main entries. *Italic* page numbers refer to illustrations and maps.

List of street names

All streets mentioned in this book that fall within the area covered by our maps are listed below. Map numbers are printed in **bold** type. Some smaller streets are not named on the maps, but the map reference given below will help you locate the correct neighborhood.

Adelaide
Angas St., **9**D5
Brougham Pl., **8**B3
Chesser St., **8**D3
Flinders St., **8**D3-9D4
Franklin St., **8**D2-3
Frome Rd., **8**B3-9C4
Gawler Pl., **8**D3
Gilbert Pl., **8**D3
Glen Osmond Rd., **9**E4-F4
Gover St., **8**A2-3
Grenfell St., **8**D3-9D4
Grote St., **8**D2-3
Hindley St., **8**D2-3
Hindmarsh Sq., **8**D3-9D4
Hutt St., **9**E4
Kensington Rd., **9**E5-6
King William Rd., **8**C3-B3
King William St., **8**E3-D3
Light Sq., **8**D2
Melbourne St., **8**B3-9B4
Montefiore Rd., **8**D2-B2
North Tce., **8**D2-9D4
O'Connell St., **8**A2-B3
Pennington Tce., **8**B2-C3
Pirie St., **8**D3-9D4
Pulteney St., **8**F3-D3
Rundle Mall, **8**D3
Rundle St., **9**D4
South Tce., **8**E2-9E5
Victoria Sq., **8**D3-E3
War Memorial Dr., **8**C1-2
Waymouth St., **8**D2-3
West Tce., **8**E2-D2

Brisbane
Adelaide St., **7**D2-C3
Albert St., **7**C2-D3
Alice St., **7**E3-D3
Ann St., **7**D2-B3
Astor Tce., **7**C2
Cordelia St., **7**E1-F2
Eagle St., **7**C3-D3
Edward St., **7**D2-3
Elizabeth St., **7**D2-3
George St., **7**D2-E3
Glenelg St., **7**E2
King George Sq., **7**D2
North Quay, **7**D1-2
Queen St., **7**D2-B3
Queen St. Mall, **7**D2
Roma St., **7**D1-2
St Paul's Tce., **7**C2-A3
Turbot St., **7**D2-C3
Wickham Tce., **7**C2

Canberra
Ainslie Ave., **2**B4-5
Anzac Pde., **2**C5-B5
Anzac Pk., **2**C5-B5
Barry Dr., **1**A3-2B4
Bunda St., **2**B4
Civic Sq., **2**B4
Clunies Ross St., **1**B2-A3
Commonwealth Ave.,
    2D4-C4
Constitution Ave., **2**B4-C5
Cooyong St., **2**B4
Kennedy St., **2**E5-F5
King Edward Tce., **2**D4-5
King George Tce., **2**D4
Limestone Ave., **2**A5-B5
London Circuit, **2**B4
Marcus Clarke St., **2**B4
Northbourne Ave.,
    2B4-A4

Parkes Way, **1**C1-2D5
Petrie Plaza, **2**B4
Wendouree Dr., **2**C5-D5
Wentworth Ave., **2**E5-F5

Melbourne
Albert St., **11**B4-5
Alexandra Ave., **11**D4-E6
Alfred Pl., **10**E3
Batman Ave., **10**C3-11D4
Batman St., **10**B1-2
Birdwood Ave., **11**D4-E5
Blackwood St., **10**A2
Bourke St., **10**C2-11B4
Bourke St. Mall, **10**C3
Burwood Hwy., **13**D4-5
Cecil St., **10**E2-F3
City Sq., **10**C3
Clarendon St., **11**C5-B5
Cohen Pl., **10**B3
Collins St., **10**C2-11B4
Courtney St., **10**A2
Coventry St., **10**F2-11E4
Domain Rd., **11**E4-6
Drummond St., **10**A3-B3
Eastern Frwy., **12**C2-3
Eastern Rd., **10**E3-11F6
Elizabeth St., **10**A2-C3
Exhibition St., **10**B3-11C4
Flinders Lane, **10**D2-11C4
Flinders St., **10**D2-C3
King St., **10**B1-D2
Lansdowne St., **11**B4-C4
La Trobe St., **10**C2-B3
Little Bourke St.,
    10C2-11B4
Little Collins St.,
    10C2-11B4

American Express Travel Guides

spanning the globe....

EUROPE
Amsterdam, Rotterdam
  & The Hague
Athens and the
  Classical Sites ‡
Barcelona & Madrid ‡
Berlin ‡
Brussels #
Dublin and Cork #
Florence and Tuscany
London #
Moscow & St Petersburg *
Paris #
Prague *
Provence and the
  Côte d'Azur *
Rome
Venice ‡
Vienna & Budapest

NORTH AMERICA
Boston and New
  England *
Los Angeles & San
  Diego #
Mexico ‡
New York #
San Francisco and
  the Wine Regions
Toronto, Montréal and
  Québec City ‡
Washington, DC

THE PACIFIC
Cities of Australia
Hong Kong & Taiwan
Singapore &
  Bangkok ‡
Tokyo #

* Paperbacks in preparation   # Paperbacks appearing January 1993
‡ Hardback pocket guides (in paperback 1993)

Clarity and quality of information, combined with outstanding maps — the ultimate in travelers' guides